THE
COMPACT
READER

SHORT ESSAYS BY
METHOD AND THEME

D0066938

NINTH EDITION

THE COMPACT READER

SHORT ESSAYS BY METHOD AND THEME

Jane E. Aaron

Ellen Kuhl Repetto

BEDFORD / ST. MARTIN'S
Boston ◆ New York

For Bedford/St. Martin's

Developmental Editor: Amy Gershman
Production Editor: Kendra LeFleur
Production Supervisor: Samuel Jones
Senior Marketing Manager: Molly Parke
Editorial Assistant: Kate Mayhew
Production Assistants: Lidia McDonald-Carr and Laura Winstead
Copyeditor: Mary Lou Wilshaw-Watts
Permissions Manager: Kalina Ingham Hintz
Senior Art Director: Anna Palchik
Text Design: Linda Robertson
Cover Design: Marine Bouvier Miller
Composition: MPS Limited, a Macmillan Company
Printing and Binding: Haddon Craftsmen, Inc., an RR Donnelley & Sons Company

President: Joan E. Feinberg
Editorial Director: Denise B. Wydra
Editor in Chief: Karen S. Henry
Director of Marketing: Karen R. Soeltz
Director of Production: Susan W. Brown
Associate Director, Editorial Production: Elise S. Kaiser
Managing Editor: Elizabeth M. Schaaf

Library of Congress Control Number: 2010928941

Manufactured in the United States of America.

5   4
h   g

For information, write: Bedford/St. Martin's, 75 Arlington Street, Boston, MA 02116   (617-399-4000)

ISBN-10: 0–312–60960–4
ISBN-13: 978–0–312–60960–3

Acknowledgments

PREFACE

The ninth edition of *The Compact Reader*, like its predecessors, combines three texts in one brief volume: a short-essay reader, a rhetorical reader, and a thematic reader. Remarkably thorough given its size, the book complements nearly three dozen professional and student essays with all the editorial apparatus of a larger book—at a lower price. The introductory chapters in Part One guide students through the process of critical reading and writing. Then ten chapters in Part Two focus on the rhetorical methods of development, with each chapter's brief selections both illustrating a method and centering on a common theme. An appendix on research and documentation offers just enough information to help students use sources effectively. This edition features a new chapter on editing, attention to visual literacy, and thirteen new essays (three of them illustrated and two of them documented), making *The Compact Reader* even more stimulating and helpful for both students and instructors.

Three Readers in One

The core of *The Compact Reader* remains its selections. Thirty-five short essays and twenty paragraphs provide interesting reading that will enliven class discussion and spark good writing. The selections represent both emerging writers—including a student in every chapter—and established writers such as Barbara Kingsolver, Langston Hughes, Dave Barry, and Anna Quindlen. Nine professional essays, four student essays, and nine paragraphs are new to this edition.

The Compact Reader's unique structure suits courses that call for brief essays with either a rhetorical or a thematic approach:

- The essays in *The Compact Reader* average just two to four pages apiece so that students can read them quickly, analyze them thoroughly, and emulate them successfully. A few longer essays, such as Dana Thomas's "The Fake Trade," help students make the transition to more challenging material.

■ Above all, the essays offer clear models for writing, but they also show the rhetorical methods—narration, example, comparison, and so on—at work in varied styles for varied purposes. In Chapters 5–13, three essays and two annotated paragraphs illustrate each method. Chapter 14, on argument, expands on this format with a more detailed introduction to the method and two additional essays that take opposing positions on a controversial issue.

■ Each rhetorical chapter also has an overlapping thematic focus that shows the method developing the same general subject and provides diverse perspectives to stimulate students' critical thinking, discussion, and writing. Three themes are new to this edition.

Narration	Recalling childhood
Description	Experiencing new places (new)
Example	Using language
Division or analysis	Looking at popular culture
Classification	Sorting friends and neighbors (new)
Process analysis	Eating well (new)
Comparison and contrast	Evaluating stereotypes
Definition	Clarifying family relationships
Cause-and-effect analysis	Understanding business and consumers
Argument and persuasion	Debating law and order

An Introduction to Reading and Writing

A thorough introduction to critical reading and the writing process appears in the four chapters of Part One:

■ Chapter 1 demonstrates the reading process, showing a student's annotations on a sample passage and providing detailed analysis of a professional essay, Barbara Lazear Ascher's "The Box Man." A new discussion of reading images, accompanied by a photograph with a student's interpretive comments, highlights the parallels between critical reading and the visual acuity most students already possess.

■ Chapter 2 covers the initial stages of composing, from assessing the writing situation through drafting, and follows a student as she responds to Ascher's essay and writes a first draft. To help students focus their writing, this chapter also offers a thorough discussion of forming and expressing a thesis.

- Chapter 3 discusses revising, from rethinking the thesis through reshaping paragraphs, adding support, and adjusting tone. The chapter includes a boxed checklist for revision as well as a revised draft of the student's response to Ascher's essay.

- Chapter 4, new to this edition, introduces the basics of editing — for grammar, clarity, emphasis, and word choice. Simple explanations, multiple examples of weak and revised sentences, and a boxed checklist teach students to recognize and repair the most common sentence-level problems. The chapter concludes with the final, edited draft of the student's response to Ascher's "The Box Man."

The Compact Reader's emphasis on the union of reading and writing carries through the entire book:

- A detailed, practical introduction to each of the ten rhetorical methods opens with a discussion of the concepts to look for when reading, analyzes two sample paragraphs that illustrate the method, and suggests specific strategies for developing an essay using the method, from choosing a subject through editing the final draft. The introductions draw connections among purpose, subject, and method, helping students analyze and respond to any writing situation. A final "Note on Thematic Connections" explains how the chapter's paragraphs and essays relate to one another.

- An updated appendix, "Working with Sources," outlines the basics of using readings and conducting research to support writing. Emphasizing the essential skills of summarizing, paraphrasing, quoting, avoiding plagiarism, and using the latest MLA documentation, this section shows students how to synthesize information and ideas from their reading to develop and support their own conclusions. The appendix ends with a sample student essay that illustrates the elements of source-based writing.

- To help students find what they need in the book, a guide to the elements of writing appears inside the back cover. This index covers Chapters 2 through 4, all the rhetorical introductions, and the appendix.

Unique Editorial Apparatus

In addition to the features already mentioned, *The Compact Reader* offers numerous aids for students and teachers:

- Complementing the section on thesis statements in Chapter 2, the introduction to each rhetorical method breaks out the discussion of forming a thesis, highlighting the importance of writing with a thesis and making the advice easy to locate.

- The introduction to each rhetorical method also features a "Focus" box that refers students to an element of revision or editing especially relevant to that method, such as verbs in narration, paragraph coherence in comparison and contrast, and tone in argument and persuasion. Each box appears with a checklist that extends the more general checklists in Chapters 3 and 4 to the particular method.

- Quotations and a journal prompt precede every essay. These pre-reading materials get students thinking and writing about the essay's topic, helping them to form and express their own ideas before they read the essay itself.

- Headnotes about the author and the essay place every selection in a context that helps focus students' reading.

- Detailed questions after each essay guide students' analysis of meaning, purpose and audience, method and structure, and language. A question labeled "Other Methods" highlights the author's use of combined methods.

- At least four writing topics after each selection give students specific direction for their own work. Among these, a "Journal to Essay" topic helps students build their journal writing into a finished essay; a "Cultural Considerations" topic leads students to consider similarities and differences among cultures; and a "Connections" topic encourages students to make thematic or rhetorical links to other selections in the book.

- Additional writing topics appear at the end of each chapter. "Writing with the Method" lists ideas for applying the chapter's method of development, and "Writing about the Theme" suggests ways to draw on the chapter's resources to explore its topic.

- A glossary at the end of the book defines and illustrates more than a hundred terms, with specific cross-references to longer discussions in the text.

Helpful Instructor's Manual and Online Resources

Resources for Teaching THE COMPACT READER, bound into the instructor's edition of the book and available as a downloadable PDF, aims to help teachers integrate the text into their courses and use it in class. It includes an overview of the book's organization and chapters, ideas for combining the reader with other course materials, and varied resources for each selection: teaching tips, a content quiz, a vocabulary quiz, and detailed answers to all the critical-reading questions. The manual also reprints one essay from each rhetorical chapter with annotations that identify the author's thesis and use of mixed methods.

Bedford/St. Martin's provides several online teaching tools at no charge. At *bedfordstmartins.com/compactreader/catalog*, instructors will find *Teaching Central*, a rich library of reference works, teaching advice, classroom materials, and adjunct support; *Bits*, an archive of creative ideas for teaching in an easily searchable blog; *The Bedford Bibliography for Teachers of Writing*; and the electronic version of *Resources for Teaching* THE COMPACT READER. In addition, content cartridges for the most common course management systems—*Blackboard, WebCT, Angel,* and *Desire2Learn*—make it easy to download course-specific digital materials.

Students also have free and open access to a range of helpful resources. At *ReWriting* (*bedfordstmartins.com/rewriting*), they can visit *Exercise Central* and practice editing with over nine thousand interactive writing and grammar exercises. Students can also find additional advice on citing sources in *Research and Documentation Online* by Diana Hacker; view sample papers and designed documents; take the *St. Martin's Tutorial on Avoiding Plagiarism*; watch videos of writers talking about writing; and learn more about reading and using visuals.

Affordable Multimedia Supplements

The Compact Reader can be packaged with a variety of innovative tools at a significant discount. *VideoCentral* is a growing collection of videos that capture real-world, academic, and student writers talking about how and why they write. *Re:Writing Plus* upgrades the basic version of *ReWriting* with hundreds of model documents, the first ever peer-review game, and full access to *VideoCentral*. And the *i-series* on CD-ROM offers interactive exercises on key rhetorical and visual concepts (*ix*), multimedia argument tutorials (*i-claim*), and hands-on practice with research and source citation (*i-cite*). To learn more, contact your Bedford/ St. Martin's sales representative, e-mail sales support at sales_support@ bfwpub.com, or visit *bedfordstmartins.com/compactreader/catalog.*

Acknowledgments

Many instructors helped to shape this edition of *The Compact Reader,* offering insights from their experience and suggestions for improvement. Many thanks to Christine Baumgarthuber, Brown University; Amy Berger, Pennsylvania State University, Berks Campus; Brenda Boudreau, McKendree University; Karin Cooper, Saddleback College; April Dolata, Northwestern Connecticut Community College; Sheila Donnelly, Orange County Community College; Roxanne Fand, University of Hawaii, Manoa; Gina Gemmel, Ohio State University; Chad Greene, Cerritos College; Jessica Hasson, Los Angeles Valley College; Kathleen Henning, Gateway Technical College; Lynn Koller, Embry-Riddle Aeronautical University; Anne Liu, Fullerton College; Charlotte Lynch, Mount San Antonio College; David McCracken, Coker College; Lori Miller, California State University, San Marcos; Pamela Monder, Community College of Vermont, Rutland; Virginia Polanski, Stonehill College; Nita Ritzke, University of Mary; and William Wright, Mesa State College. Special thanks as well to Kim Sanabria, Eugenio Maria de Hostos Community College, whose contributions to the seventh edition continue to influence the book's content and features.

The people at Bedford/St. Martin's once again contributed greatly to this project. Joan Feinberg, Karen Henry, and Steve Scipione provided encouraging and supportive leadership. Amy Gershman, assisted by Kate Mayhew, helped to conceive the book's features and select new readings, coordinated efforts with the students whose essays appear throughout, and cheerfully managed details too numerous to count. Kendra LeFleur oversaw the book's striking new design and deftly shepherded the manuscript through production. Deep and happy thanks to all.

CONTENTS

6 | DESCRIPTION: Experiencing New Places   91

9 | CLASSIFICATION: Sorting Friends and Neighbors 167

10 | PROCESS ANALYSIS: Eating Well   192

Stephanie Alaimo and Mark Koester, The Backdraft of Technology
(STUDENT ESSAY) 287

*Every time we use a self-service checkout line, the authors warn, we
pay a hidden price.*

Dana Thomas, The Fake Trade 292

*Exposing the seamy underworld of counterfeit luxury goods, an
investigative journalist explains how cheap knock-offs harm both
those who make them and those who buy them.*

Charlie LeDuff, End of the Line 300

*The author considers what happens to a factory town when its
factory shuts down.*

14 ARGUMENT AND PERSUASION: Debating Law and Order 311

The author analyzes a popular image in hip-hop music and professional sports to explain the dangers of equating violence with masculinity.

THE
COMPACT
READER

SHORT ESSAYS BY
METHOD AND THEME

PART ONE

A COMPACT GUIDE TO READING AND WRITING

1

READING

This collection of essays has one purpose: to help you become a better reader and writer. It combines examples of good writing with explanations of the writers' methods, questions to guide your reading, and ideas for your own writing. In doing so, it shows how you can adapt the processes and techniques of others as you learn to communicate clearly and effectively on paper.

Writing well is not an inborn skill but an acquired one: you will become proficient only by writing and rewriting, experimenting with different strategies, listening to the responses of readers. How, then, can it help to read the work of other writers?

- *Reading others' ideas can introduce you to new information and give you new perspectives on your own experience.* Many of the essays collected here demonstrate that personal experience is a rich and powerful source of material for writing. But the knowledge gained from reading can help pinpoint just what is remarkable in your experience. And by introducing varieties of behavior and ways of thinking that would otherwise remain unknown to you, reading can also help you understand where you fit in the scheme of things. Such insight not only reveals subjects for writing but also improves your ability to communicate with others whose experiences naturally differ from your own.

- *Reading exposes you to a broad range of strategies and styles.* Just seeing that these vary as much as the writers themselves should assure you that there is no fixed standard of writing, while it should also encourage you to find your own strategies and style. At the same time, you will see that writers do make choices to suit their subjects, their purposes, and especially their readers. Writing is rarely easy, even for the pros; but the more options you have to choose from, the more likely you are to succeed at it.

■ *Reading makes you sensitive to the role of audience in writing.* As you become adept at reading the work of other writers critically, discovering intentions and analyzing choices, you will see how a writer's decisions affect you as audience. Training yourself to read attentively and critically is a first step to becoming a more objective reader of your own writing.

Reading Attentively

This chapter offers strategies for making the most of your reading in this book and elsewhere. These strategies are reinforced in Chapters 5–14, each of which offers opportunities for careful reading with two paragraphs, one student essay, and two professional essays. Each chapter also introduces a method of developing a piece of writing:

narration	process analysis
description	comparison and contrast
example	definition
division or analysis	cause-and-effect analysis
classification	argument and persuasion

These methods correspond to basic and familiar patterns of thought and expression, common in our daily musings and conversations as well as in writing for all sorts of purposes and audiences: blogs, social-networking pages, and online discussion boards; college term papers, lab reports, and examinations; business memos and reports; letters to the editors of newspapers; articles in popular magazines.

As writers we draw on the methods, sometimes unconsciously, to give order to our ideas and even to find ideas. For instance, a writer narrates, or tells, a story of her experiences to understand and convey the feeling of living her life. As readers, in turn, we have expectations for these familiar methods. When we read a narrative of someone's experiences, for example, we expect enough details to understand what happened, we anticipate that events will be told primarily in the order they occurred, and we want the story to have a point—a reason for its being told and for our bothering to read it.

Making such expectations conscious can sharpen your skills as a critical reader and as a writer. A full chapter on each method explains how it works, shows it at work in paragraphs, and gives advice for using it to develop your own essays. The essays in each chapter provide clear examples that you can analyze and learn from (with the help of specific questions) and can refer to while writing (with the help of specific writing suggestions).

To make your reading more interesting and also to stimulate your writing, the sample paragraphs and essays in Chapters 5–14 all focus on a common subject, such as childhood, popular culture, or stereotypes. You'll see how flexible the methods are when they help five writers produce five unique pieces on the same theme. You'll also have a springboard for producing your own unique pieces, whether you take up some of the book's writing suggestions or take off with your own topics.

Reading Critically

When we look for something to watch on television or listen to on the radio, we often tune in one station after another, pausing just long enough each time to catch the program or music being broadcast before settling on one choice. Much of the reading we do is similar: we skim a newspaper, magazine, or Web site, noting headings and scanning paragraphs to get the gist of the content. But such skimming is not really reading, for it neither involves us deeply in the subject nor engages us in interaction with the writer.

To get the most out of reading, we must invest something of ourselves in the process, applying our own ideas and emotions and attending not just to the substance but to the writer's interpretation of it. This kind of reading is **critical** because it looks beneath the surface of a piece of writing. (The common meaning of *critical* as "negative" doesn't apply here: critical reading may result in positive, negative, or even neutral reactions.)

Critical reading can be enormously rewarding, but of course it takes care and time. A good method for developing your own skill in critical reading is to prepare yourself beforehand and then read the work at least twice to uncover what it has to offer.

Preparing

Preparing to read may involve just a few minutes as you form some ideas about the author, the work, and your likely response:

- ■ *What is the author's background, what qualifications does he or she bring to the subject, and what approach is he or she likely to take?* The biographical information provided before each essay in this book should help answer these questions; many periodicals and books include similar information on their authors.

- *What does the title convey about the subject and the author's attitude toward it?* Note, for instance, the quite different attitudes conveyed by these three titles on the same subject: "Safe Hunting," "In Touch with Ancient Spirits," and "Killing Animals for Fun and Profit."

- *What can you predict about your own response to the work?* What might you already know about the author's subject? Based on the title and other clues (such as headings or visuals), are you likely to agree or disagree with the author's views? *The Compact Reader* helps ready you for reading by providing two features before each selection. First, quotations from varied writers comment on the selection's general subject to give you a range of views. And second, a journal prompt encourages you to write about your thoughts on a subject before you see what the author has to say. By giving you a head start in considering the author's ideas and approach, writing *before* reading encourages you to read more actively and critically.

Reading Actively

After developing some expectations about the piece of writing, read it through carefully to acquaint yourself with the subject, the author's reason for writing about it, and the way the author presents it. (Each essay in this book is short enough to be read in one sitting.) Try not to read passively, letting the words wash over you, but instead interact directly with the work to discover its meaning, the author's intentions, and your own responses.

One of the best aids to active reading is to make notes on separate sheets of paper or, preferably (if you own the book), on the pages themselves. As you practice making notes, you will probably develop a personal code meaningful only to you. As a start, however, try this system:

- Underline or bracket passages that you find particularly effective or that seem especially important to the author's purpose.

- Circle words you don't understand so that you can look them up when you finish.

- Put question marks in the margins next to unclear passages.
- Jot down associations that occur to you, such as examples from your own experience, disagreements with the author's assumptions, or connections to other works you've read.

When you have finished such an active reading, your annotations might look like those below. (The paragraph is from the end of the essay reprinted on pp. 9–13.)

The first half of our lives is spent stubbornly denying it. As children we acquire language to make ourselves understood and soon learn from the blank *true?* stares in response to our babblings that even these, our saviors, our parents, are strangers. In adolescence when we replay earlier dramas with peers in the place of parents, we begin the quest for the best friend, that person who will receive all thoughts as if they were *What about his* her own. Later we assert that true love will find the way. *own? Audience* True love finds many ways, but no escape from exile. *= women?* The shores are littered with us, Annas and Ophelias, *Ophelia + Juliet* Emmas and Juliets, all outcasts from the dream of per- *from Shakespeare.* fect understanding. We might as well draw the night *Others also?* around us and find solace there and a friend in our *In other words,* own voice. *just give up?*

To answer questions like those in the annotations, count on rereading the essay at least once. Multiple readings increase your mastery of the material; more important, once you have a basic understanding of a writer's subject, a second and third reading will reveal details and raise questions that you might not have noticed on the first pass. Reading an essay several times also helps you to uncover how the many parts of the work—for instance, the sequencing of information, the tone, the evidence—contribute to the author's purpose.

Using a Reading Checklist

When rereading an essay, start by writing a one- or two-sentence summary of each paragraph and image—in your own words—to increase

---

CHECKLIST FOR CRITICAL READING

- Why did the author choose this subject?
- Who is the intended audience? What impression did the author wish to make on readers?
- What is the author's point? Can you find a direct statement of the thesis, or main idea, or is the thesis implied?
- What details does the author provide to support the thesis? Is the supporting evidence reliable? complete? convincing?
- How does the author organize ideas? What effect does that arrangement have on the overall impact of the work?
- What do language and tone reveal about the author's meaning, purpose, and attitude?
- How successful is the work as a whole, and why?

---

your mastery of the material (see p. 365). Then let the essay rest in your mind for at least an hour or two before approaching it again. On subsequent readings, dig beneath the essay's surface by asking questions such as those in the checklist above. Note that the questions provided after each essay in this book offer more targeted versions of the ones above. Combining the questions in the checklist with the questions for individual readings will ensure a thorough analysis of what you read.

Analyzing a Sample Essay

Critical reading—and the insights to be gained from it—can best be illustrated by examining an actual essay. The paragraph on page 7 comes from "The Box Man" by Barbara Lazear Ascher. The entire essay is reprinted here in the same format as other selections in this book, with quotations from other writers to get you thinking about the essay's subject, a suggestion for exploring your attitudes further in your journal, a note on the author, and a note on the essay.

You are where you live. —Anna Quindlen

People who are homeless are not social inadequates. They are people without homes. —Sheila McKechnie

How does it feel / To be without a home / Like a complete unknown / Like a rolling stone? —Bob Dylan

JOURNAL RESPONSE In your journal write briefly about how you typically feel when you encounter a person who appears to be homeless. Are you sympathetic? disgusted? something in between?

Barbara Lazear Ascher

Born in 1946, American writer Barbara Lazear Ascher is known for her insightful, inspiring essays. She obtained a BA from Bennington College in 1968 and a JD from Cardozo School of Law in 1979. After practicing law for two years, Ascher turned to writing full-time. Her essays have appeared in a diverse assortment of periodicals, including the *New York Times, Vogue,* the *Yale Review, Redbook,* and *National Geographic Traveler.* Ascher has also published a memoir of her brother, who died of AIDS, *Landscape Without Gravity: A Memoir of Grief* (1993), and several collections of essays: *Playing After Dark* (1986), *The Habit of Loving* (1989), and *Dancing in the Dark: Romance, Yearning, and the Search for the Sublime* (1999). She lives in New York City.

The Box Man

In this essay from *Playing after Dark,* the evening ritual of a homeless man prompts Ascher's reflection on the nature of solitude. By describing the Box Man alongside two other solitary people, Ascher distinguishes between chosen and unchosen loneliness.

The Box Man was at it again. It was his lucky night. 1

The first stroke of good fortune occurred as darkness fell and the 2 night watchman at 220 East Forty-fifth Street neglected to close the door as he slipped out for a cup of coffee. I saw them before the Box Man did.

Just inside the entrance, cardboard cartons, clean and with their top flaps intact. With the silent fervor of a mute at a horse race, I willed him toward them.

It was slow going. His collar was pulled so high that he appeared   3 headless as he shuffled across the street like a man who must feel Earth with his toes to know that he walks there.

Standing unselfconsciously in the white glare of an overhead light,   4 he began to sort through the boxes, picking them up, one by one, inspecting tops, insides, flaps. Three were tossed aside. They looked perfectly good to me, but then, who knows what the Box Man knows? When he found the one that suited his purpose, he dragged it up the block and dropped it in a doorway.

Then, as if dogged by luck, he set out again and discovered, behind the   5 sign at the parking garage, a plastic Dellwood box, strong and clean, once used to deliver milk. Back in the doorway the grand design was revealed as he pushed the Dellwood box against the door and set its cardboard cousin two feet in front—the usual distance between coffee table and couch. Six full shopping bags were distributed evenly on either side.

He eased himself with slow care onto the stronger box, reached into   6 one of the bags, pulled out a *Daily News,* and snapped it open against his cardboard table. All done with the ease of IRT Express passengers whose white-tipped, fair-haired fingers reach into attaché cases as if radar-directed to the *Wall Street Journal.* They know how to fold it. They know how to stare at the print, not at the girl who stares at them.

That's just what the Box Man did, except that he touched his tongue   7 to his fingers before turning each page, something grandmothers do.

One could live like this. Gathering boxes to organize a life. Wander-   8 ing through the night collecting comforts to fill a doorway.

When I was a child, my favorite book was *The Boxcar Children.* If I   9 remember correctly, the young protagonists were orphaned, and rather than live with cruel relatives, they ran away to the woods to live life on their own terms. An abandoned boxcar was turned into a home, a bubbling brook became an icebox. Wild berries provided abundant desserts and days were spent in the happy, adultless pursuit of joy. The children never worried where the next meal would come from or what February's chill might bring. They had unquestioning faith that berries would ripen and streams run cold and clear. And unlike Thoreau,[1] whose

---

[1] Henry David Thoreau (1817–62) was an American essayist and poet who for two years lived a solitary and simple life in the woods. He wrote of his experiences in *Walden* (1854). [Editors' note.]

deliberate living was self-conscious and purposeful, theirs had the ease of children at play.

Even now, when life seems complicated and reason slips, I long to 10 live like a Boxcar Child, to have enough open space and freedom of movement to arrange my surroundings according to what I find. To turn streams into iceboxes. To be ingenious with simple things. To let the imagination hold sway.

Who is to say that the Box Man does not feel as Thoreau did in his 11 doorway, not "crowded or confined in the least," with "pasture enough for . . . imagination." Who is to say that his dawns don't bring back heroic ages? That he doesn't imagine a goddess trailing her garments across his blistered legs?

His is a life of the mind, such as it is, and voices only he can hear. 12 Although it would appear to be a life of misery, judging from the bandages and chill of night, it is of his choosing. He will ignore you if you offer an alternative. Last winter, Mayor Koch[2] tried, coaxing him with promises and the persuasive tones reserved for rabid dogs. The Box Man backed away, keeping a car and paranoia between them.

He is not to be confused with the lonely ones. You'll find them every- 13 where. The lady who comes into our local coffee shop each evening at five-thirty, orders a bowl of soup and extra Saltines. She drags it out as long as possible, breaking the crackers into smaller and smaller pieces, first in halves and then halves of halves and so on until the last pieces burst into salty splinters and fall from dry fingers onto the soup's shimmering surface. By 6 PM, it's all over. What will she do with the rest of the night?

You can tell by the vacancy of expression that no memories linger 14 there. She does not wear a gold charm bracelet with silhouettes of boys and girls bearing grandchildren's birthdates and a chip of the appropriate birthstone. When she opens her black purse to pay, there is only a crumpled Kleenex and a wallet inside, no photographs spill onto her lap. Her children, if there are any, live far away and prefer not to visit. If she worked as a secretary for forty years in a downtown office, she was given a retirement party, a cake, a reproduction of an antique perfume atomizer and sent on her way. Old colleagues—those who traded knitting patterns and brownie recipes over the water cooler, who discussed the weather, health, and office scandal while applying lipstick and blush before the ladies' room mirror—they are lost to time and the new young employees who take their places in the typing pool.

---

[2] Edward Koch was the mayor of New York City from 1978 through 1989. [Editors' note.]

Each year she gets a Christmas card from her ex-boss. The envelope 15
is canceled in the office mailroom and addressed by memory typewriter.
Within is a family in black and white against a wooded Connecticut
landscape. The boss, his wife, who wears her hair in a gray page boy, the
three blond daughters, two with tall husbands and an occasional additional grandchild. All assembled before a worn stone wall.

Does she watch game shows? Talk to a parakeet, feed him cuttle- 16
bone, and call him Pete? When she rides the buses on her Senior Citizen
pass, does she go anywhere or wait for something to happen? Does she
have a niece like the one in Cynthia Ozick's story "Rosa," who sends
enough money to keep her aunt at a distance?

There's a lady across the way whose lights and television stay on all 17
night. A crystal chandelier in the dining room and matching Chinese
lamps on Regency end tables in the living room. She has six cats, some
Siamese, others Angora and Abyssinian. She pets them and waters her
plethora of plants—African violets, a ficus tree, a palm, and geraniums
in season. Not necessarily a lonely life except that 3 AM lights and television seem to proclaim it so.

The Box Man welcomes the night, opens to it like a lover. He moves 18
in darkness and prefers it that way. He's not waiting for the phone to
ring or an engraved invitation to arrive in the mail. Not for him a PO
number. Not for him the overcrowded jollity of office parties, the hot
anticipation of a singles' bar. Not even for him a holiday handout. People
have tried and he shuffled away.

The Box Man knows that loneliness chosen loses its sting and claims 19
no victims. He declares what we all know in the secret passages of our
own nights, that although we long for perfect harmony, communion,
and blending with another soul, this is a solo voyage.

The first half of our lives is spent stubbornly denying it. As children 20
we acquire language to make ourselves understood and soon learn from
the blank stares in response to our babblings that even these, our saviors, our parents, are strangers. In adolescence when we replay earlier
dramas with peers in the place of parents, we begin the quest for the
best friend, that person who will receive all thoughts as if they were
her own. Later we assert that true love will find the way. True love finds
many ways, but no escape from exile. The shores are littered with us,
Annas and Ophelias, Emmas and Juliets,³ all outcasts from the dream of

---

³ These are all doomed heroines of literature. Anna is the title character of
Leo Tolstoy's novel *Anna Karenina* (1876). Emma is the title character of Gustave
Flaubert's novel *Madame Bovary* (1856). Ophelia and Juliet are in Shakespeare's
plays—the lovers, respectively, of Hamlet and Romeo. [Editors' note.]

perfect understanding. We might as well draw the night around us and find solace there and a friend in our own voice.

One could do worse than be a collector of boxes.   21

Even read quickly, Ascher's essay would not be difficult to comprehend: the author draws on examples of three people to make a point at the end about solitude. In fact, a quick reading might give the impression that Ascher produced the essay effortlessly, artlessly. But close, critical reading reveals a carefully conceived work whose parts function independently and together to achieve the author's purpose.

One way to uncover underlying intentions and relations like those in Ascher's essay is to answer a series of questions about the work. The following questions proceed from the general to the specific—from overall meaning through purpose and method to word choices—and they parallel the more specific questions after the essays in this book. Here the questions come with possible answers for Ascher's essay. (The paragraph numbers can help you locate the appropriate passages in Ascher's essay as you follow the analysis.)

Meaning

What is the main idea of the essay—the chief point the writer makes about the subject, to which all other ideas and details relate? What are the subordinate ideas that contribute to the main idea?

Ascher states her main idea (or thesis) near the end of her essay: in choosing solitude, the Box Man confirms the essential aloneness of human beings (paragraph 19) but also demonstrates that we can "find solace" within ourselves (20). (Writers sometimes postpone stating their main idea, as Ascher does here. Perhaps more often, they state it near the beginning of the essay. See pp. 25–28.) Ascher leads up to and supports her idea with three examples—the Box Man (paragraphs 1–7, 11–12) and, in contrast, two women whose loneliness seems unchosen (13–16, 17). These examples are developed with specific details from Ascher's observations (such as the nearly empty purse, 14) and from the imagined lives these observations suggest (such as the remote, perhaps non-existent children, 14).

Occasionally, you may need to puzzle over some of the author's words before you can fully understand his or her meaning. Try to guess the word's meaning from its context first, and then check your guess in a dictionary. (To help master the word so that you know it next time and can draw on it yourself, use it in a sentence or more of your own.)

Purpose and Audience

Why did the author write the essay? What did the author hope readers would gain from it? What did the author assume about the knowledge and interests of readers, and how are these assumptions reflected in the essay?

Ascher seems to have written her essay for two interlocking reasons: to show and thus explain that solitude need not always be lonely and to argue gently for defeating loneliness by becoming one's own friend. In choosing the Box Man as her main example, she reveals perhaps a third purpose as well—to convince readers that a homeless person can have dignity and may achieve a measure of self-satisfaction lacking in some people who do have homes.

Ascher seems to assume that her readers, like her, are people with homes, people to whom the Box Man and his life might seem completely foreign: she comments on the Box Man's slow shuffle (paragraph 3), his mysterious discrimination among boxes (4), his "blistered legs" (11), how miserable his life looks (12), his bandages (12), the cold night he inhabits (12), the fearful or condescending approaches of strangers (12, 18). Building from this assumption that her readers will find the Box Man strange, Ascher takes pains to show the dignity of the Box Man—his "grand design" for furniture (5), his resemblance to commuters (6), his grandmotherly finger licking (7), his refusal of handouts (18).

Several other apparent assumptions about her audience also influence Ascher's selection of details, if less significantly. First, she assumes some familiarity with literature—at least with the writings of Thoreau (9, 11) and the characters named in paragraph 20. Second, Ascher seems to address women: in paragraph 20 she speaks of each person confiding in "her" friend, and she chooses only female figures from literature to illustrate "us, . . . all outcasts from the dream of perfect understanding." Finally, Ascher seems to address people who are familiar with, if not actually residents of, New York City: she refers to a New York street address (2); alludes to a New York newspaper, the *Daily News,* and a New York subway line, the IRT Express (6); and mentions the city's mayor (12). However, readers who do not know the literature Ascher cites, who are not women, and who do not know New York City are still likely to understand and appreciate Ascher's main point.

Method and Structure

What method or methods does the author use to develop the main idea, and how do the methods serve the author's subject and purpose? How does the organization serve the author's subject and purpose?

Ascher's primary support for her idea consists of three examples (Chapter 7)—specific instances of solitary people. The method of example especially suits Ascher's subject and purpose because it allows her to show contrasting responses to solitude: one person who seems to choose it and two people who don't.

As writers often do, Ascher relies on more than a single method, more than just example. She develops her examples with description (Chapter 6), vividly portraying the Box Man and the two women, as in paragraphs 6–7, so that we see them clearly. Paragraphs 1–7 in the portrayal of the Box Man involve retelling, or narrating (Chapter 5), his activities. Ascher uses division or analysis (Chapter 8) to tease apart the elements of her three characters' lives. And she relies on comparison and contrast (Chapter 11) to show the differences between the Box Man and the other two in paragraphs 13 and 17–18.

While using many methods to develop her idea, Ascher keeps her organization fairly simple. She does not begin with a formal introduction or a statement of her idea but instead starts right off with her main example, the inspiration for her idea. In the first seven paragraphs she narrates and describes the Box Man's activities. Then, in paragraphs 8–12, she explains what appeals to her about circumstances like the Box Man's and she applies those thoughts to what she imagines are his thoughts. Still delaying a statement of her main idea, Ascher contrasts the Box Man and two other solitary people, whose lives she sees as different from his (13–17). Finally, she returns to the Box Man (18–19) and zeroes in on her main idea (19–20). Though she has withheld this idea until the end, we see that everything in the essay has been controlled by it and directed toward it.

Language

How are the author's main idea and purpose revealed at the level of sentences and words? How does the author use language to convey his or her attitudes toward the subject and to make meaning clear and vivid?

One reason Ascher's essay works is that she uses specific language to portray her three examples—she shows them to us—and to let us know what she thinks about them. For instance, the language changes markedly from the depiction of the Box Man to the next-to-last paragraph on solitude. The Box Man comes to life in warm terms: Ascher watches him with "silent fervor" (paragraph 2); he seems "dogged by luck" (5); he sits with "slow care" and opens the newspaper with "ease" (6); his page turning reminds Ascher of "grandmothers" (7); it is conceivable that, in Thoreau's word, the Box Man's imagination has "pasture" to roam, that he dreams of "heroic ages" and a "goddess trailing her garments" (11). In contrast, isolation comes across as a desperate state in paragraph 20, where Ascher uses words such as "blank stares," "strangers," "exile," "littered," and "outcasts." The contrast in language helps to emphasize Ascher's point about the individual's ability to find comfort in solitude.

In describing the two other solitary people—those who evidently have not found comfort in aloneness—Ascher uses words that emphasize the heaviness of time and the sterility of existence. The first woman "drags" her meal out and crumbles crackers between "dry fingers" (13), a "vacancy of expression" on her face (14). She lacks even the trinkets of attachment—a "gold charm bracelet" with "silhouettes" of grandchildren (14). A vividly imagined photograph of her ex-boss and his family (15)—the wife with "her hair in a gray page boy," "the three blond daughters"—emphasizes the probable absence of such scenes in the woman's own life.

Ascher occasionally uses incomplete sentences (or sentence fragments, see p. 48) to stress the accumulation of details or the quickness of her impressions. For example, in paragraph 10 the incomplete sentences beginning "To" sketch Ascher's dream. And in paragraph 18 the incomplete sentences beginning "Not" emphasize the Box Man's withdrawal. Both of these sets of incomplete sentences gain emphasis from **parallelism**, the use of similar grammatical form for ideas of equal importance (see p. 53). The parallelism begins in the complete sentence preceding each set of incomplete sentences—for example, "… I long to live like a Boxcar Child, to have enough open space and freedom of movement…. To turn streams into iceboxes. To be ingenious with simple things. To let the imagination hold sway." Although incomplete sentences can be unclear, these and the others in Ascher's essay are clear: she uses them deliberately and carefully, for a purpose. (Inexperienced writers often find it safer to avoid any incomplete sentences until they have mastered the complete sentence.)

These notes on Ascher's essay show how one can arrive at a deeper, more personal understanding of a piece of writing by attentive, thoughtful analysis. Guided by the questions at the end of each essay and by your own sense of what works and why, you'll find similar lessons and pleasures in all of this book's readings.

Reading Visuals Critically

Much of what you read will have a visual component—a photograph, perhaps, or a drawing, chart, table, or graph. Sometimes these images stand alone, but often they contribute to the overall meaning and effect of a written work. A handful of the essays in this book, in fact, include visuals: Grace Patterson's "A Rock and a Hard Place" (p. 59) uses a picture to illustrate a point, William Least Heat-Moon's "Starrucca Viaduct" (p. 107) and Barbara Kingsolver's "Stalking the Vegetannual" (p. 210) both start with drawings, and Charlie LeDuff's "End of the Line" (p. 300) incorporates several photographs.

Like written texts, visual texts are composed. That is, the people who create them do with images what writers do with words: they come to the task with a purpose, an audience, and a message to convey. You can and should, therefore, "read" visuals actively. Don't simply glance over images or take them at face value. Instead, examine them closely and with a critical eye.

Reading visuals critically draws on the same skills you use for closely reading written works. The checklist for critical reading on page 8 can get you started. Determining who created an image, why, and for whom, for instance, will help you tease out details that you might have missed at first look. Examining each element of a visual composition—such as the placement and arrangement of objects, the focus, and the uses of color, light, and shadow—will give you a greater appreciation of its intent and overall effect. Notice what first captures your attention, where your eye is drawn, and how different parts of the image interact with one another to create a dominant impression. Finally, if the visual accompanies written text, such as an essay or advertisement, ask yourself what it contributes to the writer's meaning and purpose.

Consider, for example, one student's notes on a photograph of a homeless man in New York City. The picture was taken in 2005 by amateur photographer Colin Gregory Palmer and is used on the Web sites of several homeless advocacy groups, including the Homelessness Project and Push Open Doors.

relative position of man and flag = a comment on government?

dark shadows feel dangerous

cold surfaces, hard angles dominate the center

man stuffed in corner— seems powerless, insignificant

slumped over and _faceless_ (shame? or defeat?)

shoes look new—where did they come from?

As Palmer's photograph demonstrates, visual images can pack many layers of meaning into a condensed space. Learning to unpack those layers is a skill worth cultivating. (For advice on using visuals in your own writing, see p. 40).

2

DEVELOPING AN ESSAY

Analyzing a text as shown in the preceding chapter is valuable in itself: it can be fun, and the process helps you better understand and appreciate whatever you read. But it can make you a better writer, too, by showing you how to read your own work critically, broadening the range of strategies available to you, and suggesting subjects for you to write about.

The essays collected in this book are accompanied by a range of material designed to help you use your reading to write effectively. Every reading is followed by several detailed questions that will help you read it critically and examine the writing strategies that make it successful. Accompanying the questions are writing topics—ideas for you to adapt and develop into essays of your own. Some of these call for your analysis of the essay; others lead you to examine your own experiences or outside sources in light of the essay's ideas. Chapters 5–14 each conclude with two additional sets of writing topics: one group provides a range of subjects for using the chapter's method of development; the other encourages you to focus on thematic connections in the chapter.

To help you develop your writing, *The Compact Reader* also offers several tools that guide you through composing effective essays. This chapter and the next two (on revising and editing) offer specific ways to strengthen and clarify your work as you move through the **writing process**, the activities that contribute to a finished piece of writing. This process is presented as a sequence of stages: analyzing the writing situation, discovering ideas, focusing, shaping, revising, and editing. As you'll discover, these stages are actually somewhat arbitrary because writers rarely move in straight lines through fixed steps. Instead, just as they do when thinking, writers continually circle back over covered territory, each time picking up more information or seeing new relationships, until their meaning is clear to themselves and can be made clear to readers. No two writers proceed in exactly the same way, either. Still, viewing the process in stages does help sort out its many activities so that you can develop the process or processes that work best for you.

Complementing this and the next chapters' overview of the writing process are the more specific introductions to the methods of development in Chapters 5–14—narration, comparison and contrast, definition, and so on. These method introductions follow the pattern set here by also proceeding from beginning to end of the writing process, but they take up particular concerns of the method, such as organizing a narrative or clarifying a definition. (See the inside back cover for a guide to the topics covered.)

Getting Started

Every writing situation involves several elements: you communicate a *thesis* (idea) about a subject to an *audience* of readers for a particular *purpose*. At first you may not be sure of your idea or your purpose. You may not know how you want to approach your readers, even when you know who they are. Your job in getting started, then, is to explore options and make choices.

Considering Your Subject and Purpose

A subject for writing may arise from any source, including your own experience or reading, a suggestion in this book, or an assignment from your instructor. In the previous chapter, Barbara Lazear Ascher's essay on a homeless man demonstrates how an excellent subject can be found from observing one's surroundings. Whatever its source, the subject should be something you care enough about to probe deeply and to stamp with your own perspective.

This personal stamp comes from your **purpose**, your reason for writing. The purpose may be one of the following:

- To explain the subject so that readers understand it or see it in a new light.
- To persuade readers to accept or reject an opinion or to take a certain action.

■ To entertain readers with a humorous or an exciting story.

■ To express the thoughts and emotions triggered by a revealing or an instructive experience.

A single essay may sometimes have more than one purpose: for instance, a writer might both explain what it's like to have a disability and try to persuade readers to respect special parking zones for people with disabilities. Your reasons for writing may be clear to you early on, arising out of the subject and its significance for you. But you may need to explore your subject for a while—even to the point of writing a draft—before you know what you want to do with it.

Considering Your Audience

Either very early, when you first begin exploring your subject, or later, as a check on what you have generated, you may want to make a few notes on your anticipated audience. The notes are optional, but thinking about audience definitely is not. Your topic and purpose, as well as your thesis, supporting ideas, details and examples, organization, style, tone, and language—all should reflect your answers to the following questions:

■ What impression do you want to make on readers?

■ What do readers already know about your subject? What do they need to know?

■ What are readers' likely expectations and assumptions about your subject?

■ How can you build on readers' previous knowledge, expectations, and assumptions to bring them around to your view?

These considerations are obviously crucial to achieve the fundamental purpose of all public writing: communication. Accordingly, they come up again and again in the chapter introductions and the questions after each essay.

Discovering Ideas

Ideas for your writing—whether your subject itself or the many smaller ideas and details that comprise what you have to say about it—may come to you in a rush, or you may need to search for them. Writers use a variety of searching techniques, from jotting down thoughts while they pursue other activities to writing concentratedly for a set period. Here are a few techniques you might try.

Journal Writing

Many writers keep a **journal**, a record of thoughts and observations. Whether in a notebook or in a computer file, journal entries give you an opportunity to explore ideas just for yourself, free of concerns about readers who will judge what you say or how you say it. Regular journal entries can also make you more comfortable with the act of writing and build your confidence. Indeed, writing teachers often require their students to keep journals for these reasons.

In a journal you can write about whatever interests, puzzles, or disturbs you. Here are just a few possible uses:

- Record your responses to your reading in this book and other sources.
- Prepare for a class by summarizing the week's reading or the previous class's discussion.
- Analyze a relationship that's causing you problems.
- Imitate a writer you admire, such as a poet or songwriter.
- Explore your reactions to a movie or television program.
- Confide your dreams and fears.

Any of this material could provide a seed for a writing assignment, but you can also use a journal deliberately to develop ideas for assignments. One approach is built into this book: before every essay you will find several quotations and a suggestion for journal writing—all centering on the topic of the essay. In responding to the quotations and journal prompt preceding Barbara Lazear Ascher's "The Box Man" (p. 9), you might explore your feelings about homeless people or recount a particular encounter with a homeless person. One student, Grace Patterson, wrote this journal entry in response to the material preceding Ascher's essay:

> It seems that nothing works to solve the problem of homeless people. My first reaction is fear—especially if the person is really dirty or rambling on about something. I just walk away as fast as I can. Can't say I'm proud of myself though—there's always *guilt*—I should be helping. But how? I like what Bob Dylan says—a home is important, so how must it feel to be without one?

Writing for herself, Patterson felt free to explore what was on her mind, without worrying about correctness and without trying to make it clear to external readers what she meant by words such as *fear* and *guilt*. By articulating her mixed reactions to homelessness, Patterson established a personal context in which to read Ascher's essay, and that context made her a more engaged, more critical reader.

Patterson used journal writing for another purpose as well: to respond to Ascher's essay *after* she read it.

> Ascher gives an odd view of homelessness—hadn't really occurred to me that the homeless man on the street might want to be there. Always assumed that no one would want to live in filthy clothes, without a roof. What is a home anyway—shelter? decor? a clothes closet? Can your body and few "possessions" = home?

As this entry's final question makes clear, Patterson didn't come to any conclusions about homelessness or about Ascher's essay. She did, however, begin to work out ideas that would serve as the foundation for a more considered critical response later on. (Further stages of Patterson's writing process appear throughout the rest of this chapter.)

Freewriting

To discover ideas for a particular assignment, you may find it useful to try **freewriting,** or writing without stopping for a set amount of time, usually ten to fifteen minutes. In freewriting you push yourself to keep writing, following ideas wherever they lead, paying no attention to completeness or correctness or even sense. When she began composing an essay response to Barbara Lazear Ascher's "The Box Man," Grace Patterson produced this freewriting:

> Something in Ascher's essay keeps nagging at me. Almost ticks me off. What she says about the Box Man is based on certain assumptions. Like she knows what he's been through, how he feels. Can he be as content as she says? What bothers me is, how much choice does the guy really have? Just cuz he manages to put a little dignity into his life on the street and refuses handouts—does that mean he chooses homelessness? Life in a shelter might be worse than life on the street.

Notice that this freewriting is rough: the tone is very informal, as if Patterson were speaking to herself; some thoughts are left dangling; some sentences are shapeless or incomplete; a word is misspelled (*cuz* for *because*). But none of this matters because the freewriting is just exploratory. Writing fluently, without halting to rethink or edit, actually pulled insights out of Patterson. She moved from being vaguely uneasy with Ascher's essay to conceiving an argument against it. Then, with a more definite focus, she could begin drafting in earnest.

If you have difficulty writing without correcting and you compose on a word processor, you might try **invisible writing**: turn the computer's monitor off while you freewrite, so that you can't see what you're producing. When your time is up, turn the monitor back on to work with the material.

Brainstorming

Another discovery technique that helps to pull ideas from you is **brainstorming**, listing ideas without stopping to censor or change them. As in freewriting, write without stopping for ten or fifteen minutes, jotting down everything that seems even remotely related to your subject. Don't stop to reread and rethink what you have written; just keep pulling and recording ideas, no matter how silly or dull or irrelevant they seem. When your time is up, look over the list to find the promising ideas and discard the rest. Depending on *how* promising the remaining ideas are, you can resume brainstorming, try freewriting about them, or begin a draft.

Using the Methods of Development

The ten methods of development discussed in Chapters 5–14 can also help you expand your thinking. Try asking the following questions to open up ideas about your subject:

- *Narration* (Chapter 5): What is the story in the subject? How did it happen?
- *Description* (Chapter 6): How does the subject look, sound, smell, taste, and feel?
- *Example* (Chapter 7): How can the subject be illustrated? What are instances of it?
- *Division or Analysis* (Chapter 8): What are the subject's parts, and what is their relationship or significance?
- *Classification* (Chapter 9): What groups or categories can the subject be sorted into?
- *Process Analysis* (Chapter 10): How does the subject work, or how does one do it?

- *Comparison and Contrast* (Chapter 11): How is the subject similar to or different from something else?

- *Definition* (Chapter 12): What are the subject's characteristics and boundaries?

- *Cause-and-Effect Analysis* (Chapter 13): Why did the subject happen? What were or may be its consequences?

- *Argument and Persuasion* (Chapter 14): Why do I believe as I do about the subject? Why do others have different opinions? How can I convince others to accept my opinion or believe as I do?

Forming a Thesis

How many times have you read a work of nonfiction and wondered, "What's the point?" Whether consciously or not, we expect a writer to *have* a point, a central idea that he or she wants readers to take away from the work. We expect that idea to determine the content of the work—so that everything relates to it—and we expect the content in turn to demonstrate or prove the idea.

Arriving at a main idea, or **thesis**, is thus an essential part of the writing process. Sometimes your thesis will occur to you at the moment you hit on your subject—for instance, if you think of writing about the new grading policy because you want to make a point about its unfairness. More often, you will need to explore your subject for a while—even to the point of writing a draft or more—before you pin down just what you have to say. Even if your thesis will evolve, however, it's a good idea to draft it early because it can help keep you focused as you generate more ideas, seek information, and organize your thoughts.

Identifying Your Main Point

A thesis is distinct from the subject of an essay. The subject is what an essay is about; the thesis captures a writer's unique understanding of that subject. In the case of "The Box Man," for example, the subject is homelessness, but Ascher's thesis—that one homeless man's quiet dignity should serve as a model for how the rest of us go about our lives—makes a strong point that readers may not have contemplated on their own. Student writer Grace Patterson takes the same subject—homelessness—but she makes a completely different point: that a homeless person's "choice" to live on the streets is not a choice at all.

The distinction between a subject and a thesis is evident throughout this book. Each chapter of readings focuses on a single subject—such as travel, popular culture, or food—yet the individual essays demonstrate the writers' unique perspectives on particular aspects of those general topics. The readings in Chapter 5, for instance, all center on the subject of childhood, but no two take the same approach. Michael Ondaatje writes to capture the mystery of a snake that seemed immortal; Donald Hall recalls the "bliss" of hurting a playmate; Annie Dillard uses a memorable incident to explain the thrill of misbehavior; Langston Hughes writes about a church revival to make a point about innocence and faith; and Kaela Hobby-Reichstein considers the ways in which racism affected her sense of fairness.

To move from a general subject to a workable thesis for your own writing, keep narrowing your focus until you have something to say about the subject. For example, if you wanted to write about family, you'd quickly discover that the topic—which fills whole books—is too broad to work with in a brief essay. You could then narrow the subject to adoptive families, but even that covers too much territory. By consistently tightening your focus, you might eventually realize that what interests you is adopted children who want to contact their birth parents and that you want to explain how it is possible, if difficult, to locate the necessary information. In a few steps, you've turned a broad subject into a main point worth making. The process isn't always simple, but it is a necessary first step in finding a thesis.

Drafting and Revising a Thesis Sentence

Once you've narrowed your subject and have something to say about it, the best way to focus on your thesis is to write it out in a **thesis sentence** (or sentences): an assertion that makes your point about the subject. In these two sentences from the end of "The Box Man" (p. 9), Barbara Lazear Ascher asserts the main idea of her essay:

> [We are] all outcasts from the dream of perfect understanding. We might as well draw the night around us and find solace there and a friend in our own voice.

Ascher's thesis statement, while poetic, nonetheless ties together all of the other ideas and details in her essay; it also reflects her purpose in writing the essay and focuses her readers on a single point. All effective thesis sentences do this: they go beyond generalities or mere statements of fact to express the writer's opinion about the subject. Notice the differences in the following sentences Grace Patterson considered for her response to "The Box Man":

GENERAL STATEMENT   Homelessness is a serious problem in America.

STATEMENT OF FACT   Some homeless people avoid staying in temporary shelters.

EFFECTIVE THESIS SENTENCE   For the homeless people in America today, there are no good choices.

The first sentence offers an opinion, but because it's a very broad assertion that few would dispute, it fails to capture readers' interest or make a significant point. The second sentence merely expresses a fact, not a main idea worth developing in an essay. The final sentence, however, makes a strong assertion about a narrow subject and gives readers an idea of what to expect from the rest of the essay.

Because the main point of an essay may change over the course of the writing process, your own thesis sentence may also change, sometimes considerably. The following examples show how one writer shifted his opinion and moved from an explanatory to a persuasive purpose between the early stages of the writing process and the final draft.

EARLY THESIS SENTENCE   With persistence, adopted children can often locate information about their birth parents.

FINAL THESIS SENTENCE   Adopted children are unfairly hampered in seeking information about their birth parents.

The final sentence makes a definite assertion ("Adopted children are unfairly hampered") and clearly conveys the persuasive purpose of the essay to come. Thus the sentence lets readers know what to expect: an argument that adopted children should be treated more fairly when they seek information about their birth parents. Readers will also expect some discussion of what hampers an adoptee's search, what is "unfair" and "fair" in this situation, and what changes the author proposes.

Most commonly, the thesis sentence comes near the beginning of an essay, sometimes in the first paragraph, where it serves as a promise to examine a particular subject from a particular perspective. But as Ascher demonstrates by stating her thesis at the end, the thesis sentence may come elsewhere as long as it controls the whole essay. The thesis may even go unstated, as other essays in this book illustrate, but it still must govern every element of the work as if it were announced.

Organizing

Writers vary in the extent to which they arrange their material before they begin drafting, but most do establish some plan. A good time to do so is after you've explored your subject and developed a good stock of ideas about it. Before you begin drafting, you can look over what you've got and consider the best ways to organize it.

Creating a Plan

A writing plan may consist of a list of key points, a fuller list including specifics as well, or even a detailed formal outline—whatever gives order to your ideas and provides some direction for your writing.

As you'll see in later chapters, many of the methods of development suggest specific structures, most notably description, narration, classification, process analysis, and comparison and contrast. But even when the organization is almost built into the method, you'll find that some subjects demand more thoughtful plans than others. You may be able to draft a straightforward narrative of a personal experience with very little advance planning. But a nonpersonal narrative, or even a personal one involving complex events and time shifts, may require more thought about arrangement.

Though some sort of plan is almost always useful when drafting, resist any temptation at this stage to pin down every detail in its proper place. A huge investment in planning can hamper you during drafting, making it difficult to respond to new ideas and even new directions that may prove fruitful.

Thinking in Paragraphs

Most essays consist of three parts: an introduction and a conclusion (discussed in the next section) and the **body**, the most substantial and longest part, which develops the main idea or thesis.

As you explore your subject, you will discover both ideas that directly support your thesis and more specific examples, details, and other evidence that support these ideas. In the following outline of Grace Patterson's "A Rock and a Hard Place" (pp. 59–60), you can see how each supporting idea, or subpoint, helps to build the thesis sentence:

THESIS SENTENCE   For the homeless people in America today, there are no good choices.

SUBPOINT   A "good choice" is one made from a variety of options determined and narrowed down by the chooser.

SUBPOINT   Homeless people do not necessarily choose to live on the streets.

SUBPOINT   The streets are the only alternative to shelters, which are dangerous and dehumanizing.

Patterson uses specific evidence to develop each subpoint in a paragraph. In essence, the paragraphs are like mini-essays with their own main ideas and support. (See pp. 35–36 for more on paragraph structure.)

When you seek a plan in your ideas, look first for your subpoints, the main supports for your thesis. Use these as your starting points to work out your essay one chunk (or paragraph) at a time. You can sketch the supporting details and examples into your organizational plan, or you can wait until you begin drafting to get into the specifics.

Considering the Introduction and Conclusion

You'll probably have to be drafting or revising before you'll know for sure how you want to begin and end your essay. Still, it can be helpful to consider the introduction and conclusion earlier, so you have a sense of how you might approach readers and what you might leave them with.

The basic opening and closing serve readers by demonstrating your interest in their needs and expectations:

- The **introduction** draws readers into the essay and focuses their attention on the main idea and purpose, often stated in a thesis sentence.

- The **conclusion** ties together the elements of the essay and provides a final impression for readers to take away with them.

These basic forms allow considerable room for variation. Especially as you are developing your writing skills, you will find it helpful to state your thesis sentence near the beginning of the essay; but sometimes you can place it effectively at the end, or you can let it direct what you say in the essay but never state it at all. One essay may need two paragraphs of introduction but only a one-sentence conclusion, whereas another essay may require no formal introduction but a lengthy conclusion. How you begin and end depends on your subject and purpose, the kind of essay you are writing, and the likely responses of your readers. Specific ideas for opening and closing essays are included in each chapter introduction and in the Glossary under *introductions* and *conclusions*.

Drafting

However detailed your organizational plan is, you should not view it as a rigid taskmaster while you are drafting your essay. Drafting is the chance for you to give expression to your ideas, filling them out, finding relationships, drawing conclusions. If you are like most writers, you will discover much of what you have to say while drafting. In fact, if your subject is complex or difficult for you to write about, you may need several drafts just to work out your ideas and their relationships.

Writing, Not Revising

Some writers draft rapidly, rarely looking up from the paper or keyboard. Others draft more in fits and starts, gazing out the window or doodling as much as writing. Any method that works is fine, but one method rarely works: collapsing drafting and revising into one stage, trying to do everything at once.

Write first; then revise. Concentrate on *what* you are saying, not on *how* you are saying it. You pressure yourself needlessly if you try to produce a well-developed, coherent, interesting, and grammatically correct paper all at once. You may have trouble getting words on paper because you're afraid to make mistakes, or you may be distracted by mistakes from exploring your ideas fully. Awkwardness, repetition, wrong words, grammatical errors, spelling mistakes—these and other more superficial concerns can be attended to in a later draft. The same goes for considering your readers' needs: like many writers, you may find that attention to readers during the first draft inhibits the flow of ideas.

If you experience writer's block or just don't know how to begin your draft, start writing the part you're most comfortable with. Writing in paragraph chunks, as described on page 29, will also make drafting more manageable. You can start with your thesis sentence—or at least keep it in view while you draft—as a reminder of your purpose and main idea. But if you find yourself pulled away from the thesis by a new idea, you may want to let go and follow, at least for a while. If your purpose and main idea change as a result of such exploration, you can always revise your thesis accordingly.

Grace Patterson's First Draft

Some exploratory work by the student Grace Patterson appears on pages 22 and 23. What follows is the first draft she subsequently wrote on homelessness. The draft is very rough, with frequent repetitions, wandering paragraphs, and many other flaws. But such weaknesses are not important at this early stage. The draft gave Patterson the opportunity to discover what she had to say, explore her ideas, and link them in rough sequence.

Title?

In the essay, "The Box Man," Barbara Lazear Ascher says that a homeless man who has chosen solitude can show the rest of us how to "find . . . a friend in our own voice." Maybe. But her case depends on the Box Man's choice, her assumption that he *had* one.

Discussions of the homeless often use the word *choice*. Many people with enough money can accept the condition of the homeless in America when they tell themselves that many of the homeless chose their lives. That the streets are in fact what they want. But it's not fair to use the word *choice* here: the homeless don't get to choose their lives the way most of the rest of us do. For the homeless people in America today, there are no good choices.

What do I mean by a "good choice"? One made from a variety of options determined and narrowed down by the chooser. There is plenty of room for the chooser to make a decision that he will be satisfied with. When I choose a career, I expect to make a good choice. There is plenty of interesting fields worth investigating, and there is lots of rewarding work to be done. It's a choice that opens the world up and showcases its possibilities. If it came time for me to choose a career, and the mayor of my town came around and told me that I had to choose between a life of cleaning public toilets and operating a jackhammer on a busy street corner, I would object. That's a lousy choice, and I wouldn't let anyone force me to make it.

When the mayor of New York tried to take the homeless off the streets, some of them didn't want to go. People assumed that the homeless people who did not want to get in the mayor's car for a ride to a city shelter *chose* to live on the street. But just because some homeless people chose the street over the generosity of the mayor does not necessarily mean that life on the streets is their ideal. We allow ourselves as many options as we can imagine, but we allow the homeless only two: go to a shelter, or stay where you are. Who narrowed down the options for the homeless? Who benefits if they go to a shelter? Who suffers if they don't?

Homeless people are not always better off in shelters. I had a conversation with a man who had lived on the streets for a long time. The man said that he had spent some time in those shelters for the homeless, and he told me what they were like. The shelters are crowded and dirty and people have to wait in long lines for everything. People are constantly being herded around and bossed around. It's dangerous—drug dealers, beatings, theft. Dehumanizing. It matches my picture of hell. From the sound of it, I couldn't spend two hours in a shelter, never mind a whole night. I value my peace of mind and my sleep too much, not to mention my freedom and autonomy.

When homeless people sleep in the street, though, that makes the public uncomfortable. People with enough money wish the homeless would just disappear. They don't care where they go. Just out of sight. I've felt this way too but I'm as uneasy with that reaction as I am at the sight of a person sleeping on the sidewalk. And I tell myself that this is more than a question of my comfort. By and large I'm comfortable enough.

The homeless are in a difficult enough situation without having to take the blame for making the rest of us feel uncomfortable with our wealth. If we cannot offer the homeless a good set of choices, the opportunity to choose lives that they will be truly satisfied with then the least we can do is stop dumping on them (?). They're caught between a rock and a hard place: there are not many places for them to go, and the places where they can go afford nothing but suffering.

3

REVISING

The previous chapter took you through the first-draft stage of the writing process, when you have a chance to work out your ideas without regard for what others may think. This chapter describes the crucial next stage, when you actively consider your readers: revising to focus and shape your meaning.

Revision means "re-seeing." Looking at your draft as your reader would, you cut, add, and reorganize until the ideas make sense on their own. Revision is not the same as editing. In revising, you make fundamental changes in content and structure, working below the surface of the draft. Editing comes later: once you're satisfied with the revised draft, you work on the surface of sentences and words, attending to style, grammar, punctuation, and the like (see Chapter 4). The separation of these two stages is important because attention to little changes distracts from a view of the whole. If you try to edit while you revise, you'll be more likely to miss the big picture. You may also waste effort perfecting sentences you'll later decide to cut.

Reading Your Own Work Critically

Perhaps the most difficult challenge of revision is reading your own work objectively, as a reader would. To gain something like a reader's critical distance from your draft, try one or more of the following techniques:

- Put your first draft aside for at least a few hours—and preferably overnight—before attempting to revise it. You may have further thoughts in the interval, and you will be able to see your work more objectively when you return to it.

■ Ask another person to read and comment on your draft. Your teacher may ask you and your classmates to exchange drafts so that you can help each other revise. But even without such a procedure, you can benefit from others' responses. Keep an open mind to readers' comments, and ask questions when you need more information.

■ Make an outline of your draft by listing what you cover in each paragraph. Such an outline can show gaps, overlaps, and problems in organization. (See also p. 28.)

■ Read the draft out loud. Speaking the words and hearing them can help to create distance from them.

■ Imagine you are someone else—a friend, perhaps, or a particular person in your intended audience—and read the draft through that person's eyes, as if for the first time.

■ Print a double-spaced copy of your draft. It's much easier to read text on paper than on a computer screen, and you can spread out printed pages to see the whole paper at once. Once you've finished revising, transferring changes to the computer requires little effort.

Looking at the Whole Draft

Revision involves seeing your draft as a whole, focusing mainly on your purpose and thesis, the support for your thesis, and the movement among ideas. You want to determine what will work and what won't for readers—where the draft strays from your purpose, leaves a hole in the development of your thesis, does not flow logically or smoothly, digresses, or needs more details. (See the revision checklist on p. 43.) Besides rewriting, you may need to cut entire paragraphs, condense paragraphs into sentences, add passages of explanation, or rearrange sections.

Purpose and Thesis

In the press of drafting, you may lose sight of why you are writing or what your main idea is. Both your purpose and your thesis may change as you work out your meaning, so that you start in one place and end somewhere else or even lose track of where you are.

Your first goal in revising, then, is to see that your essay is well focused. Readers should grasp a clear purpose right away, and they should find that you have achieved it at the end. They should see your main idea, your thesis, very early, usually by the end of the introduction, and they should think that you have proved or demonstrated the thesis when they reach the last paragraph.

Like many writers, you may sometimes start with one thesis and finish with another, in effect writing into your idea as you draft. In many cases you'll need to rewrite your thesis statement to reflect what you actually wrote in your draft. Or you may need to upend your essay, plucking your thesis out of the conclusion and starting over with it, providing the subpoints and details to develop it. You'll probably find the second draft much easier to write because you know better what you want to say, and the next round of revision will probably be much cleaner.

Unity

When a piece of writing has **unity**, all its parts are related: the sentences build the central idea of their paragraph, and the paragraphs build the central idea of the whole essay. Readers do not have to wonder what the essay is about or what a particular paragraph has to do with the rest of the piece.

Unity in Paragraphs

Earlier we saw how the body paragraphs of an essay are almost like mini-essays themselves, each developing an idea, or subpoint, that supports the thesis. (See p. 28.) In fact, a body paragraph should have its own thesis, called its **topic**, usually expressed in a **topic sentence** or sentences. The rest of the paragraph develops the topic with specifics.

In the following paragraph from the final draft of Grace Patterson's "A Rock and a Hard Place" (pp. 59–60), the topic sentence is italicized:

> *The fact is that homeless people are not always better off in shelters.* I spoke recently with a man named Alan Doran, who had lived on the streets for a long time. He said that he had spent some time in shelters for the homeless, and he told me what they are like. They're dangerous and dehumanizing. Drug deals, beatings, and thefts are common. Because shelters are crowded, residents have to wait in long lines for everything; they also have to accept being constantly bossed around. No wonder some homeless people, including Alan, prefer the street: it affords some space to breathe, some autonomy, some peace for sleeping.

Notice that every sentence of this paragraph relates to the topic sentence. Patterson achieved this unity in revision (see pp. 44–46). In her first draft she focused the last sentences of this paragraph on herself rather than on the conditions of homeless shelters:

> It matches my picture of hell. From the sound of it, I couldn't spend two hours in a shelter, never mind a whole night. I value my peace of mind and my sleep too much, not to mention my freedom and autonomy.

If you look back at the full paragraph above, you'll see that Patterson deleted these sentences and substituted a final one that focuses on the paragraph's topic, the conditions of the shelters for the homeless themselves.

Your topic sentences will not always fall at the very beginning of your paragraphs. Sometimes you'll need to create a transition from the preceding paragraph before stating the new paragraph's topic, or you'll build the paragraph to a topic sentence at the end, or you'll divide the statement between the beginning and the end. (Patterson's second paragraph, on p. 31, works this way, defining a good choice at the beginning and a bad choice at the end.) Sometimes, too, you'll write a paragraph with a topic but without a topic sentence. In all these cases, you'll need to have an idea for the paragraph and to unify the paragraph around that idea, so that all the specifics support and develop it.

Unity in Essays

Just as sentences must center on a paragraph's main idea, so paragraphs must center on an essay's main idea, or thesis. Readers who have to ask "What is the point?" or "Why am I reading this?" generally won't appreciate or accept the point.

Look at the outline of Grace Patterson's essay on page 27. Her thesis sentence states, "For the homeless people in America today, there are no good choices," and each paragraph clearly develops this idea: what a good choice is, whether the homeless choose to live on the streets, and why shelters are not good alternatives to the streets. This unity is true of Patterson's revised draft but not of her first draft, where she drifted into considering how the homeless make other people uncomfortable. The topic could be interesting, but it blurred Patterson's focus on the homeless and their choices. Recognizing as much, Patterson deleted her entire second-to-last paragraph when she revised (see p. 46). Deleting this distracting passage also helped Patterson clarify her conclusion.

Like Patterson, you may be pulled in more than one direction by drafting, so that you digress from your thesis or pursue more than one thesis. Drafting and then revising are your chances to find and then sharpen your focus. Revising for unity strengthens your thesis.

Coherence

Writing is **coherent** when readers can follow it easily and can see how the parts relate to each other. The ideas develop in a clear sequence, the sentences and paragraphs connect logically, and the connections are clear and smooth. The writing flows.

Coherence in Paragraphs

Coherence starts as sentences build paragraphs. The example below, from the final draft of Grace Patterson's "A Rock and a Hard Place," shows several devices for achieving coherence in paragraphs:

- Repetition or restatement of key words (underlined twice in the example).

- Pronouns such as *they* and *them* that substitute for nouns such as *shelters* and *residents* (circled in the example).

- Parallelism, the use of similar grammatical structures for related ideas of the same importance (boxed in the example). See also page 53.

- Transitions that clearly link the parts of sentences and whole sentences (underlined once in the example). Transitions may indicate time (*later, soon*), place (*nearby, farther away*), similarity (*also, likewise*), difference (*in contrast, instead*), and many other relationships. See the Glossary, page 395, for a list of transitions.

The fact is that homeless people are not always better off in shelters. I spoke recently with a man named Alan Doran, who had lived on the streets for a long time. He said that he had spent some time in shelters for the homeless, and he told me what they are like. They're dangerous and dehumanizing. Drug deals, beatings, and thefts are common. Because shelters are crowded, residents have to wait in long lines for everything; they also have to accept being constantly bossed around. No wonder some homeless people, including Alan, prefer the street: it affords some space to breathe, some autonomy, some peace for sleeping.

Check all your paragraphs to be sure that each sentence connects with the one preceding and that readers will see the connection without having to stop and reread. You may not need all the coherence devices Patterson uses, or as many as she uses, but every paragraph you write will require some devices to stitch the sentences into a seamless cloth.

Coherence in Essays

Reading a coherent essay, the audience does not have to ask "What does this have to do with the preceding paragraph?"or "Where is the writer going here?" The connections are apparent, and the organization is clear and logical.

TRANSITIONS   Transitions work between paragraphs as well as within them to link ideas. When the ideas in two paragraphs are closely related, a simple word or phrase at the start of the second one may be all that's needed to show the relation. In each example below, the underlined transition opens the topic sentence of the paragraph:

> Moreover, the rising costs of health care have long outstripped inflation.

> However, some kinds of health-care plans have proved much more expensive than others.

When a paragraph is beginning a new part of the essay or otherwise changing direction, a sentence or more at the beginning will help explain the shift. In the next example, the first sentence summarizes the preceding paragraph, the second introduces the topic of the new paragraph, and the third gives the paragraph's topic sentence:

> Traditional health-care plans have thus become an unaffordable luxury for most individuals and businesses. The majority of those with health insurance now find themselves in so-called managed plans. Though they do vary, managed plans share at least two features: they pay full benefits only when the insured person consults an approved doctor, and they require prior approval for certain procedures.

Notice that underlined transitions provide further cues about the relationship of ideas.

ORGANIZATION   Although transitions can provide signposts to alert readers to movement from one idea to another, they can't achieve coherence by themselves. Just as important is an overall organization that develops ideas in a clear sequence and directs readers in a familiar pattern:

- A **spatial organization** arranges information to parallel the way we scan people, objects, or places: top to bottom, left to right, front to back, near to far, or vice versa. This scheme is especially useful for description (Chapter 6).

- A **chronological organization** arranges events or steps as they occurred in time, first to last. Such an arrangement usually organizes a narrative (Chapter 5) or a process analysis (Chapter 10) and may also help with cause-and-effect analysis (Chapter 13).

- A **climactic organization** proceeds in order of climax, usually from least to most important, building to the most interesting example, the most telling point of comparison, the most significant argument. A climactic organization is most useful for example (Chapter 7), division or analysis (Chapter 8), classification (Chapter 9), comparison and contrast (Chapter 11), definition (Chapter 12), and argument and persuasion (Chapter 14), and it may also work for cause-and-effect analysis (Chapter 13).

The introduction to each method of development in Chapters 5–14 gives detailed advice on organizing with these arrangements and variations on them.

When revising your draft for organization, try outlining it by jotting down the topic sentence of each paragraph and the key support for each topic. The exercise will give you some distance from your ideas and words, allowing you to see the structure like a skeleton. Will your readers grasp the logic of your arrangement? Will they see why you move from each idea to the next one? After checking the overall structure, be sure you've built in enough transitions between sentences and paragraphs to guide readers through your ideas.

Development

When you **develop** an idea, you provide concrete and specific details, examples, facts, opinions, and other evidence to make the idea vivid and true in readers' minds. Readers will know only as much as you tell them about your thesis and its support. Gaps, vague statements, and unsupported conclusions will undermine your efforts to win their interest and agreement.

The following undeveloped paragraph barely outlines one of four types of ex-smokers:

> The second group, evangelists, does not condemn smokers but encourages them to quit. Evangelists think quitting is easy, and they preach this message, often earning the resentment of potential converts.

Contrast the preceding bare-bones adaptation with the actual paragraphs written by Franklin E. Zimring in "Confessions of a Former Smoker":

> By contrast, the antismoking evangelist does not condemn smokers. Unlike the zealot, he regards smoking as an easily curable condition, as a social disease, and not a sin. The evangelist spends an enormous amount of time seeking and preaching to the unconverted. He argues that kicking the habit is not *that* difficult. After all, *he* did it; moreover, as he describes it, the benefits of quitting are beyond measure and the disadvantages are nil.
>
> The hallmark of the evangelist is his insistence that he never misses tobacco. Though he is less hostile to smokers than the zealot, he is resented more. Friends and loved ones who have been the targets of his preachments frequently greet the resumption of smoking by the evangelist as an occasion for unmitigated glee.

In the second sentence of both paragraphs, Zimring explicitly contrasts evangelists with zealots, the group he previously discussed. And he does more as well: he provides specific examples of the evangelist's message (first paragraph) and of others' reactions to him (second paragraph).

Development begins in sentences, when you use the most concrete and specific words you can muster to explain your meaning. (See p. 56.) At the level of the paragraph, these sentences develop the paragraph's topic. Then, at the level of the whole essay, these paragraphs develop the governing thesis.

Sometimes, you may discover that the most effective way to develop an idea is through visuals. For instance, if you support a point with numbers or statistics, presenting them in a chart or graph can make the information easier for readers to grasp. Similarly, a photograph may help to illustrate an idea or create an emotional response in your readers. If you decide to add a visual element to your draft, be sure that you have a purpose for using the image, that you provide a caption to clarify that purpose, and that you credit the source of the image. (For an effective use of a visual in a student essay, see Grace Patterson's "A Rock and a Hard Place" on p. 59. For information on crediting visual sources, see p. 379.)

The key to adequate development is a good sense of your readers' needs for information and reasons. The list of questions on page 21 can help you estimate these needs as you start to write; reconsidering the questions when you revise can help you see where your draft may fail to address, say, readers' unfamiliarity with your subject or possible resistance to your thesis.

The introduction to each method of development in Chapters 5–14 includes specific advice for meeting readers' needs when using the method to develop paragraphs and essays. When you sense that a paragraph or section of your essay is thin but you don't know how to improve it, you can also try the discovery techniques given on pages 21–25 or ask the questions for all the methods of development on page 24–25.

Tone

The **tone** of writing is like the tone of voice in speech: it expresses the writer's attitude toward his or her subject and audience. In writing we express tone with word choice and sentence structure. Notice the marked differences in these two passages discussing the same information on the same subject:

> Voice mail can be convenient, sure, but for callers it's usually more trouble than it's worth. We waste time "listening to the following menu choices," when we just want the live person at the end. All too often, there isn't even such a person!

> For callers the occasional convenience of voice mail generally does not compensate for its inconveniences. Most callers would prefer to speak to a live operator but must wait through a series of choices to reach that person. Increasingly, companies with voice-mail systems do not offer live operators at all.

The first passage is informal, expresses clear annoyance, and with *we* includes the reader in that attitude. The second passage is more formal and more objective, reporting the situation without involving readers directly.

Tone can range from casual to urgent, humorous to serious, sad to elated, pleased to angry, personal to distant. The particular tone you choose for a piece of writing depends on your purpose and your audience. For most academic and business writing, you will be trying to explain or argue a point to your equals or superiors. Your readers will be interested more in the substance of your writing than in a startling tone, and indeed an approach that is too familiar or unserious or hostile could put them off. Following these guidelines will help ensure that your tone is effective:

■ State opinions and facts calmly:

OVEREXCITED One clueless administrator was quoted in the newspaper as saying she thought many students who claim learning disabilities are faking their difficulties to obtain special treatment! Has she never heard of dyslexia, attention deficit disorder, and other well-established disabilities?

CALM Particularly worrisome was one administrator's statement, quoted in the newspaper, that many students who claim learning disabilities may be "faking" their difficulties to obtain special treatment.

■ Replace arrogance with deference:

ARROGANT I happen to know that many students would rather party or just bury their heads in the sand than get involved in a serious, worthy campaign against the school's unjust learning-disabled policies.

DEFERENTIAL Time pressures and lack of information about the issues may be what prevent students from joining the campaign against the school's unjust learning-disabled policies.

■ Replace sarcasm with plain speaking:

SARCASTIC Of course, the administration knows even without meeting students what is best for every one of them.

PLAIN SPEAKING The administration should agree to meet with each learning-disabled student to learn about his or her needs.

■ Choose words that convey reasonableness rather than negative emotions:

HOSTILE The administration coerced some students into dropping their lawsuits. [*Coerced* implies the use of threats or even violence.]

REASONABLE The administration convinced some students to drop their lawsuits. [*Convinced* implies the use of reason.]

Tone is something you want to evaluate in revision, along with whether you've achieved your purpose and whether you've developed your thesis adequately for your audience. But adjusting tone is largely a matter of replacing words and restructuring sentences, work that could distract you from an overall view of your essay. If you think your tone is off base, you may want to devote a separate phase of revision to it, after addressing unity, coherence, and the other matters discussed in this chapter.

For advice on sentence structures and word choices, see Chapter 4 on editing.

Using a Revision Checklist

The following checklist summarizes the advice on revision given in this chapter. Use the checklist to remind yourself what to look for in your first draft. But don't try to answer all the questions in a single reading of the draft. Instead, take the questions one by one, rereading the whole draft for each. That way you'll be able to concentrate on each element with minimal distraction from the others.

CHECKLIST FOR REVISION

- What is your purpose in writing? Will it be clear to readers? Do you achieve it?
- What is your thesis? Where is it made clear to readers?
- How unified is your essay? How does each body paragraph support your thesis? (Look especially at your topic sentences.) How does each sentence in the body paragraphs support the topic sentence of the paragraph?
- How coherent is your essay? Do repetition and restatement, pronouns, parallelism, and transitions link the sentences in paragraphs?
- Does the overall organization clarify the flow of ideas? How does your introduction work to draw readers in and orient them to your purpose and thesis? How does your conclusion work to pull the essay together and give readers a sense of completion?
- How well developed is your essay? Where might readers need more evidence to understand your ideas and find them convincing? Would visual images help?
- What is the tone of your essay? How is it appropriate for your purpose and your audience?

Note that the introductions to the methods of development in Chapters 5–14 also have their own revision checklists. Combining this list with the one for the method you're using will produce a more targeted set of questions. (The guide inside the back cover will direct you to the discussion you want.)

Grace Patterson's Revised Draft

Considering questions like those in the revision checklist led the student Grace Patterson to revise the rough draft we saw on pages 31–32. Patterson's revision follows. Notice that she made substantial cuts, especially of digressions near the end of the draft. She also revamped the introduction, tightened many passages, improved the coherence of paragraphs, decided to look for a photograph to illustrate one idea, and wrote a wholly new conclusion to sharpen her point. She did not try to improve her style or fix errors at this stage, leaving these activities for later editing.

~~Title?~~   *A Rock and a Hard Place*

In the essay/ "The Box Man/" Barbara Lazear Ascher says that a

homeless man who has chosen solitude can show the rest of us how to
                                                    Ascher's
"find . . . a friend in our own voice." Maybe. But ~~her~~ case depends on the

Box Man's choice, her assumption that he *had* one.

                                                              of us with
        Discussions of the homeless often use the word *choice*. Many ~~people with~~
homes would like to think
~~enough money can accept the condition of the homeless in America when~~

~~they tell themselves~~ that many of the homeless chose their lives. ~~That the~~

~~streets are in fact what they want. But it's not fair to use the word *choice*~~

~~here: the homeless don't get to choose their lives the way most of the rest of~~
        But
~~us do.~~ ⋀For the homeless people in America today, there are no good choices.

                                        A good choice is
        What do I mean by a "good choice"? ~~One~~ made from a variety of options

determined and narrowed down by the chooser. There is plenty of room for the chooser to make a decision that he will be satisfied with. When I choose

a career, I expect to make a good choice. There is plenty of interesting fields

worth investigating, and there is lots of rewarding work to be done. ~~It's a~~

~~choice that opens the world up and showcases its possibilities.~~ *However,* ~~If it came~~

~~time for me to choose a career, and~~ the mayor of my town came around and

told me that I had to choose between a life of cleaning public toilets and

operating a jackhammer on a busy street corner, I would object. That's a

lousy choice, and I wouldn't let anyone force me to make it.

When the mayor of New York tried to take ~~the~~ *people* homeless off the
streets, ~~some of them didn't want to go. People assumed that the homeless~~ *he likewise offered them a bad choice.*
~~people who did not want to~~ *They could* get in the mayor's car for a ride to a city
shelter ~~chose to live~~ *or they could stay* on the street. ~~But just because some homeless people~~ *People assumed that the homeless people*
who refused a ride to the shelter wanted to live on the street. But that
~~chose the street over the generosity of the mayor does not necessarily mean~~ *assumption is not necessarily true.*
~~that life on the streets is their ideal.~~ We allow ourselves as many options as
we can imagine, but we allow the homeless only two~~/~~ *, both unpleasant.* ~~go to a shelter, or stay~~

~~where you are. Who narrowed down the options for the homeless? Who~~

~~benefits if they go to a shelter? Who suffers if they don't?~~

Homeless people are not always better off in shelters. *Last Sunday,* I had a

conversation with a man who had lived on the streets for a long time. ~~The~~ *He*

~~man~~ said that he had spent some time in those shelters for the homeless,
[find a photo] They're dangerous and dehumanizing.
and he told me what they were like. ~~The shelters are crowded and dirty and~~
Drug dealing, beatings, and theft are common. The shelters are dirty and crowded,
~~people have to wait in long lines for everything. People are constantly being~~
so that residents have to wait in long lines for everything and are constantly
~~herded around and~~ bossed around. ~~It's dangerous—drug dealers, beatings,~~

~~theft. Dehumanizing. It matches my picture of hell. From the sound of it, I~~

No wonder some homeless people prefer the street: some space to breathe, ~~couldn't spend two hours in a shelter, never mind a whole night. I value my~~ some autonomy, some peace for sleeping. ~~peace of mind and my sleep too much, not to mention my freedom and~~ ~~autonomy.~~

~~When homeless people sleep in the street, though,~~ that makes the public uncomfortable. People with enough money wish the homeless would just disappear. They don't care where they go. Just out of sight. I've felt this way too but I'm as uneasy with that reaction as I am at the sight of a person sleeping on the sidewalk. ~~And I tell myself that this is more than a question of my comfort. By and large I'm comfortable enough.~~

The homeless are in a difficult enough situation without having to take the blame for making the rest of us feel uncomfortable with our wealth. If we cannot offer the homeless a good set of choices, the opportunity to choose lives that they will be truly satisfied with then the least we can do is stop dumping on them (?). They're caught between a rock and a hard place: there are not many places for them to go, and the places where they can go afford nothing but suffering.

Focusing on the supposed choices the homeless have may make us feel better, but it distracts attention from the kinds of choices that are really being denied the homeless. The options we take for granted—a job with decent pay, an affordable home—do not belong to the homeless. They're caught between no shelter at all and shelter that dehumanizes, between a rock and a hard place.

4

EDITING

The final stage of the writing process is **editing** to clarify and polish your work. In editing you turn from global issues of purpose, thesis, unity, coherence, organization, development, and tone to more particular issues of sentences and words. In a sense revision (the subject of the previous chapter) occurs beneath the lines, in the deeper meaning and structure of the essay. Editing occurs more *on* the lines, on the surface of the essay.

Like revision, editing requires that you gain some distance from your work so that you can see it objectively. Try these techniques:

- Work on a clean copy of your revised draft. Edit on a printout rather than on the computer: it's more difficult to spot errors on-screen.

- Read your revised draft aloud so that you can hear the words. But be sure to read what you have actually written, not what you may have intended to write but didn't.

- To catch errors, try reading your draft backward sentence by sentence. You'll be less likely to get caught up in the flow of your ideas.

- Keep a list of problems that others have pointed out in your previous writing. Add this personal checklist to the one on page 58.

Editing gets easier with practice. You can find interactive exercises for all the topics discussed in this chapter by visiting Exercise Central at *bedfordstmartins.com/rewriting*.

Making Sentences Clear and Effective

Clear and effective sentences convey your meaning concisely and precisely. In editing you want to ensure that readers will understand you easily, follow your ideas without difficulty, and stay interested in what you have to say.

Clarity

The first goal of editing is to express your ideas as clearly as possible, without errors that might distract, confuse, or annoy readers. The guidelines here can help you catch some of the most common mistakes.

- *Make sure every sentence is complete.* A complete sentence has a subject and a verb and expresses a complete thought. In contrast, a **sentence fragment** is a word group that is punctuated like a sentence but is not complete: it lacks a subject, lacks a verb, or is just part of a thought. Experienced writers sometimes use fragments deliberately, but unless you're very sure of what you're doing, add the necessary verb or subject or attach the word group to a nearby sentence:

  FRAGMENT The price of oil unpredictable and rising.
  COMPLETE The price of oil is unpredictable and rising.

  FRAGMENT Home owners are warming up to alternative heating systems. Such as heat pumps, solar panels, and pellet stoves.
  COMPLETE Home owners are warming up to alternative heating systems, such as heat pumps, solar panels, and pellet stoves.

- *Keep independent clauses separated.* An **independent clause** can be punctuated like a sentence: it has a subject and a verb, and it expresses a complete thought. Two independent clauses in a row need a clear separation: a period, a semicolon, or a comma along with *and, but, or, nor, for, so,* or *yet.* If the clauses run together with nothing between them, they create a **run-on sentence.** If they run together with only a comma between them, they create a **comma splice.** You can correct these errors most easily by punctuating each clause as its own sentence or by separating the clauses with a comma along with *and, but, or, nor, for, so,* or *yet:*

RUN-ON   Pellet stoves are especially popular suppliers can't keep up with demand.

COMMA SPLICE   Pellet stoves are especially popular, suppliers can't keep up with demand.

EDITED   Pellet stoves are especially popular. Suppliers can't keep up with demand.

EDITED   Pellet stoves are especially popular, and suppliers can't keep up with demand.

■ *Match subjects and verbs.* Use singular verbs with singular subjects and plural verbs with plural subjects. Watch especially for the following situations:

When a group of words comes between the subject and the verb, be careful not to mistake a noun in that word group (such as *pellets* below) for the subject of the sentence.

MISMATCHED   The use of construction waste to manufacture wood pellets contribute to their appeal.

MATCHED   The use of construction waste to manufacture wood pellets contributes to their appeal.

Subjects joined by *and* take plural verbs:

MISMATCHED   Low carbon emissions and the renewability of sawdust adds to the belief that pellets are environmentally friendly.

MATCHED   Low carbon emissions and the renewability of sawdust add to the belief that pellets are environmentally friendly.

■ *Check that pronouns have clearly stated antecedents.* An antecedent is the noun to which a pronoun refers. Rewrite sentences in which the reference is vague or only implied:

VAGUE   Text messaging while driving is dangerous, but it doesn't deter everyone.

CLEAR   Text messaging while driving is dangerous, but the risk doesn't deter everyone.

IMPLIED   Despite numerous studies showing that distracted driving causes accidents, they keep typing.

CLEAR   Despite numerous studies showing that distracted drivers cause accidents, they keep typing.

■ *Match pronouns and the words they refer to.* Singular nouns and pronouns take singular pronouns; plural nouns and pronouns take plural pronouns. The most common error occurs with singular indefinite pronouns such as *anybody, anyone, everyone, nobody,* and *somebody.* We often use these words to mean "many" or "all" and then mistakenly refer to them with plural pronouns:

MISMATCHED Everyone must check in before they can vote.

MATCHED Everyone must check in before he or she can vote.

MATCHED All students must check in before they can vote.

■ *Make sure that modifiers clearly modify the intended words.* A modifier describes another word in a sentence. Misplaced and dangling modifiers can be awkward or even unintentionally amusing:

MISPLACED I watched as the snow swirled around my feet in amazement.

CLEAR I watched in amazement as the snow swirled around my feet.

DANGLING Enjoying the quiet of the forest, the crack of a hunter's rifle startled me out of my reverie.

CLEAR Enjoying the quiet of the forest, I was startled out of my reverie by the crack of a hunter's rifle.

■ *Be consistent.* Don't shift needlessly between the past tense and the present tense of verbs.

INCONSISTENT We held a frantic conference to consider our options. It takes only a minute to decide to evacuate.

CONSISTENT We held a frantic conference to consider our options. It took only a minute to decide to evacuate.

Don't shift needlessly among the first person (*I, we*), second person (*you*), and third person (*he, she, they*).

INCONSISTENT We were frightened, but you had to stay calm.

CONSISTENT We were frightened, but we had to stay calm.

Don't shift needlessly between the active voice and the passive voice of verbs. (See the next page for an explanation of voice.)

INCONSISTENT The police told us to leave our belongings behind, and we were advised to notify family members.

CONSISTENT   The police told us to leave our belongings behind, and they advised us to notify family members.

Conciseness

In drafting, we often circle around our ideas, making various attempts to express them. As a result, sentences may use more words than necessary to make their points. To edit for conciseness, focus on the following changes:

■ *Put the main meaning of the sentence in its subject and verb.* Generally, the subject should name the actor, and the verb should describe what the actor did or was. Notice the difference in these two sentences (the subjects and verbs are underlined):

WORDY   According to some experts, the use of calculators by students is sometimes why they fail to develop computational skills.

CONCISE   According to some experts, students who use calculators sometimes fail to develop computational skills.

■ *Prefer the active voice.* In the active voice, a verb describes the action *by* the subject (*We grilled vegetables*), whereas in the passive voice, a verb describes the action done *to* the subject (*Vegetables were grilled*, or, adding who did the action, *Vegetables were grilled by us*). The active voice is usually more concise and more direct than the passive:

WORDY PASSIVE   Calculators were withheld from some classrooms by school administrators, and the math performance of students with and without the machines was compared.

CONCISE ACTIVE   School administrators withheld calculators from some classrooms and compared the math performance of students with and without the machines.

■ *Delete repetition and padding.* Words that don't contribute to your meaning will interfere with readers' understanding and interest. Watch out for unneeded repetition or restatement:

WORDY   Students in the schools should have ample practice in computational skills, skills such as long division and work with fractions.

CONCISE   Students should have ample practice in computational skills, such as long division and work with fractions.

Avoid empty phrases that add no meaning:

WORDY The nature of calculators is such that they remove the drudgery from computation, but can also for all intents and purposes interfere with the development of important cognitive skills.

CONCISE Calculators remove the drudgery from computation, but can also interfere with the development of important cognitive skills.

Emphasis

Once your sentences are as clear and concise as you can make them, you'll want to ensure that they give the appropriate emphasis to your ideas. Readers will look for the idea of a sentence in its subject and its verb, with modifiers clarifying or adding texture. You can emphasize important ideas by altering the structure of sentences. Following are the most common techniques.

■ *Use subordination to de-emphasize what's less important.* **Subordination** places minor information in words or word groups that modify the sentence's subject and verb:

UNEMPHATIC Computers can manipulate film and photographs, and we cannot trust these media to represent reality. [The sentence has two subject-verb structures (both underlined), and they seem equally important.]

EMPHATIC Because computers can manipulate film and photographs, we cannot trust these media to represent reality. [*Because* makes the first subject-verb group into a modifier, de-emphasizing the cause of the change and emphasizing the effect.]

■ *Use coordination to balance equally important ideas.* **Coordination** emphasizes the equality of ideas by joining them with *and, but, or, nor, for, so,* or *yet*:

UNEMPHATIC Two people may be complete strangers. A photograph can show them embracing.

EMPHATIC Two people may be complete strangers, but a photograph can show them embracing.

■ *Use the ends and beginnings of sentences to highlight ideas.* The end of a sentence is its most emphatic position, and the beginning is next most emphatic. Placing the sentence's subject and verb in one of these positions draws readers' attention to them. In these sentences the core idea is underlined:

UNEMPHATIC With computerized images, <u>filmmakers can entertain us</u>, placing historical figures alongside today's actors.

EMPHATIC <u>Filmmakers can entertain us</u> with computerized images that place historical figures alongside today's actors.

MORE EMPHATIC With computerized images that place historical figures alongside today's actors, <u>filmmakers can entertain us</u>.

- *Use short sentences to underscore points.* A very short sentence amid longer sentences will focus readers' attention on a key point:

UNEMPHATIC Such images of historical figures and fictional characters have a disadvantage, however, in that they blur the boundaries of reality.

EMPHATIC Such images of historical figures and fictional characters have a disadvantage, however. <u>They blur the boundaries of reality</u>.

Parallelism

Parallelism is the use of similar grammatical structures for elements of similar importance, either within or among sentences.

PARALLELISM WITHIN A SENTENCE Smoking can <u>worsen heart disease</u> and <u>cause lung cancer</u>.

PARALLELISM AMONG SENTENCES Smoking has less well-known effects, too. <u>It can cause</u> gum disease. <u>It can impair</u> circulation of blood and other fluids. And <u>it can reduce</u> the body's supply of vitamins and minerals.

The second example shows how parallelism can relate sentences to improve paragraph coherence (see pp. 37–38).

To make the elements of a sentence parallel, repeat the forms of related words, phrases, and sentences:

NONPARALLEL Harris expects dieters to give up <u>bread</u>, <u>dairy</u>, and <u>eating meat</u>.

PARALLEL Harris expects dieters to give up bread, dairy, and <u>meat</u>.

NONPARALLEL Harris emphasizes self-denial, but with Marconi's plan you can eat whatever you want in moderation.

PARALLEL Harris emphasizes self-denial, but Marconi emphasizes moderation.

NONPARALLEL If you want to lose weight quickly, try the Harris diet. You'll have more success keeping the weight off if you follow Marconi's plan.

PARALLEL If you want to lose weight quickly, choose the Harris diet. If you want to keep the weight off, choose Marconi.

Variety

Variety in the structure and length of sentences makes writing clearer by emphasizing important points and de-emphasizing less important points. It also helps keep readers interested. The first passage below is adapted from "How Boys Become Men," an essay by Jon Katz. The second is the passage Katz actually wrote.

UNVARIED I was walking my dog last month past the playground near my house. I saw three boys encircling a fourth. They were laughing and pushing him. He was skinny and rumpled. He looked frightened. One boy knelt behind him. Another pushed him from the front. The trick was familiar to any former boy. The victim fell backward.

VARIED Last month, walking my dog past the playground near my house, I saw three boys encircling a fourth, laughing and pushing him. He was skinny and rumpled, and he looked frightened. One boy knelt behind him while another pushed him from the front, a trick familiar to any former boy. He fell backward.

Katz's actual sentences work much better to hold and direct our attention because he uses several techniques to achieve variety:

- ■ *Vary the lengths of sentences.* The eight sentences in the unvaried adaptation range from four to thirteen words. Katz's four sentences range from three to twenty-two words, with the long first sentence setting the scene and the short final sentence creating a climax.

- ■ *Vary the beginnings of sentences.* Every sentence in the unvaried adaptation begins with its subject (*I, I, They, He, One boy, Another, The trick, The victim*). Katz, in contrast, begins the first sentence with a transition and a modifier (*Last month, walking my dog past the playground near my house...*).

■ *Vary the structure of sentences.* The sentences in the unvaried adaptation are all similar in structure, marching like soldiers down the page and making it difficult to pick out the important events of the story. Katz's version emphasizes the important events by making them the subjects and verbs of the sentences, turning the other information into modifiers that either precede or follow.

Choosing Clear and Effective Words

The words you choose can have a dramatic effect on how readers understand your meaning, perceive your attitude, and respond to your thesis.

Denotations and Connotations

The **denotation** of a word is its dictionary meaning, the literal sense without emotional overtones. A **connotation** is an emotional association the word produces in readers. Using incorrect or inappropriate words will confuse or annoy readers.

Using a word with the wrong denotation muddies meaning. Be especially careful to distinguish between words with similar sounds but different meanings, such as *sites/cites* and *whether/weather,* and between words with related but distinct meanings, such as *reward/award* and *famous/infamous.* Keeping a list of the new words you acquire will help you build your vocabulary.

Using words with strong connotations can shape readers' responses to your ideas. For example, consider the distinctions among *feeling, enthusiasm, passion,* and *mania.* Describing a group's *enthusiasm* for its cause is quite different from describing its *mania:* the latter connotes much more intensity, even irrationality. If your aim is to imply that the group's enthusiasm is excessive, and you think your readers will respond well to that characterization, then *mania* may be the appropriate word. But words can backfire if they set off inappropriate associations in readers.

Consult a dictionary whenever you are unsure of a word's meanings. For connotations, you'll find a wide range of choices in a thesaurus, which lists words with similar meanings. A thesaurus doesn't provide definitions, however, so you'll need to check unfamiliar words in a dictionary.

Concrete and Specific Words

Clear, exact writing balances abstract and general words, which provide outlines of ideas and things, with concrete and specific words, which limit and sharpen.

- **Abstract words** name ideas, qualities, attitudes, or states that we cannot perceive with our senses of sight, hearing, touch, smell, and taste: *liberty, hate, anxious, brave, idealistic*. **Concrete words**, in contrast, name objects, persons, places, or states that we can perceive with our senses: *newspaper, Mississippi River, red-faced, tangled, screeching, smoky, sweet*.

- **General words** name groups: *building, color, clothes*. **Specific words** name particular members of a group: *courthouse, red, boot-cut jeans*.

You need abstract and general words for broad statements that set the course for your writing, conveying concepts or referring to entire groups. But you also need concrete and specific words to make meaning precise and vivid by appealing to readers' senses and experiences:

VAGUE The pollution was apparent in the odor and color of the small stream.

EXACT The narrow stream, just four feet wide, smelled like rotten eggs and ran the greenish color of coffee with nonfat milk.

Concrete and specific language may seem essential only in descriptions like that of the polluted stream, but it is equally crucial in any other kind of writing. Readers can't be expected to understand or agree with general statements unless they know what evidence the statements are based on. The evidence is in the details, and the details are in concrete and specific words.

Figures of Speech

You can make your writing concrete and specific, even lively and forceful, with **figures of speech**, expressions that imply meanings beyond or different from their literal meanings. Here are some of the most common figures:

- A **simile** compares two unlike things with the use of *like* or *as: The car spun around like a top. Coins as bright as sunshine lay glinting in the chest.*

■ A **metaphor** also compares two unlike things, but more subtly, equating them without *like* or *as*: *The words shattered my fragile self-esteem. The laboratory was a prison, the beakers and test tubes her guards.*

■ **Personification** is a simile or metaphor that attributes human qualities or powers to things or abstractions: *The breeze sighed and whispered in the grasses. The city squeezed me tightly at first but then relaxed its grip.*

■ **Hyperbole** is a deliberate overstatement or exaggeration: *The dentist filled the tooth with a bracelet's worth of silver. The children's noise shook the walls and rafters.*

By briefly translating experiences and qualities into vividly concrete images, figures of speech can be economical and powerful when used sparingly. Be careful not to combine them into confusing or absurd images, such as *The players danced around the soccer field like pit bulls ready for a fight.*

In trying for figures of speech, we sometimes resort to **clichés**, worn phrases that have lost their power: *ripe old age, hour of need, heavy as lead, thin as a rail, goes on forever.* If you have trouble recognizing clichés in your writing, be suspicious of any expression you have heard or read before. When you do find a cliché, cure it by substituting plain language (for instance, *seems endless* for *goes on forever*) or by substituting a fresh figure of speech (*thin as a sapling* for *thin as a rail*).

Using an Editing Checklist

The checklist on the next page summarizes the editing advice given in this chapter and adds a few other technical concerns as well. Some of the items will be more relevant for your writing than others: you may have little difficulty with variety in sentences, but may worry that your language is too general. Concentrate your editing efforts where they're needed most, and then survey your draft to check for other problems.

Grace Patterson's Editing and Final Draft

The following paragraph comes from the edited draft of Grace Patterson's "A Rock and a Hard Place." Then Patterson's full final draft appears with notes in the margins highlighting its thesis, structure, and uses of

---

CHECKLIST FOR EDITING

- Where do sentences need editing for grammar—so that, for instance, sentences are complete, subjects and verbs agree, pronouns are used correctly, modifiers make sense, and tense is consistent?
- Is each sentence as concise as it can be?
- How well have you used sentence structure, variety, parallelism, and other techniques to emphasize ideas and hold readers' interest?
- Have you used the right words? Where can you clarify meaning with concrete and specific words or with figures of speech?
- Do any sentences need editing for punctuation, such as for appropriate use of commas and apostrophes? Concentrate on finding and correcting errors that readers have pointed out in your work before.
- Where might spelling be a problem? Look up any word you're not absolutely sure of. (You'll still have to proofread a spell-checked paper; the programs don't catch everything.)

---

the methods of development. If you compare the final version with the first draft on pages 31–32, you'll see clearly how Patterson's revising and editing transformed the essay from a rough exploration of ideas to a refined, and convincing, essay.

EDITED PARAGRAPH

~~What do I mean by~~ A "good choice"? ~~A good choice~~ is one made from a variety of options determined and narrowed down by the chooser. ~~There is plenty of room for the chooser to make a decision that he will be satisfied with.~~ When I choose a career, I expect to make a good choice. There are many interesting fields worth to investigate, and there is much rewarding work to do. ~~lots of~~ ~~be done.~~ If the mayor of my town suddenly ~~came around and~~ told me that I would have to choose between a career of cleaning ~~life~~ public toilets and one of operating a jackhammer on a busy street corner, I would object. That's a bad choice. ~~and I wouldn't let anyone force me to make it.~~

FINAL DRAFT

A Rock and a Hard Place

In the essay "The Box Man" Barbara Lazear Ascher says that a homeless man who has chosen solitude can show the rest of us how to "find…a friend in our own voice" (11). Maybe he can. But Ascher's case depends on the Box Man's choice, her assumption that he *had* one. Discussions of the homeless often involve the word *choice*. Many of us with homes would like to think that the homeless chose their lives. But for homeless people in America today, there are no good choices.

A "good choice" is one made from a variety of options determined and narrowed down by the chooser. When I choose a career, I expect to make a good choice. There are many interesting fields to investigate, and there is much rewarding work to do. If the mayor of my town suddenly told me that I would have to choose between a career of cleaning public toilets and one of operating a jackhammer on a busy street corner, I would object. That's a *bad* choice.

When the mayor of New York tried to remove the homeless people from the streets, he offered them a similarly bad choice. They could get in the mayor's car for a ride to a city shelter, or they could stay on the street. People assumed that the homeless people who refused a ride to the shelter *wanted* to live on the street. But the assumption is not necessarily true. We allow ourselves as many options as we can imagine, but we allow the homeless only two, both unpleasant.

The fact is that homeless people are not always better off in shelters. I spoke recently with a man named Alan Doran, who had lived on the streets for a long time. He said that he had spent some time in shelters for the homeless, and he told me what they are like. They're dangerous and dehumanizing. Drug deals, beatings, and thefts are common. Because shelters are crowded, residents have to wait in long

Introduction establishes point of contention with Ascher's essay

Thesis sentence (see pp. 25–28)

Definition and comparison of good choices and bad choices

Examples

Application of definition to homeless people; analysis of choice offered

Cause-and-effect analysis: why homeless avoid shelters

Description of shelter

Photograph
illustrates
Patterson's point

Fig. 1.   The line for breakfast at a homeless shelter. Notice
the stack of mats used as bedding. Brant Ward, photograph,
SF Gate. San Francisco Chronicle. 2 Dec. 2003; Web; 3 Oct. 2010.

Caption clarifies
purpose of image
and credits its
source

lines for everything (see Fig. 1); they also have to accept
being constantly bossed around. No wonder some homeless
people, including Alan, prefer the street: it affords some
space to breathe, some autonomy, some peace for sleeping.

Comparison of
shelter and street

Focusing on the supposed choices the homeless have
may make us feel better. But it distracts our attention from
something more important than our comfort: the options
we take for granted — a job with decent pay, an affordable
home — are denied the homeless. These people are caught
between no shelter at all and shelter that dehumanizes,
between a rock and a hard place.

Conclusion:
returns to good
vs. bad choices;
sums up with a
familiar image

Works Cited

Ascher, Barbara Lazear. "The Box Man." *The Compact Reader:*
    Short Essays by Method and Theme. 9th ed. Ed. Jane E. Aaron
    and Ellen Kuhl Repetto. Boston: Bedford, 2011. 9–13. Print.
Doran, Alan. Personal interview. 27 Sept. 2011.

PART TWO

SHORT ESSAYS BY
METHOD AND THEME

5

NARRATION
Recalling Childhood

You **narrate** every time you tell a story about something that happened. Narration helps us make sense of events and share our experiences with others; consequently, it is one of the longest-standing and most essential methods of communicating. (As the writer Joan Didion famously put it, "We tell stories in order to live.") You can use narration to entertain friends by retelling an amusing or a scary experience, to explain the sequence of events in a chemistry experiment, to summarize a salesclerk's actions in a letter complaining about bad customer service, to explain what went wrong in a ball game, or to persuade skeptics by means of several stories that the forestry industry is sincere about restoring clear-cut forests. Storytelling is instinctive to the ways we think and speak; it's no surprise, then, that narration should figure into so much of what we read and write.

Reading Narration

Narration relates a sequence of events that are linked in time. By arranging events in an orderly progression, a narrative illuminates the stages leading to a result. Sometimes the emphasis is on the story itself, as in fiction, biography, autobiography, some history, and much journalism. But often a narrative serves some larger point, as when a paragraph or a brief story about an innocent person's death helps to strengthen an argument for stricter handling of drunk drivers. When used as a primary means of developing an essay, such pointed narration usually relates a sequence of events that led to new knowledge or had a notable outcome. The point of the narrative—the idea the reader is to take away—then determines the selection of events, the amount of detail devoted to them, and their arrangement.

Though narration arranges events in time, narrative time is not real time. An important event may fill whole pages, even though it took only minutes to unfold; a less important event may be dispensed with in a sentence, even though it lasted for hours. Suppose, for instance, that a writer wants to narrate the experience of being mugged in order to show how courage came unexpectedly to his aid. He might provide a slow-motion account of the few minutes' encounter with the muggers, including vivid details of the setting and of the attackers' appearance, a moment-by-moment replay of his emotions, and exact dialogue. At the same time, he will compress events that merely fill in background or link main events, such as how he got to the scene of the mugging or the follow-up questioning by a police detective. And he will entirely omit many events, such as a conversation overheard at the police station, that have no significance for his point.

The point of a narrative influences not only which events are covered and how fully but also how the events are arranged. There are several possibilities:

- A straight chronological sequence is most common because it relates events in the order of their actual occurrence. It is particularly useful for short narratives, for those in which the last event is the most dramatic, or for those in which the events preceding and following the climax contribute to the point being made.

- The final event, such as a self-revelation, may come first, followed by an explanation of the events leading up to it.

- The entire story may be summarized first and then examined in detail.

- **Flashbacks**—shifts backward rather than forward in time—may recall events whose significance would not have been apparent earlier. Flashbacks are common in movies and fiction: a character in the midst of one scene mentally replays another.

In addition to providing a clear organization, writers also strive to adopt a consistent **point of view**, a position relative to the events, conveyed in two main ways:

- Pronouns indicate the storyteller's place in the story: the first-person *I* if the narrator is a direct participant; the third-person *he, she, it,* or *they* if the writer is observing or reporting.

- Verb tense indicates the writer's relation in time to the sequence of events: present (*is, run*) or past (*was, ran*).

Combining the first-person pronoun with the present tense can create great immediacy ("I feel the point of the knife in my back"). At the other extreme, combining third-person pronouns with the past tense creates more distance and objectivity ("He felt the point of the knife in his back"). In between these extremes are combinations of first person with past tense ("I felt . . .") or third person with present tense ("He feels . . ."). The choice depends on how involved the writer is in the events and on his or her purpose.

Analyzing Narration in Paragraphs

Michael Ondaatje (born 1943) is a poet, fiction writer, essayist, and filmmaker. The following paragraph is from *Running in the Family* (1982), Ondaatje's memoir of his childhood in Ceylon, now called Sri Lanka, off the southern tip of India.

After my father died, a grey cobra came into the house. My stepmother loaded the gun and fired at point blank range. The gun jammed. She stepped back and reloaded but by then the snake had slid out into the garden. For the next month this snake would often come into the house and each time the gun would misfire or jam, or my stepmother would miss at absurdly short range. The snake attacked no one and had a tendency to follow my younger sister Susan around. Other snakes entering the house were killed by the shotgun, lifted with a long stick and flicked into the bushes, but the old grey cobra led a charmed life. Finally one of the old workers at Rock Hill told my stepmother what had become obvious, that it was my father who had come to protect his family. And in fact, whether it was because the chicken farm closed down or because of my father's presence in the form of a snake, very few other snakes came into the house again.

Chronological order

Past tense

Transitions (underlined)

Point of view: participant

Purpose: to relate a colorful, mysterious story

Donald Hall (born 1928) served as poet laureate of the United States from 2006 to 2007. He is also an award-winning essayist, critic, playwright, and children's author. The following paragraph comes from his memoir *Unpacking the Boxes* (2008).

Memory is stronger when it recalls transgression. I played with a neighbor boy <u>while</u> a repairman worked on the kitchen refrigerator, which had a white coil at its top. The repairman's dented Model T, cut down to a pickup, stood beside the kitchen door on two narrow strips of breaking-apart cement. My playmate and I lifted chunks of concrete onto the pickup's bed. My mother, <u>peeking out the screen door</u>, issued a reprimand, <u>and</u> my friend and I set to undo the crime. I stood in the truck bed lifting chunks down to my accomplice, who wore an Indian headdress. I stood above the boy <u>looking down</u> on his head surrounded by feathers, <u>and</u> carefully dropped a large lump of concrete onto his skull. Oh, the bliss of targeting a head circled by feathers! He howled <u>and</u> ran home; I was sent to my room.

Chronological order

Past tense

Transitions (underlined)

Point of view: direct participant

Purpose: to express the joy of getting into trouble

Developing a Narrative Essay

Getting Started

You'll find narration useful whenever relating a sequence of events can help you make a point, sometimes to support the thesis of a larger paper, sometimes as the thesis of a paper. If you're assigned a narrative essay, probe your own experiences for a situation such as an argument involving strong emotion, a humorous or embarrassing incident, a dramatic scene you witnessed, or a learning experience like a job. If you have the opportunity to do research, you might choose a topic dealing with the natural world (such as the Big Bang scenario for the origin of the universe) or an event in history or politics (such as how a local activist worked to close down an animal-research lab).

Explore your subject by listing all the events in sequence as they happened. At this stage you may find the traditional journalist's questions helpful:

- Who was involved?
- What happened?
- When did it happen?
- Where did it happen?
- Why did it happen?
- How did it happen?

These questions will lead you to examine your subject from all angles. Then you need to decide which events should be developed in great detail because they are central to your story; which merit compression because they merely contribute background or tie the main events together; and which should be omitted altogether because they are irrelevant to the story or might clutter your narrative.

While you are weighing the relative importance of events, consider also what your readers need to know in order to understand and appreciate your narrative.

- What information will help locate readers in the narrative's time and place?

- How will you expand and compress events to keep readers' attention?

- What details about people, places, and feelings will make the events vivid for readers?

- What is your attitude toward the subject—lighthearted, sarcastic, bitter, serious?—and how will you convey it to readers in your choice of events and details?

- What should your point of view be? Do you want to involve readers intimately by using the first person and the present tense? Or does that seem overdramatic, less appropriate than the more detached, objective view that would be conveyed by the past tense or the third person or both?

Forming a Thesis

Whatever your subject, you should have some point to make about it: Why was the incident or experience significant? What does it teach or illustrate? If you can, phrase this point in a sentence before you start to draft. For instance:

> I used to think small-town life was boring, but one taste of the city made me appreciate the leisurely pace of home.

A recent small earthquake demonstrated the hazards of inadequate civil defense measures.

Sometimes you may need to draft your story before the point of it becomes clear to you, especially if the experience had a personal impact or if the event was so recent that writing a draft will allow you to gain some perspective.

Whether to state your main point outright in your essay, as a thesis sentence, depends on the effect you want to have on readers. You might use your introduction to lead to a statement of your thesis so that readers will know from the start why you are telling them your story. Then again, to intensify the drama of your story, you might decide to withhold your thesis sentence for the conclusion or omit it altogether. Remember, though, that the thesis must be evident to readers even if it isn't stated: the narrative needs a point.

Organizing

Narrative essays often begin without formal introductions, instead drawing the reader in with one of the more dramatic events in the sequence. But you may find an introduction useful to set the scene for your narrative, to summarize the events leading up to it, to establish the context for it, or to lead in to a thesis statement if you want readers to know the point of your story before they start reading it.

The arrangement of events in the body of your essay depends on the actual order in which they occurred and the point you want to make. To narrate a trip during which one thing after another went wrong, you might find a strict chronological order most effective. To narrate an earthquake that began and ended in an instant, you might sort simultaneous events into groups—say, what happened to buildings and what happened to people—or you might arrange a few people's experiences in order of increasing drama. To narrate your experience of city life, you might interweave events in the city with contrasting flashbacks to your life in a small town, or you might start by relating one especially bad experience in the city, drop back to explain how you ended up in that situation, and then go on to tell what happened afterward. Narrative time can be manipulated in any number of ways, but your scheme should have a purpose that your readers can see, and you should stick to it.

Let the ending of your essay be determined by the effect you want to leave with readers. You can end with the last event in your sequence, or the one you have saved for last, if it conveys your point and provides a strong finish. Or you can summarize the aftermath of the story if it contributes to the point. You can also end with a formal conclusion that states your point—your thesis—explicitly. Such a conclusion is especially useful if your point unfolds gradually throughout the narrative and you want to emphasize it at the finish.

Drafting

Drafting a narrative can be less of a struggle than drafting other kinds of papers, especially if you're close to the events and you use a straight chronological order. But the relative ease of storytelling can be misleading if it causes you to describe events too quickly or write without making a point. While drafting, be as specific as possible. Tell what the people in your narrative were wearing, what expressions their faces held, how they gestured, what they said. Specify the time of day, and describe the weather and the surroundings (buildings, vegetation, and the like). All these details may be familiar to you, but they won't be to your readers.

At the same time, try to remain open to what the story means to you, so that you can convey that meaning in your selection and description of events. If you know before you begin what your thesis is, let it guide you. But the first draft may turn out to be a search for your thesis, so that you'll need another draft to make it evident in the way you relate events.

In your draft you may want to experiment with dialogue—quotations of what participants said, in their words. Dialogue can add immediacy and realism as long as it advances the narrative and doesn't ramble beyond its usefulness. In reconstructing dialogue from memory, try to recall not only the actual words but also the sounds of speakers' voices and the expressions on their faces—information that will help you represent each speaker distinctly. And keep the dialogue natural sounding by using constructions typical of speech. For instance, most speakers prefer contractions such as *don't* and *shouldn't* to the longer forms *do not* and *should not*; and few speakers begin sentences with *although*, as in the formal-sounding "Although we could hear our mother's voice, we refused to answer her."

Whether you are relating events in strict chronological order or manipulating them for some effect, try to make their sequence in real time and the distance between them clear to readers. Instead of signaling sequence with the monotonous *and then...and then...and then* or *next...next...next,* use informative transitions that signal the order of events (*afterward, earlier*), the duration of events (*for an hour, in that time*), or the amount of time between events (*the next morning, a week later*). (See the Glossary under *transitions* for a list of such expressions.)

Revising and Editing

When your draft is complete, revise and edit it by answering the following questions and considering the information in the box below.

- *Is the point of your narrative clear, and does every event you relate contribute to it?* Whether or not you state your thesis, it should be obvious to readers. They should be able to see why you have lingered over some events and compressed others, and they should not be distracted by insignificant events and details.

- *Is your organization clear?* Be sure that your readers will understand any shifts backward or forward in time.

FOCUS ON VERBS

Narration depends heavily on verbs to clarify and enliven events. Weak verbs, such as forms of *make* and *be*, can sap the life from a story. Strong verbs sharpen meaning and engage readers:

WEAK   The wind made an awful noise.

STRONG   The wind roared around the house and rattled the trees.

WEAK   The noises were alarming to us.

STRONG   The noises alarmed us.

Keep in mind that verbs in the active voice (the subject does the action) usually pack more power than verbs in the passive voice (the subject is acted upon). While strengthening your verbs, also ensure that they're consistent in tense. See page 51 for a discussion of passive versus active voice and page 50 for advice on avoiding shifts in tense.

▶ To practice editing for weak and passive verbs, visit Exercise Central at *bedfordstmartins.com/rewriting.*

■ *Have you used transitions to help readers follow the sequence of events?* Transitions such as *meanwhile* or *soon afterward* serve a dual purpose: they keep the reader on track, and they link sentences and paragraphs so that they flow smoothly. (For more information, see pp. 36 and 38 and the Glossary under *transitions*.)

■ *If you have used dialogue, is it purposeful and natural?* Be sure all quoted speech moves the action ahead. And read all dialogue aloud to check that it sounds like something someone would actually say.

A Note on Thematic Connections

All the authors in this chapter saw reasons to articulate key events in their childhoods, and for that purpose narration is the obvious choice. Michael Ondaatje, in a paragraph, recalls his stepmother's inability to kill a cobra, perhaps because it embodied her dead father (p. 65). Donald Hall, in another paragraph, remembers hurting a playmate remorselessly (p. 66). Annie Dillard's essay recounts the ecstasy of being chased by an adult for pelting his car with a snowball (next page), while Langston Hughes pinpoints the moment during a church revival when he lost his faith (p. 78). And Kaela Hobby-Reichstein's narrative recalls some disturbing girlhood experiences with racism (p. 83).

We wove a web in childhood, / A web of sunny air.   —Charlotte Brontë

When she was good, / She was very, very good, / But when she was bad she was horrid.   —Henry Wadsworth Longfellow

Go directly—see what she's doing, and tell her she mustn't.   —Punch

JOURNAL RESPONSE   In a short journal entry, reflect on a time you misbehaved as a child. Was it exciting? scary? How did the adults in your life react?

Annie Dillard

A poet and essayist, Annie Dillard (born 1945) is part naturalist, part mystic. Growing up in Pittsburgh, she was an independent child given to exploration and reading. After graduating from Hollins College in the Blue Ridge Mountains of Virginia, Dillard settled in the area to investigate her natural surroundings and to write. Dillard demonstrated her intense, passionate involvement with the world of nature and the world of the mind early in her career with *Pilgrim at Tinker Creek* (1974), a series of related essays that earned her a Pulitzer Prize. Dillard's prolific output since then has spanned several genres, including poetry in volumes such as *Tickets for a Prayer Wheel* (1974) and *Mornings Like This* (1995); essays collected in *Teaching a Stone to Talk* (1982), *The Writing Life* (1989), and *For the Time Being* (1999); literary criticism in *Living by Fiction* (1982) and *Encounters with Chinese Writers* (1984); and, most recently, a novel, *The Maytrees* (2007). In 1999 she was inducted into the American Academy of Arts and Letters. Dillard now lives in North Carolina and is professor emeritus at Wesleyan University.

The Chase

In her autobiography, *An American Childhood* (1987), Dillard's enthusiasm for life in its many forms colors her recollections of her own youth. "The Chase" (editors' title) is a self-contained chapter from the book that narrates a few minutes of glorious excitement.

Some boys taught me to play football. This was fine sport. You thought   1
up a new strategy for every play and whispered it to the others. You went
out for a pass, fooling everyone. Best, you got to throw yourself mightily

at someone's running legs. Either you brought him down or you hit the ground flat out on your chin, with your arms empty before you. It was all or nothing. If you hesitated in fear, you would miss and get hurt: you would take a hard fall while the kid got away, or you would get kicked in the face while the kid got away. But if you flung yourself wholeheartedly at the back of his knees—if you gathered and joined body and soul and pointed them diving fearlessly—then you likely wouldn't get hurt, and you'd stop the ball. Your fate, and your team's score, depended on your concentration and courage. Nothing girls did could compare with it.

2 Boys welcomed me at baseball, too, for I had, through enthusiastic practice, what was weirdly known as a boy's arm. In winter, in the snow, there was neither baseball nor football, so the boys and I threw snowballs at passing cars. I got in trouble throwing snowballs, and have seldom been happier since.

3 On one weekday morning after Christmas, six inches of new snow had just fallen. We were standing up to our boot tops in snow on a front yard on trafficked Reynolds Street, waiting for cars. The cars traveled Reynolds Street slowly and evenly; they were targets all but wrapped in red ribbons, cream puffs. We couldn't miss.

4 I was seven; the boys were eight, nine, and ten. The oldest two Fahey boys were there—Mikey and Peter—polite blond boys who lived near me on Lloyd Street, and who already had four brothers and sisters. My parents approved of Mikey and Peter Fahey. Chickie McBride was there, a tough kid, and Billy Paul and Mackie Kean too, from across Reynolds, where the boys grew up dark and furious, grew up skinny, knowing, and skilled. We had all drifted from our houses that morning looking for action, and had found it here on Reynolds Street.

5 It was cloudy but cold. The cars' tires laid behind them on the snowy street a complex trail of beige chunks like crenellated castle walls. I had stepped on some earlier; they squeaked. We could have wished for more traffic. When a car came, we all popped it one. In the intervals between cars we reverted to the natural solitude of children.

6 I started making an iceball—a perfect iceball, from perfectly white snow, perfectly spherical, and squeezed perfectly translucent so no snow remained all the way through. (The Fahey boys and I considered it unfair actually to throw an iceball at somebody, but it had been known to happen.)

7 I had just embarked on the iceball project when we heard tire chains come clanking from afar. A black Buick was moving toward us down the street. We all spread out, banged together some regular snowballs, took aim, and, when the Buick drew nigh, fired.

A soft snowball hit the driver's windshield right before the driver's   8
face. It made a smashed star with a hump in the middle.

Often, of course, we hit our target, but this time, the only time in   9
all of life, the car pulled over and stopped. Its wide black door opened; a
man got out of it, running. He didn't even close the car door.

He ran after us, and we ran away from him, up the snowy Reynolds   10
sidewalk. At the corner, I looked back; incredibly, he was still after us. He
was in city clothes: a suit and tie, street shoes. Any normal adult would
have quit, having sprung us into flight and made his point. This man
was gaining on us. He was a thin man, all action. All of a sudden, we
were running for our lives.

Wordless, we split up. We were on our turf; we could lose ourselves   11
in the neighborhood backyards, everyone for himself. I paused and considered. Everyone had vanished except Mike Fahey, who was just round-
ing the corner of a yellow brick house. Poor Mikey, I trailed him. The
driver of the Buick sensibly picked the two of us to follow. The man
apparently had all day.

He chased Mikey and me around the yellow house and up a back-   12
yard path we knew by heart: under a low tree, up a bank, through a
hedge, down some snowy steps, and across the grocery store's delivery
driveway. We smashed through a gap in another hedge, entered a scruffy
backyard and ran around its back porch and tight between houses to
Edgerton Avenue; we ran across Edgerton to an alley and up our own
sliding woodpile to the Halls' front yard; he kept coming. We ran up
Lloyd Street and wound through mazy backyards toward the steep hilltop at Willard and Lang.

He chased us silently, block after block. He chased us silently over   13
picket fences, through thorny hedges, between houses, around garbage
cans, and across streets. Every time I glanced back, choking for breath,
I expected he would have quit. He must have been as breathless as we
were. His jacket strained over his body. It was an immense discovery,
pounding into my hot head with every sliding, joyous step, that this ordinary adult evidently knew what I thought only children who trained
at football knew: that you have to fling yourself at what you're doing,
you have to point yourself, forget yourself, aim, dive.

Mikey and I had nowhere to go, in our own neighborhood or out of   14
it, but away from this man who was chasing us. He impelled us forward;
we compelled him to follow our route. The air was cold; every breath
tore my throat. We kept running, block after block; we kept improvis-
ing, backyard after backyard, running a frantic course and choosing it
simultaneously, failing always to find small places or hard places to slow

him down, and discovering always, exhilarated, dismayed, that only bare speed could save us—for he would never give up, this man—and we were losing speed.

He chased us through the backyard labyrinths of ten blocks before 15 he caught us by our jackets. He caught us and we all stopped.

We three stood staggering, half blinded, coughing, in an obscure 16 hilltop backyard: a man in his twenties, a boy, a girl. He had released our jackets, our pursuer, our captor, our hero: he knew we weren't going anywhere. We all played by the rules. Mikey and I unzipped our jackets. I pulled off my sopping mittens. Our tracks multiplied in the backyard's new snow. We had been breaking new snow all morning. We didn't look at each other. I was cherishing my excitement. The man's lower pants legs were wet; his cuffs were full of snow, and there was a prow of snow beneath them on his shoes and socks. Some trees bordered the little flat backyard, some messy winter trees. There was no one around: a clearing in a grove, and we the only players.

It was a long time before he could speak. I had some difficulty at first 17 recalling why we were there. My lips felt swollen; I couldn't see out of the sides of my eyes; I kept coughing.

"You stupid kids," he began perfunctorily. 18

We listened perfunctorily indeed, if we listened at all, for the chewing 19 out was redundant, a mere formality, and beside the point. The point was that he had chased us passionately without giving up, and so he had caught us. Now he came down to earth. I wanted the glory to last forever.

But how could the glory have lasted forever? We could have run 20 through every backyard in North America until we got to Panama. But when he trapped us at the lip of the Panama Canal, what precisely could he have done to prolong the drama of the chase and cap its glory? I brooded about this for the next few years. He could only have fried Mikey Fahey and me in boiling oil, say, or dismembered us piecemeal, or staked us to anthills. None of which I really wanted, and none of which any adult was likely to do, even in the spirit of fun. He could only chew us out there in the Panamanian jungle, after months or years of exalting pursuit. He could only begin, "You stupid kids," and continue in his ordinary Pittsburgh accent with his normal righteous anger and the usual common sense.

If in that snowy backyard the driver of the black Buick had cut off 21 our heads, Mikey's and mine, I would have died happy, for nothing has required so much of me since as being chased all over Pittsburgh in the middle of winter—running terrified, exhausted—by this sainted, skinny, furious red-headed man who wished to have a word with us. I don't know how he found his way back to his car.

Meaning

1. What lesson did Dillard learn from the experience of the chase? Where is her point explicitly revealed?

2. In paragraph 2 Dillard writes, "I got in trouble throwing snowballs, and have seldom been happier since." What exactly is Dillard saying about the relationship between trouble and happiness? Do you think she is recommending "getting in trouble" as a means to happiness? Why, or why not?

3. If you do not know the meanings of the following words, try to guess them from the context of Dillard's essay. Test your guesses in a dictionary, and then try to use each word in a sentence or two of your own.

crenellated (5)	compelled (14)	perfunctorily (18, 19)
translucent (6)	improvising (14)	redundant (19)
embarked (7)	labyrinths (15)	exalting (20)
impelled (14)	obscure (16)	

Purpose and Audience

1. What seems to be Dillard's purpose in "The Chase": to encourage children to get into trouble? to encourage adults to be more tolerant of children who get into trouble? to do something else?

2. In her first paragraph, Dillard deliberately shifts from the first-person point of view (using *me*) to the second (using *you*). What is the effect of this shift, and how does it contribute to Dillard's purpose?

Method and Structure

1. Why do you think Dillard chose narration to illustrate her point about the difference between children and adults? What does she gain from this method? What other methods might she have used?

2. In this straightforward narrative, Dillard expands some events and summarizes others: for instance, she provides much more detail about the chase in paragraph 12 than in paragraphs 13 and 14. Why might she first provide and then pull back from the detail in paragraph 12?

3. How does the last sentence of paragraph 2 — "I got in trouble throwing snowballs, and have seldom been happier since" — serve to set up the story Dillard is about to tell?

4. **OTHER METHODS** Dillard makes extensive use of description (Chapter 6). Locate examples of this method and analyze what they contribute to the essay as a whole.

Language

1. How would you characterize Dillard's style? How does the style reflect the fact that the adult Dillard is writing from a child's point of view?

2. What does Dillard mean by calling the man who chases her "sainted" (paragraph 21)? What is her attitude toward this man? What words and passages support your answer?

3. Consider Dillard's description of cars: traveling down the street, they looked like "targets all but wrapped in red ribbons" (paragraph 3), and their tires in the snow left "a complex trail of beige chunks like crenellated castle walls" (5). What is the dominant impression created here?

Writing Topics

1. **JOURNAL TO ESSAY** Write a narrative essay about the incident of misbehavior you explored in your journal entry (p. 72). Use the first person *I*, strong verbs, and plenty of descriptive details to render vividly the event and its effects on you and others.

2. Write a narrative essay about a time you discovered that an "ordinary adult" knew some truth you thought only children knew. What was that truth, and why did you believe until that moment that only children knew it? What did this adult do to change your mind?

3. Though Dillard focuses on a time when no harm was done, the consequences of throwing snowballs at moving cars could be quite serious. Rewrite the essay from the point of view of someone who would *not* glorify the children's behavior—the man driving the Buick, for instance, or one of the children's parents. How might one of these people narrate these events? On what might he or she focus?

4. **CULTURAL CONSIDERATIONS** Childhood pranks like throwing snowballs at cars are tolerated more in some cultural groups than in others. In a narrative essay, retell an event in your childhood when you felt you were testing the rules of behavior in your culture. Make your motivations as clear as possible, and reflect on the results of your action.

5. **CONNECTIONS** Annie Dillard and Alaina Wong ("China Doll," p. 242) share an exuberant attitude toward their childhoods, at least toward the small portions they describe in their essays. But Wong focuses on a concrete, specific object, while Dillard focuses on an event. Write an essay examining the effects each essay has on you, and why. What techniques does each writer use to create these effects?

Nothing is more restful than conformity. —Elizabeth Bowen

We all try to be alike in our youth. —Alec Tweedie

This above all: to thine own self be true, / And it must follow, as the night the day, / Thou canst not then be false to any man. —William Shakespeare

JOURNAL RESPONSE When have you experienced a powerful desire to think, look, or act like others, especially your peers? Write a journal entry about your experience.

Langston Hughes

A poet, fiction writer, playwright, critic, and humorist, Langston Hughes described his writing as "largely concerned with depicting Negro life in America." He was born in 1902 in Joplin, Missouri, and grew up in Illinois, Kansas, and Ohio. After dropping out of Columbia University in the early 1920s, Hughes worked at odd jobs while struggling to gain recognition as a writer. His first book of poems, *The Weary Blues* (1925), helped seed the Harlem Renaissance, a flowering of African American music and literature centered in the Harlem district of New York City during the 1920s. The book also generated a scholarship that enabled Hughes to finish college at Lincoln University. In all of his work—including *The Negro Mother* (1931), *The Ways of White Folks* (1934), *Shakespeare in Harlem* (1942), *Montage of a Dream Deferred* (1951), and *Ask Your Mama* (1961)—Hughes captured and projected the rhythms of jazz and the distinctive speech, subtle humor, and deep traditions of African American people. He died in New York City in 1967.

Salvation

A chapter in Hughes's autobiography, *The Big Sea* (1940), "Salvation" is a simple yet compelling narrative about a moment of deceit and disillusionment for a boy of twelve. As you read Hughes's account, notice how the opening two sentences set up every twist of the story.

I was saved from sin when I was going on thirteen. But not really saved. 1
It happened like this. There was a big revival at my Auntie Reed's church.
Every night for weeks there had been much preaching, singing, praying,

and shouting, and some very hardened sinners had been brought to Christ, and the membership of the church had grown by leaps and bounds. Then just before the revival ended, they held a special meeting for children, "to bring the young lambs to the fold." My aunt spoke of it for days ahead. That night, I was escorted to the front row and placed on the mourner's bench with all the other young sinners, who had not yet been brought to Jesus.

My aunt told me that when you were saved you saw a light, and some- 2 thing happened to you inside! And Jesus came into your life! And God was with you from then on! She said you could see and hear and feel Jesus in your soul. I believed her. I have heard a great many old people say the same thing and it seemed to me they ought to know. So I sat there calmly in the hot, crowded church, waiting for Jesus to come to me.

The preacher preached a wonderful rhythmical sermon, all moans 3 and shouts and lonely cries and dire pictures of hell, and then he sang a song about the ninety and nine safe in the fold, but one little lamb was left out in the cold. Then he said: "Won't you come? Won't you come to Jesus? Young lambs, won't you come?" And he held out his arms to all us young sinners there on the mourner's bench. And the little girls cried. And some of them jumped up and went to Jesus right away. But most of us just sat there.

A great many old people came and knelt around us and prayed, 4 old women with jet-black faces and braided hair, old men with work-gnarled hands. And the church sang a song about the lower lights are burning, some poor sinners to be saved. And the whole building rocked with prayer and song.

Still I kept waiting to see Jesus. 5

Finally all the young people had gone to the altar and were saved, 6 but one boy and me. He was a rounder's son named Westley. Westley and I were surrounded by sisters and deacons praying. It was very hot in the church, and getting late now. Finally Westley said to me in a whisper: "God damn! I'm tired o' sitting here. Let's get up and be saved." So he got up and was saved.

Then I was left all alone on the mourner's bench. My aunt came and 7 knelt at my knees and cried, while prayers and songs swirled all around me in the little church. The whole congregation prayed for me alone, in a mighty wail of moans and voices. And I kept waiting serenely for Jesus, waiting, waiting—but he didn't come. I wanted to see him, but nothing happened to me. Nothing! I wanted something to happen to me, but nothing happened.

I heard the songs and the minister saying: "Why don't you come? My   8
dear child, why don't you come to Jesus? Jesus is waiting for you. He wants
you. Why don't you come? Sister Reed, what is this child's name?"

"Langston," my aunt sobbed.   9

"Langston, why don't you come? Why don't you come and be   10
saved? Oh, Lamb of God! Why don't you come?"

Now it was really getting late. I began to be ashamed of myself,   11
holding everything up so long. I began to wonder what God thought
about Westley, who certainly hadn't seen Jesus either, but who was now
sitting proudly on the platform, swinging his knickerbockered legs and
grinning down at me, surrounded by deacons and old women on their
knees praying. God had not struck Westley dead for taking his name in
vain or for lying in the temple. So I decided that maybe to save further
trouble, I'd better lie, too, and say that Jesus had come, and get up and
be saved.

So I got up.   12

Suddenly the whole room broke into a sea of shouting, as they saw   13
me rise. Waves of rejoicing swept the place. Women leaped in the air.
My aunt threw her arms around me. The minister took me by the hand
and led me to the platform.

When things quieted down, in a hushed silence, punctuated by a   14
few ecstatic "Amens," all the new young lambs were blessed in the name
of God. Then joyous singing filled the room.

That night, for the last time in my life but one—for I was a big   15
boy twelve years old—I cried. I cried, in bed alone, and couldn't stop.
I buried my head under the quilts, but my aunt heard me. She woke up
and told my uncle I was crying because the Holy Ghost had come into
my life, and because I had seen Jesus. But I was really crying because I
couldn't bear to tell her that I had lied, that I had deceived everybody in
the church, that I hadn't seen Jesus, and that now I didn't believe there
was a Jesus anymore, since he didn't come to help me.

Meaning

1. What is the main point of Hughes's narrative? What change occurs in
   him as a result of his experience?

2. What finally makes Hughes decide to get up and be saved? How does
   this decision affect him afterward?

3. What do you make of the title and the first two sentences? What is
   Hughes saying here about "salvation"?

4. If you are unfamiliar with any of the following words, try to guess what they mean from the context of Hughes's essay. Test your guesses in a dictionary, and then try to use each word in a sentence or two of your own.

dire (3)   rounder (6)   deacons (6)

Purpose and Audience

1. Why do you think Hughes wrote "Salvation" as part of his autobiography more than two decades after the experience? Was his purpose simply to express feelings prompted by a significant event in his life? Did he want to criticize his aunt and the other adults in the congregation? Did he want to explain something about childhood or about the distance between generations? What passages support your answer?

2. What does Hughes seem to assume about his readers' familiarity with the kind of service he describes? What details help make the procedure clear?

3. How do dialogue, lines from hymns, and details of other sounds (paragraphs 3–10) help re-create the increasing pressure Hughes feels? What other details contribute to this sense of pressure?

Method and Structure

1. Why do you think Hughes chose narration to explore the themes of this essay? Can you imagine an argumentative essay (Chapter 14) that would deal with the same themes? What might its title be?

2. Where in his narrative does Hughes insert explanations, compress time by summarizing events, or jump ahead in time by omitting events? Where does he expand time by drawing moments out? How does each of these insertions and manipulations of time relate to Hughes's main point?

3. In paragraph 1 Hughes uses several transitions to signal the sequence of events and the passage of time: "for weeks," "Then just before," "for days ahead," "That night." Where does he use similar signals in the rest of the essay?

4. **OTHER METHODS** Hughes's narrative also explains a process (Chapter 10): we learn how a revival meeting works. Why is this process analysis essential to the essay?

Language

1. What does Hughes's language reveal about his adult attitudes toward his experience? Does he feel anger? bitterness? sorrow? guilt? shame? amusement? What words and passages support your answer?

2. Hughes relates his experience in an almost childlike style, using many short sentences and beginning many sentences with *And*. What effect do you think he is trying to achieve with this style?

3. Hughes expects to "see" Jesus when he is saved (paragraphs 2, 5, 7), and afterward his aunt thinks that he has "seen" Jesus (15). What does each of them mean by *see*? What is the significance of the difference in Hughes's story?

Writing Topics

1. **JOURNAL TO ESSAY** Continuing from your journal entry (p. 78), write a narrative essay about a time when others significantly influenced the way you thought, looked, or acted—perhaps against your own true beliefs or values. What was the appeal of the others' attitudes, appearance, or behavior? What did you gain by conforming? What did you lose? Use specific details to explain how and why the experience affected you.

2. Hughes says, "I have heard a great many old people say the same thing and it seemed to me they ought to know" (paragraph 2). Think of a piece of information or advice that you heard over and over again from adults when you were a child. Write a narrative essay about an experience in which you were helped or misled by that information or advice.

3. **CULTURAL CONSIDERATIONS** It seems that Hughes wants to be saved largely because of the influence of his family and his community. Westley (paragraphs 6 and 11) represents another kind of influence, peer pressure, that often works against family and community. Think of an incident in your own life when you felt pressured by peers to go against your parents, religion, school, or another authority. Write a narrative essay telling what happened and making it clear why the situation was important to you. What were the results?

4. **CONNECTIONS** When Hughes doesn't see Jesus and then lies to satisfy everyone around him, he feels betrayed and pained. How does Hughes's experience differ from the one cheerfully reported by Michael Ondaatje (p. 65), in which a potentially deadly snake is said to be Ondaatje's deceased father, "come to protect his family"? Write an essay analyzing what elements these narratives have in common and any significant differences between them.

> Racism and class hatred are a learned activity, and as a kid I found myself in a society that was all too ready to teach it. —Henry A. Giroux

> Sometimes, I feel discriminated against, but it does not make me angry. It merely astonishes me. How can any deny themselves the pleasure of my company? —Zora Neale Hurston

> I have a dream that my four little children will one day live in a nation where they will not be judged by the color of their skin but by the content of their character. —Martin Luther King, Jr.

JOURNAL RESPONSE   In a journal entry, look back on a time when you were surprised by another person's opinion of one of your friends. Try to convey how your perspectives differed and why your point of view seemed more logical to you at the time. Has your perspective changed now that you're an adult?

Kaela Hobby-Reichstein

Kaela Hobby-Reichstein was born in 1981 and grew up in Philadelphia. A teacher got her interested in writing while she was a high-school student at Germantown Friends School, and she immersed herself in writing projects as an undergraduate at the University of Massachusetts, Amherst. Hobby-Reichstein worked to support herself as she completed her undergraduate thesis and spent some time in the African country of Ghana before graduating with a degree in African American studies in 2007. She currently works for the African Chamber of Commerce of the Pacific Northwest, a nonprofit trade organization located in Seattle.

Learning Race
(Student Essay)

Hobby-Reichstein, who reports that she is "still fascinated by race," first wrote this essay while in high school and rewrote it for her required freshman writing course in 1999. In her narrative she recounts two episodes from her childhood to re-create the gradual discovery of an ugly truth.

A few weeks ago as we sat down for lunch, my best friend, Ryan, asked   1
me when I learned what race was. My mind searched and searched, but I couldn't pin down an answer. It was not an easy question. I have known

Ryan since I was two. We grew up in neighboring apartments where we shared a wall as well as each other's toys and families. I can't remember a time without her or the exact moment I realized I was white, she was black, and what that meant. Of course, I always knew the creamy pink color of my skin and deep brown color of her skin weren't the same, but really understanding this took me many years.

My first memory is from kindergarten, Ms. Oakleaf's class at C. W. 2 Henry Elementary School. It was a normal day. The room, like most kindergarten classrooms, was overflowing with bright colors and various animal posters. The kids sat at their respective tables scratching their heads because of the recent lice invasion in our cubbies. Ms. Oakleaf stood at the front of the class swimming in her dated plaid pants suit and announced our next project.

"Children, would you all please stand in front of your easels."   3

Our chairs made an extremely annoying metallic noise as we jumped 4 from our plastic seats and pushed each other on the way to our easels.

"I would like you to put on your smocks and paint a picture of your 5 family for me."

At my easel, I velcroed my smock behind my neck and assessed the 6 colors they had set out for us. There was the usual red, yellow, blue, green, purple, and orange as well as two new colors, skin colors, brown and peach. First, I painted a rainbow in the top left corner of my paper because back then there were rainbows in everything I painted. Second, I painted a stick figure of myself with colorful clothing, curly blue hair and peach skin. I dipped my finger into the paint to make sure it was the right color. Next to me I painted my father. I chose the brown paint for him because his skin is darker than mine. Next to my father I painted my mother with peach paint. And next to her I painted my half brother in brown paint. My color selection seemed logical to me. In Ryan's family, she and her mom were the same color, brown. Her father and her stepbrother were peach, like me. Girls in a family were one color and boys in a family were another.

Ms. Oakleaf came around when we had all finished our paintings 7 and informed me my painting was wrong. She had met my family and knew all four of us were white. At the time, she wouldn't explain why it was wrong. She told me to talk to my parents about it when I got home, which I did. When my mom's Honda pulled up in front of the school, I ran outside, with my painting in hand. I asked her if Dad was light black or dark white and told her I thought he was light black. She laughed for a long time and then told me my father was not black but white. I painted a new picture of my family that night with all peach people and a rainbow in the corner and learned that my family and I were white and Ryan and her mom were black.

Though I was now aware that people were different colors, I 8 didn't really know what those colors meant. My mother cooked mostly bland foods: oatmeal, boiled chicken, and potatoes. Ryan's family ate grits, crabs, fried chicken, and added lots of spices to everything. My mom told me to say "Ryan and I" rather than "me and Ryan." Ryan's mom said "y'all" and "ain't." Ryan's family loved listening to loud music, and my family didn't really listen to music at all. Ryan's Barbies were black. My mom felt Barbie degraded women. Ryan's mom used a pick when she did her hair, and my mom used a brush, though we both screamed just as loud. There were no concrete things that made her black and me white, and growing up across the hall from each other, I'm sure we had picked up a number of each other's cultural attributes.

It was also with Ryan that I learned about bigotry. I think I was 9 in fourth grade, though I'm not really sure. Her father was driving us to dinner at her grandmother's house. Her grandmother lived in Fort Richmond, which could be described as a blue-collar Italian neighborhood, where the rest of her father's family lived. The streets were lined with old American cars. Along the river, factories that employed most of the neighborhood puffed out huge clouds of smoke. Everyone lived in a row house and therefore knew everyone else's business. It was the middle of the summer, and as we pulled up we saw a group of kids gathered around the fire hydrant cooling off and joking around in the powerful spray. We begged her dad to let us go play with the other kids, and he parked the car as we ran down the street toward the kids. As we got closer, they looked up. Their eyes froze on our little bodies, and their smiles turned to frowns.

"Get out of here." 10

"What do you think you are doing?" 11

"You don't belong here, monkey." 12

"Nigger lover, get that nigger out of here." 13

We stopped and stared at them, examining their faces for reasons, 14 logic, justification. They threw rocks at us and we ran. At that moment, I learned the feeling of hatred and it hurt. My head ached from sobbing, my body hurt from running so hard and fast, and my stomach turned remembering the looks on their faces and the way the words rolled off their tongues. My eyes burned with injustice as I imagined being able to fry them with a look. Shards of childlike innocence caught in my throat, making it impossible to respond or even speak. It is a feeling that I have felt many times since then and has yet to soften. I felt it when I saw

Ryan's mom put a pretty peach Band-Aid on her smooth chocolate leg, trying not to notice the obvious color clash. I felt it when my next-door neighbor was called a "dirty black man" by a judge in a courtroom full of white people. I felt it when a black man on the bus called me a cracker and spit on my jacket.

So that is how I learned race, to tell the differences between me   15 and so many, to see the bigotry and the hate differences can inspire. It is knowledge that I am glad I have. My awareness of the differences between Ryan and me have helped me understand her and myself better. We still talk every Sunday though we now live three hundred miles apart. My knowledge of hatred has helped me understand right and wrong. My experiences have made me stronger, and it is strength that allows me to speak my mind and possibly end some ignorance and hatred in the process.

Meaning

1. In paragraph 1, Hobby-Reichstein writes that "really understanding" the meaning of race "took...many years." Where in the essay (if at all) does she share her understanding of what race means? How did Hobby-Reichstein feel about the differences between herself and her best friend as a child? How does she feel about them now?

2. Why did Hobby-Reichstein believe that "girls in a family were one color and boys in a family were another" (paragraph 6)? What does that belief reveal about her understanding of difference?

3. If you are unsure of the meanings of any of the following words, try to guess them from the context of Hobby-Reichstein's essay. Look the words up in a dictionary to test your guesses, and then use each word in a sentence or two of your own.

respective (2)	degraded (8)	justification (14)
swimming (2)	attributes (8)	
grits (8)	bigotry (9)	

Purpose and Audience

1. It can be very difficult to recall a painful experience in your life, yet Hobby-Reichstein chooses to do so. What do you believe is her purpose in recording these episodes from her childhood: to understand her experiences? to tell her peers about her childhood? to do something else?

2. How does dialogue help re-create the discomfort and shock Hobby-Reichstein felt as a child? Is her repetition of other people's racial slurs (such as "monkey" in paragraph 12, "nigger" in paragraph 13, and "cracker" in paragraph 14) offensive or effective? Why do you think so?

Method and Structure

1. What features of narration make it ideal for describing childhood experiences like the ones documented by Hobby-Reichstein?

2. Although Hobby-Reichstein uses chronological order to organize her experiences, the two major episodes she recounts took place four years apart and her final examples are taken from her adult life. Why do you believe she jumps between time periods? How does this manipulation of narrative time serve the overall purpose of the essay?

3. **OTHER METHODS** In the middle of her narration (paragraph 8), Hobby-Reichstein compares and contrasts (Chapter 11) her white family with her friend's biracial family. What differences and similarities does she highlight? Why do you think she chose these details for her comparison? What do they contribute to the purpose of her narrative?

Language

1. Hobby-Reichstein uses many figures of speech to enrich her prose, particularly when she recounts her emotional response to the taunts of the young boys: "shards of childlike innocence caught in [her] throat," her "eyes burned with injustice," and she fantasized about "being able to fry them with a look" (paragraph 14). How effective are her figures of speech in reflecting how she felt about her experiences? How do they contribute to the overall meaning of her essay?

2. Although the topic of race is very complicated, Hobby-Reichstein uses relatively simple sentence structures through most of her essay. How does the rhythm of her sentences reinforce her purpose?

Writing Topics

1. **JOURNAL TO ESSAY** In "Learning Race," Hobby-Reichstein revisits two moments when she was surprised to discover that other people saw her best friend in a much different light than she did. In your journal entry (p. 83), you also recalled a moment when you were surprised by another person's opinion of one of your friends. Elaborate on that memory in a brief narrative essay. Include details of the episode that will make this

memory more vivid and real for your readers. What perspective can you bring to your experience now that you didn't have then?

2. "Learning Race" relies on narrative to recount a difficult and troubling learning experience. Using the same method, write an essay in which you recapture one of the happiest or most exciting discoveries of your childhood: for example, finding a favorite hiding place, learning a skill such as skating or playing a musical instrument, making an unexpected friend, or receiving something you deeply desired. Use straightforward chronological time if that works best, or, like Hobby-Reichstein, compress narrative time to emphasize the most significant moments.

3. **CULTURAL CONSIDERATIONS** Many scientists and cultural critics argue that there are no significant biological differences between people of varying colors and ethnicities. Race, they say, is a *social construction*: in other words, our understandings of racial difference are the result of what we're taught by society, not a scientific truth. Hobby-Reichstein's narrative explores one instance of this kind of cultural education: as a child she saw no differences between black and white until adults pointed them out to her, and she continues to reject the labels she was given. Write an essay in which you explore your own understandings of race and try to pinpoint where they came from. When did you first learn that skin color matters in American culture? Do you believe that there are real differences between races, or do you lean toward the idea that skin color is irrelevant? Explain your answer, giving plenty of details from your own experiences.

4. **CONNECTIONS** Like Hobby-Reichstein, Leanita McClain, in "The Middle-Class Black's Burden" (p. 230), writes poignantly about the frustration of being classified by skin color. These two women address similar issues, but their perspectives are quite different. In an essay of your own, compare the tones and viewpoints of these two authors.

Narration

Select one of the following topics, or any other topic they suggest, for an essay developed by narration. Be sure to choose a topic you care about so that narration is a means of communicating an idea, not an end in itself.

FRIENDS AND RELATIONS

1. Gaining independence
2. A friend's generosity or sacrifice
3. A wedding or funeral
4. An incident from family legend

THE WORLD AROUND YOU

5. An interaction you witnessed while taking public transportation
6. A storm, a flood, an earthquake, or another natural event
7. The history of your neighborhood
8. A school event, such as a meeting, demonstration, or celebration
9. A time when a poem, story, film, song, or other work changed you

LESSONS OF DAILY LIFE

10. An especially satisfying run, tennis match, bicycle tour, or other sports experience
11. A time when you confronted authority
12. A time when you had to deliver bad news
13. A time when a long-anticipated possession proved disappointing
14. Your biggest social blunder

FIRSTS

15. Your first day of school, as a child or more recently
16. The first time you met someone who became important to you
17. The first performance you gave

ADVENTURES

18. An episode of extrasensory perception
19. An intellectual journey: discovering a new field, pursuing a subject, solving a mystery
20. A trip to an unfamiliar place

WRITING ABOUT THE THEME

Recalling Childhood

1. While growing up inevitably involves fear, disappointment, and pain, there is usually security and happiness as well. Michael Ondaatje clearly finds comfort in his dead father's reappearance as a cobra (p. 65), Donald Hall (p. 66) and Annie Dillard both relish the joy of misbehaving (p. 72), and Kaela Hobby-Reichstein believes that her childhood experiences with racism strengthened her relationship with her best friend (p. 83). Write a narrative essay about a similarly mixed experience from your childhood, making sure to describe your feelings vividly so that your readers share them with you.

2. The vulnerability of children is a recurring theme in the essays and paragraphs in this chapter. Michael Ondaatje, Langston Hughes (p. 78), and Kaela Hobby-Reichstein all write in some way about psychological pain. After considering each writer's situation individually, write an essay analyzing the differences among these situations. Based on these narratives, which writers seem to have the most in common? Which of their responses seem unique to children? Which are most likely to be outgrown?

3. Childhood is full of epiphanies, or sudden moments of realization, insight, or understanding. Langston Hughes and Annie Dillard both report such moments at the ends of their essays: Hughes loses faith in a Jesus who would not help him in church, and Dillard recognizes that any experience of glorious happiness must end. Write a narrative essay in which you tell of events leading to an epiphany when you were growing up. Make sure both the events themselves and the nature of the epiphany are vividly clear.

6

DESCRIPTION
Experiencing New Places

Whenever you use words to depict or re-create a scene, an object, a person, or a feeling, you use **description**. A mainstay of conversation between people, description is likely to figure in almost any writing situation: an e-mail home may describe a new roommate's spiky yellow hair; a laboratory report may describe the colors and odors of chemicals; a business memo may examine the tastes and textures of competitors' low-fat potato chips; an insurance claim may explain the condition of an apartment after a kitchen fire. Because the method builds detail and brings immediacy to a subject for readers, description is an important part of most essay writing as well.

Reading Description

Description draws on perceptions of the five senses—sight, sound, smell, taste, and touch — to understand and communicate a particular experience of the world. A writer's purpose in writing and his or her involvement with the subject will largely determine how objective or subjective a description is.

- **Objective description** strives for precision and objectivity, trying to convey the subject impersonally, without emotion. This is the kind of description required in scientific writing—for instance, a medical diagnosis or a report on an experiment in psychology—where cold facts and absence of feeling are essential for readers to judge the accuracy of procedures and results. It is also the method of news reports and of reference works such as encyclopedias.

- **Subjective description**, in contrast, draws explicitly on emotions, giving an impression of the subject filtered through firsthand experience. Instead of withdrawing to the background, the writer invests feelings in the subject and lets those feelings determine which details he or she will describe and how he or she will describe them. State of mind—perhaps loneliness, anger, or joy—can be re-created by reference to sensory details such as numbness, heat, or sweetness.

In general, writers favor objective description when their purpose is explanation and subjective description when their purpose is self-expression or entertainment. But the categories are not exclusive, and most descriptive writing mixes the two. A news report on a tropical storm, for instance, might objectively describe bent and broken trees, fallen wires, and lashing rain, but the reporter's selection of details gives a subjective impression of the storm's fearsomeness.

Whether objective or subjective or a mixture of the two, effective description requires a **dominant impression**—a central theme or idea about the subject to which readers can relate all the details. The dominant impression may be something a writer sees in the subject, such as the apparent purposefulness of city pedestrians or the expressiveness of an actor. Or it may derive from an emotional response to the subject, perhaps pleasure (or depression) at all the purposefulness of the city pedestrians, perhaps admiration (or disdain) for the actor's technique. Whatever its source, the dominant impression serves as a unifying principle that guides both the writer's selection of details and the reader's understanding of the subject.

One aid in creating a dominant impression is a consistent **point of view**, the position from which a writer approaches a subject. Point of view in description has two main elements:

- A real or imagined *physical* relation to the subject: a writer could view a mountain, for instance, from the bottom looking up, from fifteen miles away across a valley, or from an airplane passing overhead. The first two points of view are fixed because the writer remains in one position and scans the scene from there; the third is moving because the writer changes position.

- A *psychological* relation to the subject, a relation partly conveyed by pronouns. In subjective description, where feelings are part of the message, writers might use *I* and *you* freely to narrow the distance between themselves and the subject and between themselves and the reader. But in the most objective, impersonal description, writers will use *one* ("One can see the summit") or avoid self-reference altogether in order to appear distant from and unbiased toward the subject.

Once a physical and psychological point of view has been established, readers come to depend on it. Thus a sudden and inexplicable shift from one view to another—zooming in from fifteen miles away to the foot of a mountain, abandoning *I* for the more removed *one*—can disorient readers and distract them from the dominant impression.

Analyzing Description in Paragraphs

Helene Cooper is a White House correspondent for the *New York Times*. Born in 1966 to members of Liberia's ruling class, she enjoyed a privileged childhood until violent uprisings forced her family to seek asylum in the United States in 1980. This paragraph, from her memoir *The House at Sugar Beach* (2008), describes her first impressions upon returning to Africa as an adult.

Arriving on West African soil for the first time is unlike any other arrival in the world. The first thing that hits you is the smell: a combination of coal fires, dried fish, humid air, and the sea. After smell comes the feel of the air. It is heavy, even when the sun is shining and there is not a cloud in the sky. You can never escape the humidity of the West African coastline, and in the interior, even more so. It is air so heavy that it weighs on your tongue, as if you can open your mouth and take a sip. It is a soup, a big hot pot of soupy air, fetid under the equatorial sun.

Specific, concrete details (under-lined once)

Figures of speech (underlined twice)

Point of view: fixed; psychologically somewhat distant

Dominant impression: oppressive humidity

Matthew Power (born 1974) is a freelance travel writer and a contributing editor for *National Geographic Adventurer* and *Harper's* magazine. The following paragraph comes from "The Magic Mountain," a feature article for *Harper's* about Payatas, a fifty-acre garbage dump in the Philippines.

As we come over a rise, my first glimpse of Payatas is hallucinatory: a great smoky-gray mass that towers above the trees and shanties creeping up to its edge. On the rounded summit, almost the same color as the thunderheads that mass over the city in the afternoons, a tiny backhoe crawls along a contour, seeming to float in the sky. As we approach, shapes and colors emerge out of the gray. What at first seemed to be flocks of seagulls spiraling upward in a hot wind reveal themselves to be cyclones of plastic bags. The huge hill itself appears to shimmer in the heat, and then its surface resolves into a moving mass of people, hundreds of them, scuttling like termites over a mound. From this distance, with the wind blowing the other way, Payatas displays a terrible beauty, inspiring an amoral wonder at the sheer scale and collective will that built it, over many years, from the accumulated detritus of millions of lives.

Specific, concrete details (underlined once)

Figures of speech (underlined twice)

Point of view: moving; psychologically close

Dominant impression: disarming beauty

Developing a Descriptive Essay

Getting Started

The subject for a descriptive essay may be any object, place, person, or state of mind that you have observed closely enough or experienced sharply enough to invest with special significance. A chair, a tree, a room, a shopping mall, a movie actor, a passerby on the street, a feeling of fear, a sense of achievement — anything you have a strong impression of can prompt effective description.

Observe your subject directly, if possible, or recall it as completely as you can. Jot down the details that seem to contribute most to the impression you're trying to convey. You needn't write the description of the details yet — that can wait for drafting — but you do want to capture the possibilities in your subject.

You should start to consider the needs and expectations of your readers early on. If the subject is something readers have never seen or felt before, you will need enough objective details to create a complete picture in their minds. A description of a friend, for example, might focus on his distinctive voice and laugh, but readers will also want to know something about his appearance. If the subject is essentially abstract, like an emotion, you will need details to make it concrete for readers. And if the subject is familiar to readers, as a shopping mall or an old spruce tree on campus probably would be, you will want to skip obvious objective information in favor of fresh observations that will make readers see the subject anew.

Forming a Thesis

When you have your subject, specify in a sentence the dominant impression that you want to create for readers. The sentence will help keep you on track while you search for the sensory details that will make your description concrete and vivid. It should evoke a quality or an atmosphere or an effect, as these examples do:

> His fierce anger at the world shows in every word and gesture.
>
> The mall is a thoroughly unnatural place, like a space station in a science-fiction movie.

Such a sentence can serve as the thesis of your essay. You don't necessarily need to state it outright in your draft; sometimes you may prefer to let the details build to a conclusion. But the thesis should hover over the essay nonetheless, governing the selection of every detail and making itself as clear to readers as if it were stated.

Organizing

Though the details of a subject may not occur to you in any particular order, you should arrange them so that readers are not confused by shifts among features. You can give readers a sense of the whole subject in the introduction to the essay: objective details of location or size or shape, the incident leading to a state of mind, or the reasons for describing a familiar object. In the introduction, also, you may want to state your thesis—the dominant impression you will create.

The organization of the body of the essay depends partly on point of view and partly on dominant impression. If you take a moving point of view—say, strolling down a city street—the details will probably arrange themselves naturally. But a fixed point of view, scanning a subject from one position, requires your intervention. When the subject is a landscape, a person, or an object, you'll probably want to use a spatial organization: near to far, top to bottom, left to right, or vice versa. (See also p. 39.) Other subjects, such as a shopping mall, might be better treated in groups of features: shoppers, main concourses, insides of stores. Or a description of an emotional state might follow the chronological sequence of the event that aroused it (thus overlapping description and narration, the subject of the previous chapter). The order itself is not important, as long as there is an order that channels readers' attention.

Drafting

The challenge of drafting your description will be bringing the subject to life. Whether it is in front of you or in your mind, you may find it helpful to consider the subject one sense at a time—what you can see, hear, smell, touch, taste. Of course, not all senses will be applicable to all subjects; a chair, for instance, may not have a noticeable odor, and you're unlikely to know its taste. But proceeding sense by sense can help you uncover details, such as the smell of a tree or the sound of a person's voice, that you may have overlooked.

Examining one sense at a time is also one of the best ways to conceive of concrete words and figures of speech to represent sensations and feelings. For instance, does *acid* describe the taste of fear? Does an actor's appearance suggest the smell of soap? Does a shopping mall smell like new dollar bills? In creating distinct physical sensations for readers, such representations make meaning inescapably clear. (See pp. 55–57 and the box on the next page for more on specific, concrete language and figures of speech.)

Revising and Editing

When you are ready to revise and edit, use the following questions and box as a guide.

- *Have you in fact created the dominant impression you intended to create?* Check that you have plenty of specific details and that each one helps to pin down one crucial feature of your subject. Cut irrelevant details that may have crept in. What counts is not the number of details but their quality and the strength of the impression they make.

- *Are your point of view and organization clear and consistent?* Watch for confusing shifts from one vantage point or organizational scheme to another. Watch also for confusing and unnecessary shifts in pronouns, such as from *I* to *one* or vice versa. Any shifts in point of view or organization should be clearly essential for your purpose and for the impression you want to create.

FOCUS ON CONCRETE AND SPECIFIC LANGUAGE

For readers to imagine your subject, you'll need to use concrete, specific language that appeals to their experiences and senses. (See p. 56 for the meanings of *concrete* and *specific*.) When editing your description, keep a sharp eye out for vague words such as *delicious, handsome, loud,* and *short* that force readers to create their own impressions or, worse, leave them with no impression at all. Use details that call on readers' sensory experiences, say why delicious or why handsome, how loud or how short. When stuck for a word, conjure up your subject and see it, hear it, touch it, smell it, taste it.

▶ To practice editing for concrete and specific language, visit Exercise Central at *bedfordstmartins.com/rewriting.*

A Note on Thematic Connections

The writers represented in this chapter all set out to explore their reactions to the places they encountered on their travels. They probably didn't decide consciously to write a description, but turned to the method intuitively as they chose to record the perceptions of their senses. In a paragraph, Helene Cooper captures the dense unpleasantness of humidity in West Africa (p. 93). In another paragraph, Matthew Power describes the surprising images inspired by the first sight of an enormous landfill in the Philippines (p. 94). Marta K. Taylor's experience of a family trip through the American desert climaxes in the glory of a lightning storm (next page). Amanda Fields's essay on a subway ride contemplates what it means to be a woman in Egypt (p. 102). And William Least Heat-Moon's description of a bridge in Pennsylvania ponders the "beauty of plainness" (p. 107).

Memory is the diary that we all carry about with us. —Oscar Wilde

A childhood is what anyone wants to remember of it. —Carol Shields

I might have seen more of America when I was a child if I hadn't had to spend so much of my time protecting my half of the back seat from incursions by my sister. —Calvin Trillin

JOURNAL RESPONSE Recall a childhood event such as a family outing, a long car ride, a visit to an unfamiliar place, or an incident in your neighborhood. Imagine yourself back in that earlier time and write down details of what you experienced and how you felt.

Marta K. Taylor

Marta K. Taylor was born in 1970 and raised in Los Angeles. She attended a "huge" public high school there before being accepted into Harvard University. She graduated from Harvard in 1992 with a degree in chemistry and from Harvard Medical School in 1998. She is now a physician in Philadelphia, where she specializes in ear, nose, and throat surgery.

Desert Dance

(Student Essay)

Taylor wrote this description of a nighttime ride when she was a freshman in college taking the required writing course. The essay was published in the 1988–89 edition of *Exposé*, a collection of student writing published by Harvard.

We didn't know there was a rodeo in Flagstaff. All the hotels were filled, 1 except the really expensive ones, so we decided to push on to Winslow that night. Dad must have thought we were all asleep, and so we should have been, too, as it was after one AM and we had been driving all day through the wicked California and Arizona desert on the first day of our August Family Trip. The back seat of our old station wagon was down, allowing two eleven-year-old kids to lie almost fully extended and still leaving room for the rusty green Coleman ice-chest which held the packages of pressed turkey breast, the white bread, and the pudding snack-pacs that Mom had cleverly packed to save on lunch expenses and quiet the inevitable "Are we there yet?" and "How much farther?"

Jon was sprawled out on his back, one arm up and one arm down, reminding me of Gumby or an outline chalked on the sidewalk in a murder mystery. His mouth was wide open and his regular breath rattled deeply in the back of his throat somewhere between his mouth and his nose. Beside the vibration of the wheels and the steady hum of the engine, no other sound disturbed the sacred silence of the desert night. 2

From where I lay, behind the driver's seat, next to my twin brother on the old green patchwork quilt that smelled like beaches and picnics—salty and a little mildewed—I could see my mother's curly brown head slumped against the side window, her neck bent awkwardly against the seat belt, which seemed the only thing holding her in her seat. Dad, of course, drove—a motionless, soundless, protective paragon of security and strength, making me feel totally safe. The back of his head had never seemed more perfectly framed than by the reflection of the dashboard lights on the windshield; the short, raven-colored wiry hairs that I loved so much caught and played with, like tinsel would, the greenish glow with red and orange accents. The desert sky was starless, clouded. 3

Every couple of minutes, a big rig would pass us going west. The lights would illuminate my mother's profile for a moment and then the roar of the truck would come and the sudden, the violent sucking rush of air and we would be plunged into darkness again. Time passed so slowly, unnoticeably, as if the whole concept of time were meaningless. 4

I was careful to make no sound, content to watch the rising and falling of my twin's chest in the dim light and to feel on my cheek the gentle heat of the engine rising up through the floorboards. I lay motionless for a long time before the low rumbling, a larger sound than any eighteen-wheeler, rolled across the open plain. I lifted my head, excited to catch a glimpse of the rain that I, as a child from Los Angeles, seldom saw. A few seconds later, the lightning sliced the night sky all the way across the northern horizon. Like a rapidly growing twig, at least three or four branches, it illuminated the twisted forms of Joshua trees and low-growing cacti. All in silhouette — and only for a flash, though the image stayed many moments before my mind's eye in the following black. 5

The lightning came again, this time only a formless flash, as if God were taking a photograph of the magnificent desert, and the long, straight road before us—empty and lonely—shone like a dagger. The trees looked like old men to me now, made motionless by the natural strobe, perhaps to resume their feeble hobble across the sands once the shield of night returned. The light show continued on the horizon though the expected rain never came. The fleeting, gnarled fingers grasped out and were gone; the fireworks flashed and frolicked and faded over and 6 over—danced and jumped, acting out a drama in the quick, jerky move-ments of a marionette. Still in silence, still in darkness.

I watched the violent, gaudy display over the uninhabited, endless   7 expanse, knowing I was in a state of grace and not knowing if I was dream-ing but pretty sure I was awake because of the cramp in my neck and the pain in my elbow from placing too much weight on it for too long.

Meaning

1. What does Taylor mean by "state of grace" in paragraph 7? What as-sociations does this phrase have? To what extent does it capture the dominant impression of this essay?

2. If you do not know the meaning of any of the words below, try to guess it from its context in Taylor's essay. Test your guesses in a dictionary, and then try to use each word in a sentence or two of your own.

paragon (3)	gnarled (6)	marionette (6)
silhouette (5)	frolicked (6)	gaudy (7)
strobe (6)		

Purpose and Audience

1. Why does Taylor open with the sentence "We didn't know there was a rodeo in Flagstaff"? What purposes does the sentence serve?

2. Even readers familiar with the desert may not have had Taylor's experience of it in a nighttime lightning storm. Where does she seem especially careful about describing what she saw? What details sur-prised you?

Method and Structure

1. What impression or mood is Taylor trying to capture in this essay? How does the precise detail of the description help to convey that mood?

2. Taylor begins her description inside the car (paragraphs 1–5) and then moves out into the landscape (5–7), bringing us back into the car in her final thought. Why does she use such a sequence? Why do you think she devotes roughly equal space to each area?

3. Taylor's description is mainly subjective, invested with her emotions. Point to elements of the description that reveal emotion.

4. **OTHER METHODS** Taylor's description relies in part on narration (see Chap-ter 5). How does narrative strengthen the essay's dominant impression?

Language

1. How does Taylor's tone help convey the "state of grace" she feels inside the car? Point out three or four examples of language that establish that mood.

2. Why do you think Taylor titles her essay "Desert Dance"?

3. Notice the words Taylor uses to describe Joshua trees (paragraphs 5–6). If you're already familiar with the tree, how accurate do you find Taylor's description? If you've never seen a Joshua tree, what do you think it looks like, based on Taylor's description? (Look the tree up online or in an encyclopedia to test your impression.)

4. Taylor uses similes to make her description vivid and immediate. Find several examples, and comment on their effectiveness. (See p. 56 for more on similes.)

5. Taylor's last paragraph is one long sentence. Does this long sentence work with or against the content and mood of the paragraph? Why and how?

Writing Topics

1. **JOURNAL TO ESSAY** Using subjective description, expand your journal entry about a childhood event (p. 98) into an essay. Recalling details of sight, sound, touch, smell, even taste, build a dominant impression for readers of what the experience was like for you.

2. Taylor's essay illustrates her feelings not only about the desert but also about her father, mother, and twin brother. Think of a situation when you were intensely aware of your feelings about another person (friend or relative). Describe the situation and the person in a way that conveys those feelings.

3. **CULTURAL CONSIDERATIONS** Though she had evidently seen the desert before, Taylor had not seen it the way she describes it in "Desert Dance." Write an essay in which you describe your first encounter with something new—for instance, a visit to the home of a friend from a different social or economic background, a visit to a big city or a farm, an unexpected view of your own backyard. Describe what you saw and your responses. How, if at all, did the experience change you?

4. **CONNECTIONS** Both Taylor and Ashley Rhodes, in "Fatherhood Is Essential" (p. 259), express strong feelings toward their fathers. In a brief essay, analyze how these writers convey their sense of the father-daughter relationship so that their emotions are concrete, not vague. Focus on their words and especially on their figures of speech. (See pp. 56–57 for more on figures of speech.)

> Travel in all the four quarters of the earth, yet you will find nothing anywhere. Whatever there is, is only here. —Ramakrishna
>
> Perhaps travel cannot prevent bigotry, but by demonstrating that all peoples cry, laugh, eat, worry, and die, it can introduce the idea that if we try and understand each other, we may even become friends. —Maya Angelou
>
> One's destination is never a place but rather a new way of looking at things. —Henry Miller

JOURNAL RESPONSE You've probably ventured beyond your hometown at least once in your life, perhaps on a family vacation, on a road trip with friends, or to the town or city where your current school is located. Think of one such trip and how the place you visited seemed strange to you. Were you surprised by people's behavior or unfamiliar with local customs? Could you understand the language or local dialect? Was the landscape different? In your journal, describe any discomfort you felt. (If you've never traveled, think of a place you'd like to go and imagine what it might be like to be there.)

Amanda Fields

A fiction writer and teacher, Amanda Fields (born 1977) grew up in Knoxville, Illinois. She earned a BA from Millikin University in Decatur, Illinois, in 1999, an MA in English from Iowa State University in 2001, and an MFA in creative nonfiction from the University of Minnesota in 2005. Her short story "Boiler Room," about life on a family farm, was published in *Indiana Review* and nominated for a Pushcart Prize in 2007. Fields taught creative writing, literature, and composition at the University of Minnesota while pursuing her degree and currently teaches writing at the American University in Cairo, Egypt.

Cairo Tunnel

In the following essay published in the online magazine *Brevity* in 2009, Fields relates a touching experience from her time as an American woman living and working in a predominantly Muslim country: an unexpected moment of cross-cultural understanding.

I nudge through the turnstile, putting the stiff yellow ticket in my pocket 1
and crossing a footbridge to the other side of the tracks, where I head

toward the cluster of women on the platform. It's rush hour. Morning salutations compete with beehive intensity. I scoot forward and back. Soon, the Metro barrels up, and the women's car, painted with a red stick-lady in a triangle skirt, sighs open.

I shove and fold in with a throng of women heading to low-paying 2 public sector jobs, or to clean expatriates' houses such as mine, or to public school. Once inside, there is no need to hold onto the metal bars, already bombarded with curled hands, wrapped over and bullying each other. We are like books on a shelf, supporting each other's weight.

A short woman, eyes looming behind a black mask, presses her gloved 3 hands flat against my chest. I only see the eyes, dark and liquid—she is without a mouth or nose or ears or cheekbones or eyebrows. I look down the length of my buttoned blouse, to her fingertips, to my skin. Still, I can smell her sour breath, and she can probably smell mine. I find my hands and legs in immovable positions. Someone tentatively touches my hair, probably a little girl.

It is April, and hot. A single fan rotates. I can see the dust on its 4 blades, and the windows are dingy and cracked, and through them the slums of Cairo whip by, the crumbling grey buildings, the jumbled sand and trash.

The back of my shirt grows slick. At each stop, more women force 5 themselves in, and I begin to feel the pressure on my ribs, the itchy cloth of the woman in *niqab*[1] against my bare arms. Even schoolgirls, writhing with giggles, are a burden to the rest of us. All is gravity and physicality. The Metro rattles into a dark tunnel, one weak bulb lighting the car. We might squeeze each other to death.

I was warned about taking the Metro in Cairo. My upper-class stu- 6 dents had warned that there would be staring, pushing, insults. And that was just in the women's car. I had heard stories of women taunting each other for the tint of their skin, of women in *niqab* shouting about Allah and bared flesh. Desperate women would sneak on the Metro without a ticket and peddle tissues and crumbling cosmetics for a few pounds.[2] Cover your arms, said my students. Deny the American University, they advised.

I try to breathe deeply, my chest barely moving beneath the wom- 7 an's hands. I once heard a rumor about a study of Cairo's traffic patterns. The Japanese scientists couldn't figure out how it worked, how there

---

[1] A *niqab* is a veil that covers a woman's head and face. [Editors' note.]

[2] Unit of currency. One Egyptian pound is equivalent to approximately 18 US cents. [Editors' note.]

weren't multiple car accidents every second. I have learned to put faith in this inscrutability.

Some of the women look at me with frankness, but I cannot sense   8
what they see. They cling to each other in something more than physical necessity. Most of them look tired.

Behind me, a fleeting space opens. I grapple for a handhold, clench-   9
ing a breast, then a stomach. "Sorry," I mutter.

Then a woman in lime-colored *hijab*[3] says, "Welcome." Her makeup   10
is minimal, like mine. She wears a pantsuit, an oversized purse against her hip. She smiles.

When I respond in stilted Arabic, other women smile, eyes crinkling.   11
The woman in *niqab* looks up. As we near Sadat station, a schoolgirl taps my shoulder to let me know it is time to start shoving toward the door, assuming, rightly, that I'm going to the university.

The car slows to the blur of hundreds of faces, hundreds of clamor-   12
ing women. I try to stick with the schoolgirl as we push through women staying, women going, women trying to get on before others can depart. The woman with the lime-colored *hijab* prods me forward. As we pass, a Sudanese girl gets spun in a circle as easily as a rack of clothes, her braids flying.

A sea of women — we crest, then topple out, gripping each other,   13
pressing, patting in a womanly empathy so familiar in Cairo. I can't understand how I'm not falling, how I'm not getting trampled. I can't understand how we carry each other in such smooth uncertainty. And all the while, women are laughing. I am laughing. We have this in common.

Meaning

1. Fields devotes the majority of her essay to describing the unpleasantness of riding in the women's car of the Metro, but her perception changes markedly toward the end. What causes her shift in attitude?

2. Why did the author's students try to discourage her from taking the subway?

3. How might Fields's last sentence have two meanings?

4. "Cairo Tunnel" does not include a thesis statement. Does Fields have a main point, and if so, what is it? How can you tell?

---

[3] A *hijab* is a headscarf that covers a woman's hair but leaves her face exposed. [Editors' note.]

5. If you're unsure of any of the following words, try to guess what they mean from the context of Fields's essay. Then look them up to see if you were right. Use each word in a sentence or two of your own.

salutations (1) Allah (6) clamoring (12)
expatriates (2) inscrutability (7) crest (13)
looming (3) stilted (11) empathy (13)
writhing (5)

Purpose and Audience

1. How does Fields make her experience vivid and clear for readers who have never been in Cairo or on a crowded train?

2. In a blog entry about her efforts to write "Cairo Tunnel," Fields comments, "Other things happened in the space of that event, so I had to make thematic decisions, removing details that still seem poignant. . . . For instance, I removed a man who harassed me. . . . [His] behavior is something that women in Egypt endure daily. In the end, though, that man represented an element of Cairo beneath which the reality of women, and discussions about women, too often disappear." Do you agree with Fields that omitting the episode strengthened her essay? Why or why not?

Method and Structure

1. What dominant impression of the subway ride does Fields create?

2. What point of view does the author take toward her subject?

3. **OTHER METHODS** "Cairo Tunnel" uses narration (Chapter 5) as much as it uses description. While Fields relies on chronological order for most of the essay, in paragraphs 6 and 7 she flashes back to past warnings and rumors. What do these previous episodes contribute to her meaning and purpose?

Language

1. Note Fields's frequent use of the first person (*I* and *we*) and of the present tense. What does she achieve with this point of view?

2. How many of the five senses does Fields appeal to in her description? Find words or phrases that seem especially precise in conveying sensory impressions.

3. In several places throughout her essay, Fields uses figures of speech to add depth to her description. Locate two examples that you find especially striking and explain their effect. (If necessary, see *figures of speech* in the Glossary.)

Writing Topics

1. **JOURNAL TO ESSAY**   Expanding on your journal entry (p. 102), write a descriptive essay about the discomfort you felt when you first visited a new place. Consider not only what made you uncomfortable, but why you reacted the way you did. You may, if you wish, use your essay as an opportunity to contemplate the broader significance of your experience.

2. Through most of her essay, Fields sees the other women on the subway as foreign, so different and strange that sharing a space with them makes her anxious. But as an American living and working in Cairo, Fields is the foreigner in this situation. Imagine the scenario she describes from the point of view of the Egyptian passengers. How might they have perceived her?

3. **CULTURAL CONSIDERATIONS**   Fields briefly mentions the *niqab* and *hijab* worn by other women on the train. Although she expresses no opinion about these garments, they are highly controversial in Western and Muslim cultures alike—the face-shielding *niqab* especially. Search the Web for an overview of the major positions on the issue and decide what you think. (See the Appendix for tips on finding and using sources.) Do veils oppress women or liberate them? Should wearing them be banned (or required) in certain communities or situations? Why?

4. **CONNECTIONS**   Both Fields and William Least Heat-Moon, in "Starrucca Viaduct" (p. 107), write about trains: Fields from the perspective of a harried commuter and Heat-Moon from the perspective of an admiring tourist. Compare and contrast what public transportation means to them. How do their respective points of view affect their experiences and attitudes? Be sure to include examples from both essays to support your comparison.

Beauty is in the eye of the beholder. —Margaret Wolfe Hungerford

And all the loveliest things there be / Come simply, so it seems to me. —Edna St. Vincent Millay

The absence of flaw in beauty is itself a flaw. —Havelock Ellis

JOURNAL RESPONSE Think of a building or public art installation that has been criticized for being ugly, plain, or otherwise ineffective. List some of the reasons critics give for disliking it. Next to each item in that list, explain why others might disagree.

William Least Heat-Moon

One of America's leading travel writers, William Least Heat-Moon consistently applies a journalist's eye for detail and a folksy, understated style to the physical and cultural landscape of rural America. He was born in 1939 in Kansas City, Missouri, to parents of Irish-English and Osage extraction, and in his extensive travels across the United States he has attended closely to the distinctive people and places he has encountered in small towns and little-known byways. After graduating from the University of Missouri at Columbia in 1961, Heat-Moon stayed on to earn a PhD in literature and a BA in photojournalism. He has contributed narratives of his journeys to many periodicals, including the *Atlantic, Esquire,* the *New Yorker,* the *New York Times,* and *Whole Earth Review.* Heat-Moon is best known, however, for his meticulously researched travelogues: *Blue Highways* (1982), *PrairyErth* (1991), *This Land Is Your Land* (1997), *River-Horse* (1999), and most recently *Roads to Quoz* (2008). When he's not meandering about the country, Heat-Moon makes his home in Columbia, Missouri.

Starrucca Viaduct

In *Roads to Quoz* Heat-Moon chronicles the sixteen-thousand-mile quest he and his wife, "Q," made in search of American "quoz," an archaic term for "anything strange, incongruous, or peculiar." They found one such instance in a nineteenth-century railroad trestle, lovingly described in this excerpt.

Where is the traveler who has never experienced arriving at a destination only to find anticipation surpassing reality? If the worth of the objective depends on expected awe, then one's disappointment may double. How many times have you heard "Is that it? Is that all of it? Isn't there more?" The gorge wasn't deep enough, the mountain high enough, the famed roller coaster frightful enough.

But for the Starrucca (Star-RUCK-ah), the first time I came upon the   2 1848 masonry railroad bridge, it was unquestionably enough, and the longer I looked, it became more than enough, both at that moment and in recollection: its age, height, length, and solidity, its unembellished grace, its beauty of plainness — qualities residents living in its shadows almost take for granted. If they cherish it, to them it's still just "the stone bridge."

The Starrucca Viaduct at Lanesboro, Pennsylvania, circa 1880.

Q and I arrived beneath it one morning when the sun had about fin-   3 ished turning the eastern face of the viaduct into seventeen golden portals. Surrounded by interrupted woodlands, the tall arches of big blocks of bluestone appeared to be a rock wall of massive doorways opening into some country beyond America, a land that finds use and beauty in structures of yore. A few old two-storey houses with backyards extending right up to the big stone piers introduced a dollop of reality and a sense of scale. Atop the sharp peaks of their steeply pitched roofs was space to set a seven-storey building which would reach only to the level of the viaduct parapets edging the deck carrying the tracks that, when first laid were a section of the longest railroad (at less than five-hundred miles) in the world.

By the time of completion of the span, thirteen years before com-   4 mencement of the Civil War, the surrounding hills had been heavily timbered off, and the bridge stood better revealed than today. It looked even longer and higher, much in the way a closely cropped head makes ears look bigger. Pieces of opened forest had returned to beautify the valley while somewhat minifying the span, although it could still call to mind a great, multiple-arched, classical Roman aqueduct, especially the one of the first century AD called the Claudian.[1]

A ten-storey-high bridge a thousand-feet long is big enough to reach 5 across most American rivers, yet under it, a child could toss a pebble over Starrucca Creek and in many places wade to the opposite bank without wetting more than a shirttail. To say this another way, the span is about forty times longer and a hundred times higher than necessary to get over the stream. Because the Susquehanna River is less than a half-mile west, a visitor can be forgiven for thinking the contractor built the bridge above the wrong waterway. It was, of course, not the creek but its rather deep Appalachian valley that the old Erie Railroad — on a route from the Hudson River to Lake Erie — needed to cross. Even though Starrucca Creek is a fraction of the width of the Mississippi, its valley is deeper than anything the big river flows through in its two-thousand-mile descent.

America has other huge bridges. Only twenty-five miles southwest, 6 to name one, is the great Tunkhannock Creek Viaduct, a splendid 1915 monument of reinforced concrete. But, beyond that, since alterations to the rebuilt High (or Aqueduct) Bridge[2] over the Harlem River north of Manhattan, no longer is there a span anywhere in the country (and few in the world) of such size *and* age as the Starrucca. Designed to support fifty-ton engines of the mid-nineteenth century, its pure and scarcely modified masonry, 160 years later, carried two-hundred-ton locomotives with monstrous loads behind them, and until not long ago might bear two trains at once. The Starrucca Viaduct, in architecture and undeserved anonymity, stands supreme.

Meaning

1. Does Heat-Moon describe purely for the sake of describing, or does he have a thesis he wants to convey? If so, where does he most explicitly state this thesis?

---

[1] Considered the grandest architectural example of the imperial Roman aqueducts, the Claudian was six miles long, featured arches as high as 109 feet, and carried more than 300 million gallons of water a day. [Editors' note.]

[2] Completed in 1848, the High (Aqueduct) Bridge transported water and pedestrians until the 1960s. The bridge is now under renovation and should be reopened to foot traffic in 2010. [Editors' note.]

2. What is the dominant impression Heat-Moon creates of the Starrucca Viaduct? Why, according to the author, might people living near the bridge not share his impression?

3. Explain what Heat-Moon means by the "beauty of plainness" (paragraph 2). Why would he characterize as *plain* a structure as massive and imposing as the Starrucca Viaduct?

4. Based on their context in the essay, try to guess the meanings of any of the following words that you don't know. Test your guesses in a dictionary, and then try out your knowledge of each word by using it in sentences of your own.

viaduct (title, 3, 6)	yore (3)	commencement (4)
objective (1)	piers (3)	timbered (4)
gorge (1)	dollop (3)	aqueduct (4)
masonry (2)	parapets (3)	shirttail (5)
unembellished (2)	span (4, 6)	descent (5)
portals (3)		

Purpose and Audience

1. Why do you think Heat-Moon felt compelled to write about the Starrucca Viaduct? Consider whether he might have had a dual purpose.

2. What kind of audience is Heat-Moon writing for? Architects? Historians? Tourists? People from Lanesboro, Pennsylvania? Someone else? How do you know?

Method and Structure

1. What is the effect of the quotation Heat-Moon includes in the first paragraph?

2. Heat-Moon's description of the bridge relies almost entirely on sight. Why doesn't he involve more of the senses, such as smell or sound? Does their absence weaken or strengthen his description in any way? Why?

3. Why does Heat-Moon include the nineteenth-century illustration of the bridge? How does this image differ from and resemble Heat-Moon's description?

4. How does the author organize his description? What is the effect of this organization?

5. **OTHER METHODS** Paragraphs 4 and 6 compare and contrast (Chapter 11) the Starrucca Viaduct with other very large stone bridges. How do these comparisons help Heat-Moon make his point?

Language

1. Notice that Heat-Moon's first three paragraphs include several shifts in person such as *the traveler, one, you, I* (see p. 50). Trace these shifts and consider their effect. Is Heat-Moon writing carelessly, or does he shift person for a purpose? What do Heat-Moon's shifts contribute to, or take away from, his essay? Explain your answer.

2. What is the effect of the vivid imagery in paragraph 5? In what way does this imagery explain Heat-Moon's enjoyment of the bridge?

3. Heat-Moon uses several figures of speech, such as "It looked even longer and higher, much in the way a closely cropped head makes ears look bigger" (paragraph 4). Find two or three other figures of speech and analyze how each contributes to Heat-Moon's meaning and helps convey his attitude toward the bridge. (If necessary, consult *figures of speech* in the Glossary.)

Writing Topics

1. **JOURNAL TO ESSAY** Using Heat-Moon's essay as a model, write a descriptive essay about something that you consider beautiful but others do not. Your subject could be a building or work of art, such as the one you described in your journal entry (p. 107), or something else: a person, an animal, a natural phenomenon, an object you hold dear. You may use details from your own experience and observation, use information culled from your reading and general knowledge, or, as Heat-Moon does, use material from both sources.

2. Reread Heat-Moon's essay, paying particular attention to his use of concrete words and figures of speech that appeal to readers' fancy. Choose the details and language that you find most powerful or suggestive, and write a brief essay explaining how they contribute to Heat-Moon's dominant impression of the Starrucca Viaduct.

3. In a travel magazine or the travel section of a newspaper, read a description of a place you are unfamiliar with. Then write a comparison of that piece and Heat-Moon's essay, explaining which you find more interesting and why. To what extent do the authors' purposes and audiences account for the differences you perceive in the essays?

4. **CULTURAL CONSIDERATIONS**   In opening his essay with the disappointment of travelers who "arriv[e] at a destination only to find anticipation surpassing reality" (paragraph 1), Heat-Moon implies that people travel to be entertained. Is this a fair assumption? For what other reasons might someone go on a trip? In an essay, use classification (Chapter 9) to list as many reasons for traveling as you can you think of, considering both the travelers' goals and the effects such journeys may have on them and the places they visit.

5. **CONNECTIONS**   Both Heat-Moon and Marta Taylor, in "Desert Dance" (p. 98), create a fairy-tale sense of monsters in their essays. Compare the way Taylor describes the Joshua trees as old men in paragraphs 5 and 6 of her essay to Heat-Moon's suggestions, in paragraphs 3–5 of "Starrucca Viaduct," that the Susquehanna valley is populated by giants. How does each writer combine striking images and original figures of speech to convey a strong sense of unreality? Do you think one author's imagery is more successful than the other's? Why?

WRITING WITH THE METHOD

Description

Select one of the following topics, or any topic they suggest, for an essay developed by description. Be sure to choose a topic you care about so that description is a means of communicating an idea, not an end in itself.

PEOPLE

1. An exceptionally neat or messy person
2. A person whose appearance and mannerisms are at odds with his or her real self
3. A person you admire or respect
4. An irritating child
5. A person who intimidates you (teacher, salesperson, doctor, police officer, fellow student)

PLACES AND SCENES

6. A shopping mall, yard sale, or flea market
7. A frightening place
8. A prison cell, police station, or courtroom
9. Your home
10. The devastation caused by a natural disaster
11. A scene of environmental destruction
12. The scene at a concert (rock, rap, country, folk, classical, jazz)

ANIMALS AND THINGS

13. Birds at a bird feeder
14. A work of art
15. A pet or an animal in a zoo
16. A prized possession
17. The look and taste of a favorite or detested food

SENSATIONS

18. Waiting for important news
19. Being freed of some restraint
20. Sunday afternoon
21. Writing
22. Skating, running, bodysurfing, skydiving, or some other activity
23. Extreme hunger, thirst, cold, heat, or fatigue

WRITING ABOUT THE THEME

Experiencing New Places

1. Although we tend to think of travel as a form of entertainment or relaxation, some of the writers in this chapter recognize that unfamiliar places can be difficult to come to terms with. Amanda Fields's description of the subway in Cairo (p. 102), Matthew Power's description of Payatas (p. 94), and Helene Cooper's description of West African humidity (p. 93) are most notable in this respect, but even William Least Heat-Moon's examination of an oversized bridge (p. 107) emphasizes the unsettling effects of its weirdness. Write a descriptive essay about a place that is special to you, emphasizing its strangeness rather than its beauty.

2. All of the writers in this chapter demonstrate strong feelings for the place, thing, or phenomenon they describe, but the writers vary considerably in the ways they express their feelings. For example, Amanda Fields's own discomfort on the Cairo Metro colors all of her perceptions, whereas Marta Taylor's description of an electrical storm mixes serenity and awe. Write an essay analyzing the tone of these and the three other selections in this chapter: Helene Cooper's paragraph on the land of her childhood, Matthew Power's paragraph on a Philippine landfill, and William Least Heat-Moon's "Starrucca Viaduct." Discuss which pieces you find most effective and why.

3. Each writer in this chapter vividly describes a specific place or thing that represents some larger, abstract concept: for example, Marta Taylor's desert lightning represents the awesomeness of nature, and Amanda Field's subway car represents cultural stereotypes. Think of a specific, tangible place or thing in your life that represents some larger, abstract idea and write a descriptive essay exploring this relationship.

7

EXAMPLE
Using Language

An **example** represents a general group or an abstract concept or quality. Steven Spielberg is an example of the group of movie directors. A friend's calling at 2:00 AM is an example of her inconsiderateness—or desperation. We habitually use examples to bring broad ideas down to specifics so that others will take an interest in them and understand them. You might use examples to entertain friends with the idea that you're accident prone, to convince family members that a sibling is showing self-destructive behavior that requires intervention, to demonstrate to voters that your local fire department deserves a budget increase, or to convince your employer that competing companies' benefits packages are more generous. Examples are so central to human communication, in fact, that you will find them in nearly everything you read and use them in nearly everything you write.

Reading Examples

The chief purpose of examples is to make the general specific and the abstract concrete. Since these operations are among the most basic in writing, it is easy to see why illustration or exemplification (the use of example) is among the most common methods of writing. Examples appear frequently in essays developed by other methods. In fact, as diverse as they are, all the essays in this book employ examples for clarity, support, and liveliness. If the writers had not used examples, we might have only a vague sense of their meaning or, worse, might supply mistaken meanings from our own experiences.

While nearly indispensable in any kind of writing, exemplification may also serve as the dominant method of developing an essay. When a writer's primary goal is to convince readers of the truth of a general statement—whether a personal observation or a controversial assertion—using examples is a natural choice. Any of the following generalizations, for instance, might form the central assertion of an essay developed by example:

- Generalizations about trends: "MP3 players are forcing the recording industry to rethink the way it does business."
- Generalizations about events: "Some fans at the championship game were more competitive than the players."
- Generalizations about institutions: "A mental hospital is no place for the mentally ill."
- Generalizations about behaviors: "The personalities of parents are sometimes visited on their children."
- Generalizations about rituals: "A funeral benefits the dead person's family and friends."

How many examples are necessary to support a generalization? That depends on a writer's subject, purpose, and intended audience. Two basic patterns are possible:

- A single **extended example** of several paragraphs or several pages fills in needed background and gives the reader a complete view of the subject from one angle. For instance, the purpose of a funeral might be made clear with a narrative and descriptive account of a particular funeral, the family and friends who attended it, and the benefits they derived from it.
- **Multiple examples**, from a few to dozens, illustrate the range covered by the generalization. The competitiveness of a team's fans might be captured with three or four examples. But supporting the generalization about mental hospitals might demand many examples of patients whose illnesses worsened in the hospital or (from a different angle) many examples of hospital practices that actually harm patients.

Sometimes a generalization merits support from both an extended example and several briefer examples, a combination that provides depth along with range. For instance, half the essay on mental hospitals might be devoted to one patient's experiences and the other half to brief summaries of others' experiences.

When you read essays developed by illustration and exemplification, pay attention to how writers use examples to develop a point. Rarely will a simple list do an idea justice. Effective writers, you will see, not only provide examples but also explain how those examples support their ideas.

Analyzing Examples in Paragraphs

Deborah Tannen (born 1945), a respected scholar with a knack for popular writing, is widely known for her prolific work on how men and women communicate. The following paragraph is from the book *Talking from 9 to 5* (1994), Tannen's best-selling exploration of gender differences in workplace communication.

Women are often told they apologize too much. The reason they're told to stop doing it is that, to many men, apologizing seems synonymous with putting oneself down. But there are many times when "I'm sorry" isn't self-deprecating, or even an apology; it's an automatic way of keeping both speakers on an equal footing. For example, a well-known columnist once interviewed me and gave me her phone number in case I needed to call her back. I misplaced the number and had to go through the newspaper's main switchboard. When our conversation was winding down and we'd both made ending-type remarks, I added, "Oh, I almost forgot—I lost your direct number, can I get it again?" "Oh, I'm sorry," she came back instantly, even though she had done nothing wrong and *I* was the one who'd lost the number. But I understood she wasn't really apologizing; she was just automatically reassuring me she had no intention of denying me her number.

Generalization and topic sentence (underlined)

Single detailed example

William Lutz (born 1940) is an expert on doublespeak, which he defines as "language that conceals or manipulates thought. It makes the bad seem good, the negative appear positive, the unpleasant appear attractive or at least tolerable." In this paragraph from his book *Doublespeak* (1989), Lutz illustrates one use of this deceptive language.

<u>Because it avoids or shifts responsibility, double-speak is particularly effective in explaining or at least glossing over accidents.</u> An air force colonel in charge of safety wrote in a letter that rocket boosters weighing more than 300,000 pounds "have an explosive force upon surface impact that is sufficient to exceed the accepted overpressure threshold of physiological damage for exposed personnel." In English: if a 300,000-pound booster rocket falls on you, you probably won't survive. In 1985 three American soldiers were killed and sixteen were injured when the first stage of a Pershing II missile they were unloading suddenly ignited. There was no explosion, said Major Michael Griffen, but rather "an unplanned rapid ignition of solid fuel."

Generalization and topic sentence (underlined)

Two examples

Developing an Essay by Example

Getting Started

You need examples whenever your experiences, observations, or reading lead you to make a general statement; the examples give readers evidence for the statement so that they see its truth. An appropriate subject for an example paper is likely to be a general idea you have formed about people, things, the media, or any other feature of your life. Say, for instance, that you have noticed while watching television that many programs aimed at teenagers deal with sensitive topics such as drug abuse, domestic violence, or chronic illness. There is a promising subject: teen dramas that address controversial social issues.

After choosing a subject, you should make a list of all the pertinent examples that occur to you. This stage may take some thought and even some further reading or observation. When you're making this list, focus on identifying as many examples as you can, but keep your intended readers at the front of your mind: what do they already know about your subject, and what do they need to know in order to accept your view of it?

Forming a Thesis

Having several examples of a subject is a good starting place, but you will also need a thesis that ties the examples together and gives them a point. A clear thesis is crucial for an example paper because without it readers can only guess what your illustrations are intended to show.

To move from a general subject toward a workable thesis, try making a generalization based on what you know of individual examples, for instance:

> Some teen dramas do a surprisingly good job of dramatizing and explaining difficult social issues.

> Some teen dramas trivialize difficult social issues in their quest for higher ratings.

Either of these statements could serve as the thesis of an essay, the point you want readers to take away from your examples.

Avoid the temptation to start with a broad statement and then try to drum up a few examples to prove it. A thesis such as "Teenagers do poorly in school because they watch too much television" would require factual support gained from research, not the lone example of your brother. If your brother performs poorly in school and you attribute his performance to his television habits, then narrow your thesis so that it accurately reflects your evidence—perhaps "In the case of my brother, at least, the more time spent watching television the poorer the grades."

After arriving at your thesis, you should narrow your list of examples down to those that are most pertinent, adding new ones as necessary to persuade readers of your point. For instance, in illustrating the social value of teen dramas for readers who believe television is worthless or even harmful, you might concentrate on the programs or individual episodes that are most relevant to readers' lives, providing enough detail about each to make readers see the relevance.

Organizing

Most example essays open with an introduction that engages readers' attention and gives them some context to relate to. You might begin the paper on teen dramas, for instance, by briefly narrating the plot of one episode. The opening should lead into your thesis sentence so that readers know what to expect from the rest of the essay.

Organizing the body of the essay may not be difficult if you use a single example, for the example itself may suggest a distinct method of development (such as narration) and thus an arrangement. But an essay using multiple examples usually requires close attention to arrangement so that readers experience not a list but a pattern. Some guidelines:

- With a limited number of examples—say, four or five—use a climactic organization (p. 39), arranging examples in order of increasing importance, interest, or complexity. Then the strongest and most detailed example provides a dramatic finish.

- With many examples—ten or more—find some likenesses among them that will allow you to treat them in groups. For instance, instead of covering fourteen teen dramas in a shapeless list, you might group them by subject into shows dealing with family relations, those dealing with illness, and the like. (This is the method of classification, discussed in Chapter 9.) Covering each group in a separate paragraph or two would avoid the awkward string of choppy paragraphs that might result from covering each example independently. And arranging the groups themselves in order of increasing interest or importance would further structure your presentation.

To conclude your essay, you may want to summarize by elaborating on the generalization of your thesis now that you have supported it. But the essay may not require a conclusion at all if you believe your final example emphasizes your point and provides a strong finish.

Drafting

While you draft your essay, remember that your examples must be plentiful and specific enough to support your generalization. If you use fifteen different examples, their range should allow you to treat each one briefly, in one or two sentences. But if you use only three examples, say, you will have to describe each one in sufficient detail to make up for their small number. And, obviously, if you use only a single example, you must be as specific as possible so that readers see clearly how it illustrates your generalization.

Revising and Editing

To be sure you've met the expectations that most readers hold for examples, revise and edit your draft by considering the following questions and the information in the box.

- *Is your generalization fully supported by your examples?* If not, you may need to narrow your thesis statement or add more evidence to prove your point.

- *Are all examples, or parts of a single example, obviously relevant to your generalization?* Be careful not to get sidetracked by interesting but unrelated information.

- *Are the examples specific?* Examples bring a generalization down to earth only if they are well detailed. For an essay on the social value of teen dramas, for instance, simply naming representative programs and their subjects would not demonstrate their social value. Each drama would need a plot or character summary that shows how the program fits and illustrates the generalization.

- *Do the examples, or the parts of a single example, cover all the territory mapped out by your generalization?* To support your generalization, you need to present a range of instances that fairly represents the whole. An essay would be misleading if it failed to acknowledge that not *all* teen dramas have social value. It would also be misleading if it presented several shows as representative examples of socially valuable teen programming when in fact they were the *only* instances of such television.

FOCUS ON SENTENCE VARIETY

While accumulating examples and detailing them during drafting—both essential tasks for a successful essay—you may find yourself writing strings of similar sentences. As you review your draft, be alert to repetitive sentence structures and look for opportunities to change them: try coordinating and subordinating ideas, varying the beginnings and endings of sentences, shortening some and lengthening others, and so on. Editing for sentence variety will ensure that your labor isn't too obvious and that your writing is more interesting. For more on sentence variety, turn to pages 54 and 55.

▶ To practice editing for sentence variety, visit Exercise Central at *bedfordstmartins.com/rewriting*.

A Note on Thematic Connections

The authors represented in this chapter all have something to say about language—how we use it, abuse it, or change from it. Their ideas probably came to them through examples as they read, talked, and listened, so naturally they use examples to demonstrate those ideas. In one paragraph, Deborah Tannen draws on a single example to show the layers of meaning a simple phrase can convey (p. 117). In another, William Lutz uses two examples to illustrate how evasive doublespeak can be (p. 118). Kim Kessler's essay explores the emergence of the expression *blah blah blah* to end sentences (opposite). Anita Jain finds unexpected meaning in her father's use of pronouns (p. 128). And Perri Klass's essay grapples with why doctors use peculiar and often cruel jargon and how it affects them (p. 133).

Sometimes speech is no more than a device for saying nothing. —Simone de Beauvoir

Continual eloquence is tedious. —Blaise Pascal

One way of looking at speech is to say it is a constant stratagem to cover nakedness. —Harold Pinter

JOURNAL RESPONSE Pick a conversation filler that you have noticed, such as *you know* or *I mean*. Why do people use these fillers? Do you use them yourself? Write a journal entry reacting to these words and phrases.

Kim Kessler

Kimberly Anne Kessler was born in 1975 in New York City and grew up mostly in Greenwich, Connecticut. A political science major, she graduated from Brown University in 1997, worked in magazine publishing for several years, and earned a law degree from New York University in 2003. Kessler is currently a defense attorney specializing in white-collar crime.

Blah Blah Blah
(Student Essay)

Kessler published this essay in the *Brown Daily Herald* in 1996, after noticing, she says, that she and her friends "had basically stopped talking to each other in complete sentences." With ample examples and analysis, Kessler questions the uses of the title expression in place of words that the speaker, for some reason, doesn't want to utter.

"So he says to me, 'Well it just happened. I was this and that and blah blah blah.'" 1

That's an actual quote. That was the statement one of my oh-so- 2 articulate friends made as an explanation of a certain situation. The thing about it is that I figured I knew exactly what he meant. The more important thing about it, the thing that makes this quote notable, is that I feel as though I've been hearing it all over the place these days. It has come to my attention in the last few weeks, maybe even in the last couple of months, that it is common for peers of mine to finish their sentences with "blah blah blah." Some people have their own less common versions of the phrase—e.g., "yadda yadda" or "etc., etc."—but it all amounts to the same thing. Rather than completing a thought or detailing an explanation, sentences simply fade away into a symbol of generic rhetoric.

I'm not quite sure what I think about this recently noticed phenom- 3 enon quite yet. What does it mean that I can say "blah blah blah" to you and you consider it to be an acceptable statement?

I guess that there are a couple of good reasons for why this is going 4 on. First, it's a commentary on just how trite so many of those conversations we spend our time having really are. Using the phrase is a simple acknowledgment of the fact that what is about to be said has been said so many times before that it is pretty much an exercise in redundancy to say it again. Some folks "blah blah blah" me (yeah, it's a verb) when they're using the phrase as a shortcut; they are eager to get to the part of their story that *does* distinguish it from all the other stories out there. Other times people "blah blah blah" me when they think that it is not worth their time or their energy to actually recount a story for my sake. In this case I feel dismissed, rejected. You can get "blah blahed" (past tense) in an inclusive way, too. In this scenario the "blah blah" construction is used to refer to something that both you and the speaker understand. This reflects a certain intimacy between the speaker and the listener, an intimacy that transcends the need for the English language that strangers would need in order to communicate.

I have discovered quite a different use for the phrase. I have found 5 that because "blah blah" is an accepted part of our everyday discourse, and because people assume that with this phrase what you are referring to is indeed the same thing that they are thinking of, it is very easy to use this construction to lie. Well, maybe "lie" isn't the best word. It's usually more of a cover-up than a lie. I'll give an example to demonstrate my meaning here.

I'm walking across campus at some time on some Monday. I get 6 accosted by some acquaintance and have the gratuitous "How was your weekend?" conversation. He's asking me about my Saturday night. I reply: "It was good, you know . . . went out to dinner then to a party, blah blah blah." The acquaintance smiles and nods and then goes merrily on his way, his head filled with thoughts of me and my normal Saturday night. What he will never know (as long as he's not reading this) is that I ended that night walking many, many blocks home alone in the rain without a coat, carrying on my back, of all things, a trombone. He also does not know about the mini-breakdown and moment of personal evaluation that my lonely, wet, trombone-carrying state caused me to have under a streetlight in the middle of one of those many blocks. He does not know these things because he has constructed his own end to my night to fill in for my "blah blah blah." (I hope you can all handle that open display of vulnerability. It's not very often that I share like that.)

"Blah blah blah" implies the typical. I tend to use it in place of the   7
atypical, usually the atypical of the most embarrassing sort. For me, it's a cop-out. The accepted use of the phrase has allowed me a refuge, a wall of meaningless words with which to protect myself. I'm definitely abusing the term.

Maybe there are a couple of you readers who would want to inter-   8
ject here and remind me that not everybody tells the *whole* truth *all* of the time. (I'd guess that there would even be a hint of sarcasm in your voice as you said this to me.) Well, I realize that. I just feel the slightest twinge of guilt because my withholding of the truth has a deceptive element to it.

But, hey, maybe I'm not the only one. Maybe everyone is manipu-   9
lating the phrase "blah blah blah." What if none of us really knows what anyone else is talking about anymore? What are the repercussions of this fill-in-the-blank type of conversation? I feel myself slipping into that very annoying and much too often frequented realm of the overly analytical, so I'm going to stop myself. To those of you who are concerned about this "blah blah" thing I am going to offer the most reasonable solution that I know of—put on your Walkman[1] and avoid it all. The logic here is that the more time you spend with your Walkman on, the less time you spend having those aforementioned gratuitous conversations, and therefore the fewer "blah blahs" you'll have to deal with.

Meaning

1. How does Kessler's use of the phrase *blah blah blah* differ from the normal use, and why does her use bother her?

2. What is the "symbol of generic rhetoric" referred to in paragraph 2? What does Kessler mean by these words? (Consult a dictionary if you're not sure.) Does this sentence state Kessler's main idea? Why, or why not?

3. Try to guess the meanings of any of the following words you are unsure of, based on their context in Kessler's essay. Look the words up in a

---

[1] Portable audiocassette player. [Editors' note.]

dictionary to test your guesses, and then use each word in a sentence of your own.

articulate (2)	transcends (4)	atypical (7)
phenomenon (3)	discourse (5)	interject (8)
trite (4)	accosted (6)	repercussions (9)
redundancy (4)	gratuitous (6)	

Purpose and Audience

1. What seems to be Kessler's purpose in this essay: to explain the various ways the phrase *blah blah blah* can be used? to argue against the overuse of the phrase? to do something else?

2. Whom did Kessler assume as her audience? (Look back at the note on the essay, p. 123, if you're not sure.) How do her subject, evidence, and tone reflect such an assumption?

Method and Structure

1. Why do you think Kessler chose to examine this linguistic phenomenon through examples? How do examples help her achieve her purpose in a way that another method might not? (Hint: What is lost when you skip from paragraph 5 to 7?)

2. What generalizations do the examples in paragraphs 4 and 6 support?

3. Which paragraphs fall into the introduction, body, and conclusion of Kessler's essay? What function does each part serve?

4. **OTHER METHODS**   Kessler's essay attempts to define the indefinable, an expression that would seem to have no meaning. What meanings does she find for *blah blah blah*? How does this use of definition (Chapter 12) help Kessler achieve her purpose?

Language

1. How would you characterize Kessler's tone: serious? light? a mix of both? How does this tone reflect her intended audience and her attitude toward her subject?

2. Point out instances of irony in the essay. (See *irony* in the Glossary.)

3. What does Kessler achieve by addressing the reader directly throughout the essay?

Writing Topics

1. **JOURNAL TO ESSAY** Reread your journal entry (p. 123), and then listen carefully for the conversation filler you've selected in the speech of your friends, the talk you observe on campus or in online chat rooms, and the dialogue in television shows and movies. Form a generalization about the way the filler functions and the purpose or purposes it serves, and then, in an essay, support that generalization with plenty of examples.

2. Write an essay expressing your opinion of Kessler's essay. For instance, how did you react to her complaint that most of her conversations with her peers were "trite" or "gratuitous"? Do you think she is too critical of her peers? Agree or disagree with Kessler, supporting your opinion with your own examples.

3. **CULTURAL CONSIDERATIONS** Although Kessler never explicitly says so, the phenomenon she writes about seems to apply mainly to people of her own generation. Think of an expression that you use when among a group to which you belong (family, ethnic group, others of your own gender, and so on) but feel constrained from using outside the group. Write an essay explaining and illustrating the uses of the expression in the group and the problems you experience using it elsewhere.

4. **CONNECTIONS** To what extent, if at all, does *blah blah blah* resemble the jargon of the medical profession as discussed by Perri Klass in "She's Your Basic LOL in NAD" (p. 133)? After reading Klass's essay, list the purposes she believes medical jargon serves. Does *blah blah blah* serve similar or different purposes for Kessler and her peers? Spell your answer out in an essay, drawing on Klass's and Kessler's essays as well as your own experience for evidence.

The purpose of polite behavior is never virtuous. Deceit, surrender, and concealment: these are not virtues. —June Jordan

Chivalry is a poor substitute for justice, if one cannot have both. Chivalry is something like the icing on cake, sweet, but not nourishing. —Nellie McClung

There is not a single outward mark of courtesy that does not have a deep moral basis. —Johann Wolfgang von Goethe

JOURNAL RESPONSE Think of a traditional form of politeness that some people now object to. Examples might include holding a door open, addressing a customer as *ma'am*, or offering to help an older person cross the street. Why do some people interpret such behaviors as common courtesy, while others consider them rude or insulting? Write down as many reasons as you can.

Anita Jain

Anita Jain was born in 1973 in New Delhi, India, and grew up in the United States, living in eleven different school districts before her family made a permanent home in the Sacramento, California, area. Jain is a successful financial reporter who has worked out of Mexico City, London, Singapore, New York, and New Delhi. She is also the author of a best-selling memoir, *Marrying Anita* (2008), that details her frustrations with American dating norms and her experience of returning to India to seek a husband through traditional means such as arranged marriage. Jain now lives in New Delhi, a city she found unexpectedly modern and cosmopolitan.

A Nameless Respect

In "A Nameless Respect" (Editors' title), an excerpt from *Marrying Anita*, Jain takes a careful look at the way her parents address each other. Her father, she discovers, has found a subtle way to accord his wife a measure of equality traditionally denied Indian women of her generation.

My father's interests tend toward daytime talk shows and his latest cash-generating shenanigans, which at this moment is day trading. But while he may not be highbrow in his pursuits or refined in his habits, a distinct nobility of mind and dignity of character underlie his ideas and actions regarding gender relations.

Disgusted with the poor treatment of women he observed growing 2
up in 1940s India, my father became an ardent feminist. He was hardly
poised to become one, born into a lower-middle-class family of seven
brothers and one sister in Meerut, an industrial town two hours outside
of Delhi. It was a town earlier immortalized in history as the one whose
hotheads gave India its first insurrection against imperial rule, the 1857
mutiny against the British. Although my paternal grandfather ensured
that all his children received a proper education—all of them went on
to study engineering—I suspect the Hindi-language public schools my
father and his siblings attended may have given short shrift to ideas
stemming from the Enlightenment such as equality, justice, and liberty.
Given a background destined to turn a man into a brute, or at least one
not especially attuned to his feminine side, my father managed to chart
a personal philosophy predicated on the belief that women are equal to
men and should be treated so accordingly, every day, in every conversation.

As in many languages other than English, there are several ways to 3
say "you" in Hindi. (The English language is veritably impoverished when
it comes to the second-person pronoun, our default for the second-person
plural across the vast English-speaking world being the inelegant "you
guys.") There is the formal *aap* that is used for elders and unfamiliar people, the familiar *tum* used with friends and siblings, and beneath that, the
somewhat rough-hewn *tu,* which can be deployed with affection, as parents do with their children or between close friends, but can also be crude,
unrefined, and imperious when directed at servants or underlings.

My mother, in accordance with her generation and small-town 4
middle-class manners, was expected to address my father with the formal
aap. In my mother's era, it was also considered disrespectful for a woman
to utter her husband's name, as in "Rajiv, dinner's ready!" or "Amit, what a
day I had today," or even when referring to him in the third person ("Ashok
and I would like our son to be a doctor."). To this day, I have never heard
my mother mouth my father's name, Naresh. When calling out to him, she
says, "Listen up!" or "Do you hear?" When referring to him in conversation
with other Indians, she just uses "he." To avoid confusing non-Indians who
would not understand her delicacy, she will say "My husband." As a childish prank, I used to try to trick her and get her to voice his name by asking
her the correct pronunciation or employing some other ruse, but she would
always manage to get around repeating his name.

In every conversation in the forty years my parents have been mar- 5
ried, my father also addresses my mother as *aap* and has similarly never
uttered her name, Santosh. When conversing with others, he will refer

to her as "she" much as she does with him. I've never actually seen any other Indian man do this. Other uncles address their wives with the middle form *tum*, or even the boorish *tu*, while most often wives reply with *aap*. I've also seen many couples of my parents' generation, having perhaps established a good rapport or being from a more modern background, address each other equally with *tum* as well as refer to each other by name. Indeed this is what modern couples do now and what I would expect to do when speaking Hindi with a partner. If my father had simply done what most men of his generation did and employed the middle form of *you*, it hardly would mark him as a discourteous or ill-mannered husband, and I daresay many men in the West would do the same. But my father believed that if women were equal to men, then certainly one should start at the beginning, as it were: linguistic parity.

I still marvel at the depth of principle and reserve of restraint that   6
would keep a man from ever letting his wife's name slip, even after forty years. For a woman, of course, it's hardly unusual to fathom that she would continue to use the respectful form when addressing her husband, seeing as females in all societies have been inculcated to behave in a manner that is seen as befitting their gender. But for a man in a traditional society, it is nothing short of extraordinary.

Meaning

1. What is Jain's thesis? Underline the sentence that you believe best demonstrates her main idea.

2. What pronouns does Jain discuss, and why is her father's use of one of them so extraordinary to her?

3. Why have Jain's mother and father never referred to each other by name? Consider each parent individually.

4. If you are uncertain of the meanings of any of the words listed below, try to guess them from the context of Jain's essay. Then look them up to see how close your definitions were to those in the dictionary. Test out the new words by using each of them in a sentence or two.

shenanigans (1)	deployed (3)	discourteous (5)
ardent (2)	imperious (3)	linguistic (5)
insurrection (2)	accordance (4)	parity (5)
imperial (2)	ruse (4)	fathom (6)
predicated (2)	boorish (5)	inculcated (6)
veritably (3)	rapport (5)	

Purpose and Audience

1. "A Nameless Respect" expresses the author's admiration for her father. Is Jain's praise weakened by her references to his shortcomings in the first paragraph? Why, or why not?

2. What assumptions does Jain seem to make about her readers—their gender or age, their marital status, their attitudes toward traditional gender roles, their knowledge of Indian culture and history, and so on?

3. Jain does not specify what she means by "the poor treatment of women . . . in 1940s India" (paragraph 2). Is it fair for her to expect that readers will understand the generalization? Does she offer clarification anywhere else in the essay?

Method and Structure

1. Why do you think that Jain does not give examples of her parents' uses of language until halfway through the essay? Does this delay make the essay weaker or more interesting for you?

2. Weigh the evidence that Jain gives to support her opinions. Which evidence is personal, and which is not? Are both the personal and the impersonal equally effective? Why, or why not?

3. **OTHER METHODS** Where in this essay can you find an instance of classification (Chapter 9)? How is this classification central to Jain's subject and purpose?

Language

1. How would you characterize Jain's tone in this essay—for instance, sarcastic, argumentative, admiring, humorous, serious, flippant, ambivalent, irritated, confused, enthusiastic? Give examples to support your analysis. How is the tone appropriate (or not) for the audience you identified in "Purpose and Audience" question 2?

2. Jain uses a combination of academic vocabulary and colloquialisms, sometimes in the same breath. (If necessary, see *colloquial language* in the Glossary.) For instance, she refers to "hotheads [who] gave India its first insurrection against imperial rule" (paragraph 2) and expresses amazement "at the depth of principle and reserve of restraint that would keep a man from ever letting his wife's name slip" (6). Locate additional examples of formal and informal language. What is the effect of combining them as Jain does?

Writing Topics

1. **JOURNAL TO ESSAY**   Reread your journal entry and the quotations at the beginning of Jain's essay (p. 128). Using specific examples, write an essay arguing that a form of politeness has outlived its usefulness. Under what circumstances did the courtesy originate, and why was it considered polite? What has changed to render it objectionable to some people? Are they right to object? Is there some other behavior that should take its place?

2. With Jain's essay as a model, write an essay of your own that uses examples to explain why you admire another person. You might write about a parent, as Jain does, or about anyone who has had a positive influence on you.

3. In her conclusion, Jain comments that "females in all societies have been inculcated to behave in a manner that is seen as befitting their gender" (paragraph 6). She seems to believe, in other words, that women everywhere willingly adhere to rigidly defined gender roles. What do you think of this assertion? Can you think of examples that contradict it? Write an essay that examines Jain's assumption. Whether you agree with her or not, offer plenty of evidence to support your conclusions.

4. **CULTURAL CONSIDERATIONS**   As Jain points out, the English language has only one form of the second-person pronoun *you*. Jain characterizes this quality as a weakness but then goes on to suggest ways in which different levels of the pronoun's formality in Hindi can be used to reinforce inequality. Focusing on a single example, write an essay in which you contemplate the influence of language on culture, and vice versa. How might multiple forms of the pronoun *you*, for instance, reflect social hierarchies? Why did feminists fight to eliminate the generic male pronoun from American English (until the late twentieth century, it was standard practice to use *he*, *his*, and *man* to refer to both men and women)? Why does France have a government commission charged with banning words like *weekend, volleyball*, and *surfer* from the French language? Other examples may come to mind; write about what interests you most.

5. **CONNECTIONS**   In "I Want a Wife" (p. 264), Judy Brady also writes about what was expected of wives forty years ago. Read her essay and consider what she might think of Naresh Jain's effort to treat his wife as an equal. Would "linguistic parity" be enough for Brady? What aspects of the Jains' marriage might she criticize? What aspects might she applaud?

A passage is not plain English—still less is it good English—if we are obliged to read it twice to find out what it means. —Dorothy Sayers

I'm bilingual. I speak English and I speak educationese.
—Shirley Hufstedler

You and I come by road or rail, but economists travel on infrastructure. —Margaret Thatcher

JOURNAL RESPONSE What words or expressions have you encountered in your college courses or in your college's rules and regulations that have confused, delighted, or irritated you? Write a brief journal entry describing the language and its effects on you.

Perri Klass

Perri Klass is a pediatrician, a writer, and a knitter. She was born in 1958 in Trinidad and grew up in New York City and New Jersey. Klass obtained a BA from Harvard University in 1979, finished Harvard Medical School in 1986, and teaches journalism and pediatrics at New York University. Her publications are extensive: short stories and articles in *Mademoiselle*, *Antioch Review*, the *New England Journal of Medicine*, and other periodicals; several novels, including *Other Women's Children* (1990) and *The Mercy Rule* (2009); five essay collections; a memoir, *Every Mother Is a Daughter* (2005); and the parenting guide *Quirky Kids* (2003). Klass is the president and medical director of Reach Out and Read, a nonprofit group that works with pediatricians to distribute books to disadvantaged children.

She's Your Basic LOL in NAD

Most of us have felt excluded, confused, or even frightened by the jargon of the medical profession—that is, by the special terminology and abbreviations for diseases and procedures. In this essay Klass uses examples of such language, some of it heartless, to illustrate the pluses and minuses of becoming a doctor. The essay first appeared in 1984 as a "Hers" column in the *New York Times*.

"Mrs. Tolstoy is your basic LOL in NAD, admitted for a soft rule-out MI,"   1
the intern announces. I scribble that on my patient list. In other words
Mrs. Tolstoy is a Little Old Lady in No Apparent Distress who is in the

hospital to make sure she hasn't had a heart attack (rule out a myocardial infarction). And we think it's unlikely that she has had a heart attack (a *soft* rule-out).

If I learned nothing else during my first three months of working in the hospital as a medical student, I learned endless jargon and abbreviations. I started out in a state of primeval innocence, in which I didn't even know that "s̄ CP, SOB, N/V" meant "without chest pain, shortness of breath, or nausea and vomiting." By the end I took the abbreviations so for granted that I would complain to my mother the English professor, "And can you believe I had to put down *three* NG tubes last night?"

"You'll have to tell me what an NG tube is if you want me to sympathize properly," my mother said. NG, nasogastric—isn't it obvious?

I picked up not only the specific expressions but also the patterns of speech and the grammatical conventions; for example, you never say that a patient's blood pressure fell or that his cardiac enzymes rose. Instead, the patient is always the subject of the verb: "He dropped his pressure." "He bumped his enzymes." This sort of construction probably reflects that profound irritation of the intern when the nurses come in the middle of the night to say that Mr. Dickinson has disturbingly low blood pressure. "Oh, he's gonna hurt me bad tonight," the intern may say, inevitably angry at Mr. Dickinson for dropping his pressure and creating a problem.

When chemotherapy fails to cure Mrs. Bacon's cancer, what we say is, "Mrs. Bacon failed chemotherapy."

"Well, we've already had one hit today, and we're up next, but at least we've got mostly stable players on our team." This means that our team (group of doctors and medical students) has already gotten one new admission today, and it is our turn again, so we'll get whoever is next admitted in emergency, but at least most of the patients we already have are fairly stable, that is, unlikely to drop their pressures or in any other way get suddenly sicker and hurt us bad. Baseball metaphor is pervasive: a no-hitter is a night without any new admissions. A player is always a patient—a nitrate player is a patient on nitrates, a unit player is a patient in the intensive-care unit, and so on, until you reach the terminal player.

It is interesting to consider what it means to be winning, or doing well, in this perennial baseball game. When the intern hangs up the phone and announces, "I got a hit," that is not cause for congratulations. The team is not scoring points; rather, it is getting hit, being bombarded with new patients. The object of the game from the point of view of the doctors, considering the players for whom they are already responsible, is to get as few new hits as possible.

These special languages contribute to a sense of closeness and profes- 8
sional spirit among people who are under a great deal of stress. As a medical student, it was exciting for me to discover that I'd finally cracked the
code, that I could understand what doctors said and wrote and could use
the same formulations myself. Some people seem to become enamored
of the jargon for its own sake, perhaps because they are so deeply thrilled
with the idea of medicine, with the idea of themselves as doctors.

I knew a medical student who was referred to by the interns on 9
the team as Mr. Eponym because he was so infatuated with eponymous
terminology,[1] the more obscure the better. He never said "capillary pul-
sation" if he could say "Quincke's pulses." He would lovingly tell over
the multinamed syndromes—Wolff-Parkinson-White, Lown-Ganong-
Levine, Henoch-Schonlein—until the temptation to suggest Schleswig-
Holstein or Stevenson-Kefauver or Baskin-Robbins became irresistible to
his less reverent colleagues.

And there is the jargon that you don't ever want to hear yourself 10
using. You know that your training is changing you, but there are certain changes you think would be going a little too far.

The resident was describing a man with devastating terminal pan- 11
creatic cancer. "Basically he's CTD," the resident concluded. I reminded
myself that I had resolved not to be shy about asking when I didn't
understand things. "CTD?" I asked timidly.

The resident smirked at me. "Circling The Drain."   12

The images are vivid and terrible. "What happened to Mrs. Melville?" 13

"Oh, she boxed last night." To box is to die, of course.   14

Then there are the more pompous locutions that can make the 15
beginning medical student nervous about the effects of medical training. A friend of mine was told by his resident, "A pregnant woman with
sickle-cell represents a failure of genetic counseling."

Mr. Eponym, who tried hard to talk like the doctors, once explained 16
to me, "An infant is basically a brainstem preparation." A brainstem
preparation, as used in neurological research, is an animal whose higher
brain functions have been destroyed so that only the most primitive
reflexes remain, like the sucking reflex, the startle reflex, and the root-
ing reflex.

The more extreme forms aside, one most important function of medical 17
jargon is to help doctors maintain some distance from their patients.

---

[1] *Eponymous* means "named after"—in this case, medical terminology is
named after researchers. [Editors' note.]

By reformulating a patient's pain and problems into a language that the patient doesn't even speak, I suppose we are in some sense taking those pains and problems under our jurisdiction and also reducing their emotional impact. This linguistic separation between doctors and patients allows conversations to go on at the bedside that are unintelligible to the patient. "Naturally, we're worried about adreno-CA," the intern can say to the medical student, and lung cancer need never be mentioned.

I learned a new language this past summer. At times it thrills me to   18
hear myself using it. It enables me to understand my colleagues, to communicate effectively in the hospital. Yet I am uncomfortably aware that I will never again notice the peculiarities and even atrocities of medical language as keenly as I did this summer. There may be specific expressions I manage to avoid, but even as I remark them, promising myself I will never use them, I find that this language is becoming my professional speech. It no longer sounds strange in my ears—or coming from my mouth. And I am afraid that as with any new language, to use it properly you must absorb not only the vocabulary but also the structure, the logic, the attitudes. At first you may notice these new alien assumptions every time you put together a sentence, but with time and increased fluency you stop being aware of them at all. And as you lose that awareness, for better or for worse, you move closer and closer to being a doctor instead of just talking like one.

Meaning

1. What point does Klass make about medical jargon in this essay? Where does she reveal her main point explicitly?

2. What useful purposes does medical jargon serve, according to Klass? Do the examples in paragraphs 9–16 serve these purposes? Why, or why not?

3. Try to guess the meanings of any of the following words that are unfamiliar. Check your guesses in a dictionary, and then use each word in a sentence or two of your own.

primeval (2)	syndromes (9)	locutions (15)
terminal (6)	reverent (9)	jurisdiction (17)
perennial (7)	pompous (15)	

Purpose and Audience

1. What does Klass imply when she states that she began her work in the hospital "in a state of primeval innocence" (paragraph 2)? What does this phrase suggest about her purpose in writing the essay?

2. From what perspective does Klass write this essay: that of a medical professional? someone outside the profession? a patient? someone else? To what extent does she expect her readers to share her perspective? What evidence in the essay supports your answer?

3. Given that she is writing for a general audience, does Klass take adequate care to define medical terms? Support your answer with examples from the essay.

Method and Structure

1. Why does Klass begin the essay with an example rather than a statement of her main idea? What effect does this example produce? How does this effect support her purpose in writing the essay?

2. Although Klass uses many examples of medical jargon, she avoids the dull effect of a list by periodically stepping back to make a general statement about her experience or the jargon—for instance, "I picked up not only the specific expressions but also the patterns of speech and the grammatical conventions" (paragraph 4). Locate other places—not necessarily at the beginnings of paragraphs—where Klass breaks up her examples with more general statements.

3. **OTHER METHODS** Klass uses several other methods besides example, among them classification (Chapter 9), definition (Chapter 12), and cause-and-effect analysis (Chapter 13). What effects—positive and negative—does medical jargon have on Klass, other students, and doctors who use it?

Language

1. What is the tone of this essay? Is Klass trying to be humorous or tongue-in-cheek about the jargon of the profession, or is she serious? Where in the essay is the author's attitude toward her subject the most obvious?

2. Klass refers to the users of medical jargon as both *we/us/our* (paragraphs 1, 5, 6, 17) and *they/our* (7), and sometimes she shifts from *I* to *you* within a paragraph (4, 18). Do you think these shifts are effective or distracting? Why? Do the shifts serve any function?

3. Klass obviously experienced both positive and negative feelings about mastering medical jargon. Which words and phrases in the last paragraph reflect positive feelings, and which negative?

Writing Topics

1. **JOURNAL TO ESSAY** When she attended medical school, Perri Klass discovered a novel language to learn and with it some new attitudes.

Working from your journal entry (p. 133), write an essay about new languages and attitudes you have encountered in college. Have you been confronted with different kinds of people (professors, other students) from the ones you knew before? Have you had difficulty understanding some words people use? Have you found yourself embracing ideas you never thought you would or speaking differently? Have others noticed a change in you that you may not have been aware of? Have you noticed changes in your pre-college friends? Focus on a particular kind of obstacle or change, using specific examples to convey this experience to readers.

2. Klass likens her experience learning medical jargon to that of learning a new language (paragraph 18). If you are studying or have learned a second language, write an essay in which you explain the "new alien assumptions" you must make "every time you put together a sentence." Draw your examples not just from the new language's grammar and vocabulary but from its underlying logic and attitudes. For instance, does one speak to older people differently in the new language? make requests differently? describe love or art differently?

3. Klass's essay explores the "separation between doctors and patients" (paragraph 17). Has this separation affected you as a patient or as a relative or friend of a patient? If so, write an essay about your experiences. Did the medical professionals rely heavily on jargon? Was their language comforting, frightening, irritating? Based on your experience and on Klass's essay, do you believe that the separation between doctors and patients is desirable? Why, or why not?

4. **CULTURAL CONSIDERATIONS** Most groups focused on a common interest have their own jargon. If you belong to such a group—for example, runners, football fans, food servers, engineering students—spend a few days listening to yourself and others use this language and thinking about the purposes it serves. Which aspects of this language seem intended to make users feel like insiders? Which seem to serve some other purpose, and what is it? In an essay, explain what this jargon reveals about the group and its common interest, using as many specific examples as you can.

5. **CONNECTIONS** Both Klass and Anita Jain, in "A Nameless Respect" (p. 128), suggest that the way we speak can create closeness to or distance from other people. Write an essay in which you examine the way members of a group—say, faculty members, relatives, politicians, or people from a particular region—use language to establish the nature of their relationships.

Example

Select one of the following statements, or any other statement they suggest, and agree or disagree with it in an essay developed by example. The statement you choose should concern a topic you care about so that the example or examples are a means of communicating an idea, not an end in themselves.

FAMILY

1. In happy families, talk is the main activity.
2. Grandparents relate more closely to their grandchildren than to their children.
3. Sooner or later, children take on the personalities of their parents.

BEHAVIOR AND PERSONALITY

4. Rudeness is on the rise.
5. Facial expressions often communicate what words cannot say.
6. Our natural surroundings when we are growing up contribute to our happiness or unhappiness as adults.

EDUCATION

7. The best college courses are the difficult ones.
8. Education is an easy way to get ahead in life.
9. Students at schools with enforced dress codes behave better than students at schools without such codes.

POLITICS AND SOCIAL ISSUES

10. Talk radio can influence public policy.
11. Drug or alcohol addiction is not restricted just to "bad" people.
12. Unemployment is hardest on those over fifty years old.
13. The best popular musicians treat social and political issues in their songs.

RULES FOR LIVING

14. Murphy's Law: If anything can go wrong, it will go wrong, and at the worst possible moment.
15. With enough motivation, a person can accomplish anything.
16. Lying may be justified by the circumstances.

WRITING ABOUT THE THEME

Using Language

1. Deborah Tannen (p. 117), William Lutz (p. 118), Anita Jain (p. 128), and Perri Klass (p. 133) discuss the power of language with a good deal of respect. Tannen refers to its social uses, Lutz to its effectiveness "in explaining . . . accidents," Jain to its effect on intimate relationships, and Klass to its support as she became a doctor. Think of a time when you were in some way profoundly affected by language, and write an essay about this experience. Provide as many examples as necessary to illustrate both the language that affected you and how it made you feel.

2. Kim Kessler (p. 123), Anita Jain, and Perri Klass all write about forms of language that do not obey traditional rules and are considered inappropriate by some people. As you see it, what are the advantages and disadvantages of using nonstandard language when speaking? How effective are these forms of language as ways to communicate? Write an essay answering these questions, using examples from the selections and your own experience.

3. Perri Klass writes that medical jargon "contribute[s] to a sense of closeness and professional spirit among people who are under a great deal of stress" (paragraph 8) and that it helps "doctors maintain some distance from their patients" (17). Write an essay in which you analyze the function of "doublespeak," as presented by William Lutz. Who, if anyone, is such language designed to help? The accident victims? Survivors of these victims? Someone else? Can a positive case be made for this language?

8

DIVISION OR ANALYSIS
Looking at Popular Culture

Division and **analysis** are interchangeable terms for the same method. *Division* comes from a Latin word meaning "to force asunder or separate." *Analysis* comes from a Greek word meaning "to undo." Using this method, we separate a whole into its elements, examine the relations of the elements to one another and to the whole, and reassemble the elements into a new whole informed by the examination.

Analysis (as we will call it) is the foundation of **critical thinking**, the ability to see beneath the surface of things, images, events, and ideas; to uncover and test assumptions; to see the importance of context; and to draw and support independent conclusions. The method, then, is essential to college learning, whether in discussing literature, reviewing a psychology experiment, or interpreting a business case. It is also fundamental in the workplace, from choosing a career to making sense of market research. Analysis even informs and enriches life outside of school or work, whether we ponder our relationships with others, decide whether a movie was worthwhile, evaluate a politician's campaign promises, or determine whether a new video game system is worth buying.

We use analysis throughout this book when looking at paragraphs and essays. And it is the basic operation in at least four other methods discussed in other chapters: classification (Chapter 9), process analysis (Chapter 10), comparison and contrast (Chapter 11), and cause-and-effect analysis (Chapter 13).

Reading Division or Analysis

At its most helpful, division or analysis peers inside an object, institution, work of art, policy, or any other whole. It identifies the parts, examines how the parts relate, and leads to a conclusion about the meaning, significance, or value of the whole. The subject of any analysis is usually singular—a freestanding, coherent unit, such as a bicycle or a poem, with its own unique constitution of elements. (In contrast, classification, the subject of the next chapter, usually starts with a plural subject, such as bicycles or the poems of the Civil War, and groups them according to their shared features.) A writer chooses the subject and with it a **principle of analysis**, a framework that determines how the subject will be divided and thus what elements are relevant to the discussion.

Sometimes the principle of analysis is self-evident, especially when the subject is an object, such as a bicycle or a camera, that can be "undone" in only a limited number of ways. Most of the time, however, the principle depends on the writer's view of the whole. In academic disciplines, businesses, and the professions, distinctive principles are part of what the field is about and are often the subject of debate within the field. In art, for instance, some critics see a painting primarily as a visual object and concentrate on its composition, color, line, and other formal qualities; other critics see a painting primarily as a social object and concentrate on its content and context (cultural, economic, political, and so on). Both groups use a principle of analysis that is a well-established way of looking at a painting, yet each group finds different elements and thus meaning in a work.

Writers have a great deal of flexibility in choosing a principle of analysis, but the principle also must meet certain requirements: it should be appropriate for the subject and the field or discipline; it should be significant; and it should be applied thoroughly and consistently. Analysis is not done for its own sake but for a larger goal of illuminating the subject, perhaps concluding something about it, perhaps evaluating it. But even when the method culminates in evaluation—in the writer's judgment of the subject's value—the analysis should represent the subject as it actually is, in all its fullness and complexity. In analyzing a movie, for instance, a writer may emphasize one element, such as setting, and even omit some elements, such as costumes; but the characterization of the whole must still apply to *all* the elements. If it does not, readers can be counted on to notice; so the writer must single out any wayward element(s) and explain why they do not substantially undermine the framework and thus weaken the opinion.

Analyzing Division or Analysis in Paragraphs

Jon Pareles (born 1953) is the chief critic of popular music for the *New York Times*. The following paragraph comes from "Gather No Moss, Take No Prisoners, but Be Cool," a review of a concert by the rock guitarist Keith Richards.

Mr. Richards shows off by not showing off. He uses rhythm chords as a goad, not a metronome, slipping them in just ahead of a beat or skipping them entirely. The distilled twang of his tone has been imitated all over rock, but far fewer guitarists have learned his guerrilla timing, his coiled silences. When he switches to lead guitar, Mr. Richards goes not for long lines, but for serrated riffing, zinging out three or four notes again and again in various permutations, wringing from them the essence of the blues. The phrasing is poised and suspenseful, but it also carries a salutary rock attitude: that less is more, especially when delivered with utter confidence.

> Principle of analysis (topic sentence underlined): elements of Richards's "not showing off"
> 1. Rhythm chords as goad (or prod)
> 2. Timing
> 3. Silences
> 4. Riffing (or choppy playing)
> 5. Confident, less-is-more attitude

Luci Tapahonso (born 1953) is a poet and teacher. This paragraph is from her essay "The Way It Is," which appears in *Sign Language*, a book of photographs (by Skeet McAuley) of life on the reservation for some Navajo and Apache Indians.

It is rare and, indeed, very exciting to see an Indian person in a commercial advertisement. Word travels fast when that happens. Nunzio's Pizza in Albuquerque, New Mexico, ran commercials featuring Jose Rey Toledo of Jemez Pueblo talking about his "native land—Italy" while wearing typical Pueblo attire—jewelry, moccasins, and hair tied in a chongo. Because of the ironic humor, because Indian grandfathers specialize in playing tricks and jokes on their grandchildren, and because Jose Rey Toledo is a respected and well-known elder in the Indian communities, word of this commercial

> Principle of analysis: elements of the commercial that appealed to Indians
> 1. Rarity of an Indian in a commercial
> 2. Indian dress
> 3. Indian humor
> 4. Indian tradition
> 5. Respected Indian spokesperson

spread fast among Indians in New Mexico. It was the
cause of recognition and celebration of sorts on the
reservations and in the pueblos. His portrayal was not   6. Realism
in the categories which the media usually associate
with Indians but as a typical sight in the Southwest.
It showed Indians as we live today—enjoying pizza as   Topic sentence
one of our favorite foods, including humor and fun as   (underlined)
part of our daily lives, and recognizing the importance   summarizes
of preserving traditional knowledge.   elements.

Developing an Essay by Division or Analysis

Getting Started

Analysis is one of the readiest methods of development: almost anything
whole can be separated into its elements, from a lemon to a play by
Shakespeare to an economic theory. In college and at work, many writing assignments will demand analysis with a verb such as *analyze, criticize, discuss, evaluate, interpret,* or *review.* If you need to develop your own
subject for analysis, think of something whose meaning or significance
puzzles or intrigues you and whose parts you can distinguish and relate
to the whole—for instance, an object such as a machine, an artwork
such as a poem, a media product such as a news broadcast, an institution such as a hospital, a relationship such as stepparenting, or a social
issue such as sheltering the homeless.

Dissect your subject, looking at the actual physical thing if possible,
imagining it in your mind if necessary. Make detailed notes of all the
elements you see, their distinguishing features, and how those features
work together. In analyzing someone's creation, tease out the creator's
influences, assumptions, intentions, conclusions, and evidence. You may
have to go outside the work for some of this information—researching
an author's background, for instance, to uncover the political biases that
may underlie his or her opinions. Even if you do not use all this information in your final draft, it will help you see the elements and help keep
your analysis true to the subject.

If you begin by seeking meaning or significance in a subject, you will
be more likely to find a workable principle of analysis and less likely to
waste time on a hollow exercise. Each question below suggests a distinct

approach to the subject's elements—a distinct principle of analysis—that makes it easier to isolate the elements and see their connections.

To what extent is an enormously complex hospital a community in itself?

What is the function of the front-page headlines in the local tabloid newspaper?

Why did a certain movie have such a powerful effect on you and your friends?

Forming a Thesis

A clear, informative thesis sentence (or sentences) is crucial in division or analysis because readers need to know the purpose and structure of your analysis in order to follow your points. If your exploratory question proves helpful as you gather ideas, you can also use it to draft a thesis sentence: answer it in such a way that you state your opinion about your subject and reveal your principle of analysis.

QUESTION To what extent is an enormously complex hospital a community in itself?

THESIS SENTENCE The hospital encompasses such a wide range of personnel and services that it resembles a good-size town.

QUESTION What is the function of the front-page headlines in the local tabloid newspaper?

THESIS SENTENCE The newspaper's front page routinely appeals to readers' fear of crime, anger at criminals, and sympathy for victims.

QUESTION Why did a certain movie have such a powerful effect on you and your friends?

THESIS SENTENCE The film is a unique and important statement of the private terrors of adolescence.

Note that all three thesis statements imply an explanatory purpose— an effort to understand something and share that understanding with the reader. The third thesis sentence, however, suggests a persuasive purpose as well: the writer hopes that readers will accept her evaluation of the film.

These thesis sentences clearly convey the writers' approaches to their subjects. In contrast, the following sentence does not. With "do anything," it overstates and yet fails to specify a framework for analysis.

VAGUE Advertisers will do anything to sell their products.

Compare this thesis sentence with the actual one from "Racism and Sexism in Advertising," an essay by student writer Shafeeq Sadiq. Here it is apparent that the writer will focus on the racist and sexist elements in advertising:

> CLEAR   Often, these advertising gimmicks reinforce racial stereotypes and portray women in a negative light.

A well-focused thesis sentence benefits not only your readers but also you as writer, because it gives you a yardstick to judge the completeness, consistency, and supportiveness of your analysis. Don't be discouraged, though, if your thesis sentence doesn't come to you until *after* you've written a first draft and had a chance to discover your interest. Writing about your subject may be the best way for you to find its meaning and significance.

Organizing

In the introduction to your essay, let readers know why you are bothering to analyze your subject: Why is the subject significant? How might the essay relate to the experiences of readers or be useful to them? A subject unfamiliar to readers might be summarized or described, or part of it (an anecdote or a quotation, say) might be used to tantalize readers. A familiar subject might be introduced with a surprising fact or an unusual perspective. An evaluative analysis might open with an opposing viewpoint.

In the body of the essay, you'll need to explain your principle of analysis according to the guidelines above. The arrangement of elements and analysis should suit your subject and purpose: you can describe the elements and then offer your analysis, or you can introduce and analyze elements one by one. You can arrange the elements themselves from least to most important, least to most complex, most to least familiar, spatially, or chronologically. Devote as much space to each element as it demands: there is no requirement that all elements be given equal space and emphasis if their complexity or your framework dictates otherwise.

Most analysis essays need a conclusion that assembles the elements, returning readers to a sense of the whole subject. The conclusion can restate the thesis, summarize what the essay has contributed, consider the influence of the subject or its place in a larger picture, or (especially in an evaluation) assess the effectiveness or worth of the subject.

Drafting

If your subject or your view of it is complex, you may need at least two rough drafts of an analysis essay—one to discover what you think and one to clarify your principle, cover each element, and support your points with concrete details and vivid examples (including quotations if the subject is a written work). Plan on two drafts if you're uncertain of your thesis when you begin; you'll probably save time in the long run by attending to one goal at a time. Especially because the analysis essay says something about the subject by explaining its structure, you need to have a clear picture of the whole and relate each part to it.

As you draft, be sure to consider your readers' needs as well as the needs of your subject and your own framework:

- If the subject is unfamiliar to your readers, you'll need to carefully explain your principle of analysis, define all specialized terms, distinguish parts from one another, and provide ample illustrations.

- If the subject is familiar to readers, your principle of analysis may not require much justification (as long as it's clear), but your details and examples must be vivid and convincing.

- If readers may dispute your way of looking at your subject, be careful to justify as well as explain your principle of analysis.

Whether readers are familiar with your subject or not, always account for any evidence that may seem not to support your opinion—either by showing why, in fact, the evidence is supportive or explaining why it is unimportant. (If contrary evidence refuses to be dispensed with, you may have to rethink your approach.)

Revising and Editing

When you revise and edit your essay, use the following questions and the box on the next page to uncover any weaknesses remaining in your analysis.

- *Is your principle of analysis clear?* The significance of your analysis and your view of the subject should be apparent throughout your essay.

- *Is your analysis complete?* Have you identified all elements according to your principle of analysis and determined their relations to one another and to the whole? If you have omitted some elements from your discussion, will the reason for their omission be clear to readers?

FOCUS ON PARAGRAPH COHERENCE

With several elements that contribute to the whole of a subject, an analysis will be easy for your readers to follow only if you frequently clarify what element you are discussing and how it fits with your principle of analysis. To help readers keep your analysis straight, rely on the techniques of paragraph coherence discussed on pages 37–39, especially on transitions and on repetition. *Transitions*, like those listed in the Glossary, act as signposts to tell readers where you, and they, are headed. And repetition, or restatement, of labels for your principle of analysis or for individual elements makes clear the topic of each sentence.

- *Is your analysis consistent?* Is your principle of analysis applied consistently to the entire subject (including any elements you have omitted)? Do all elements reflect the same principle, and are they clearly separate rather than overlapping? You may find it helpful to check your draft against your list of elements or your outline or to outline the draft itself.

- *Is your analysis well supported?* Is the thesis supported by clear assertions about parts of the subject, and are the assertions supported by concrete, specific evidence (sensory details, facts, quotations, and so on)? Do not rely on your readers to prove your thesis.

- *Is your analysis true to the subject?* Is your thesis unforced, your analysis fair? Is your new whole (your reassembly of the elements) faithful to the original? Be wary of leaping to a conclusion that distorts the subject.

A Note on Thematic Connections

Because popular culture is everywhere, and everywhere taken for granted, it is a tempting and challenging target for writers. Having chosen to write critically about a disturbing, cheering, or intriguing aspect of popular culture, all the authors represented in this chapter naturally pursued the method of division or analysis. The paragraph by Jon Pareles dissects the unique playing style of the rock guitarist Keith Richards (p. 143). The other paragraph, by Luci Tapahonso, analyzes a pizza commercial that especially appealed to Native Americans (p. 143). Dave Barry's essay asks just what drivers experience when they sit behind the wheel of a Humvee (opposite). Andrew Warren's essay ponders the value of *The Simpsons* (p. 154). And Thomas de Zengotita's essay considers what it is about the television show *American Idol* that makes it so irresistible to viewers (p. 160).

> The purpose of life is to produce and consume automobiles. —Jane Jacobs

> It is only here, in your very own castle of rubber and steel, that you can for a short but blissful time throw off the cloak of civilizations and be the raging Hun you always wanted to be. —Adair Lara

> Whither goest thou, America, in thy shiny car in the night? —Jack Kerouac

JOURNAL RESPONSE What do you drive: a hand-me-down wreck? a sporty convertible? a muscular sport-utility vehicle? an environmentally friendly hybrid? an occasional rental? Write about your first or current car, describing why you chose it, what you use it for, and the reasons you like or dislike it. If you don't have access to a car, do you hope to acquire one someday? What, when, and why—or why not?

Dave Barry

Dave Barry (born 1947) is known for finding laugh-out-loud humor in the most mundane elements of daily life. Raised in Armonk, New York, Barry earned a BA in English from Haverford College and worked as a small-town reporter and business-writing consultant before joining the *Miami Herald* in 1983. Barry's weekly column, for which he won the Pulitzer Prize for commentary in 1988, was syndicated in hundreds of newspapers (he took an indefinite break in 2004). He is the author of more than two dozen best-selling humor books, including *The Taming of the Screw* (1983), *Dave Barry Is Not Making This Up* (2001), and *Dave Barry's Money Secrets* (2006). Barry is currently working on children's books and playing guitar with the Rock Bottom Remainders, a rock band composed of popular writers, among them Amy Tan, Barbara Kingsolver (p. 210), and Stephen King.

Humvee Satisfies a Man's Lust for Winches

In this column, first published on January 7, 2001, Barry launches his trademark wit at a favorite target: grown men's toys. Why would anybody pay in excess of $100,000 for a car? The answer, Barry suggests, is that it gives men a (false) sense of masculinity.

It is time for our popular feature "Stuff That Guys Need." Today's topic 1
is: the Humvee.

Most Americans became aware of the Humvee (military shorthand for 2
HUgely Masculine VEEhickle) during the Gulf War, when US troops, driv-
ing Humvees equipped with missile launchers, kicked Iraq's butt and taught
Saddam Hussein a lesson that he would not forget for several weeks.[1]

After the war, a few wealthy Californians got hold of Humvees. 3
This led to some mishaps, most notably when Arnold Schwarzenegger,
attempting to open his garage door, accidentally launched a missile. Fortunately, it landed in a noncelebrity neighborhood.

But once the "bugs" were ironed out, the Humvee became available 4
for civilian purchase. I test-drove one recently thanks to my coworker
Terry Jackson, who is the *Miami Herald*'s automotive writer and TV critic.
That's correct: this man gets paid to drive new cars AND watch television. If he ever dies and goes to heaven, it's going to be a big letdown.

When I arrived at Terry's house, there was a bright-yellow Humvee 5
sitting in his driveway, covered with puddles of drool deposited by passing guys. In terms of styling, the Humvee is as masculine as a vehicle
can get without actually growing hair in its wheel wells. It's a big, boxy
thing with giant tires and many studly mechanical protuberances. It
looks like something you'd buy as part of a toy action-figure set called
"Sergeant Bart Groin and His Pain Platoon."

Terry told me this particular Humvee model cost $101,000, which 6
sounds like a lot of money until you consider its features. For example,
it has dashboard switches that enable you to inflate or deflate your tires
as you drive. Is that cool, or WHAT? In a perfect guy universe, this feature
would seriously impress women.

GUY: Look! I can inflate the tires as I drive! 7

WOMAN: Pull over right now, so we can engage in wanton carnality! 8

Unfortunately, the real world doesn't work this way. I know this 9
because when I took my wife for a ride in the Humvee, we had this
conversation:

ME: Look! I can inflate the tires as I drive! 10

MY WIFE: *Why?* 11

Another feature that my wife did not appreciate was the winch. This 12
Humvee had a SERIOUS winch in front ("It can pull down a house," noted

---

[1] In 1991, Americans led a successful United Nations effort to force Iraqis
out of neighboring Kuwait. Saddam Hussein, the longtime dictator of Iraq, was
captured during the war that began in 2003. He was tried and executed in 2006.
[Editors' note.]

Terry). There's nothing like the feeling of sitting in traffic, knowing that you have a MUCH bigger winch than any of the guys around you. Plus, a winch can be mighty handy in an emergency. Like, suppose some jerk runs you off the road into a ditch. After a tow truck pulls you out, you could find out where the jerk lives, then use your winch to pull down his house.

The Humvee also boasts an engine. Terry offered to show it to me, 13 but I have a strict policy of not looking at engines, because whenever I do, a mechanic appears and says "There's your problem right there" and charges me $758. I can tell you this, however: the Humvee engine is LOUD. I picture dozens of sweating men under the hood, furiously shoveling coal as Leonardo DiCaprio and Kate Winslet run gaily past.[2]

As for comfort: despite the Humvee's ruggedness, when it's cruising on 14 the highway, the "ride" is surprisingly similar to that of a full-size luxury sedan being dragged across a boulder field, on its roof. But a truly masculine, big-winched man does not need comfort. All he needs is the knowledge that he can take his vehicle into harsh and unforgiving terrain. And I gave the Humvee the toughest challenge you can give a car in America. That's right: I drove it to a shopping mall just before Christmas.

Perhaps you think I was foolhardy. Well, people said that the Portu- 15 guese explorer Vasco da Gama was foolhardy, too, and do you remember what he did? Neither do I. But if he had not done it, I doubt that Portugal would be what it is today: a leading producer of cork.

And thus I found myself piloting the Humvee through the mall 16 parking structure at roughly the speed of soybean growth, knowing that I was competing for the one available parking space with roughly 20,000 other motorists, but also knowing that ALL of them would have to stop their vehicles if they wanted to inflate or deflate their tires. The pathetic wimps! I could not help but cackle in a manly way. My wife was rolling her eyes at me, but by God I got us safely into and out of there, and I doubt that I used more than 300 gallons of fuel.

Meaning

1. In paragraph 5, Barry writes, "The Humvee is as masculine as a vehicle can get without actually growing hair in its wheel wells." How does this statement illustrate Barry's main idea?

2. A *winch* is a vehicle-mounted crank used for pulling items. How does Barry's use of the word in his title function as a pun, or a play on the

---

[2] DiCaprio and Winslet starred in the 1997 film *Titanic*. The doomed steamship was powered by manually fed coal furnaces. [Editors' note.]

similar sound of two words with very different meanings? How does the pun predict Barry's point about Humvees?

3. If any of the following words are new to you, try to guess their meanings from the context of Barry's essay. Test your guesses in a dictionary, and then use each new word in a sentence or two.

protuberances (5)   carnality (8)   foolhardy (15)
wanton (8)

Purpose and Audience

1. What is Barry's purpose in writing this essay: to persuade readers to purchase a Humvee? to explain why the vehicle is popular? to make fun of his coworker? to do something else?

2. Barry is relentless in his mockery of men who drive (or want to drive) Humvees. Find at least three examples of statements that are either obviously untrue or greatly exaggerated. What is the effect of Barry's use of hyperbole, and how does it contribute to his purpose? (If necessary, see *hyperbole* in the Glossary.)

Method and Structure

1. What is Barry's principle of analysis, and into what elements does he divide the Humvee? Be specific, supporting your answer with examples from the text.

2. How does Barry use the method of analysis for comic effect? In what ways does analysis lend itself particularly well to a humorous subject such as this one?

3. **OTHER METHODS** In addition to analysis, Barry employs description (Chapter 6) and example (Chapter 7) to illustrate the masculine appeal of Humvees, and he uses comparison and contrast (Chapter 11) to explore the differences in how men and women perceive several of the vehicle's features. Locate examples of each of these methods in Barry's essay. What do they add to his analysis of Humvees?

Language

1. What is Barry's tone? How seriously does he take his subject?

2. Note Barry's frequent use of informal language and colloquial phrases, such as "Is that cool, or WHAT?" (paragraph 6). What does he achieve with this attitude? (If necessary, see *colloquial language* in the Glossary.)

Writing Topics

1. **JOURNAL TO ESSAY** Building on your journal entry (p. 149), write an essay in which you analyze the benefits and drawbacks of your current (or desired) means of transportation. Make a list of all the elements that constitute a particular vehicle or public conveyance (such as a bus or subway). In your essay examine each element to show what it contributes to the whole. Be sure your principle of analysis is clear to readers.

2. Barry jokes about the Humvee's poor gas mileage in the last paragraph of his essay, but his earlier reference to the Gulf War of 1991 (paragraph 2) subtly invokes many people's concern that American reliance on fossil fuels has significant environmental and political consequences. Write a serious argumentative essay that addresses the issue of America's use of fossil fuels. To what extent should automotive manufacturers be required to meet environmental standards? Under what circumstances, if any, should personal choice be limited in the name of global responsibility? Be sure to include examples to support your opinions.

3. **CULTURAL CONSIDERATIONS** Throughout his essay, Barry implies that the men who are drawn to Humvees are trying to compensate for something they think they lack. Most of us, however, have experienced a moment (or perhaps many moments) when we were tempted to buy something to make us feel better about ourselves — an impulse that some say is the direct result of advertising practices that create insecurities in order to exploit them. (Consider, for instance, weight loss ads suggesting that a size 10 woman is fat, or the current push for tooth whitening.) Choose an example of advertising that you think appeals to a real or invented insecurity to sell a product, and analyze its message in a brief essay. Are the advertiser's techniques effective? ethical? entertaining? Be sure to identify a principle of analysis for your response and to support your argument with details from the advertisement.

4. **CONNECTIONS** Like Barry, Marta Taylor, in "Desert Dance" (p. 98), describes the strength and power conferred on the male driver of a car. The two writers, however, offer very different interpretations of masculine roles and responsibilities. Whose concept of automotive masculinity strikes you as more realistic or insightful? Why? Explain your answer in an essay, using plenty of details from both readings to support your thesis.

Junk is the ideal product . . . the ultimate merchandise. No sales talk necessary. The client will crawl through a sewer and beg to buy.
—William S. Burroughs

Your responsibility as a parent is not as great as you might imagine. . . . If your child simply grows up to be someone who does not use the word *collectible* as a noun, you can consider yourself an unqualified success. —Fran Liebowitz

Toys were lots of fun before they became capitalist tools.
—Beth Copeland Vergo

JOURNAL RESPONSE Do you own, or did you ever own, merchandise tied to a movie or TV show, such as *Star Wars* drink glasses, a *Family Guy* T-shirt, or *Smurfs* bedding? Write about why you wanted a particular item or set of items and what, if anything, they still mean to you.

Andrew Warren III

Andrew Warren III was born in 1981 and grew up in Boston. He graduated from the Boston Latin School and worked as a computer technician for several years before completing a BA in English, with a minor in computer science, from the University of Massachusetts, Boston, in 2009. An aspiring technical writer, Warren reports that his interests include "eating, cooking, watching movies, playing video games, and generally just being a nerd." He lives in Quincy, Massachusetts, and currently holds internships in technical writing and in quality assurance at a company that specializes in network security systems.

Throwing Darts at *The Simpsons*
(Student Essay)

In this entertaining analysis of the most enduring scripted prime-time show in the history of television (twenty-two years and counting), Warren offers detailed examples and information from a source to support a fresh take on *The Simpsons*. He wrote this essay for a composition class, then at his instructor's suggestion submitted it to *Lux*, the literary magazine of the University of Massachusetts, Boston. Warren reports that he revised the finished essay twice before it was published, tightening the focus, dropping some of the deeper analysis, improving the style, and in the process trimming it to half its original length.

"C'mon dude . . . let's open it," my friend Sean begged. We were hanging
out in our apartment and, yet again, he wanted to play darts with my
Simpsons dart board—a repeated episode throughout 2001. It was resting
on an end table in its unopened box, cellophane wrapper still intact. I had
purchased it earlier that year for $30 from a collectibles dealer on eBay,
so I had to protect it every few weeks from Sean or others who wanted
to actually play a game of darts. The board was, and still is, a snazzy
decoration—a large, colorful square adorned with the images of Homer
and Bart Simpson, Moe the Bartender, Barney, and Krusty the Clown.
I too have occasionally thought about ripping open the plastic and chuck-
ing darts at the board ("playing darts" gives me too much credit), badly
scarring the cork and surrounding walls. But I haven't had the heart.

I began watching *The Simpsons*, a satirical cartoon sitcom about
a nuclear small-town American family, every day starting in 1992 or
1993—whenever the first episodes began running in syndication. Before
then I didn't really understand the show. I don't think I was old enough.
But starting in junior high school, the rest of my friends and I, including
Sean, used the show as a milestone for good taste. Those first years—up
to 1998—are simply brilliant. (That is a fact, and I'll argue with anyone
who disagrees with me to the death.) Those who understood the show
received instant respect and inclusion (unless you were a jerk). Many
conversations evolved out of strings of quotes from the show's characters, and obscure references to various scenes became daily jokes. We
developed a sentimental attachment to *The Simpsons* that extended far
beyond the daily twenty-five minute television commitment into the
cores of our lives, due not only to the resonant pleasure of the viewing
experience, but also due to the reinforced social connections my peers
and I had crafted among ourselves.

Amazingly, before I even started watching *The Simpsons*, it had
already reached its zenith in the public sphere. The show was the biggest
pop culture event of 1990 (Turner, 25). Bart, the spiky haired scion of
the Simpson clan, led the charge, as images of him and other members
of the family graced the covers of some of the most prominent media
rags: "*Time* and *Newsweek, Rolling Stone, TV Guide,* and *Mad Magazine,*
even *Mother Jones*" (Turner, 25). In the wake of the advertising juggernaut
came the merchandise. This feverish love affair was dubbed "Bart-mania"
by the media, and most mainstream retailers had racks of clothing and
shelves of merchandise dedicated to *The Simpsons*—especially Bart. But
unlike most other pop culture phenomena, which tend to implode
immediately like an explosion starved for oxygen, *The Simpsons* did
not die off; and although the ratings slightly declined after the initial

buzz dissipated, the show improved (this is a completely objective fact, I swear), revealing an ever deeper well of ironic and analytical satire of society and the media through carefully, hilariously employed humor.

One of the show's favorite, and funniest, satirical vehicles is Krusty   4 the Clown, Bart Simpson's childhood hero and a symbol of everything that is wrong with the entertainment industry. He is a morally destitute, corrupt, addicted, all-purpose wretch; he is also the most prominent icon in the lives of the Simpson family. The children watch his television show daily. Many episodes begin with the familiar scene of the children sitting in front of the tube after school, faces illuminated by the glow, watching the mindless string of gags that compose the Krusty the Clown Show. Sometimes Krusty is included in the absurd adventures in which the Simpsons are involved each week. Yet the most present he is to them is through the omnipresent, narcissistically personified branding in his merchandise, which constitutes the primary source of his fortunes. Bart's room is a virtual shrine to the entertainer, with many of his material goods bearing the visage and logo of Krusty and his media enterprise. Other examples of Krusty's products, sporting the Krusty Brand Seal of Approval (practically a guarantee that you *will* be injured; see the "Kamp Krusty" episode for explicit examples), are not even connected to toys and playthings. Some of the more blatant, hyperbolic examples are Krusty's Non-Narkotik Kough Syrup for Kids, Krusty's Sulfuric Acid, and the terrifying Krusty's Home Pregnancy Test (Warning: May Cause Birth Defects). So, although the TV experience ends at the same time every day, the relation to Krusty picks up again via his ever-present merchandise.

The writers of *The Simpsons* were well aware of a similar situation   5 developing between the show, its fans, and the Fox Broadcasting Company. Krusty was first introduced to lampoon the uncannily predictable seedy side behind most childhood icons, but later his omnipresence shifted into a satire of the entire enterprise of television and fandom. Like Bart and the rest of the citizens of Springfield, my sentiments have been reinforced through repeated viewing of syndicated broadcasts. Years ago, watching *The Simpsons* was a required activity—I needed my fix—and the Fox Broadcasting Company, well aware of this need since the initial Nielsen-reinforced popularity boom of 1990, produced tons of real-world merchandise spaces in order to occupy the space in between viewings of the show, expanding the potential to make more money. Several years later, I purchased my dart board, a product with a vague association with the show at best (there has only been one scene, in Moe's Tavern, in which characters playing darts has been featured on *The Simpsons*), just as Bart's allegiance to Krusty is exemplified in all-consuming collection of non-clown or even comedy related merchandise from the show: dolls, bedding and bedroom furniture, decorative posters, and various other artifacts which round out and define his daily existence. They declare his love for his hero. Fans of *The Simpsons* do the same. I've seen countless posters, bottle openers, and other stuff like my dart board present in my peers' living quarters since the madness began.

So, I recently rediscovered my once-treasured *Simpsons* dart board   6 in my bedroom. It was up on top of a bookshelf, mostly hidden from view by a movie poster I stuck in front of it. I pulled it down, brushed off the dust, and examined its packaging—still mint. Its value on Ebay has declined to around $8 (plus shipping), most likely due to a drop in interest in the show and the merchandising blitz following the less than mediocre movie release. I'm not surprised, as I rarely watch the reruns anymore (and never the Sunday episode premieres). My relationship with my dart board is now relatively empty. I see it as nothing more than a toy, certainly not the symbol of something else I once loved. The show's creators have been reminding us all along that something like the dart board is only worth as much as the public's interest in it. In the first episode in which we meet Krusty's character, his merchandise is burned by the citizens of Springfield when the public is tricked into believing that he robbed a convenience store at gunpoint. Our connections to merchandise are only as strong as the quality of the strongest memories of the events which give the products their value. I guess that leaves only one thing: does anyone want to play a game of darts?

Works Cited

"Kamp Krusty." *The Simpsons:* The Complete Fourth Season. 1992. 20th Cent. Fox, 2004. DVD-ROM. Disc 1.

Turner, Chris. *Planet Simpson*. Cambridge: Da Capo, 2004. Print.

Meaning

1. In your own words, explain Warren's thesis. Where does he state it explicitly?

2. Why, according to Warren, has he been reluctant to take his *Simpsons* dart board out if its original packaging? What finally makes him decide to open it?

3. What does Warren mean in paragraph 6 when he refers to "the less than mediocre movie release"? What movie is he talking about? Did he like it or not?

4. If you are unfamiliar with any of the following words, try to guess their meanings from the context in which Warren uses them. Look up the words in a dictionary to check your guesses, and then use each one in a sentence or two of your own.

adorned (1)	phenomena (3)	narcissistically (4)
satire/satirical (2, 3, 4)	implode (3)	visage (4)
syndication/	dissipated (3)	hyperbolic (4)
syndicated (2, 5)	destitute (4)	lampoon (5)
resonant (2)	icon (4)	uncannily (5)
zenith (3)	omnipresent/	
juggernaut (3)	omnipresence (4, 5)	

Purpose and Audience

1. What do you think Warren's purpose was in writing this essay: to get more people to watch *The Simpsons*? to explain why his dart board has lost its value? to convince merchandisers to change their ways? to do something else?

2. What assumptions does Warren seem to make about his readers—their gender or age, their attitudes toward *The Simpsons*, their attitudes toward advertising and merchandising, and so on?

3. In paragraph 3, Warren cites two pieces of information from a source. What does this information add to his analysis?

Method and Structure

1. Why do you think Warren chose the method of analysis to talk about the role of merchandising in the long-term success of *The Simpsons*? How does the method help Warren achieve his purpose?

2. What principle of analysis does Warren apply to his examination of *The Simpsons*? Why is that principle particularly well suited to his subject?

3. What does Warren accomplish in his first and last paragraphs?

4. **OTHER METHODS** Warren's analysis essay is also a model of comparison and contrast (Chapter 11) because he examines the similarities between Krusty the Clown fans and *Simpsons* fans. Why do you think Warren devotes so much attention to Krusty? What makes the comparison significant?

Language

1. How would you describe Warren's tone? How seriously does he take his subject? Is the tone appropriate, given his purpose?

2. Notice the many sentences and phrases Warren encloses in parentheses, such as "That is a fact, and I'll argue with anyone who disagrees with me to the death" (paragraph 2). What is the function of these parenthetical remarks? What do they contribute to the writer's purpose?

Writing Topics

1. **JOURNAL TO ESSAY** Expand your journal entry about pop culture merchandise (p. 154) into a full essay analyzing a single item. Describe the item and why you wanted it, considering your feelings about the characters it represents. Include a discussion of what the merchandise means to you now, explaining why it is or is not still part of your life. Make sure your essay has a controlling thesis that draws together all the points of your analysis. Document any sources you consult, as Warren does (see pp. 369–80).

2. How did you react to Warren's essay? Do you agree with his assessment of *The Simpsons* and his suggestion that merchandising both helped the show succeed and contributed to its decline? Or do you find his evaluation of the show's worth one-sided, his examples and opinions too personal to form the basis of an analysis? Write an essay that responds to Warren's conclusions. Be sure to include examples to support your view.

3. **CULTURAL CONSIDERATIONS** In the Western world, we watch a lot of television: most of us watch it every day. Some people feel that TV can expand our vision of the world by showing us different people and places and exposing us to new ideas and issues. Others argue that TV narrows our views, inundating us with shallow content designed to please the crowd. What is your opinion about the effects of TV? Do you think that your viewing habits have an essentially positive or negative effect on you? Write an essay in which you explain how you think TV affects you.

4. **CONNECTIONS** In "Humvee Satisfies a Man's Lust for Winches" (p. 149), Dave Barry says of the sport-utility vehicle that "It looks like something you'd buy as part of a toy action-figure set called 'Sergeant Bart Groin and His Pain Platoon,'" suggesting that the Humvee is in some respects an example of military merchandising. And like *The Simpsons*, the Humvee has experienced a decline in popularity (to the point that General Motors sold the line to a Chinese company in 2010). In an essay, consider how Warren's understanding of the role of consumer sentiment in merchandising might explain the Humvee's fate.

Television—teacher, mother, secret lover! —Homer Simpson

Television is chewing gum for the eyes. —Frank Lloyd Wright

The medium is the message. —Marshall McLuhan

JOURNAL RESPONSE Reflect for a few moments on your favorite show on TV. Write a journal entry explaining what you like about the show, trying to get down as many details as you can.

Thomas de Zengotita

A contributing editor for *Harper's Magazine*, Thomas de Zengotita (born 1943) earned a PhD in anthropology from Columbia University in 1985 and teaches at both the Dalton School (a private preparatory school in Manhattan) and New York University's Draper Graduate Program. His essays have appeared in the *Nation, Shout Magazine,* the scholarly journal *Cultural Anthropology,* and his blog on the *Huffington Post.* De Zengotita's interest in the influences of mass media led him to develop the analytic concept of *mediation,* which theorizes that every aspect of our consciousness is filtered through what we see and hear in popular culture. He elaborates on this central idea of his critical work in *Mediated: How the Media Shapes Your World and the Way You Live in It* (2005), his widely acclaimed first book.

American Idol Worship

A major tenet of de Zengotita's theory of mediation is that the media flatter audiences by suggesting that popular culture is ultimately about the people who consume it. (As he explains it, contemporary media offer "a place where everything is addressed to us, everything is for us, and nothing is beyond us anymore.") In this essay, written in 2006 and published in both the *Los Angeles Times* and the *Christian Science Monitor,* de Zengotita examines how this flattery works in one of the most popular media productions going—the television show *American Idol.*

When the ratings numbers came in after last week's Grammy Awards, the   1
news wasn't good for the professionals. A show that features amateurs had attracted a far bigger audience than had one with the likes of Madonna, Coldplay, and U2. . . . *American Idol* drew almost twice as many viewers as the awards show. What's going on here? Why does this reality show consistently attract the weekly attention of close to 35 million viewers?

It's a nexus of factors shaping the "virtual revolution" unfolding all 2
around us, on so many fronts. Think chat rooms, *MySpace.com*, blogs, life
journals illustrated with photos snapped by cell phones, flash-mobbing,
marathon running, focus groups, talk radio, e-mails to news shows,
camcorders, sponsored sports teams for tots—and every garage band in
town with its own CD. What do all these platforms have in common?
They are all devoted to otherwise anonymous people who don't want
to be mere spectators. In this virtual revolution, it's not workers against
capitalists—that's so nineteenth century. In our mediated world, it's
spectators against celebrities, with spectators demanding a share of the
last scarce resource in the overdeveloped world—attention. The *American
Idol* format combines essential elements of this revolution.

Have you followed the ruckus over why people don't have heroes 3
anymore—in the old-fashioned statesman, warrior, genius, artist kind
of way? People concerned with education are especially alarmed. They
invest a lot of energy in trying to rekindle an aura of greatness around
the Founding Fathers. But it's hopeless. Ask natural-born citizens of the
mediated world who their heroes are, and their answers fall into one of
two categories: somebody in their personal lives or performers—above
all, pop music performers.

The "everyday hero" answer reflects the virtual revolution, but what 4
about performers? Why are they so important to their fans? Because,
in concert especially, these new kinds of heroes create an experience of
belonging that their fans would otherwise never know, living as they do
in a marketplace of lifestyles that can make one's existence feel optional.
That's why there's a religious quality to a concert when the star meets
the audience's awesome expectations and creates, in song and persona,
a moment in which each individual feels personally understood and,
at the same time, fused with other fans in a larger common identity.
"Performer heroes" are, in the end, all about us. They don't summon us
to serve a cause—other than the one of being who we are. So, naturally,
they have been leaders of the virtual revolution. From their perch on
high, they make us the focus of attention.

American Idol takes the next step. It unites both aspects of the 5
relationship—in the climactic final rounds, a fan becomes an idol; the
ultimate dream of our age comes true before our eyes and in our hearts.

That's mediational magic. 6

And don't forget the power of music. *American Idol* wouldn't be 7
what it is if, say, amateur actors were auditioning. You can disagree with
someone about movie stars and TV shows and still be friends. But you
can't be friends with someone who loves the latest boy band, in a totally

unironic way, if you are into Gillian Welch. That's because tastes in pop music go right to the core of who you are, with a depth and immediacy no other art form can match. Music takes hold of you on levels deeper than articulated meaning. That's why words, sustained by music, have such power. There is nothing like a song for expressing who we are.

That brings us to the early rounds of *American Idol,* in which con-   8 testants are chosen for the final competition in Hollywood. The conventional wisdom is that they're an exercise in public humiliation, long a staple of reality TV. That's not wrong, as far as it goes, but it isn't just any old humiliation exercise—it is the most excruciating form of voluntary personal humiliation the human condition allows for because it involves the most revealing kind of performance there is, this side of pornography. During this phase of the show, the audience, knowing it will eventually fuse in a positive way with a finalist idol, gets to be in the most popular clique on the planet, rendering snarky judgments on one of the most embarrassing pools of losers ever assembled.

American Idol gives you so many ways to feel good about yourself.   9 No wonder it's a hit.   10

Meaning

1. What is de Zengotita's thesis? Where does he state it explicitly? Try to summarize the central meaning of de Zengotita's analysis in a sentence or two of your own.

2. According to de Zengotita, what elements define the "virtual revolution" (paragraph 2)? How does *American Idol* bring together these elements to create an irresistible media experience?

3. What do you think de Zengotita means when he writes, "*American Idol* . . . unites both aspects of the relationship—in the climactic final rounds, a fan becomes an idol; the ultimate dream of our age comes true before our eyes and in our hearts. . . . That's mediational magic" (paragraphs 5 and 6)? According to de Zengotita, how does *American Idol* transform both the contestants and the audience?

4. Try to guess the meanings of any of the following words that you are unsure of, based on their context in de Zengotita's essay. Test your guesses in a dictionary, and then try to use each word in a sentence of your own.

nexus (2)	persona (4)	excruciating (8)
ruckus (3)	climactic (5)	clique (8)
rekindle (3)	unironic (7)	snarky (8)
aura (3)	articulated (7)	

Purpose and Audience

1. What do you think was de Zengotita's purpose in writing this essay? Does he want to shock, inform, persuade, or entertain his readers? Something else? What evidence from the text supports your viewpoint?

2. What assumptions does de Zengotita make about his audience? Does he assume that his readers are familiar with *American Idol?* with his theory of *mediation?* How familiar with the show (or the author's theory) would readers have to be in order to understand de Zengotita's analysis?

Method and Structure

1. De Zengotita's immediate subject of analysis is *American Idol,* but he's also using the show to examine a wider phenomenon. What is that wider phenomenon? How does the author's analysis of *American Idol* explain it?

2. What is de Zengotita's principle of analysis, and what elements of *American Idol* does he analyze? How does he reassemble these elements into a new whole? Support your answer with evidence from the essay.

3. De Zengotita begins his essay by contrasting *American Idol*'s ratings with those for the Grammy Awards. How does beginning with this comparison foreshadow the conclusions he draws about the implications of the "virtual revolution" in popular culture?

4. **OTHER METHODS**   In addition to division, de Zengotita uses cause-and-effect analysis (Chapter 13) to show how *American Idol*'s individual elements explain its popularity. What does this cause-and-effect analysis add to the analysis of *American Idol?* What would be lost without it?

Language

1. As is the case with most of de Zengotita's writing, this essay combines loose, informal language—"What's going on here?" (paragraph 1) and "that's so nineteenth century" (2)—with scholarly vocabulary to explore a complex idea. What do you suppose is the author's purpose in employing these different levels of diction? What is the effect on you as a reader? (If necessary, see *diction* in the Glossary.)

2. Throughout his essay, de Zengotita shifts back and forth between first person (*we, us, our*), second person (*you*), and third person (*they/them*). Can you find an underlying purpose for the different uses? Do the shifts add to or detract from the essay's overall effect? Why?

Writing Topics

1. **JOURNAL TO ESSAY** In your journal entry (p. 160) you reflected on your favorite television show. Now write a more formal essay in which you describe that TV show and explain what makes it so enjoyable for you. Just as de Zengotita took *American Idol* apart to understand its popularity, explain what elements contribute to the appeal of the show you selected. Does its appeal rest mostly on the actors involved, the places depicted, the story line, or other features? Does it make you think about who you are as a person or change your view of the world? If it is merely good "entertainment," describe what makes it so.

2. Although the idea of *mediation* may seem complicated, it boils down to a relatively simple concept: de Zengotita believes that popular culture influences the way we perceive the world and ourselves. What do you think of this notion? Do the media control how you think, or can you pick and choose among its offerings without being affected in any meaningful way? Write an essay that uses the concept of mediation to explore your relationship with an aspect of popular culture of your choosing (for example, you might examine how a fashion or "lifestyle" magazine has changed the way you look at yourself, or describe how a song changed your attitude toward a problem you were facing). Or, if you don't accept the concept of mediation, write an essay that uses examples from your own experience to explain why you disagree with de Zengotita. If time allows, consider doing additional research on de Zengotita's theories to inform your analysis.

3. **CULTURAL CONSIDERATIONS** American television programs are watched all over the world: *Baywatch*, for example, is one of the most popular shows in Germany, and *Desperate Housewives* is popular in China. Many global viewers say they watch the programming to improve their English language skills or to learn about American culture. But what are they learning? Write an essay that focuses on a particular type of show—network news, for example, or medical dramas—and explores how a non-American viewer might interpret it. Does the program provide an accurate depiction of life in the United States, or does it distort reality?

4. **CONNECTIONS** De Zengotita and Dave Barry, in "Humvee Satisfies a Man's Lust for Winches" (p. 149), both refer to popular culture's power to make us feel better about ourselves. At the same time, both writers suggest that such good feelings are superficial at best, maybe even harmful on a deeper level. Write an essay in which you analyze the effects of popular culture on self-esteem, drawing on both essays and your own understanding of this issue.

Division or Analysis

Select one of the following topics, or any other topic they suggest, for an essay developed by analysis. Be sure to choose a topic you care about so that analysis is a means of communicating an idea, not an end in itself.

PEOPLE, ANIMALS, AND OBJECTS

1. The personality of a friend or relative
2. The personality of a typical politician, teacher, or other professional
3. An animal such as a cat, dog, horse, cow, spider, or bat
4. A machine or an appliance such as a car engine, harvesting combine, laptop computer, hair dryer, toaster, or sewing machine
5. A nonmotorized vehicle such as a skateboard, in-line skate, bicycle, or snowboard
6. A building such as a hospital, theater, or sports arena

IDEAS

7. The perfect city
8. The perfect crime
9. A theory or concept in a field such as psychology, sociology, economics, biology, physics, engineering, or astronomy
10. The evidence in a political argument (written, spoken, or reported in the news)
11. A liberal arts education

ASPECTS OF CULTURE

12. A style of dress or "look," such as that associated with the typical business-person, bodybuilder, rap musician, or outdoors enthusiast
13. A typical hero or villain in science fiction, romance novels, war movies, or movies or novels about adolescents
14. A television or film comedy
15. A literary work: short story, novel, poem, essay
16. A visual work: painting, sculpture, building
17. A musical work: song, concerto, symphony, opera
18. A performance: sports, acting, dance, music, speech
19. The slang of a particular group or occupation

WRITING ABOUT THE THEME

Looking at Popular Culture

1. The essays by Dave Barry (p. 149), Andrew Warren (p. 154), and Thomas de Zengotita (p. 160) all include the theme that what you see—whether in consumer products, advertising, or entertainment—is not all you get. Think of something you have used, seen, or otherwise experienced that made you suspect a hidden message or agenda. Consider, for example, a childhood toy, a popular breakfast cereal, a political speech, a magazine, a textbook, a video game, a movie, or a visit to a theme park such as Disney World. Using the essays in this chapter as models, write an analysis of your subject, making sure to divide it into distinct elements and to conclude it by reassembling those elements into a new whole.

2. Andrew Warren and Thomas de Zengotita both write seriously about television, a subject that some people would consider trivial and unworthy of critical attention. How informative and useful are such analyses of popular culture? Where does each essay tell us something significant about ourselves, or in contrast, where does it fail in trying to make the trivial seem important? Is popular culture—television, magazines, Hollywood movies, self-help books, toys, fast-food restaurants—best looked at critically, best ignored, or best simply enjoyed? Explain your answers in an essay, using plenty of examples to support your thesis.

3. Thomas de Zengotita argues that popular culture is moving in a new direction that shifts power to the audience. How do de Zengotita's observations affect your reading of the other selections in this chapter? For instance, does Jon Pareles (p. 143) present Keith Richards as an "everyday hero" or a "performer hero"? Did Native American viewers appreciate the advertisement described by Luci Tapahonso (p. 143) because it made them the center of attention? Are some men drawn to Humvees because those vehicles make them feel powerful, as Dave Barry playfully suggests? How does de Zengotita's idea that the media is ultimately about its consumers resonate with Andrew Warren's explanation for the declining value of *Simpsons* merchandise? Write an essay using de Zengotita's concept of mediation to explain the appeal (or lack of appeal) of one or several of the popular culture examples in this chapter. Quote de Zengotita's analysis and passages from other writers as necessary, being sure to use proper citation format (see pp. 372–80) to acknowledge your sources.

9

CLASSIFICATION
Sorting Friends and Neighbors

We **classify** when we sort things into groups: kinds of cars, styles of writing, types of customers. Because it creates order, classification helps us make sense of our experiences and our surroundings. With it, we see the correspondences among like things and distinguish them from unlike things, similarities and distinctions that can be especially helpful when making a decision or encouraging others to see things from a new perspective. You use classification when you prioritize your bills, sort your laundry, or organize your music collection; you might also draw on the method to choose among types of cell phone plans, to propose new pay scales at your workplace, or to argue at a town meeting that some types of community projects are more valuable than others. Because classification helps us name things, remember them, and discuss them with others, it is also a useful method for developing and sharing ideas in writing.

Reading Classification

Writers classify primarily to explain a pattern in a subject that might not have been noticed before: a sportswriter, for instance, might observe that basketball players tend to fall into one of three groups based on the aggressiveness of their play. Sometimes, writers also classify to persuade readers that one group is superior: a sportswriter might argue that one style of basketball play is more effective than the other two.

Classification involves a three-step process:

1. Separate things into their elements, using the method of division or analysis (previous chapter).
2. Isolate the similarities among the elements.
3. Group or classify the things based on those similarities, matching like with like.

The following diagram illustrates a classification essay that appears later in this chapter, "The People Next Door" by Jonathan R. Gould, Jr. (p. 180). Gould's subject is neighbors, and he sees four distinct kinds:

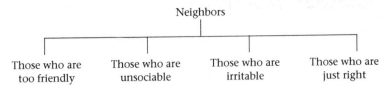

All the members of Gould's overall group share at least one characteristic: they have been Gould's neighbors. The members of each subgroup also share at least one characteristic: they are too friendly, for instance, or unsociable. The people in each subgroup are independent of each other, and none of them is essential to the existence of the subgroup: the kind of neighbor would continue to exist even if at the moment Gould didn't live next door to such a person.

The number of groups in a classification scheme depends entirely on the basis for establishing the classes in the first place. There are two systems:

- In a **complex classification** like that used for neighbors, each individual fits firmly into one class because of at least one distinguishing feature shared with all members of that class but not with any members of any other classes. All the too-friendly neighbors are overly friendly, but none of the unsociable, irritable, or just-right neighbors is.

- In a **binary** or **two-part classification**, two classes are in opposition to each other, such as constructive and destructive neighbors. Often, one group has a certain characteristic that the other group lacks. For instance, neighbors could be classified into those who respect your privacy and those who don't. A binary scheme is useful to emphasize the possession of a particular characteristic, but it is limited if it specifies nothing about the members of the "other" class except that they lack the trait. (An old joke claims that there are two kinds of people in the world—those who classify and all others.)

Sorting items demands a **principle of classification** that determines the groups by distinguishing them. For instance, Gould's principle in identifying four groups of neighbors is their behavior toward him and his family. Principles for sorting a year's movies might be genre (action-adventure, comedy, drama); place of origin (domestic, foreign); or cost of production (low-budget, medium-priced, high-budget). The choice of a principle depends on the writer's main interest in the subject.

Although a writer may emphasize one class over the others, the classification itself must be complete and consistent. A classification of movies by genre would be incomplete if it omitted comedies. It would be inconsistent if it included action-adventures, comedies, dramas, low-budget films, and foreign films: such a system mixes *three* principles (genre, cost, origin); it omits whole classes (what about high-budget domestic dramas?); and it overlaps other classes (a low-budget foreign action-adventure would fit in three different groups).

Analyzing Classification in Paragraphs

Nelson George (born 1957) is a filmmaker, television producer, journalist, novelist, and noted historian and critic of African American music. This paragraph is adapted from "Strangers on His Street," a memoir of the changes in his New York City neighborhood, first published in the *New York Times* in 2009.

When I moved to the neighborhood, a significant number of white home owners were living on the glorious brownstone "South" streets like Oxford, Porter, and Elliot, but their presence was dwarfed by two kinds of black folks. First, there were the working-class people who drank at Frank's bar on Fulton Street, ate Sunday brunch at Two Steps Down on Dekalb Avenue, and avoided eye contact with the minor-league clockers selling crack cocaine and marijuana outside a bodega on Lafayette near Fort Greene Place. Then there were aspiring young black artists like me . . . a wave of young writers, designers, cartoonists, dancers, actors, and musicians who gave parties, walked the streets, and worked hard at becoming good and famous. A few did both. But in the

Principle of classification (topic sentence underlined): black residents of the Fort Greene neighborhood

1. Working-class people: focused on daily life

2. Artists: focused on future success

last half-dozen years, many of my contemporaries have
departed. . . . Black artists still live in Fort Greene, but they
are only a piece of the neighborhood's color palette.

Kevin Roose (born 1987) is a recent Brown University graduate who chose
to spend his semester abroad at Liberty University, a private Christian college.
Roose's goal was to demystify the culture of born-again Christianity by immersing
himself in it. This paragraph is from The Unlikely Disciple (2009), his book about
the experience. (Joey and Travis are two of the friends he made on campus.)

Joey proceeded to tell me that there are several
tiny pockets of non-Christians at Liberty (and by "non-
Christians," of course, he means "nonevangelicals").
One is composed of varsity athletes who came to Liberty on sports scholarships, either not realizing or not
caring that Liberty was an evangelical school. Another
is a group of international students, predominantly
Buddhists from Asia, whose parents wanted them in a
school with conservative social rules and were willing
to ignore the religious discrepancy. Then there are people
who came to Liberty because it was a decent, affordable
school close to home. Travis originally came to Liberty
for reasons one and three—he wanted to play football,
and he lives an hour or so from campus. He got cut
from the team during his freshman year, but he decided
to stay at Liberty, even though his beliefs didn't match
up with the school's doctrinal statement.

*Principle of classifica-
tion (topic sentence
underlined): nonevan-
gelical students*

*1. Athletes on
scholarship*

*2. International
students*

*3. Budget-
minded locals*

*Placement of a
friend among
the groups*

Developing an Essay by Classification

Getting Started

Classification essays are often assigned in college: you might be asked to
identify the major schools of therapy for a psychology class, for instance,
or to categorize difficult personality types for a business communication
course. When you need to develop your own subject for a classification
essay, think of one large class of things whose members you've noticed

fall into subclasses, such as study habits, midnight grocery shoppers, or political fund-raising appeals. Be sure that your general subject forms a class in its own right—that all its members share at least one important quality. Then look for your principle of classification, the quality or qualities that distinguish some members from others, providing poles for the members to group themselves around. One such principle for political fund-raising appeals might be the different methods of delivery, such as direct marketing, media advertising, meetings, or the Internet.

While generating ideas for your classification, keep track of them in a list, diagram, or outline to ensure that your principle is applied thoroughly (all classes) and consistently (each class relating to the principle). Fill in the list, diagram, or outline with the distinguishing features of each class and with examples that will clarify your scheme.

Forming a Thesis

You will want to state your principle of classification in a thesis sentence so that you know where you're going and your readers know where you're taking them. Be sure the sentence also conveys a *reason* for the classification so that the essay does not become a dull list of categories. The following tentative thesis sentence is mechanical; the revision is more interesting.

> TENTATIVE THESIS SENTENCE Political fund-raising appeals are delivered in many ways.

> REVISED THESIS SENTENCE Of the many ways to deliver political fund-raising appeals, the three that rely on personal contact are generally the most effective.

(Note that the revised thesis sentence implies a further classification based on whether the appeals involve personal contact or not.)

Organizing

The introduction to a classification essay should make clear why the classification is worthwhile: What situation prompted the essay? What do readers already know about the subject? What use might they make of the information you will provide? Unless your principle of classification is self-evident, you may want to explain it briefly—though save extensive explanation for the body of the essay.

In the body of the essay, the classes may be arranged in order of decreasing familiarity or increasing importance or size—whatever pattern provides the emphasis you want and clarifies your scheme for readers. You should at least mention each class, but some classes may demand considerable space and detail.

A classification essay often ends with a conclusion that restores the wholeness of the subject. Among other uses, the conclusion might summarize the classes, comment on the significance of one particular class in relation to the whole, or point out a new understanding of the whole subject gained from the classification.

Drafting

For the first draft of your classification, your main goal will be to establish your scheme: spelling out the purpose and principle of classification and defining the groups so that they are complete and consistent, covering the subject without mixing principles or overlapping. The more you've been able to plan your scheme, the less difficult the draft will be. If you can also fill in the examples and other details needed to develop the groups, do so.

Be sure to consider your readers' needs as you draft. For a subject familiar to readers, such as study habits, you probably wouldn't need to justify your principle of classification, but you would need to enliven the classes themselves with vivid examples. For an unfamiliar subject, in contrast, you might need to take considerable care in explaining the principle of classification as well as in detailing the classes.

Revising and Editing

The following questions and the information in the box can help you revise and edit your classification.

- *Will readers see the purpose of your classification?* Let readers know early why you are troubling to classify your subject, and keep this purpose evident throughout the essay.

- *Is your classification complete?* Your principle of classification should create categories that encompass every representative of the general subject. If some representatives will not fit the scheme, you may have to create a new category or revise the existing categories to include them.

> **FOCUS ON PARAGRAPH DEVELOPMENT**
>
> A crucial aim of revising a classification is to make sure each group is clear: what's counted in, what's counted out, and why. It's not unusual to get so focused on identifying and sorting categories during the draft stage that you neglect the details. In that case, you'll need to go back and provide examples, comparisons, and other particulars to make the groups clear as you develop the paragraph(s) devoted to each group. These details pin down a group, making it distinct from other groups and clear in itself. For more on developing paragraphs through specifics, see pp. 39–41.

■ *Is your classification consistent?* Consistency is essential to save readers from confusion or irritation. Make sure all the classes reflect the same principle and that they do not overlap. Remedy flaws by adjusting the classes or creating new ones.

A Note on Thematic Connections

Writers classify people more than any other subject, perhaps because the method gives order and even humor to our relationships with each other. The authors in this chapter explore the connections that give people a sense of where they fit in with friends and neighbors. In a paragraph, Nelson George identifies two types of black residents in his neighborhood, workers and artists (p. 169). Also in a paragraph, Kevin Roose sorts students at his school by their reasons for attending (p. 170). Brandon Griggs's essay identifies a dozen irritating behaviors among *Facebook* friends (next page). Jonathan Gould's essay finds four kinds of next-door neighbors (p. 180). And Marion Winik's essay categorizes her friends into nine groups (p. 184).

Now the cliques are moving online. —Kim Komando

Rather than bringing me closer to others, the time that I spend online isolates me from the most important people in my life: my family, my friends, my neighborhood, my community. —Clifford Stoll

There are three kinds of death in this world. There's heart death, there's brain death, and there's being off the network. —Guy Almes

JOURNAL RESPONSE Do you have a *MySpace* page? A *Facebook* account? A *Twitter* following? Write a short journal entry about how you connect with your friends online. How would your relationships suffer, or improve, if you didn't have access to a social-networking tool?

Brandon Griggs

Brandon Griggs (born 1960) is a journalist who writes about culture and technology. He went to high school in Washington, DC, graduated from Tufts University in 1982, and studied at Columbia University's Graduate School of Journalism under a fellowship with the National Arts Journalism Program. Griggs held a staff writing position as the "Culture Vulture" for the *Salt Lake Tribune* for fifteen years before taking his current position as a technology-section producer for *CNN.com*. He is the author of *Utah Curiosities: Quirky Characters, Roadside Oddities and Other Offbeat Stuff* (2008), a guide to the state's peculiar legends and unconventional tourist attractions.

The Most Annoying Facebookers

In this 2009 article for *CNN.com*, Griggs draws on his personal experience and his sense of humor to call attention to behaviors that are guaranteed to alienate anyone's network of friends.

Facebook, for better or worse, is like being at a big party with all your   1
friends, family, acquaintances, and coworkers. There are lots of fun, interesting people you're happy to talk to when they stroll up. Then there are the other people, the ones who make you cringe when you see them coming. This article is about those people.

Sure, *Facebook* can be a great tool for keeping up with folks who ₂ are important to you. Take the status update, the 160-character message that users post in response to the question, "What's on your mind?" An artful, witty, or newsy status update is a pleasure—a real-time, tiny window into a friend's life.

But far more posts read like navel-gazing diary entries, or worse, ₃ spam. A recent study categorized 40 percent of *Twitter* tweets as "pointless babble," and it wouldn't be surprising if updates on *Facebook*, still a fast-growing social network, break down in a similar way.

Combine dull status updates with shameless self-promoters, "friend- ₄ padders," and that friend of a friend who sends you quizzes every day, and *Facebook* becomes a daily reminder of why some people can get on your nerves.

Here are twelve of the most annoying types of *Facebook* users: ₅

The Let-Me-Tell-You-Every-Detail-of-My-Day Bore. "I'm waking ₆ up." "I had Wheaties for breakfast." "I'm bored at work." "I'm stuck in traffic." You're kidding! How fascinating! No moment is too mundane for some people to broadcast unsolicited to the world. Just because you have 432 *Facebook* friends doesn't mean we all want to know when you're waiting for the bus.

The Self-Promoter. OK, so we've probably all posted at least once ₇ about some achievement. And sure, maybe your friends really do want to read the fascinating article you wrote about beet farming. But when almost EVERY update is a link to your blog, your poetry reading, your 10k results, or your art show, you sound like a bragger or a self-centered careerist.

The Friend-Padder. The average *Facebook* user has 120 friends on ₈ the site. Schmoozers and social butterflies—you know, the ones who make lifelong pals on the subway—might reasonably have 300 or 400. But 1,000 "friends"? Unless you're George Clooney or just won the lottery, no one has that many. That's just showing off.

The Town Crier. "Michael Jackson is dead!!!" You heard it from me ₉ first! Me, and the 213,000 other people who all saw it on TMZ. These Matt Drudge[1] wannabes are the reason many of us learn of breaking news not from TV or news sites but from online social networks. In their rush to trumpet the news, these people also spread rumors, half-truths, and innuendo. No, Jeff Goldblum did not plunge to his death from a New Zealand cliff.

The TMIer. "Brad is heading to Walgreens to buy something for ₁₀ these pesky hemorrhoids." Boundaries of privacy and decorum don't

---

[1] Creator and editor of the *Drudge Report,* an online news and gossip site.

seem to exist for these too-much-information updaters, who unabashedly offer up details about their sex lives, marital troubles, and bodily functions. Thanks for sharing.

The Bad Grammarian. "So sad about Fara Fauset but Im so gladd 11 its friday yippe." Yes, I know the punctuation rules are different in the digital world. And, no, no one likes a spelling-Nazi schoolmarm. But you sound like a moron.

The Sympathy-Baiter. "Barbara is feeling sad today." "Man, am I 12 glad that's over." "Jim could really use some good news about now." Like anglers hunting for fish, these sad sacks cast out their hooks—baited with vague tales of woe—in the hopes of landing concerned responses. Genuine bad news is one thing, but these manipulative posts are just pleas for attention.

The Lurker. The Peeping Toms of *Facebook*, these voyeurs are too 13 cautious, or maybe too lazy, to update their status or write on your wall. But once in a while, you'll be talking to them and they'll mention something you posted, so you know they're on your page, hiding in the shadows. It's just a little creepy.

The Crank. These curmudgeons, like the trolls who spew hate in 14 blog comments, never met something they couldn't complain about. "Carl isn't really that impressed with idiots who don't realize how idiotic they are." (Actual status update.) Keep spreading the love.

The Paparazzo. Ever visit your *Facebook* page and discover that 15 someone's posted a photo of you from last weekend's party—a photo you didn't authorize and haven't even seen? You'd really rather not have to explain to your mom why you were leering like a drunken hyena and French-kissing a bottle of Jagermeister.

The Obscurist. "If not now then when?" "You'll see . . ." "Grist for 16 the mill." "John is, small world." "Dave thought he was immune, but no. No, he is not." (Actual status updates, all.) Sorry, but you're not being mysterious—just nonsensical.

The Chronic Inviter. "Support my cause." "Sign my petition." "Play 17 Mafia Wars with me." "Which 'Star Trek' character are you?" "Here are the 'Top 5 cars I have personally owned.'" "Here are '25 Things about Me.'" "Here's a drink." "What drink are you?" "We're related!" "I took the 'What President Are You?' quiz and found out I'm Millard Fillmore! What president are you?"

You probably mean well, but stop. Just stop. I don't care what presi- 18 dent I am—can't we simply be friends? Now excuse me while I go post the link to this story on my *Facebook* page.

Meaning

1. Does Griggs have a thesis? Where in the essay does he make his point clear?

2. In which category or categories, if any, does Griggs place himself? How can you tell?

3. In paragraph 7, Griggs remarks of "every-detail-of-my-day" posts, "You're kidding! How fascinating!" Does he really mean to say that such information interests him? (Hint: look up *irony* in the Glossary.)

4. Try to guess the meanings of any of the following words that are unfamiliar to you. Test your guesses in a dictionary, and then come up with a sentence or two using each new word.

   mundane (6)   unabashedly (10)   curmudgeons (14)
   unsolicited (6)   anglers (12)   paparazzo (15)
   innuendo (9)   voyeurs (13)   chronic (17)
   decorum (10)

Purpose and Audience

1. How can we tell that Griggs intends to entertain us with his essay? Do you detect any other purpose?

2. What assumptions does Griggs make about the readers of his essay? Are the assumptions correct in your case?

Method and Structure

1. How does Griggs use the method of classification for comic effect? In what ways does classification lend itself particularly well to a humorous subject such as this one?

2. What is the one quality that all members of Griggs's subject share, and what principle of classification does he use to sort them?

3. If Griggs's subject is *Facebook,* why does he mention a study of *Twitter* in his introduction (paragraph 4)? What do that study's findings have to do with his thesis?

4. **OTHER METHODS** In addition to classification, Griggs relies heavily on example (Chapter 7) to make his point. Why do you think he uses so many direct quotations from *Facebook* status updates? What would the essay lose if Griggs didn't provide these examples?

Language

1. Examine Griggs's tone. How would you characterize his attitude toward his subject? Is he angry, resigned, hopeful, something else? Does his overall tone strengthen his essay or weaken it? Why? (If necessary, see pp. 41–43 on tone.)

2. Find three places where Griggs uses hyperbole (see p. 57 for a definition). What effect does this figure of speech have in this essay?

3. Consider the labels Griggs devises for each category. What connotations do these words and phrases have? How do they contribute to his overall point? (If necessary, see p. 55 on connotation.)

4. Notice that Griggs addresses his readers directly, as *you*. What is the effect of this choice? How does it contribute to his purpose?

Writing Topics

1. **JOURNAL TO ESSAY**   Building on your journal entry about your use of social-networking sites (p. 174), write a response to Griggs's essay. Does it amuse you? anger you? embarrass you? make you feel something else? Does it make you want to change your habits when writing status updates? Do you find Griggs's categories, examples, and conclusions fair? Why, or why not? Support your response with details from Griggs's essay and examples from your own experience.

2. Defend one of the groups of *Facebook* users that Griggs finds annoying. Write an essay explaining why someone might engage in a particular posting behavior, such are sharing minor moments or seeking sympathy, and consider what good might come of it, both for the poster and for his or her network of friends.

3. Using Griggs's essay as a model, write an essay that classifies a group of people (teachers, bosses, or salesclerks, for example) for the purpose of getting readers to examine their own behaviors. Sort your subject into classes according to a consistent principle, and provide plenty of details to clarify the classes you decide on. In your essay, be sure to explain to your readers why the classification should persuade them to change their ways.

4. **CULTURAL CONSIDERATIONS**   In questioning how anyone could have 1,000 friends, Griggs reveals an assumption that online friendship is nothing more than a digital extension of real-world friendship. Do you agree, or is the definition of *friend* unique to each context? How do online communities function differently than face-to-face communities do, and

what distinct purposes are served by each? Write an essay answering these questions. As evidence for your response, you may want to discuss how, if at all, your own real-world and online friendships correlate with each other.

5. **CONNECTIONS** Griggs and Jonathan R. Gould, Jr., in "The People Next Door" (p. 180), use similar means to achieve humorous effects. Write an essay in which you compare and contrast the tone, style, and use of language in each essay. How does each writer make his readers laugh? Is one more successful than the other, and why?

We make our friends; we make our enemies; but God makes our next-door neighbor. —G. K. Chesterton

Good fences make good neighbors. —Proverb

For what do we live, but to make sport for our neighbours, and laugh at them in our turn? —Jane Austen

JOURNAL RESPONSE Jot down a list of neighbors you have now and have had in the past. Then write a short journal entry about the different kinds of neighbors you have encountered.

Jonathan R. Gould, Jr.

Jonathan R. Gould, Jr., was born in 1968 in Little Falls, New York, and grew up on a dairy farm in nearby Fort Plain. Graduating from Little Falls Baptist Academy, he was valedictorian of his class. He served three years in the US Army, specializing in administration and computer programming. At the State University of New York (SUNY) at Oneonta, he was an honors student, received the Provost Award for academic distinction, and obtained a BS in mathematics education.

The People Next Door

(Student Essay)

From his experiences in many different settings, Gould identifies four types of neighbors, only one of which could be considered truly neighborly. Gould wrote this essay in 1994 for a writing course at SUNY.

I have moved more often than I care to remember. However, one thing 1 always stays the same no matter where I have been. There is always a house next door, and that house contains neighbors. Over time, I have begun putting my neighbors into one of four categories: too friendly, unsociable, irritable, and just right.

Neighbors who are too friendly can be seen just about anywhere. 2 I mean that both ways. They exist in every neighborhood I have ever lived in and seem to appear everywhere I go. For some strange reason these people become extremely attached to my family and stop in as many as eight to ten times a day. No matter how tired I appear to be, nothing short of opening the door and suggesting they leave will make them go home at night. (I once told an unusually friendly neighbor that his house was on fire, in an attempt to make him leave, and he still took ten minutes to say goodbye.) What is truly interesting about these people is their strong desire to cook for us even though they have developed no culinary skill whatsoever. (This has always proved particularly disconcerting since they stay to watch us eat every bite as they continually ask if the food "tastes good.")

The unsociable neighbor is a different story altogether. For reasons 3 of his own, he has decided to pretend that we do not exist. I have always found that one or two neighbors of this type are in my neighborhood. It is not easy to identify these people, because they seldom leave the shelter of their own house. To be honest, the only way I know that someone lives in their building is the presence of a name on the mailbox and the lights shining through the windows at night. My wife often tries to befriend these unique people, and I have to admire her courage. However, even her serenity is shaken when she offers our neighbors a fresh-baked apple pie only to have them look at her as if she intended to poison them.

Probably the most difficult neighbor to deal with is the irritable 4 neighbor. This individual probably has several problems, but he has reduced all those problems down to one cause—the proximity of my family to his residence. Fortunately, I have only encountered this type of neighbor in a handful of settings. (He is usually too busy with one group of "troublemakers" to pick up a new set.) The times that I have encountered this rascal, however, have proved more than enough for my tastes. He is more than willing to talk to me. Unfortunately, all he wants to tell me is how miserable my family is making him. Ignoring this individual has not worked for me yet. (He just adds my "snobbishness" to his list of faults that my family displays.) Interestingly, this fellow will eat anything my wife (bless her soul) might make in an attempt to be sociable. Even though he never has anything good to say about the food, not a crumb will be left on the plate when he is finished (which leads me to wonder just how starved and impoverished he must be).

At the risk of sounding like Goldilocks, there is also a neighbor who 5 is "just right." One of the most wonderful things about this neighbor is that there has always been at least one everywhere I have gone. We meet often (though not too often), and our greetings are always sincere. Occasionally, our families will go out to eat or to shop, or just sit and talk. We tend to spend as much time at their house as they do at ours (two to three times a month), and everyone knows just when it is time to say goodnight. For some reason, this neighbor knows how to cook, and we frequently exchange baked goods as well as pleasantries. For obvious reasons, this type of neighbor is my favorite.

As I mentioned before, each type of neighbor I have encountered is a   6
common sight in any neighborhood. I have always felt it was important to identify the type of neighbors that were around me. Then I am better able to maintain a clear perspective on our relationship and understand their needs. After all, people do not really change; we just learn how to live with both the good and the bad aspects of their behavior.

Meaning

1. Where does Gould state his thesis?

2. What is the difference between unsociable and irritable neighbors in Gould's classification?

3. From their context in Gould's essay, try to guess the meanings of any of the following words that are unfamiliar to you. Check your definitions against a dictionary's, and then write a sentence or two using each new word.

culinary (2)	proximity (4)	pleasantries (5)
disconcerting (2)	impoverished (4)	

Purpose and Audience

1. Why do you suppose Gould wrote this essay? Where does he give the clearest indication?

2. Does Gould make any assumptions about his audience? Does he seem to be writing for a certain type of reader?

Method and Structure

1. Why do you think Gould chose the method of classification to write about the subject of neighbors? How does the method help him achieve his purpose?

2. What is Gould's principle of classification? Do you think his classification is complete and consistent? How else might he have sorted neighbors?

3. Why do you think Gould stresses the fact that he has encountered most of these types of neighbors everywhere he has lived?

4. What does Gould accomplish in his conclusion?

5. **OTHER METHODS**   Gould's categories lend themselves to comparison and contrast (Chapter 11). Based on his descriptions, what are the differences between the too-friendly neighbor and the just-right neighbor?

Language

1. What is Gould's tone? How seriously does he take the problem of difficult neighbors?

2. Point out several instances of hyperbole or overstatement in the essay. What effect do these have?

Writing Topics

1. **JOURNAL TO ESSAY** In your journal entry (p. 180) you began a process of classification by focusing on neighbors you have had. Now think of a group to which you belong—a religious organization, your family, a club or committee, even a writing class. Write a classification essay in which you sort the group's members into categories according to a clear principle of classification. Be sure to label and define each type for your readers, to provide examples, and to position yourself in one of the categories. What does your classification reveal about the group as a whole?

2. Most of us have had at least one colorful or bothersome neighbor at some time or another—a busybody, a recluse, a borrower. Write a descriptive essay (with some narration) about an interesting neighbor you have known or a narrative essay (with some description) about a memorable run-in with a neighbor.

3. **CULTURAL CONSIDERATIONS** "Good fences make good neighbors," says a character in Robert Frost's poem "Mending Wall," and many people in our live-and-let-live society would seem to agree. Is the best neighbor an invisible one? Or do we lose something when we ignore those who are literally closest to us? Write an essay giving a definition of what it means to be a good neighbor. Or, if you prefer, write an essay in which you compare and contrast neighboring habits in different types of communities you have lived in or know of.

4. **CONNECTIONS** Both Gould and Marion Winik, in "What Are Friends For?" (p. 184), classify common relationships: Gould distinguishes four categories of neighbors, while Winik pinpoints nine types of friends. Write an essay in which you compare the two essays. How persuasive do you find each writer's groups? Which comes closest to your own experiences with neighbors or friends? Why?

> I get by with a little help from my friends. —John Lennon and Paul McCartney
>
> If a man does not make new acquaintances as he advances through life, he will soon find himself alone. —Samuel Johnson
>
> We need new friends. Some of us are cannibals who have eaten their old friends up; others must have ever-renewed audiences before whom to reenact an ideal version of their lives. —Logan Pearsall Smith

JOURNAL RESPONSE Draw up a list of your friends. Include people you see on a regular basis and others you haven't seen for a while. Can you sort them into categories—for instance, by the places you see them, the things you discuss with them, the ways they make you feel, or their importance to you?

Marion Winik

Marion Winik was born in New York City in 1958. She received her BA from Brown University and her MFA from Brooklyn College. Perhaps best known as a commentator for National Public Radio's *All Things Considered*, Winik regularly publishes pieces in print periodicals such as *Parenting, Cosmopolitan, Reader's Digest,* and the *Utne Reader*. Her books include *Telling: Confessions, Concessions, and Other Flashes of Light* (1995) and *First Comes Love* (1997), a memoir about life with her gay, AIDS-infected husband. She's also the author of *The Lunch Box Chronicles* (1999), which deals with single parenthood in the nineties, and *Above Us Only Sky* (2005), a collection of essays on "family and friendship and faith."

What Are Friends For?

In "What Are Friends For?" Winik locates various kinds of friends, from "Faraway" to "Hero" to "Friends You Love to Hate." The essay appears in Winik's collection *Telling: Confessions, Concessions, and Other Flashes of Light.*

I was thinking about how everybody can't be everything to each other, 1 but some people can be something to each other, thank God, from the ones whose shoulder you cry on to the ones whose half-slips you borrow to the nameless ones you chat with in the grocery line.

Buddies, for example, are the workhorses of the friendship world, 2 the people out there on the front lines, defending you from loneliness and boredom. They call you up, they listen to your complaints, they celebrate your successes and curse your misfortunes, and you do the same for them in return. They hold out through innumerable crises before concluding that the person you're dating is no good, and even then understand if you ignore their good counsel. They accompany you to a movie with subtitles or to see the diving pig at Aquarena Springs. They feed your cat when you are out of town and pick you up from the airport when you get back. They come over to help you decide what to wear on a date. Even if it is with that creep.

What about family members? Most of them are people you just got 3 stuck with, and though you love them, you may not have very much in common. But there is that rare exception, the Relative Friend. It is your cousin, your brother, maybe even your aunt. The two of you share the same views of the other family members. Meg never should have divorced Martin. He was the best thing that ever happened to her. You can confirm each other's memories of things that happened a long time ago. Don't you remember when Uncle Hank and Daddy had that awful fight in the middle of Thanksgiving dinner? Grandma always hated Grandpa's stamp collection; she probably left the windows open during the hurricane on purpose.

While so many family relationships are tinged with guilt and obli- 4 gation, a relationship with a Relative Friend is relatively worry free. You don't even have to hide your vices from this delightful person. When you slip out Aunt Joan's back door for a cigarette, she is already there.

Then there is that special guy at work. Like all the other people at 5 the job site, at first he's just part of the scenery. But gradually he starts to stand out from the crowd. Your friendship is cemented by jokes about coworkers and thoughtful favors around the office. Did you see Ryan's hair? Want half my bagel? Soon you know the names of his turtles, what he did last Friday night, exactly which model CD player he wants for his birthday. His handwriting is as familiar to you as your own.

Though you invite each other to parties, you somehow don't quite 6 fit into each other's outside lives. For this reason, the friendship may not survive a job change. Company gossip, once an infallible source of entertainment, soon awkwardly accentuates the distance between you. But wait. Like School Friends, Work Friends share certain memories which acquire a nostalgic glow after about a decade.

A Faraway Friend is someone you grew up with or went to school 7 with or lived in the same town as until one of you moved away. Without a Faraway Friend, you would never get any mail addressed in handwriting. A Faraway Friend calls late at night, invites you to her wedding, always says she is coming to visit but rarely shows up. An actual visit from a Faraway Friend is a cause for celebration and binges of all kinds. Cigarettes, Chips Ahoy, bottles of tequila.

Faraway Friends go through phases of intense communication, then 8 may be out of touch for many months. Either way, the connection is always there. A conversation with your Faraway Friend always helps to put your life in perspective: when you feel you've hit a dead end, come to a confusing fork in the road, or gotten lost in some crackerbox subdivision of your life, the advice of the Faraway Friend—who has the big picture, who is so well acquainted with the route that brought you to this place—is indispensable.

Another useful function of the Faraway Friend is to help you remem- 9 ber things from a long time ago, like the name of your seventh-grade history teacher, what was in that really good stir-fry, or exactly what happened that night on the boat with the guys from Florida.

Ah, the Former Friend. A sad thing. At best a wistful memory, at 10 worst a dangerous enemy who is in possession of many of your deepest secrets. But what was it that drove you apart? A misunderstanding, a betrayed confidence, an unrepaid loan, an ill-conceived flirtation. A poor choice of spouse can do in a friendship just like that. Going into business together can be a serious mistake. Time, money, distance, cult religions: all noted friendship killers. You quit doing drugs, you're not such good friends with your dealer anymore.

And lest we forget, there are the Friends You Love to Hate. They call 11 at inopportune times. They say stupid things. They butt in, they boss you around, they embarrass you in public. They invite themselves over. They take advantage. You've done the best you can, but they need professional help. On top of all this, they love you to death and are convinced they're your best friend on the planet.

So why do you continue to be involved with these people? Why do 12 you tolerate them? On the contrary, the real question is, What would you do without them? Without Friends You Love to Hate, there would be nothing to talk about with your other friends. Their problems and their irritating stunts provide a reliable source of conversation for everyone they know. What's more, Friends You Love to Hate make you feel good about yourself, since you are obviously in so much better shape than they are. No matter what these people do, you will never get rid of them. As much as they need you, you need them too.

At the other end of the spectrum are Hero Friends. These people are 13 better than the rest of us, that's all there is to it. Their career is something you wanted to be when you grew up—painter, forest ranger, tireless doer of good. They have beautiful homes filled with special handmade things presented to them by villagers in the remote areas they have visited in their extensive travels. Yet they are modest. They never gossip. They are always helping others, especially those who have suffered a death in the family or an illness. You would think people like this would just make you sick, but somehow they don't.

A New Friend is a tonic unlike any other. Say you meet her at a 14 party. In your bowling league. At a Japanese conversation class, perhaps. Wherever, whenever, there's that spark of recognition. The first time you talk, you can't believe how much you have in common. Suddenly, your life story is interesting again, your insights fresh, your opinion valued. Your various shortcomings are as yet completely invisible.

It's almost like falling in love.   15

Meaning

1. What is Winik's thesis? How does it relate to the question she poses in the title?

2. What label does Winik assign to each category of friend that she establishes? What functions does each group fulfill?

3. Winik concludes her essay by describing the experience of meeting a New Friend (paragraph 14). How is a New Friend different from other types of friends, and why does Winik compare this experience with falling in love?

4. Try to guess the meanings of the following words from their context in Winik's essay. Look up the words in a dictionary to check your guesses. Then use each word in a sentence or two of your own.

counsel (2)	binges (7)	lest (11)
tinged (4)	crackerbox (8)	inopportune (11)
cemented (5)	wistful (10)	butt in (11)
infallible (6)	ill-conceived (10)	tonic (14)
nostalgic (6)		

Purpose and Audience

1. Winik begins her essay by saying, "I was thinking about . . ." (paragraph 1). What does this introductory sentence reveal about her purpose?

2. Is the essay addressed to both male and female readers? In your opinion, is it accessible to both sexes? Why, or why not? According to the information presented in this essay, does Winik believe that friends can be of either sex?

Method and Structure

1. Some people would not think of classifying relationships as intimate as friendships into such clear-cut categories. Does Winik's choice of method surprise you? Do you find it effective? What does this method enable her to do?

2. What is Winik's principle of classification? Does she group her friends based on differences among them independent of her or on differences in their relationships with her? Why do you think she just mentions but doesn't explain School Friends (paragraph 6)? Do you understand what she means by this category? Is it a flaw in the essay that Winik does not explain the category?

3. In paragraph 3, Winik asks, "What about family members?" as a transition to the category of Relative Friends. Study how she moves from one category to another in the rest of the essay. Are her transitions appropriate and effective? Why, or why not?

4. **OTHER METHODS**   How does Winik use definition (Chapter 12) to differentiate her categories of friends? Where in the essay does she seem to take the most care with definition? Why do you think she gives more attention to some categories than to others?

Language

1. Winik sometimes uses actual lines from conversation but without quotation marks. For example, in paragraph 3 she writes, "The two of you share the same views of the other family members. Meg should never have divorced Martin. He was the best thing that ever happened to her." Locate two other passages where dialogue blends into the text. What is the effect of this use of dialogue?

2. Winik sometimes omits words (such as *If* at the beginning of "You quit doing drugs, you're not such good friends with your dealer anymore," paragraph 10) or uses sentence fragments (such as "Even if it is with that creep," 2). Why do you think she chooses to break some rules of writing?

3. Winik uses several metaphors in the essay—for example, "Buddies . . . are the workhorses of the friendship world" (paragraph 2). Find other examples of metaphor. What do they contribute to the essay? (If necessary, review *metaphor* in the Glossary.)

Writing Topics

1. **JOURNAL TO ESSAY** Write an essay about one of the categories of friends that you described in your journal entry (p. 184)—for example, friends you study with, childhood friends, or friends you confide in. Using the method of classification, examine the *functions* this category of friends performs. What activities do you do with them that you don't do with others? What do you talk about? How relaxed or tense, happy or irritated, do they make you feel? Why are they significant to you? For each function, provide plenty of examples for readers.

2. Winik uses classification to explore friendship. Use the same method to develop your own essay about people with whom you do *not* get along. What categories do they fall into—for example, are some gossipy, others arrogant, still others unreliable? (Detail the categories with plenty of examples.) What does your dislike of these types of people ultimately reveal about you and your values?

3. **CULTURAL CONSIDERATIONS** Americans have a reputation for being very friendly, so that a stranger might smile, wish you a nice day, or even suggest having coffee together. What, in your view, is the appropriate way to interact (or not interact) with a stranger? In answering, ignore situations that might be risky, such as deserted nighttime streets or strangers who look clearly threatening. Think instead of a safe situation, such as a long line at the grocery store or coffee shop or the waiting room of a doctor's office. What are your "rules" for initiating conversation and for responding to a stranger's overtures? What informs your rules: experience? personality? upbringing? To what extent do you think your rules are invented by you or bred into you?

4. **CONNECTIONS** Kaela Hobby-Reichstein's essay "Learning Race" (p. 83), like Winik's essay, touches on the importance of friendship. Hobby-Reichstein, however, writes about a category that is missing from Winik's classification: the best friend. Use Hobby-Reichstein's experience (or your own) to write a paragraph that adds the best friend to Winik's classification. As you draft, consider both what makes a person a best friend and why that kind of relationship is important to a person.

Classification

Select one of the following topics, or any other topic they suggest, for an essay developed by classification. Be sure to choose a topic you care about so that classification is a means of communicating an idea, not an end in itself.

PEOPLE

1. Boring people
2. Laundromat users
3. Teachers or students
4. Parents or children

PSYCHOLOGY AND BEHAVIOR

5. Ways of punishing misbehavior
6. Obsessions
7. Diets
8. Dreams

THINGS

9. Buildings on campus
10. Junk foods
11. Computer games
12. Trucks

SPORTS AND PERFORMANCE

13. Styles of baseball pitching, tennis serving, or another sports skill
14. Gym members
15. Styles of dance, guitar playing, acting, or another performance art

COMMUNICATIONS MEDIA

16. Talk-show hosts
17. Online discussion groups
18. Sports announcers
19. Magazines or newspapers

WRITING ABOUT THE THEME

Sorting Group Identities

1. Kevin Roose (p. 170) classifies students at Liberty College according to why they chose to enroll there. Write a brief essay in which you classify students at your college or university or at a competing school. You may devise your own classification system, if you wish, or you might try adapting the categories of one of the other writers in this chapter to this subject. For instance, are some students workers and some dreamers, like the people in Nelson George's (p. 169) neighborhood? Do they exhibit, in person, any of the characteristics that Brandon Griggs complains about in "The Most Annoying Facebookers" (p. 174)? Are they, like Jonathan Gould's neighbors, "too friendly, unsociable, irritable, and just right" (p. 180)? Have you developed friendships on campus similar to any of the types Marion Winik describes in "What Are Friends For" (p. 184)?

2. Brandon Griggs, Jonathan Gould, and Marion Winik all classify and label people with some intention to amuse readers. However, not all labels used to classify people are harmless. Consider, for example, labels based on gender or race or sexual orientation. Write an essay in which you discuss both the benefits and the costs of assigning labels to people — for those using the labels, for those being labeled, and for society as a whole. Give plenty of specific examples.

3. Groups of friends and neighbors often form distinct communities, such as Brandon Griggs's *Facebook* friends, Jonathan Gould's mutually supportive neighbors, or the artists on Nelson George's block. Write an essay in which you offer your definition of *community*. Consider not only what constitutes a group identity but also why people might seek (or reject) a connection with others. What do communities offer their members, and what do they demand of individuals in return?

10

PROCESS ANALYSIS
Eating Well

Game rules, repair manuals, cookbooks, science textbooks—these and many other familiar works are essentially process analyses. They explain how to do something (play Monopoly, patch a hole in the wall), how to make something (an omelet), or how something happens (how our hormones affect our behavior, how a computer stores and retrieves data). That is, they explain a sequence of actions with a specified result (the **process**) by dividing it into its component steps (the **analysis**). You might use process analysis to explain how a hybrid engine saves gas or how a student organization can influence cafeteria menus. You also use process analysis when you want to teach someone how to do something, such as create a Web page or follow a new office procedure.

Process analysis overlaps several other writing methods discussed in this book. The analysis component is the method examined in Chapter 8—dividing a thing or concept into its elements. And we analyze a process much as we analyze causes and effects (Chapter 13), except that cause-and-effect analysis asks mainly *why* something happens or *why* it has certain results, whereas process analysis asks *how*. Process analysis also overlaps narration (Chapter 5), for the steps involved are almost always presented in chronological sequence. But narration recounts a unique sequence of events with a unique result, whereas process analysis explains a series of steps with the same predictable result. You might narrate a particularly exciting baseball game, for instance, but you would analyze the process—the rules—of any baseball game.

Reading Process Analysis

Almost always, the purpose of process analysis is to explain, but sometimes a parallel purpose is to prove something about a process or to
evaluate it: a writer may want to show how easy it is to change a tire, for
instance, or urge aspiring marathon runners to follow a training regimen
on the grounds of its safety and effectiveness.

Processes occur in several varieties, including mechanical (a car engine),
natural (cell division), psychological (acquisition of sex roles), and political
(the electoral process). Process analyses generally fall into one of two types:

- A **directive** process analysis tells how to do or make something:
  bake a cake, tune a guitar, negotiate a deal, write a process analysis.
  It outlines the steps in the process completely so that the reader who
  follows them can achieve the specified result. Generally, a directive process analysis addresses the reader directly, using the second-
  person *you* ("You should think of negotiation as collaboration rather
  than competition") or the imperative (commanding) mood of verbs
  ("Add one egg yolk and stir vigorously"). (See also p. 195.)

- An **explanatory** process analysis provides the information necessary
  for readers to understand the process, but more to satisfy their curios-
  ity than to teach them how to perform it. It may address the reader
  directly, but the third-person *he, she, it,* and *they* are more common.

Whether directive or explanatory, process analyses usually follow
a chronological sequence. Most processes can be divided into phases or
stages, and these in turn can be divided into steps. The stages of changing a tire, for instance, may be jacking up the car, removing the flat,
putting on the spare, and lowering the car. The steps within, say, jacking up the car may be setting the emergency brake, blocking the other
wheels, loosening the lug nuts, positioning the jack, and raising the car.
Following a chronological order, a writer covers the stages in sequence
and, within each stage, covers the steps in sequence.

To ensure that the reader can duplicate the process or understand
how it unfolds, a process analysis must fully detail each step and specify
the reasons for it. In addition, the writer must ensure that the reader
grasps the sequence of steps, their duration, and where they occur. To
this end, transitional expressions that signal time and place—such as
after five minutes, meanwhile, to the left, and *below*—can be invaluable.

Though a chronological sequence is usual for process analysis, the
sequence may be interrupted or modified to suit the material. A writer

may need to pause in a sequence to provide definitions of specialized terms or to explain why a step is necessary or how it relates to the preceding and following steps. Instructions on how to change a tire, for instance, might stop briefly to explain that the lug nuts should be loosened slightly *before* the car is jacked up in order to prevent the wheel from spinning once the weight is off the tire.

Analyzing Processes in Paragraphs

L. Rust Hills (1924–2008) was a fiction editor, writing teacher, and writer. This paragraph comes from "How to Eat an Ice-Cream Cone," which appears in his book *How to Do Things Right* (1972).

In trying to make wise and correct decisions about the ice-cream cone in your hand, you should always keep the objectives in mind. The main objective, of course, is to get the cone under control. Secondarily, one will want to eat the cone calmly and with pleasure. Real pleasure lies not simply in eating the cone but in eating it *right*. Let us assume that you have darted to your open space and made your necessary emergency repairs. The cone is still dangerous—still, so to speak, "live." But you can now proceed with it in an orderly fashion. First, revolve the cone through the full three hundred and sixty degrees, snapping at the loose gobs of ice cream; turn the cone by moving the thumb away from you and the forefinger toward you, so the cone moves counterclockwise. Then with the cone still "wound," which will require the wrist to be bent at the full right angle toward you, apply pressure with the mouth and tongue to accomplish overall realignment, straightening and settling the whole mess. Then, unwinding the cone back through the full three hundred and sixty degrees, remove any trickles of ice cream. From here on, some supplementary repairs may be necessary, but the cone is now defused.

Margin annotations:

Directive process analysis: tells how to eat an ice-cream cone

Goals of the process

Transitions signaling sequence, time, and place (underlined)

Process divided into three distinct steps

Test for correct performance of step

Reason for step

Result of the process

Jane E. Brody (born 1941) is a nutritionist whose weekly *New York Times* column, "Personal Health," has been syndicated in more than one hundred newspapers for three decades. This paragraph is from her guide to sensible eating, *Jane Brody's Nutrition Book* (1981).

When you think about it, it's impossible to lose—as many . . . diets suggest—10 pounds of *fat* in ten days, even on a total fast. A pound of body fat represents 3,500 calories. To lose 1 pound of fat, you must expend 3,500 more calories than you consume. Let's say you weigh 170 pounds and, as a moderately active person, you burn 2,500 calories a day. If your diet contains only 1,500 calories, you'd have an energy deficit of 1,000 calories a day. In a week's time that would add up to a 7,000-calorie deficit, or 2 pounds of real fat. In ten days, the accumulated deficit would represent nearly 3 pounds of lost body fat. Even if you ate nothing at all for ten days and maintained your usual level of activity, your caloric deficit would add up to 25,000 calories (2,500 calories a day times 10). At 3,500 calories per pound of fat, that's still only 7 pounds of lost fat. So if you want to lose fat, which is all you should want to lose, the loss must be gradual—at most a pound or two a week.

Explanatory process analysis: tells how weight loss happens

Process divided into steps

Transitions (underlined) signal sequence

Goal of process

Developing an Essay by Process Analysis

Getting Started

You'll find yourself writing process analyses for your courses in school (for instance, explaining how a drug affects brain chemistry), in memos at work (recommending a new procedure for approving cost estimates), or in life outside work (giving written directions to your home). To find a subject when an assignment doesn't make one obvious, examine your interests or hobbies or think of something whose workings you'd like to research in order to understand them better. Explore the subject by listing chronologically all the necessary stages and steps.

Remember your readers while you are generating ideas. Consider how much background information they need, where specialized terms must be defined, and where examples must be given. Especially if you are providing instructions, consider what special equipment readers will need, what hitches they may encounter, and what the interim results should be. To build a table, for instance, what tools would readers need? What should they do if the table wobbles even after the corners are braced? What should the table feel like after the first sanding or the first varnishing?

Forming a Thesis

While you are exploring your subject, decide on the point of your analysis and express it in a thesis sentence that will guide your writing and tell your readers what to expect. The simplest thesis states what the process is and outlines its basic stages. For instance:

> Building a table is a three-stage process of cutting, assembling, and finishing.

But you can increase your readers' interest in the process by also conveying your reason for writing about it. You might assert that a seemingly difficult process is actually quite simple, or vice versa:

> Changing a tire does not require a mechanic's skill or strength; on the contrary, a ten-year-old child can do it.

> Windsurfing may look easy, but it demands the knowledge of an experienced sailor and the balance of an acrobat.

You might show how the process demonstrates a more general principle:

> The process of getting a bill through Congress illustrates majority rule at work.

Or you might assert that a process is inefficient or unfair:

> The state's outdated registration procedure forces new car buyers to waste hours standing in line.

Regardless of how you structure your thesis sentence, try to make it clear that your process analysis has a point. Usually you will want to include a direct statement of your thesis in your introduction so that readers know what you're writing about and why the process should matter to them.

Organizing

Many successful process analyses begin with an overview of the process to which readers can relate each step. In such an introduction you can lead up to your thesis sentence by specifying when or where the process occurs, why it is useful or interesting or controversial, what its result is, and the like. Especially if you are providing instructions, you can also use the introduction (perhaps a separate paragraph) to provide essential background information, such as the materials readers will need.

After the introduction, you should present the stages distinctly, perhaps one or two paragraphs for each, and usually in chronological order. Within each stage, also chronologically, you then cover the necessary steps. This chronological sequence helps readers see how a process unfolds or how to perform it themselves. Try not to deviate from it unless you have good reason to—perhaps because your process requires you to group simultaneous steps or your readers need definitions of terms, reasons for steps, connections between separated steps, and other explanations.

A process essay may end simply with the result. But you might conclude with a summary of the major stages, with a comment on the significance or usefulness of the process, or with a recommendation for changing a process you have criticized. For a directive process essay, you might state the standards by which readers can measure their success or give an idea of how much practice may be necessary to master the process.

Drafting

While drafting your process analysis, concentrate on getting in as many details as you can: every step, how each relates to the one before and after, how each contributes to the result. In revising you can always delete unnecessary details and connective tissue if they seem cumbersome, but in the first draft it's better to overexplain than underexplain.

Drafting a process analysis is a good occasion to practice a straightforward, concise writing style, for clarity is more important than originality of expression. Stick to plain language and uncomplicated sentences. If you want to dress up your style a bit, you can always do so after you have made yourself clear.

Revising and Editing

When you've finished your draft, ask a friend to read it. If you have explained a process, he or she should be able to understand it. If you have given directions, he or she should be able to follow them, or imagine following them. Then examine the draft yourself against the following questions and the information in the box.

- *Have you adhered to a chronological sequence?* Unless there is a compelling and clear reason to use some other arrangement, the stages and steps of your analysis should proceed in chronological order. If you had to depart from that order—to define or explain or to sort out simultaneous steps—the reasons should be clear to your readers.

- *Have you included all necessary steps and omitted any unnecessary digressions?* The explanation should be as complete as possible but not

---

FOCUS ON CONSISTENCY

While drafting a directive process analysis telling readers how to do something, you may start off with subjects or verbs in one form and then shift to another form because the original choice felt awkward:

INCONSISTENT   To keep the car from rolling while changing the tire, one should first set the car's emergency brake. Then one should block the other three tires with objects like rocks or chunks of wood. Before raising the car, you should loosen the lug nuts of the wheel.

To repair inconsistencies, start with a subject that is both comfortable and sustainable. Avoid shifts by using you, or use the commanding form of verbs, in which you is understood as the subject:

CONSISTENT   To keep the car from rolling while changing the tire, you should set the car's emergency brake. Then you should block the other three tires with objects like rocks or chunks of wood.

CONSISTENT   To keep the car from rolling while changing the tire, first set the car's emergency brake. Then block the other three tires with objects like rocks or chunks of wood.

See pages 50–51 for more on shifts and how to avoid them.

▶ To practice editing for shifts, visit Exercise Central at bedfordstmartins.com/rewriting.

cluttered with information, however interesting, that contributes nothing to the readers' understanding of the process.

■ *Have you accurately gauged your readers' need for information?* You don't want to bore readers with explanations and details they don't need. But erring in the other direction is even worse, for your essay will achieve little if readers cannot understand it.

■ *Have you shown readers how each step fits into the whole process and relates to the other steps?* If your analysis seems to break down into a multitude of isolated steps, you may need to organize them more clearly into stages.

■ *Have you used plenty of informative transitions?* Transitions such as *at the same time* and *on the other side of the machine* indicate when steps start and stop, how long they last, and where they occur. (A list of such expressions appears in the Glossary under *transitions.*) The expressions should be as informative as possible; signals such as *first . . . second . . . third . . . fourteenth* and *next . . . next* do not help indicate movement in space or lapses in time, and they quickly grow tiresome.

A Note on Thematic Connections

The authors represented in this chapter set out to examine the steps involved in maintaining a healthy relationship with food, and for that purpose process analysis is the natural choice of method. In a paragraph, L. Rust Hills provides meticulous instructions for eating an ice-cream cone without making a mess (p. 194). In another paragraph, Jane E. Brody explains to dieters how calories translate into pounds (p. 195). Glenn Erikson's essay recommends a way for adults to keep their sanity in a children's theme restaurant (next page). Lars Eighner's essay details an eating strategy of the homeless and very poor: scavenging in trash bins (p. 205). And in an excerpt from a book that has helped to galvanize the local foods movement, Barbara Kingsolver creates an imaginary plant to explain the seasonality of produce (p. 210).

The ordinary human being would sooner starve than live on brown bread and raw carrots. —George Orwell

Americans now spend more money on fast food than on higher education. —Eric Schlosser

Fast food chains know that they are ordinary. They *want* to be ordinary. —Margaret Visser

JOURNAL RESPONSE What kinds of restaurants do you regularly visit: fast food places that specialize in burgers, tacos, or pizza? the school cafeteria? casual family chains like Applebee's or the Olive Garden? fancy, special-occasion destinations? Write about the restaurant food you most enjoy, describing when and how often you eat it and the reasons you do so. (If you've sworn off restaurants, explain why you prefer to eat at home.)

Glenn Erikson

Glenn Erikson was born in 1960 and grew up in Omaha, Nebraska. He graduated from high school in 1979 and held several jobs before finding his niche at the Lozier Corporation, a manufacturer of store fixtures, in 1995. Erikson returned to school in 2002, attending Metropolitan Community College in Omaha while raising his daughter and son. Erikson continues to work at the distribution center of the Lozier Corporation and enjoys watching Nebraska Cornhusker football with his coworkers and spending time with his grandson.

How to Survive at Chuck E. Cheese

(Student Essay)

In the following how-to essay, Erikson explains how a parent can endure, and maybe even enjoy, a family outing at a children's theme restaurant. Erikson wrote this piece for a composition class and published it in the *Metropolitan*, a student magazine produced by his campus writing center, in 2002.

Before you begin your adventure at Chuck E. Cheese, be aware that this 1 is not your ordinary pizzeria. Chuck E. Cheese is a child's dream to eat at.

However, for adults, it is a living hell if you're not totally prepared both financially and emotionally. To prepare yourself financially, you must first look through your coupon box and hope you have a coupon for Chuck E. Cheese to lessen your expenses. Next, stop off at your local ATM machine and withdraw enough money to cover your high-priced adventure.

Now that you are equipped financially, prepare yourself mentally. When you enter this carnival extravaganza called Chuck E. Cheese, try to remember how exciting a place like this would have been to you when you were a child. For instance, when I was a kid, I was excited when I had the opportunity to go to Shakey's Pizza because they had a couple of pinball machines there. However, Shakey's can't compare to Chuck E. Cheese. Think of this experience as a chance to rekindle some childhood excitement. Who knows: you just might enjoy yourself! 2

As you enter Chuck E. Cheese, don't be alarmed at the kids screaming and crying as they are being dragged out of the restaurant by their stressed-out parents. As you walk in, take a couple of deep breaths to calm the hairs that are standing up on the back of your neck. You notice a doorman as you enter, and you may think, "Great, a cover charge." Don't worry. There's no cover charge; the pizza prices are high enough to cover the restaurant's expenses. The doorman is there for security. While waiting in line, you'll see him stamp the hand of each member of your party. Upon leaving, the doorman checks everybody's stamp, making sure that no child leaves with someone else. That ensures that your kids are safe and won't be subject to any violence at this fun place. 3

After you get inside, go over to the pizza counter. Look over the coupon you brought with you, decide what pizza you want, and give the coupon to the pizza cashier with your order. Prepare to pay an outrageous price, even with the coupon. As you leave the counter, remember to take your order number so that your pizza can be delivered to your table. After going through the self-service beverage stand, find a table for your family. This might seem like an impossible task on a Friday or Saturday night since these two nights are the busiest of the week to go out for dinner, especially at Chuck E. Cheese. 4

As you seat yourselves, you may notice a large stage covered by a big curtain up in the front of the room. Then all of a sudden, you hear a band playing. Looking toward the stage, you see some oversized mechanical zoo animals playing musical instruments and singing. All the children in the audience become quiet and watch in amazement this modern-day technology band. After a short time, your hot, steaming pizza arrives at your table, and you watch the expression on your children's faces. Their eyes gleam with excitement as they are each handed a slice of pizza. 5

Once the pizza is gone, you're ready to leave and you start walk- 6
ing toward the exit. Before you can escape, though, your children yell,
"Mom/Dad, we have games to play!" With that, you know you're not
going to get out of Chuck E. Cheese easily.

When you walk into the gameroom, the only thing you can hear 7
is children screaming and the ding, bing, dong of the video games. As
you start to feel overwhelmed by the noise and craziness, take control of
your emotions: don't freak out. How do you think your children would
react if they walked into an adult's workplace? They would probably
have a lot of nervousness, just like you do right now walking into a
kid's playland. Instead of feeling tense, try to revert back to your childhood and just enjoy yourself. You'll not only have a good time, you will
probably improve your relationship with your child.

So reach into your right front pocket, pull out your wallet, buy a 8
handful of tokens, and hand them to your children. Join right in playing video games, skeeball, and any of the other games that are there.
Depending on how well you score in these games, you will receive a
certain number of tickets. Take the tickets to the counter, where you can
redeem them for imported Chinese trinkets. You discover that you are
having a blast, and in no time at all, the tokens are gone and so is your
budget for Chuck E. Cheese.

The time has come to leave. When you inform the children that it 9
is time to go, they whine and cry to stay and play one more game. Be
firm and don't budge in your decision, even if you almost have to drag
your children out to the car. On your way out, you will see other families
entering Chuck E. Cheese. You can see the excitement and glee in the
children's eyes, while on the other hand you see doubt on some of the
parents' faces. If one of the parents asks, "Is it bad in there tonight?"
reply, "It's all that you make it."

Driving home in the car, reflect on your adventure. The children 10
may be surprised at how much fun their old fuddy-duddy parent could
be. I remember having that exact feeling toward my dad also after a trip
to Shakey's Pizza. It's funny how some things don't change.

Meaning

1. What is Chuck E. Cheese? How does Erikson ensure that readers who have
   never been there will nonetheless understand what the place is like?

2. In his introduction, Erikson identifies three things readers will need in
   preparation for their outing. What are they? Why are they essential to
   successful completion of the process he describes?

3. If you are not familiar with any of the following words, try to guess their meanings based on their context in Erikson's essay. Check your guesses in a dictionary, and then use each new word in a sentence or two.

extravaganza (2) gleam (5) fuddy-duddy (10)
rekindle (2) skeeball (8)

Purpose and Audience

1. Why do you think Erikson chose this topic for his essay? Does he have a reason for writing beyond explaining what it's like to spend an evening at Chuck E. Cheese?

2. Erikson finds some unpleasantness in the restaurant, calling it a "living hell" (paragraph 1) with "kids screaming and crying" (3), "stressed-out parents" (3), and "noise and craziness" (7). Do these observations fit in with Erikson's purpose? Why, or why not?

3. What statements and references show that Erikson is trying to appeal to other parents? What assumptions does he make about his audience?

Method and Structure

1. Assuming that Erikson has a larger purpose in mind than merely teaching readers how to make it through an evening at Chuck E. Cheese, how does his process analysis help accomplish this purpose?

2. At several points in his essay, Erikson breaks from chronology to explain the reasons for a step. Identify at least two of these digressions. What do they contribute to Erikson's main idea?

3. Point out transitional words and phrases that Erikson uses as guideposts in his process analysis.

4. **OTHER METHODS** Where and how does Erikson use comparison and contrast (Chapter 11) to establish the significance of his subject?

Language

1. How seriously does Erikson take his subject? How can you tell?

2. What is the effect of "ding, bing, dong" in paragraph 7?

Writing Topics

1. **JOURNAL TO ESSAY** Building on your journal entry (p. 200), write an essay in which you analyze your preferences as a consumer of restaurant food. Make a list of all the elements that constitute this activity and the

setting in which it occurs. In your essay, examine each element to show what it contributes to the whole. Be sure your principle of analysis is clear to readers.

2. Using Erikson's essay as a model, write a directive process analysis explaining how to do something that is significant to you but that others may not know about. For instance, you might tell readers how to protect a home from intruders, how to thwart identity thieves, how to reduce one's carbon footprint, or how to become a foster parent. Be sure to explain why your subject is meaningful and to identify all the steps involved.

3. Erikson's explanation of how to enjoy Chuck E. Cheese is written from a wary parent's perspective. If you have been to that restaurant, or to one like it, try writing a directive process analysis that explains, from the children's point of view, how to drive parents crazy.

4. **CULTURAL CONSIDERATIONS**   Early in his essay, Erikson casually mentions the possibility of child abduction: "The doorman is there for security. While waiting in line, you'll see him stamp the hand of each member of your party. Upon leaving, the doorman checks everybody's stamp, making sure that no child leaves with someone else. That ensures your kids are safe and won't be subject to any violence at this fun place" (paragraph 3). Although Erikson's comments are meant to be reassuring, they do remind us that many parents fear their children will be kidnapped from public places. In your opinion, how real and serious is this threat? Do parents need to be extra vigilant with their children, or do the media overstate the risk of child abduction by sensationalizing isolated incidents? Why do you think so? You may want to provide evidence from experts to support your opinion; see pages 362–85 for information on finding and using sources.

5. **CONNECTIONS**   Like Erikson, Ashley Rhodes, in "Fatherhood Is Essential" (p. 259), suggests that parents must sometimes sacrifice their own comfort to strengthen their relationships with their children. Write an essay that compares these writers' beliefs about the rewards and responsibilities of parenting. Is one more realistic than the other? Cite specific examples from both essays to support your conclusions.

Waste not, want not. —Proverb

Our modern industrial economy takes a mountain covered with trees, lakes, and running streams and transforms it into a mountain of junk, garbage, slime pits, and debris. —Edward Abbey

What counts as trash depends on who's counting. —Susan Strasser

JOURNAL RESPONSE In a journal entry, comment on one example of material or energy waste, such as plastic shopping bags, disposable razors, or gas-guzzling cars. Where do you observe the waste happening? What causes it? Is it a significant problem? Should, or can, anything be done about it?

Lars Eighner

An essayist and fiction writer, Lars Eighner was born in 1948 in Texas and attended the University of Texas at Austin. He has contributed essays to *Threepenny Review* and stories to that periodical as well as to *Advocate Men, The Guide,* and *Inches.* He published a volume of short fiction, *Bayou Boys and Other Stories,* in 1985. In 1988 Eighner became homeless after leaving a job he had held for ten years as an attendant in a mental hospital. His memoir about living on the streets, *Travels with Lizbeth* (1993), was critically acclaimed and sold enough copies to get him back on his feet. He now lives in a small apartment in Austin and supports himself as a novelist and fiction writer.

Dumpster Diving

This essay from a 1992 issue of *Utne Reader* was abridged from a prize-winning piece published in *Threepenny Review* and later included in *Travels with Lizbeth.* Eighner explains a process that you probably do not want to learn: how to subsist on what you can scavenge from trash. But, as Eighner observes, scavenging has lessons to teach about value.

I began Dumpster diving about a year before I became homeless.   1

I prefer the term *scavenging.* I have heard people, evidently meaning   2
to be polite, use the word *foraging,* but I prefer to reserve that word for gathering nuts and berries and such, which I also do, according to the season and opportunity.

I like the frankness of the word *scavenging*. I live from the refuse 3
of others. I am a scavenger. I think it a sound and honorable niche,
although if I could I would naturally prefer to live the comfortable consumer life, perhaps—and only perhaps—as a slightly less wasteful consumer owing to what I have learned as a scavenger.

Except for jeans, all my clothes come from Dumpsters. Boom boxes, 4
candles, bedding, toilet paper, medicine, books, a typewriter, a virgin
male love doll, coins sometimes amounting to many dollars: all came
from Dumpsters. And yes, I eat from Dumpsters, too.

There is a predictable series of stages that a person goes through in 5
learning to scavenge. At first the new scavenger is filled with disgust and
self-loathing. He is ashamed of being seen.

This stage passes with experience. The scavenger finds a pair of run- 6
ning shoes that fit and look and smell brand-new. He finds a pocket cal-
culator in perfect working order. He finds pristine ice cream, still frozen,
more than he can eat or keep. He begins to understand: people do throw
away perfectly good stuff, a lot of perfectly good stuff.

At this stage he may become lost and never recover. All the Dumpster 7
divers I have known come to the point of trying to acquire everything
they touch. Why not take it, they reason, it is all free. This is, of course,
hopeless, and most divers come to realize that they must restrict themselves to items of relatively immediate utility.

The finding of objects is becoming something of an urban art. Even 8
respectable, employed people will sometimes find something tempting
sticking out of a Dumpster or standing beside one. Quite a number of
people, not all of them of the bohemian type, are wiling to brag that
they found this or that piece in the trash.

But eating from Dumpsters is the thing that separates the dilettanti 9
from the professionals. Eating safely involves three principles: using the
senses and common sense to evaluate the condition of the found materials; knowing the Dumpsters of a given area and checking them regularly;
and seeking always to answer the question "Why was this discarded?"

Yet perfectly good food can be found in Dumpsters. Canned goods, 10
for example, turn up fairly often in the Dumpsters I frequent. I also have
few qualms about dry goods such as crackers, cookies, cereal, chips, and
pasta if they are free of visible contaminants and still dry and crisp.
Raw fruits and vegetables with intact skins seem perfectly safe to me,
excluding, of course, the obviously rotten. Many are discarded for minor
imperfections that can be pared away.

A typical discard is a half jar of peanut butter—though non- 11
organic peanut butter does not require refrigeration and is unlikely to
spoil in any reasonable time. One of my favorite finds is yogurt—often

discarded, still sealed, when the expiration date has passed—because it will keep for several days, even in warm weather.

No matter how careful I am I still get dysentery at least once a 12 month, oftener in warm weather. I do not want to paint too romantic a picture. Dumpster diving has serious drawbacks as a way of life.

I find from the experience of scavenging two rather deep lessons. 13 The first is to take what I can use and let the rest go. I have come to think that there is no value in the abstract. A thing I cannot use or make useful, perhaps by trading, has no value, however fine or rare it may be.

The second lesson is the transience of material being. I do not sup- 14 pose that ideas are immortal, but certainly they are longer-lived than material objects.

The things I find in Dumpsters, the love letters and rag dolls of so 15 many lives, remind me of this lesson. Now I hardly pick up a thing without envisioning the time I will cast it away. This, I think, is a healthy state of mind. Almost everything I have now has already been cast out at least once, proving that what I own is valueless to someone.

I find that my desire to grab for the gaudy bauble has been largely 16 sated. I think this is an attitude I share with the very wealthy—we both know there is plenty more where whatever we have came from. Between us are the rat-race millions who have confounded their selves with the objects they grasp and who nightly scavenge the cable channels for they know not what.

I am sorry for them. 17

Meaning

1. Eighner ends his essay with the statement "I am sorry for them." Whom is he sorry for, and why? How does this statement relate to the main point of Eighner's essay?

2. How does Eighner decide what to keep when he digs through Dumpsters? How does he decide a thing's value? What evidence in the essay supports your answer?

3. If you do not know the meanings of the following words, try to guess them from their context in Eighner's essay. Then look them up in a dictionary, and use each one in a sentence or two of your own:

scavenging (2)	qualms (10)	bauble (16)
foraging (2)	contaminants (10)	sated (16)
refuse (3)	dysentery (12)	confounded (16)
niche (3)	transience (14)	
dilettanti (9)	gaudy (16)	

Purpose and Audience

1. How does paragraph 2 reveal that Eighner's purpose is not simply to explain how to scavenge but also to persuade his readers to examine any stereotypes they may hold about scavengers?

2. In paragraphs 10 and 11 Eighner goes into considerable detail about the food he finds in Dumpsters. Why do you think he does this?

Method and Structure

1. Eighner identifies three main stages "a person goes through in learning to scavenge" (paragraph 5). What are these stages, and do all scavengers experience each one? Support your answer with evidence from the essay.

2. **OTHER METHODS**   In paragraph 2 Eighner uses definition (Chapter 12) to distinguish *foraging* from *scavenging*. What is the distinction he makes? How does it relate to the overall meaning of the essay?

Language

1. Eighner says of his life as a scavenger, "I think it a sound and honorable niche, although if I could I would naturally prefer to live the comfortable consumer life" (paragraph 3). How would you characterize the tone of this statement? Where else in the essay do you find this tone?

2. Eighner's style is often formal: consider the word choice and order in such phrases as "I think it a sound and honorable niche" (paragraph 3) and "who nightly scavenge the cable channels for they know not what" (16). Find at least three other instances of formal style. What is the effect of this language, and how does it further Eighner's purpose? (If necessary, consult *style* in the Glossary.)

Writing Topics

1. **JOURNAL TO ESSAY**   Take off from the comments you made in your journal entry (p. 205) to write an essay about protection of the environment. Do you regard waste and pollution as critical problems? Do you believe that the government is taking adequate steps to protect the environment? Do you believe that the actions of individuals can make a difference? Your essay may but need not be an argument: that is, you could explain your answer to any of these questions or argue a specific point. Either way, use examples and details to support your ideas.

2. Eighner writes that since he became a scavenger he hardly "pick[s] up a thing without envisioning the time I will cast it away. This, I think, is a healthy state of mind" (paragraph 15). Do you agree? What associations do you have with material objects that cause you to support or deny Eighner's claim? Do you own things that matter a great deal to you, or would it be relatively easy to cast many of your possessions away? Write an essay arguing either for or against Eighner's position, making sure to provide your own illustrations to support your argument.

3. Eighner writes that he and the very wealthy share the attitude that "there is plenty more where whatever we have came from" (paragraph 16). In your experience, how true is this statement? Do you agree that one needs to be very poor or very rich to feel this way? Is this state of mind a response to the amount of money one has, or can it be developed independently, regardless of one's wealth or lack of it? Write an essay describing how you think people arrive at a belief that "there is plenty more" available of whatever it is they have.

4. **CULTURAL CONSIDERATIONS** Eighner attempts to teach his readers how to scavenge, certainly, but he also attempts to persuade readers to examine their stereotypes about the homeless. Write an essay in which you examine your stereotypes about homeless people. Describe both personal encounters and media images, and discuss how these experiences led to your beliefs. Finally, consider the extent to which "Dumpster Diving" changed your perspective.

5. **CONNECTIONS** If you live in or have visited an urban area, you have probably seen people picking through dumpsters or garbage cans, looking for items such as food, clothing, and bottles or cans that can be returned for a deposit. Consider your own experiences and observations as well as the information and ideas in Eighner's essay and in Barbara Lazear Ascher's "The Box Man" (p. 9). Write an essay proposing a solution to the social problems of extreme poverty and homelessness.

Eat food. Not too much. Mostly plants. —Michael Pollan

Did you ever stop to taste a carrot? Not just eat it, but taste it? You can't taste the beauty and energy of the earth in a Twinkie. —Astrid Alauda

A vegetable garden in the beginning looks so promising and then after all little by little it grows nothing but vegetables, nothing, nothing but vegetables. —Gertrude Stein

JOURNAL RESPONSE Current dietary guidelines recommend eating at least five servings of fruits and vegetables a day. Assuming you wanted to follow this advice, how easy, or difficult, would it be for you to do so? In your journal, consider what vegetables you eat, how often you eat them, and why you like or dislike them.

Barbara Kingsolver

Barbara Kingsolver is a well-known naturalist and best-selling author of more than a dozen novels, short-story and poetry collections, and nonfiction books, including *The Bean Trees* (1988), *The Poisonwood Bible* (1998), *Small Wonder* (2002), *Animal, Vegetable, Miracle* (2007), and *The Lacuna* (2009). She was born in 1955 in Annapolis, Maryland, grew up in rural Kentucky, and earned a BA in biology from DePauw University and an MS in ecology and evolutionary biology from the University of Arizona. Kingsolver worked briefly as a lab assistant before taking an office position at the University of Arizona and building a career as a writer. An activist with a strong sense of social justice, Kingsolver has written that "good art is political, whether it means to be or not, insofar as it provides the chance to understand points of view alien to our own." She lives in the Appalachian region of Virginia with her husband and two daughters.

Stalking the Vegetannual

Animal, Vegetable, Miracle documents a year in the life of Kingsolver and her family, when they moved to an ancestral farm and challenged themselves to eat only what they could produce themselves or obtain from local growers. In this excerpt from the book, Kingsolver advises how to recognize what vegetables are in season, a skill largely lost in a society accustomed to seeing strawberries and asparagus in the supermarket year-round.

If potatoes can surprise some part of their audience by growing leaves, it   1
may not have occurred to everyone that lettuce has a flower part. It does,
they all do. Virtually all nonanimal foods we eat come from flowering
plants. Exceptions are mushrooms, seaweeds, and pine nuts. If other
exotic edibles exist that you call food, I salute you.

Flowering plants, known botanically as angiosperms, evolved from   2
ancestors similar to our modern-day conifers. The flower is a handy
reproductive organ that came into its own during the Cretaceous era,[1]
right around the time when dinosaurs were for whatever reason getting downsized. In the millions of years since then, flowering plants
have established themselves as the most conspicuously successful terres-
trial life forms ever, having moved into every kind of habitat, in infinite
variations. Flowering plants are key players in all the world's ecotypes:
the deciduous forests, the rain forests, the grasslands. They are the desert cacti and the tundra scrub. They're small and they're large, they fill
swamps and tolerate drought, they have settled into most every niche in
every kind of place. It only stands to reason that we would eat them.

Flowering plants come in packages as different as an oak tree and a   3
violet, but they all have a basic life history in common. They sprout and
leaf out; they bloom and have sex by somehow rubbing one flower's boy
stuff against another's girl parts. Since they can't engage in hot pursuit,
they lure a third party, such as bees, into the sexual act—or else (depending on species) wait for the wind. From that union comes the blessed event,
babies made, in the form of seeds cradled inside some form of fruit. Finally,
sooner or later—because after *that*, what's the point anymore?—they die.

---

[1] Roughly 145–65 million years ago. [Editors' note.]

Among the plants known as annuals, this life history is accomplished all in a single growing season, commonly starting with spring and ending with frost. The plant waits out the winter in the form of a seed, safely protected from weather, biding its time until conditions are right for starting over again. The vegetables we eat may be leaves, buds, fruits, or seeds, but each comes to us from some point along this same continuum, the code all annual plants must live by. No variations are allowed. They can't set fruit, for example, before they bloom. As obvious as this may seem, it's easy enough to forget in a supermarket culture where the plant stages constantly present themselves in random order.

To recover an intuitive sense of what will be in season throughout   4
the year, picture a season of foods unfolding as if from one single plant. Take a minute to study this creation—an imaginary plant that bears over the course of one growing season a cornucopia of all the different vegetable products we can harvest. We'll call it a vegetannual. Picture its life passing before your eyes like a time-lapse film: first, in the cool early spring, shoots poke up out of the ground. Small leaves appear, then bigger leaves. As the plant grows up into the sunshine and the days grow longer, flower buds will appear, followed by small green fruits. Under midsummer's warm sun, the fruits grow larger, riper, and more colorful. As days shorten into the autumn, these mature into hard-shelled fruits with appreciable seeds inside. Finally, as the days grow cool, the vegetannual may hoard the sugars its leaves have made, pulling them down into a storage unit of some kind: a tuber, bulb, or root.

So goes the year. First the leaves: spinach, kale, lettuce, and chard   5
(here, that's April and May). Then more mature heads of leaves and flower heads: cabbage, romaine, broccoli, and cauliflower (May–June). Then tender young fruit-set: snow peas, baby squash, cucumbers (June), followed by green beans, green peppers, and small tomatoes (July). Then more mature, colorfully ripened fruits: beefsteak tomatoes, eggplants, red and yellow peppers (late July–August). Then the large, hard-shelled fruits with developed seeds inside: cantaloupes, honeydews, watermelons, pumpkins, winter squash (August–September). Last come the root crops, and so ends the produce parade.

Plainly these don't all come from the same plant, but each comes   6
from a *plant*, that's the point—a plant predestined to begin its life in the spring and die in the fall. (A few, like onions and carrots, are attempting to be biennials, but we'll ignore that for now.) Each plant part we eat must come in its turn—leaves, buds, flowers, green fruits, ripe fruits, hard fruits—because that is the necessary order of things for an annual plant. For the life of them, they can't do it differently.

Some minor deviations and a bit of overlap are allowed, but in   7
general picturing an imaginary vegetannual plant is a pretty reliable
guide to what will be in season, wherever you live. If you find yourself eating a watermelon in April, you can count back three months
and imagine a place warm enough in January for this plant to have
launched its destiny. Mexico maybe, or southern California. Chile is
also a possibility. If you're inclined to think this way, consider what
it took to transport a finicky fruit the size of a human toddler to your
door, from that locale.

Our gardening forebears meant watermelon to be the juicy, barefoot   8
taste of a hot summer's end, just as a pumpkin is the trademark fruit of late
October. Most of us accept the latter, and limit our jack-o'lantern activities to the proper botanical season. Waiting for a watermelon is harder.
It's tempting to reach for melons, red peppers, tomatoes, and other late-
summer delights before the summer even arrives. But it's actually possible
to wait, celebrating each season when it comes, not fretting about its being
absent at all other times because something else good is at hand.

If many of us would view this style of eating as deprivation, that's   9
only because we've grown accustomed to the botanically outrageous
condition of having everything, always. This may be the closest thing
we have right now to a distinctive national cuisine. Well-heeled North
American epicures are likely to gather around a table where whole con-
tinents collide discreetly on a white tablecloth: New Zealand lamb with
Italian porcinis,[2] Peruvian asparagus, and a hearty French Bordeaux. The
date on the calendar is utterly irrelevant.

I've enjoyed my share of such meals, but I'm beginning at least to   10
notice when I'm consuming the United Nations of edible plants and
animals all in one seating. (Or the WTO,[3] is more like it.) On a winter's
day not long ago I was served a sumptuous meal like this, finished off
with a dessert of raspberries. Because they only grow in temperate zones,
not the tropics, these would have come from somewhere deep in the
Southern Hemisphere. I was amazed that such small, eminently bruis-
able fruits could survive a zillion-mile trip looking so good (I myself look
pretty wrecked after a mere red-eye from California), and I mumbled
some reserved awe over that fact. I think my hostess was amused by my
country-mouse naiveté. "This is New York," she assured me. "We can get
anything we want, any day of the year."

---

[2] Mushrooms. [Editors' note.]

[3] World Trade Organization. [Editors' note.]

So it is. And I don't wish to be ungracious, but we get it at a price. Most   11
of that is not measured in money, but in untallied debts that will be paid
by our children in the currency of extinctions, economic unravelings, and
global climate change. I do know it's impolite to raise such objections at
the dinner table. Seven raspberries are not (I'll try to explain someday to
my grandkids) the end of the world. I ate them and said "Thank you." . . .

The business of importing foods across great distances is not, by its   12
nature, a boon to Third World farmers, but it's very good business for oil
companies. Transporting a single calorie of a perishable fresh fruit from
California to New York takes about 87 calories worth of fuel. That's as
efficient as driving from Philadelphia to Annapolis, and back, in order to
walk three miles on a treadmill in a Maryland gym. . . .

In many social circles it's ordinary for hosts to accommodate veg-   13
etarian guests, even if they're carnivores themselves. Maybe the world
would likewise become more hospitable to diners who are queasy about
fuel-guzzling foods, if that preference had a name. Petrolophobes? Sea-
sonaltarians? Local eaters, Homeys? Lately I've begun seeing the term
locavores, and I like it: both scientifically and socially descriptive, with
just the right hint of "Livin' *la vida loca.*"[4]

Slow Food International has done a good job of putting a smile on   14
this eating style, rather than a pious frown, even while sticking to the
quixotic agenda of fighting overcentralized agribusiness. The engaging
strategy of the Slowies (their logo is a snail) is to celebrate what we have,
standing up for the pleasures that seasonal eating can bring. They have
their work cut out for them, as the American brain trust seems mostly
blank on that subject. Consider the frustration of the man who wrote in
this complaint to a food columnist: having studied the new food pyramid
brought to us by the US Dietary Guidelines folks (impossible to decipher
but bless them, they do keep trying), he had his marching orders for "2
cups of fruit, 2½ cups of vegetables a day." So he marched down to his
grocery and bought (honest to Pete) eighty-three plums, pears, peaches,
and apples. Outraged, he reported that virtually the entire lot was "rotten,
mealy, tasteless, juiceless, or hard as a rock and refusing to ripen."

Given the date of the column, this had occurred in February or March.   15
The gentleman lived in Frostburg, Maryland, where they would still have
been deeply involved in a thing called winter. I'm sure he didn't really
think tasty tree-ripened plums, peaches, and apples were hanging outside
ripe for the picking in the orchards around . . . um, *Frost*-burg. Probably he
didn't think "orchard" at all—how many of us do, in the same sentence
with "fruit"? Our dietary guidelines come to us without a roadmap.

---

[4] Spanish for "the crazy life." [Editors' note.]

Concentrating on local foods means thinking of fruit invariably as   16
the product of an orchard, and a winter squash as the fruit of an early-
winter farm. It's a strategy that will keep grocery money in the neighborhood where it gets recycled into your own school system and local businesses. The green spaces surrounding your town stay green, and farmers
who live nearby get to grow more food next year, for you. But before
any of that, it's a win-win strategy for anyone with taste buds. It begins
with rethinking a position that is only superficially about deprivation.
Citizens of frosty worlds unite, and think about marching past the off-
season fruits: you have nothing to lose but mealy, juiceless, rock-hard
and refusing to ripen.

Meaning

1. What, according to Kingsolver, is a *vegetannual*? What does it have to do
   with her purpose for writing?

2. Identify two possible meanings of the word *stalking* in Kingsolver's title.
   How does the word help preview the focus of her essay?

3. Kingsolver comments in paragraph 9 that "we've grown accustomed
   to the botanically outrageous condition of having everything, always."
   What does she mean? Why is this situation "outrageous"?

4. Some of the following words may be new to you. Before looking them
   up in a dictionary, try to guess their meanings from their context in
   Kingsolver's essay. Then use each new word in a sentence or more.

botanical (2, 8, 9)	tuber (4)	sumptuous (10)
conifers (2)	predestined (6)	temperate (10)
terrestrial (2)	biennials (6)	eminently (10)
ecotypes (2)	deviations (7)	untallied (11)
deciduous (2)	forebears (8)	boon (12)
tundra (2)	latter (8)	hospitable (13)
scrub (2)	fretting (8)	pious (14)
annuals (3, 6)	deprivation (9, 16)	quixotic (14)
continuum (3)	epicures (9)	invariably (16)
cornucopia (4)	discreetly (9)	

Purpose and Audience

1. Why does Kingsolver withhold her thesis statement until the very last
   sentence of her essay? How would you have reacted to her main idea if
   she had opened with it?

2. Kingsolver's chief assumption about her readers is evident in paragraph 9.
   What is it?

Method and Structure

1. Why do you think Kingsolver chose the method of process analysis to explore her subject? What does the method allow her to convey about the practice of eating fruits and vegetables that are not in season locally?

2. Despite the fact that her purpose goes beyond mere explanation, does Kingsolver explain the process of plant growth clearly enough for you to understand how it works and why it matters? What are the main stages of the process?

3. Take a close look at the drawing that opens the essay. What does it represent? Where in her essay does Kingsolver discuss it, and what does it have to do with her subject?

4. **OTHER METHODS**   The process analysis portion of "Stalking the Veget-annual" seems to come to an end at paragraph 9. Why do you suppose Kingsolver turns to example (Chapter 7), cause-and-effect analysis (Chapter 13), and argument and persuasion (Chapter 14) to complete her thoughts?

Language

1. How would you describe Kingsolver's tone? How can you tell that the author is personally invested in the process she is explaining? (See pp. 41–43 for more on tone.)

2. Notice Kingsolver's use of personification to explain the life cycle of plants in paragraph 3. (If necessary, see p. 57 for a definition of personification.) What does this figure of speech add to (or detract from) her analysis?

3. How does the author attempt to make her ideas accessible while also maintaining her sophistication? In your opinion, is this essay difficult to read, easy to read, or something in between? Why?

Writing Topics

1. **JOURNAL TO ESSAY**   In your journal entry (p. 210), you wrote about the vegetables you eat. Now that you've read Kingsolver's essay, do you have any misgivings about your habits? Has she inspired you to change the way you look at food? Why, or why not? Explain your answers in a brief essay.

2. How do you react to Kingsolver's essay? Do you agree with her that a person's food choices have broad-ranging environmental and economic consequences? Or do you think her local foods solution is impractical and

overly idealistic? Write an essay of your own responding to Kingsolver's ideas. Be sure to include examples to support your view.

3. **CULTURAL CONSIDERATIONS** Our attitudes toward foods are often influenced by the family, community, or larger culture in which we grew up. Think of feelings that you have about a particular food that seem at least partly due to other people. In an essay describe the food and your feelings about it and explain the origins of your feelings as best you can.

4. **CONNECTIONS** In "Dumpster Diving" (p. 205), Lars Eighner comments that he is accustomed to "gathering nuts and berries and such . . . according to the season and opportunity." But, unlike Kingsolver, he doesn't have much choice in what or when he eats. Or does he? Write an essay that considers what these two writers, who live under very different circumstances, share in their attitudes toward food and the environment.

Process Analysis

Select one of the following topics, or any other topic they suggest, for an essay developed by process analysis. Be sure to choose a topic you care about so that process analysis is a means of communicating an idea, not an end in itself.

TECHNOLOGY AND THE ENVIRONMENT

1. How an engine or other machine works
2. How the Internet works
3. Setting up a recycling program in a home or an office
4. How solar energy can be converted into electricity

EDUCATION AND CAREER

5. How children learn to dress themselves, play with others, read, or write
6. Reading a newspaper
7. Interviewing for a job
8. Succeeding in biology, history, computer science, or another course
9. Coping with a bad boss

ENTERTAINMENT AND HOBBIES

10. Performing a magic trick
11. Throwing a really *bad* party
12. Climbing a mountain
13. Playing a sport or a musical instrument
14. Making great chili or some other dish

FAMILY AND FRIENDS

15. Offering constructive criticism to a friend
16. Driving your parents, brother, sister, friend, or roommate crazy
17. Minimizing sibling rivalry
18. Making new friends in a new place

WRITING ABOUT THE THEME

Eating Well

1. Many of the essays in this chapter offer techniques for overcoming difficulties with eating: L. Rust Hills equates an ice-cream cone with a live bomb (p. 194); Jane Brody emphasizes the challenges faced by dieters (p. 195); Glenn Erikson describes the restaurant Chuck E. Cheese as "a living hell" (p. 200); Lars Eighner reports experiencing "disgust and self-loathing" while scavenging (p. 205); and even Barbara Kingsolver faces social obstacles in her quest to avoid nonlocal foods (p. 210). Using these works as models, write a process analysis about an activity you find simultaneously difficult and rewarding, making sure to convey both feelings to your readers.

2. Barbara Kingsolver attends dinner parties that feature exotic foods imported from around the globe, and Glenn Erikson pays an "outrageous price" so his kids can eat pizza in a funhouse, while Lars Eighner subsists on the food that other people throw away. How do you feel about this kind of discrepancy? Is eating well a basic human right, or is food just another commodity governed by the laws of supply and demand? Can the problem of world hunger be solved? Explain your answers in an essay. Be sure to back up your general statements with specific examples and other evidence.

3. Some writers in this chapter reveal mixed feelings about the business side of eating. Jane Brody expresses concern about the safety and effectiveness of commercial weight-loss plans. Glenn Erikson experiences both pleasure and terror in a chain restaurant. And Barbara Kingsolver speaks of "fighting overcentralized agribusiness." How do you feel about the food and diet industries? Do you trust the companies that grow, process, and distribute the food you eat? What do you think accounts for your attitude? Drawing on the readings in this chapter and your own experience, write an essay that explains why you do, or don't, have faith in the food industry.

11

COMPARISON AND CONTRAST
Evaluating Stereotypes

An insomniac watching late-night television faces a choice between two World War II movies broadcasting at the same time. To make up his mind, he uses the dual method of comparison and contrast:

- **Comparison** shows the similarities between two or more subjects: the similar broadcast times and topics of the two movies force the insomniac to choose between them.

- **Contrast** shows the differences between subjects: the different actors, locations, and reputations of the two movies make it possible for the insomniac to choose one.

As in the example, comparison and contrast usually work together, because any subjects that warrant side-by-side examination usually resemble each other in some respects and differ in others. (Since comparison and contrast are so closely related, the terms *comparison* and *compare* will be used from now on to designate both.) You use the method instinctively whenever you need to choose among options—for instance, two political candidates, four tiers of company health benefits, or several pairs of running shoes. You might also use comparison to make sense of competing proposals for calming traffic in a congested neighborhood, to explain how nursing has changed in the past ten years, or to understand why some environmentalists warn of global warming while others are concerned about global cooling. Writers, too, often draw on the method, especially when a comparison can explain something that may be unfamiliar to their readers.

Reading Comparison and Contrast

Writers generally use comparison for one of two purposes:

- To **explain** the similarities and differences between subjects so as to make either or both of them clear.
- To **evaluate** subjects so as to establish their advantages and disadvantages, strengths and weaknesses.

The explanatory comparison does not take a position on the relative merits of the subjects; the evaluative comparison does, and it usually concludes with a preference or a suggested course of action. An explanatory comparison in a health magazine, for example, might show the similarities and differences between two popular diet plans; an evaluative comparison on the same subject might argue that one plan is better than the other.

Whether explanatory or evaluative, comparisons treat two or more subjects in the same general class or group: tax laws, religions, attitudes toward marriage, diseases, advertising strategies, diets, contact sports, friends. A writer may define the class to suit his or her interest—for instance, a television critic might focus on medical dramas, on cable news programs, or on classic situation comedies. The class likeness ensures that the subjects share enough features to make comparison worthwhile. With subjects from different classes, such as an insect and a tree, the similarities are so few and differences so numerous—and both are so obvious—that explaining them would be pointless.

In putting together a comparison, a writer selects subjects from the same class and then, using division or analysis, identifies the features shared by the subjects. These **points of comparison** are the attributes of the class and thus of the subjects within the class. For instance, the points of comparison for diets may be forbidden foods, allowed foods, speed of weight loss, and nutritional quality; for air pollutants they may be sources and dangers to plants, animals, and humans. These points help to arrange similarities and differences between subjects, and, more important, they ensure direct comparison rather than a random listing of unrelated characteristics.

In an effective comparison, a thesis or controlling idea governs the choice of class, points of comparison, and specific similarities and differences, while also making the comparison worthwhile for the reader.

With two or more subjects, several points of comparison, many similarities and differences, and a particular emphasis, comparison clearly requires a firm organizational hand. Writers have two options for arranging a comparison:

- **Subject-by-subject**, in which the points of comparison are grouped under each subject so that the *subjects* are covered one at a time.

- **Point-by-point**, in which the subjects are grouped under each point of comparison so that the *points* are covered one at a time.

The following brief outlines illustrate the different arrangements as they might be applied to diets:

Subject-by-subject	*Point-by-point*
Harris's diet	Speed of weight loss
Speed of weight loss	Harris's diet
Required self-discipline	Marconi's diet
Nutritional risk	Required self-discipline
Marconi's diet	Harris's diet
Speed of weight loss	Marconi's diet
Required self-discipline	Nutritional risk
Nutritional risk	Harris's diet
	Marconi's diet

Since the subject-by-subject arrangement presents each subject as a coherent unit, it is particularly useful for comparing impressions of subjects: the dissimilar characters of two friends, for instance. However, covering the subjects one at a time can break an essay into discrete pieces and strain readers' memories, so this arrangement is usually confined to essays that are short or that compare several subjects briefly. For longer comparisons requiring precise treatment of the individual points—say, an evaluation of two proposals for a new student-aid policy—the point-by-point arrangement is more useful. Its chief disadvantage is that the reader can get lost in the details and fail to see any subject as a whole. Because each arrangement has its strengths and weaknesses, writers sometimes combine the two in a single work, using the divided arrangement to introduce or summarize overall impressions of the subjects and using the alternating arrangement to deal specifically with the points of comparison.

Analyzing Comparison and Contrast in Paragraphs

Michael Dorris (1945–97) was a fiction and nonfiction writer who, as a member of the Modoc tribe, explored Native American issues and experiences. The following paragraph comes from "Noble Savages? We'll Drink to That," first published in the *New York Times* in April 1992.

For centuries, flesh and blood Indians have been assigned the role of a popular-culture metaphor. Today, their evocation instantly connotes fuzzy images of Nature, the Past, Plight, or Summer Camp. War-bonneted apparitions pasted to football helmets or baseball caps act as opaque, impermeable curtains, solid walls of white noise that for many citizens block or distort all vision of the nearly two million Native Americans today. And why not? Such honoring relegates Indians to the long ago and thus makes them magically disappear from public consciousness and conscience. What do the 300 federally recognized tribes, and their various complicated treaties governing land rights and protections, their crippling teenage suicide rates, their manifold health problems have in common with jolly (or menacing) cartoon caricatures, wistful braves, or raven-tressed Mazola girls?

> Subject-by-subject organization
>
> 1. The image in popular culture
>
> Comparison clarified by transitions (underlined once) and repetition (underlined twice)
>
> 2. The reality of Native American life

Julia Álvarez (born 1950) is a novelist, poet, essayist, and teacher. Born in New York and raised in the Dominican Republic until the age of ten when her family fled political upheaval, Álvarez often writes about the complexities of immigration and bicultural identity. In this paragraph from her essay "A White Woman of Color," she examines class tensions within her immediate family.

It was Mami's family who were *really* white. They were white in terms of race, and white also in terms of class. From them came the fine features, the pale skin, the lank hair. Her brothers and uncles went to schools abroad and had important businesses in the country. . . .

> Point-by-point organization
>
> 1. Education

Not that Papi's family weren't smart and enterprising, all twenty-five brothers and sisters. (The size of the family in and of itself was considered very country by some members of Mami's family.) Many of Papi's brothers had gone to the university and become professionals. But their education was totally island—no fancy degrees from Andover and Cornell and Yale, no summer camps or school songs in another language. Papi's family still lived in the interior versus the capital, in old-fashioned houses without air conditioning, decorated in ways my mother's family would have considered, well, taste-less. . . . They were *criollos*—creoles—rather than cosmo-politans, expansive, proud, colorful. . . . Their features were less aquiline than Mother's family's, the skin darker, the hair coarse and curly. Their money still had the smell of the earth on it and was kept in a wad in their back pock-ets, whereas my mother's family had money in the Chase Manhattan Bank, most of it with George Washington's picture on it, not Juan Pablo Duarte's.

> Comparison clarified by transitions (underlined once) and repetition (underlined twice)

> 2. Housing

> 3. Appearance

> 4. Money

Developing an Essay by Comparison and Contrast

Getting Started

Whenever you observe similarities or differences between two or more members of the same general class—activities, people, ideas, things, places—you have a possible subject for comparison and contrast. Just be sure that the subjects are worth comparing and that you can do the job in the space and time allowed. For instance, if you have a week to complete a three-page paper, don't try to show all the similarities and differences between country-and-western music and rhythm and blues. The effort can only frustrate you and irritate your readers. Instead, limit the subjects to a manageable size—for instance, the lyrics of a represen-tative song in each type of music—so that you can develop the compari-sons completely and specifically.

To generate ideas for a comparison, explore each subject separately to pick out its characteristics, and then explore the subjects together to see what characteristics one suggests for the other. Look for points of comparison. Early on, you can use division or analysis (Chapter 8) to identify points of comparison by breaking the subjects' general class into its elements. A song lyric, for instance, could be divided into story line or plot, basic emotion, and special language such as dialect or slang. After you have explored your subjects fully, you can use classification (Chapter 9) to group your characteristics under the points of comparison. For instance, you might classify characteristics of two proposals for a new student-aid policy into qualifications for aid, minimum and maximum amounts to be made available, and repayment terms.

As you gain increasing control over your material, consider also the needs of your readers:

- Do they know your subjects well, or will you need to take special care to explain one or both of them?

- Will your readers be equally interested in similarities and differences, or will they find one more enlightening than the other?

Forming a Thesis

While you are shaping your ideas, you should also begin formulating your controlling idea, your thesis. The first thing you should do is look over your points of comparison and determine whether they suggest an explanatory or evaluative approach.

The thesis of an evaluative comparison will generally emerge naturally because it coincides with your purpose of supporting a preference for one subject over another:

THESIS SENTENCE (EVALUATION) The two diets result in similarly rapid weight loss, but Harris's requires much more self-discipline and is nutritionally much riskier than Marconi's.

In an explanatory comparison, however, your thesis will need to do more than merely reflect your general purpose in explaining. It should go beyond the obvious and begin to identify the points of comparison. For example:

TENTATIVE THESIS SENTENCE (EXPLANATION) Rugby and American football are the same in some respects and different in others.

REVISED THESIS SENTENCE (EXPLANATION) Though rugby requires less strength and more stamina than American football, the two games are very much alike in their rules and strategies.

These examples suggest other decisions you must make when formulating a thesis:

- Will you emphasize both subjects equally or stress one over the other?
- Will you emphasize differences, similarities, or both?

Keeping your readers in mind as you make these decisions will make it easier to use your thesis to shape the body of your essay. For instance, if you decide to write an evaluative comparison and your readers are likely to be biased against your preference or recommendation, you will need to support your case with plenty of specific reasons. If the subjects are equally familiar or important to your readers (as the diets are in the previous example), you'll want to give them equal emphasis, but if one subject is unfamiliar (as rugby is in this country), you will probably need to stress it over the other.

Knowing your audience will also help you decide whether to focus on similarities, differences, or both. Generally, you'll stress the differences between subjects your readers consider similar (such as diets) and the similarities between subjects they are likely to consider different (such as rugby and American football).

Organizing

Your readers' needs and expectations can also help you plan your essay's organization. An effective introduction to a comparison essay often provides some context for readers—the situation that prompts the comparison, for instance, or the need for the comparison. Placing your thesis sentence in the introduction also informs readers of your purpose and point, and it may help keep you focused while you write.

For the body of the essay, choose the arrangement that will present your material most clearly and effectively. Remember that the subject-by-subject arrangement suits brief essays comparing dominant impressions of the subjects, whereas the point-by-point arrangement suits longer essays requiring emphasis on the individual points of comparison. If you are torn between the two—wanting both to sum up each subject and to show the two side by side—then a combined arrangement may be your wisest choice.

A rough outline like the models on page 222 can help you plan the basic arrangement of your essay and also the order of the subjects and points of comparison. If your subjects are equally familiar to your readers and equally important to you, then it may not matter which subject you treat first, even in a subject-by-subject arrangement. But if one subject is less familiar or if you favor one, then that one should probably come second. You can also arrange the points themselves to reflect their importance and your readers' knowledge: from least to most significant or complex, from most to least familiar. Be sure to use the same order for both subjects.

Most readers know intuitively how comparison and contrast works, so they will expect you to balance your comparison feature for feature as well. In other words, all the features mentioned for the first subject should be mentioned as well for the second, and any features not mentioned for the first subject should not suddenly materialize for the second.

The conclusion to a comparison essay can help readers see the whole picture: the chief similarities and differences between two subjects compared in a divided arrangement, or the chief characteristics of subjects compared in an alternating arrangement. In addition, you may want to comment on the significance of your comparison, advise readers on how they can use the information you have provided, or recommend a specific course of action for them to follow. As with all other methods of development, the choice of conclusion should reflect the impression you want to leave with readers.

Drafting

Drafting your essay gives you the chance to spell out your comparison so that it supports your thesis or, if your thesis is still tentative, to find your idea by writing into it. You can use paragraphs to help manage the comparison as it unfolds:

- In a subject-by-subject arrangement, if you devote two paragraphs to the first subject, try to do the same for the second subject. For both subjects, try to cover the points of comparison in the same order and group the same ones in paragraphs.

- In a point-by-point arrangement, balance the paragraphs as you move back and forth between subjects. If you treat several points of comparison for the first subject in one paragraph, do the same for the second subject. If you apply a single point of comparison to both subjects in one paragraph, do the same for the next point of comparison.

This way of drafting will help you achieve balance in your comparison and see where you may need more information to flesh out your subjects and your points. If the finished draft seems to march too rigidly in its pattern, you can always loosen things up when revising.

Revising and Editing

When you are revising and editing your draft, use the following questions and the information in the box to be certain that your essay meets the principal requirements of the comparative method.

- *Are your subjects drawn from the same class?* The subjects must have notable differences *and* notable similarities to make comparison worthwhile—though, of course, you may stress one group over the other.

- *Does your essay have a clear purpose and say something significant about the subject?* Your purpose of explaining or evaluating *and* the point you are making should be evident in your thesis *and* throughout the essay. A vague, pointless comparison will quickly bore readers.

- *Do you apply all points of comparison to both subjects?* Even if you emphasize one subject, the two subjects must match feature for feature. An unmatched comparison may leave readers with unanswered questions or weaken their confidence in your authority.

- *Does the pattern of comparison suit readers' needs and the complexity of the material?* Although readers will appreciate a clear organization and roughly equal treatment of your subjects and points of comparison, they will also appreciate some variety in the way you move

---

FOCUS ON PARALLELISM

With several points of comparison and alternating subjects, a comparison will be easier for your readers to follow if you emphasize the relative importance of the subjects in each of the points you are discussing. To help readers keep your comparison straight, take advantage of the technique of parallelism discussed on pages 53–54. Parallelism—the use of similar grammatical structures for elements of similar importance—balances a comparison and clarifies the relationship between elements. At the same time, lack of parallelism can distract or confuse readers.

▶ To practice editing for parallelism, visit Exercise Central at *bedfordstmartins.com/ rewriting.*

back and forth. You needn't devote a sentence to each point, first for one subject and then for the other, or alternate subjects sentence by sentence through several paragraphs. Instead, you might write a single sentence on one point or subject but four sentences on the other—if that's what your information requires.

A Note on Thematic Connections

Each writer represented in this chapter uses comparison and contrast to understand or challenge stereotypes that have been applied to a minority group. A paragraph by Michael Dorris contrasts media images of Native Americans with the group's reality (p. 223). Another paragraph, by Julia Álvarez, evaluates the differences between the "cosmopolitan" and "creole" sides of a Dominican family (p. 223). Leanita McClain distinguishes her experience as a middle-class African American from the misperceptions of both blacks and whites (next page), while Cheryl Peck describes how hostility toward overweight people has affected her (p. 236). And Alaina Wong explains how playing with dolls helped a young girl come to terms with her Chinese features (p. 242).

What is repugnant to every human being is to be reckoned always as a member of a class and not as an individual person. —Dorothy L. Sayers

It is utterly exhausting being black in America—physically, mentally, and emotionally. While many minority groups and women feel similar stress, there is no respite or escape from your badge of color.
—Marian Wright Edelman

Prejudices are the chains forged by ignorance to keep men apart.
—Countess of Blessington

JOURNAL RESPONSE Prejudice is so pervasive in our society that it is hard to avoid. Think of a time when somebody made an assumption about you because of your membership in a group (as an ethnic, religious, or sexual minority; as a club member; as a woman or man; as a "jock," "nerd," "homeboy," and so on). Write a journal entry about the incident and how it made you feel.

Leanita McClain

An African American journalist, Leanita McClain earned a reputation for honest, if sometimes bitter, reporting on racism in America. She was born in 1952 on Chicago's South Side and grew up in a housing project there. She attended Chicago State University and the Medill School of Journalism at Northwestern University. Immediately after graduate school she began working as a reporter for the *Chicago Tribune,* and over the next decade she advanced to writing a twice-weekly column and serving as the first African American member of the paper's editorial board. Long suffering from severe depression, she committed suicide in 1984, at the age of thirty-two.

The Middle-Class Black's Burden

McClain wrote this essay for the "My Turn" column in *Newsweek* magazine in October 1980, and it was reprinted in a collection of her essays, *A Foot in Each World* (1986). As her comparison makes disturbingly clear, McClain's position as an economically successful African American subjected her to mistaken judgments by both blacks and whites.

I am a member of the black middle class who has had it with being pat- 1
ted on the head by white hands and slapped in the face by black hands
for my success.

Here's a discovery that too many people still find startling: when 2
given equal opportunities at white-collar pencil pushing, blacks want
the same things from life that everyone else wants. These include the
proverbial dream house, two cars, an above-average school, and a vacation for the kids at Disneyland. We may, in fact, want these things
more than other Americans because most of us have been denied them
so long.

Meanwhile, a considerable number of the folks we left behind in 3
the "old country," commonly called the ghetto, and the militants we
left behind in their antiquated ideology can't berate middle-class blacks
enough for "forgetting where we came from." We have forsaken the
revolution, we are told, we have sold out. We are Oreos, they say, black
on the outside, white within.

The truth is, we have not forgotten; we would not dare. We are sim- 4
ply fighting on different fronts and are no less war weary, and possibly
more heartbroken, for we know the black and white worlds can meld,
that there can be a better world.

It is impossible for me to forget where I came from as long as I am 5
prey to the jive hustler who does not hesitate to exploit my childhood
friendship. I am reminded, too, when I go back to the old neighborhood in fear—and have my purse snatched—and when I sit down to a
business lunch and have an old classmate wait on my table. I recall the
girl I played dolls with who now rears five children on welfare, the boy
from church who is in prison for murder, the pal found dead of a drug
overdose in the alley where we once played tag.

My life abounds in incongruities. Fresh from a vacation in Paris, 6
I may, a week later, be on the milk-run Trailways bus in Deep South back-
country attending the funeral of an ancient uncle whose world stretched
only fifty miles and who never learned to read. Sometimes when I wait
at the bus stop with my attaché case, I meet my aunt getting off the bus
with other cleaning ladies on their way to do my neighbors' floors.

But I am not ashamed. Black progress has surpassed our greatest 7
expectations; we never even saw much hope for it, and the achievement
has taken us by surprise.

In my heart, however, there is no safe distance from the wretched 8
past of my ancestors or the purposeless present of some of my contemporaries; I fear such a fate can reclaim me. I am not comfortably middle
class; I am uncomfortably middle class.

I have made it, but where? Racism still dogs my people. There are 9 still communities in which crosses are burned on the lawns of black families who have the money and grit to move in.

What a hollow victory we have won when my sister, dressed in her 10 designer everything, is driven to the rear door of the luxury high rise in which she lives because the cab driver, noting only her skin color, assumes she is the maid, or the nanny, or the cook, but certainly not the lady of any house at this address.

I have heard the immigrants' bootstrap tales, the simplistic reproach 11 of "why can't you people be like us." I have fulfilled the entry requirements of the American middle class, yet I am left, at times, feeling unwelcome and stereotyped. I have overcome the problems of food, clothing and shelter, but I have not overcome my old nemesis, prejudice. Life is easier, being black is not.

I am burdened daily with showing whites that blacks are people. 12 I am, in the old vernacular, a credit to my race. I am my brothers' keeper, and my sisters,' though many of them have abandoned me because they think that I have abandoned them.

I run a gauntlet between two worlds, and I am cursed and blessed by 13 both. I travel, observe, and take part in both; I can also be used by both. I am a rope in a tug of war. If I am a token in my downtown office, so am I at my cousin's church tea. I assuage white guilt. I disprove black inadequacy and prove to my parents' generation that their patience was indeed a virtue.

I have a foot in each world, but I cannot fool myself about either. 14 I can see the transparent deceptions of some whites and the bitter hopelessness of some blacks. I know how tenuous my grip on one way of life is, and how strangling the grip of the other way of life can be.

Many whites have lulled themselves into thinking that race relations are just grand because they were the first on their block to discuss crab grass with the new black family. Yet too few blacks and whites in this country send their children to school together, entertain each other, or call each other friend. Blacks and whites dining out together draw stares. Many of my coworkers see no black faces from the time the train pulls out Friday evening until they meet me at the coffee machine Monday morning. I remain a novelty.

Some of my "liberal" white acquaintances pat me on the head, hinting that I am a freak, that my success is less a matter of talent than of luck and affirmative action. I may live among them, but it is difficult to live with them. How can they be sincere about respecting me, yet hold my fellows in contempt? And if I am silent when they attempt to sever me from my own, how can I live with myself?

Whites won't believe I remain culturally different; blacks won't   17
believe I remain culturally the same.

I need only look in a mirror to know my true allegiance, and I am   18
painfully aware that, even with my off-white trappings, I am prejudged
by my color.

As for the envy of my own people, am I to give up my career, my   19
standard of living, to pacify them and set my conscience at ease? No.
I have worked for these amenities and deserve them, though I can never
enjoy them without feeling guilty.

These comforts do not make me less black, nor oblivious to the woe   20
in which many of my people are drowning. As long as we are denigrated
as a group, no one of us has made it. Inasmuch as we all suffer for every
one left behind, we all gain for every one who conquers the hurdle.

Meaning

1. McClain states, "My life abounds in incongruities" (paragraph 6). What does the word *incongruities* mean? How does it apply to McClain's life?

2. What is the "middle-class black's burden" to which the title refers? What is McClain's main idea?

3. McClain writes that "there is no safe distance from the wretched past of my ancestors or the purposeless present of some of my contemporaries" (paragraph 8). What do you think she means by this statement?

4. If any of the following words are new to you, try to guess their meanings from their context in McClain's essay. Check your guesses against a dictionary's definitions, and then try to use each word in a sentence or two of your own.

proverbial (2)	nemesis (11)	tenuous (14)
antiquated (3)	vernacular (12)	amenities (19)
ideology (3)	gauntlet (13)	oblivious (20)
berate (3)	assuage (13)	denigrated (20)
reproach (11)		

Purpose and Audience

1. What seems to be McClain's primary purpose in this piece? Does she simply want to express her frustration at whites and blacks, or is she trying to do something else here?

2. Is McClain writing primarily to whites or to blacks or to both? What feelings do you think she might evoke in white readers? in black readers? What is *your* reaction to this essay?

3. McClain's essay poses several questions, including "I have made it, but where?" (paragraph 9) and "How can they be sincere about respecting me, yet hold my fellows in contempt?" (16). What is the purpose of such questions?

Method and Structure

1. What exactly is McClain comparing here? What are her main points of comparison?

2. Paragraph 6 on "incongruities" represents a turning point in McClain's essay. What does she discuss before this paragraph? What does she discuss after?

3. McClain uses many expressions to make her comparison clear, such as "Meanwhile" (paragraph 3) and "different fronts" (4). Locate three more such expressions, and explain what relationship each one establishes.

4. **OTHER METHODS**   McClain relies on many other methods to develop her comparison. Locate one instance each of description (Chapter 6), narration (Chapter 5), example (Chapter 7), and cause-and-effect analysis (Chapter 13). What does each contribute to the essay?

Language

1. McClain sets the tone for this essay in the very first sentence. How would you describe this tone? Is it appropriate, do you think?

2. In her opening sentence, does McClain use the words *patted* and *slapped* literally? How would you explain her use of these words in the context of her essay?

3. Notice McClain's use of parallelism in paragraph 8: "I am not comfortably middle class; I am uncomfortably middle class." Locate two or three other uses of parallelism. How does this technique serve McClain's comparison? (For more on parallelism, see p. 53 and *parallelism* in the Glossary.)

4. In paragraph 16, McClain uses quotation marks around the term *liberal* in reference to her white acquaintances. Why do you think she uses the quotation marks here? What effect does this achieve?

Writing Topics

1. **JOURNAL TO ESSAY**   McClain writes about prejudices that plague her, and in your journal entry (p. 230) you recorded a personal experience of being prejudged because of your membership in a group. Now write

a narrative in which you recount this experience in more detail. How were you perceived, and by whom? What about this perception was accurate? What was unfair? How did the experience affect you? Write for a reader who is not a member of the group in question, being sure to include enough detail to bring the experience to life.

2. McClain's essay reports in part her experience of conflict resulting from her growth beyond the boundaries of her childhood and community. Think of a time when you outgrew a particular group or community. What conflicts and satisfactions did you experience? Write an essay comparing your experience with McClain's.

3. **CULTURAL CONSIDERATIONS**   Are there any ways in which you feel, like McClain, that you have "a foot in each world" (paragraph 14)? These worlds might be related to race and affluence, as McClain's worlds are, or they might be aligned by gender, social class, religion, or some other characteristic. Write an essay describing your own experience in balancing these two worlds. Are there ways in which you appreciate having a dual membership, or is it only a burden? What have you learned from your experience?

4. **CONNECTIONS**   Like McClain, Judy Brady, in "I Want a Wife" (p. 264), writes with strong emotion about the burdens of being oppressed by others. Both essays were written several decades ago. In an essay of your own, consider to what extent their perspectives are timely or dated. Could McClain and Brady make the same claims today?

Thou seest I have more flesh than another man, and therefore more frailty. —William Shakespeare

Except for smoking, obesity is now the number one preventable cause of death in this country. Three hundred thousand people die of obesity every year. —Dr. C. Everett Koop

Fat people may not be chortling all day long, but they're a hell of a lot nicer than the wizened and shriveled. —Suzanne Britt

JOURNAL RESPONSE If you're like most people, you've probably been dissatisfied with your size at one point or another, whether you wanted to be taller or shorter, lose a few pounds, build some muscle, or simply avoid weight gain. Write a journal entry in which you describe your attitude toward your body. What, if anything, would you change about it? Why?

Cheryl Peck

Cheryl Peck (born 1951) has always lived in Michigan—first with her parents and four younger siblings on a nonworking farm; now in Three Rivers with her "Beloved," Nancy, and her cat, Babycakes. She attended the University of Michigan and holds a full-time job in a welfare office. After friends encouraged her to write down the personal stories she was always amusing them with, Peck started submitting humorous and poignant articles to a Kalamazoo lesbian newsletter and giving readings at a community church. Her self-published essay collection *Fat Girls and Lawn Chairs* (2004) caught the attention of an editor at Warner Books, who brought the essays to a wider audience and cult-favorite status. Peck followed it a year later with *Revenge of the Paste Eaters: Memoirs of a Misfit* (2005) and is currently "contemplating writing a book about something more interesting than my own life."

Fatso

In most of her writing, Peck uses her ample size—"three hundred pounds (plus change)"—to fuel her self-deprecating brand of humor. This essay from *Revenge of the Paste Eaters*, however, takes a decidedly different approach to the weight issues that have plagued the author all her life.

My friend Annie and I were having lunch and we fell into a discussion of   1
people of size. She told me she had gone to the fair with a friend of hers
who is a young man of substance, and while he was standing in the mid-
way, thinking about his elephant ear,[1] someone walked past him, said,
"You don't need to eat that," and kept on walking away. Gone before
he could register what had been said, much less formulate a stunning
retort.

And that person was probably right: he did not need to eat that   2
elephant ear. Given what they are made of, the question then becomes:
Who *does* need to eat an elephant ear? And to what benefit? Are elephant
ears inherently better for thin people than for fat ones? Do we suppose
that that one particular elephant ear will somehow alter the course of
this man's life in some way that all of the elephant ears before it, or all
of the elephant ears to follow, might not? And last but not least, what
qualifies any of us for the mission of telling other people what they
should or should not eat?

I have probably spent most of my life listening to other people tell   3
me that as a middle-class white person, I have no idea what it is like to
be discriminated against. I have never experienced the look that tells
me I am not welcome, I have never been treated rudely on a bus, I have
never been reminded to keep my place, I have never been laughed at,
ridiculed, threatened, snubbed, not waited on, or received well-meaning
service I would just as soon have done without. I have never had to
choose which streets I will walk down and which streets I will avoid. I
have never been told that my needs cannot be met in this store. I have
never experienced that lack of social status that can debilitate the soul.

My feelings were not hurt when I was twelve years old and the shoe   4
salesman measured my feet and said he had no women's shoes large
enough for me, but perhaps I could wear the boxes.

I have never been called crude names, like "fatso" or "lard-bucket."...   5
My nickname on the school bus was never "Bismarck," as in the famous
battleship. No one ever assumed I was totally inept in all sports except
those that involved hitting things because—and everyone knows—the
more weight you can put behind it, the farther you can kick or bat or just
bully the ball.

I have never picked up a magazine with the photograph of a naked   6
woman of substance on the cover, to read, in the following issue, thirty
letters to the editor addressing sizism, including the one that said, "She

---

[1] Fried dough. [Editors' note.]

should be ashamed of herself. She should go on a diet immediately and demonstrate some self-control. She is going to develop diabetes, arthritis, hypertension, and stroke, she will die an ugly death at an early age and she will take down the entire American health system with her." And that would, of course, be the only letter I remember. I would not need some other calm voice to say, "You don't know that—and you don't know that the same fate would not befall a thin woman."

No one has ever assumed I am lazy, undisciplined, prone to self-pity, and emotionally unstable purely based on my size. No one has ever told me all I need is a little self-discipline and I too could be thin, pretty—a knockout, probably, because I have a "pretty face"—probably very popular because I have a "good personality." My mother never told me boys would never pay any attention to me because I'm fat. 7

I have never assumed an admirer would never pay any attention to me because I'm fat. I have never mishandled a sexual situation because I have been trained to think of myself as asexual. Unattractive. Repugnant. 8

Total strangers have never walked up to me in the street and started to tell me about weight loss programs their second cousin in Tulsa tried with incredible results, nor would they ever do so with the manner and demeanor of someone doing me a nearly unparalleled favor. I have never walked across a parking lot to have a herd of young men break into song about loving women with big butts. When I walk down the street or ride my bicycle, no one has ever hung out the car window to yell crude insults. When I walk into the houses of friends I have never been directed to the "safe" chairs as if I just woke up this morning this size and am incapable of gauging for myself what will or will not hold me. 9

I have never internalized any of this nonexistent presumption of who I am or what I feel. I would never discriminate against another woman of substance. I would never look at a heavy person and think, "self-pitying, undisciplined tub of lard." I would never admit that while I admire beautiful bodies, I rarely give the inhabitants the same attention and respect I would a soul mate because I do not expect they would ever become a soul mate. I would never tell you that I was probably thirty years old before I realized you really *can* be too small or too thin, or that the condition causes real emotional pain. 10

I have never skipped a high school reunion until I "lose a few pounds." I have never hesitated to reconnect with an old friend. I will appear anywhere in a bathing suit. If my pants split, I assume—and I assume everyone assumes—it was caused by poor materials. 11

I have always understood why attractive women are offended when men whistle at them. 12

I have never felt self-conscious standing next to my male friend   13
who is five foot ten and weighs 145 pounds.

I am not angry about any of this.   14

Meaning

1. Throughout her essay Peck repeats that she has never experienced, done, or felt any of the things she describes. Is she telling the truth? How do you know? (Hint: look up *irony* in the Glossary.)

2. How does Peck feel about the discrimination she faces as an overweight woman? Why does she feel this way?

3. Several times in her essay, Peck refers to people "of substance" (paragraphs 1, 6, and 10). How might this phrase have a double meaning?

4. If any of the following words are new to you, try to guess their meanings from their context in Peck's essay. Check your guesses against a dictionary's definitions, and then try to use each word in a sentence or two of your own.

register (1)	crude (5)	demeanor (9)
retort (1)	prone (7)	gauging (9)
debilitate (3)	asexual (8)	presumption (10)

Purpose and Audience

1. For whom is Peck writing? Fat people? Thin people? Herself? What clues in the essay bring you to your conclusion?

2. What lesson might readers take from Peck's essay?

Method and Structure

1. What, precisely, is Peck comparing and contrasting in this essay? Identify a few of the points of comparison she uses to develop her main idea. Which of these points seem most important to her?

2. Where does Peck's comparison begin? How does she use a subtle shift in point of view to indicate that she does, indeed, know "what it is like to be discriminated against" (paragraph 3)? (If necessary, see *point of view* in the Glossary.)

3. **OTHER METHODS**   Peck's comparison relies heavily on example (Chapter 7), focusing on a series of hurtful incidents from her own life. Choose two examples, and consider what each contributes to Peck's point.

Language

1. Peck is cautious in the words she uses to refer to overweight people, preferring terms such as "woman of substance" (paragraphs 6 and 10) and "heavy person" (10) over the judgmental terms that some people have used to describe her (and that she has caught herself thinking about others). Why, then, does she use the obviously insulting "Fatso" as the title of her essay?

2. Peck uses the phrase "I have never" repeatedly (seventeen times, to be exact), as well as variations such as "I would never" and "I have not." What is the effect of this repetition?

3. How would you characterize the tone of this essay? How does it affect you as a reader?

Writing Topics

1. **JOURNAL TO ESSAY** In your journal entry (p. 236), you described your attitude toward your body. Where do you think that attitude came from? Was it influenced in any way by your family, your friends, or the media? Write an essay in which you examine how other people's opinions affect a person's self-image. In your essay, describe your own thoughts about the ideal body, and explain the origins of those thoughts as best you can.

2. Peck's essay is in some respects an imagined response to the person who insulted her friend's friend. Think of a time when a stranger made an inappropriate or insensitive comment directed at you or someone close to you (or of a time when you overheard such a remark intended for someone else). Write an essay that responds to the person in question, explaining why his or her comment was offensive.

3. Write an essay expressing your opinion of Peck's essay. For instance, how would you respond to her complaint that people treat overweight individuals unfairly? Does she overlook important considerations about health? Do you think she exaggerates any of her points? Agree or disagree with Peck, supporting your opinion with your own examples.

4. **CULTURAL CONSIDERATIONS** American society is famously obsessed with people's size. Media outlets have focused recently on what has been described as an "obesity epidemic," and weight loss is a multibillion-dollar industry in this country. But in many cultures (Samoan and Polynesian, for example), large bodies are prized over small ones. Identify one such culture, and find two or three brief sources that explain that

culture's attitudes toward body shape (a librarian can help you). Write an essay that compares that culture's standards of physical beauty with America's. Which culture's ideals seem more reasonable to you? Express your preference in a clear thesis statement and support your evaluation with details. Be sure to document your sources, referring to pages 369–80 of the Appendix as necessary.

5. **CONNECTIONS** Peck suggests that discrimination against people of size is comparable, if not equivalent, to discrimination against people of color. In "The Middle-Class Black's Burden" (p. 230), Leanita McClain describes her own experiences with racial discrimination, and like Peck, she is angry. How do you think McClain would respond to Peck's characterization of race? Write an imaginary conversation between these two authors, inventing dialogue that mimics each writer's language and reflects the point of view she takes in her essay.

If Barbie is so popular, why do you have to buy her friends?
—Steven Wright

I think they should have a Barbie with a buzz cut.   —Ellen DeGeneres

Barbie is just a doll.   —Mary Schmich

JOURNAL RESPONSE   Think of a toy you wanted desperately when you were a child. Write a brief journal entry that explains why you wanted it. What was so special about it? If you did receive the toy, did it live up to your expectations? If you didn't get it, how did you react to your disappointment?

Alaina Wong

Alaina Wong was born in 1981 and grew up in New Jersey. As an English major at the University of Pennsylvania, she served as managing editor of *Mosaic*, a magazine for Asian American students. Wong graduated in 2002 and worked for several years in the marketing department at the publishing company Simon & Schuster. She is currently a marketing manager in the children's division at Penguin Books.

China Doll
(Student Essay)

Wong wrote "China Doll" when she was a college junior as a submission for the teen anthology *YELL-Oh Girls! Emerging Voices Explore Culture, Identity, and Growing Up Asian American* (2001). The essay, Wong explains, "provides a whimsical glimpse into the mind of a child, detailing the ways girls may come to terms with their Asian features, which so often contrast with the media-defined ideal of beauty."

I wanted Princess Barbie, with long blond hair that you could brush and   1
a beautiful shiny gown. She even came with a shimmery white tiara, which, in my eight-year-old mind, crowned her at the top of her Barbie world. My parents looked at me expectantly as I tore through the wrapping paper in childlike excitement. As the pile of shredded paper around me grew larger, so did my anticipation.

But instead of a beautiful princess with golden tresses, what I found 2
was an unfamiliar black-haired "friend" of Barbie, who wore a floral
wrap skirt over a pink bathing suit.

Disappointment passed over my eyes as I examined the doll more 3
closely. With her dark hair and slanted eyes, she was a dull comparison
to her blond friend. My other dolls were all alike and beautiful with their
clouds of blond (or light-brown) hair, broad, toothy smiles, and wide-
open eyes. Even Ken had a perfectly painted-on coif of blond hair and
flashed a winning grin. I didn't think this new doll would go riding in
Barbie's convertible with Ken. Why would he pick her when he already
had so many blond friends to choose from? Besides, instead of a wide
movie-star grin, her lips were curved into a more secretive, sly smile. I
wondered what secrets she was hiding. Maybe she had crooked teeth.

I announced that I loved my new doll. I didn't want my mom and 4
dad to feel bad. Maybe the store didn't have any more Princess Barbie
dolls, so they had to buy me the leftovers, or the ones that no one
wanted. I looked at the name of this new black-haired addition to my
perfect Barbie family. Kira. Kira didn't even have shoes, though her feet
were still arched up, as if they were waiting expectantly for their missing
shoes. She seemed incomplete. She was probably missing lots of things
besides her shoes. My other Barbies all had colorful plastic high heels to
complement their fashionable dresses. Their outfits were perfect.

"Alaina," my mom said, "get your things ready so I can drive you 5
over to Sarah's house!" I threw the dark-haired doll into my backpack
with the other Barbies I was bringing; Sarah and I always shared the
latest additions to our Barbie collections. Everyone always said that
Sarah would grow up to look like Goldie Hawn, some famous movie
star. I didn't think I would grow up to look like anybody important, not
unless I was like Cinderella, and a fairy godmother went Zap! so I could
be transformed, like magic. Sarah's hair fell in soft waves down her back,
while my own black hair was slippery and straight, like uncooked spa-
ghetti. I bet Sarah had gotten the Princess Barbie for Christmas.

I liked going over to Sarah's house. Her mom didn't care if we ate 6
raspberries from the backyard without washing them. The last time I
went there, I saw my best friend pluck a juicy purple berry right off the
bush and into her mouth. I was amazed that she didn't care about dirt.
Sarah's mom let us taste cookie dough from the batter when she baked
cookies. I guess only Chinese people cared about germs. My mother
never baked cookies anyway. Baking cookies is what white mothers do
all the time—they like to make things from "scratch" that turn out soft
and chewy, while Chinese mothers buy cookies from the supermarket

that are dry and go crunch, unless you dip them in milk. Sarah's mother made the best macaroni and cheese too. Obviously she made it from "scratch." I hoped I was eating lunch there today.

After we pulled into Sarah's driveway, I jumped out of the car and 7 said good-bye to my mom. Inside, Sarah and I ran up the stairs so I could look at her new dollhouse. On the way, we passed piles of laundry warm from the dryer, toys spread out on the floor in front of the TV, and newspapers scattered on the kitchen table. I was jealous. Sarah's mother probably didn't make them clean up every time someone came over.

Upstairs, I dumped my Barbies out of my backpack so we could 8 compare our collections. Before I could even look at her dolls, Sarah turned to me.

"Look what I got!" she said proudly. 9

I knew it. Sarah had gotten the Princess Barbie. 10

And what did I have to show her? A plain Barbie friend with a funny 11 name, Kira, in an ordinary bathing suit and a skirt that was just a piece of cloth that needed to be tied; it didn't even slip on like real clothes. My doll had straight black hair, no shoes, and worst of all, she didn't even know how to smile right.

"Well . . . she has pretty flowers on her skirt," Sarah said helpfully. 12 "And she looks kind of like you!"

She did? But I didn't want to look like this strange new "friend" of 13 Barbie. Everyone knew that the Barbies with the blond hair were the best. They were the original ones. And they always got to wear the prettiest dresses. I noticed something, but I didn't want to say it out loud. The best dolls, the most glamorous ones, were always the ones that seemed to look like Sarah.

"Sarah, honey," her mom called. "Why don't you help me bring up 14 some cookies for you and Alaina?"

My best friend turned to me. "I'll be right back!" she chirped. "If 15 you want to, your dolls can try on Princess Barbie's clothes," she offered generously.

Sarah skipped out of the room, her blond pigtails swinging around 16 her head. I turned to my Kira doll, regarding her simple outfit. I highly doubted that Princess Barbie's costume would look right on her. Whoever heard of a black-haired doll with slanted eyes wearing a crown? Maybe it wouldn't even fit right. Hesitatingly, I picked up Sarah's Princess Barbie. She really was beautiful. Slowly, I slipped off her gown and dressed her in one of the extra doll outfits, a shiny purple top and silver pants. Princess Barbie continued smiling blankly at me. I was glad she didn't mind that I had changed her clothes.

Carefully, I buttoned my Kira doll into the glittery princess gown. 17
No Velcro closures here; this dress was glamorous, like what a princess
would wear in real life. The sunlight through Sarah's bedroom window
made the dress sparkle, as if my plain dark-haired Kira doll was actually a
princess. The doll's secretive smile began to comfort me, as if we shared a
secret together. We both knew this wasn't her real gown, but maybe she
could be princess for a day. Just maybe. I stared at her. Finally I placed
Barbie's iridescent tiara on top of Kira's jet-black hair. And what do you
know? It fit perfectly.

Meaning

1. In her opening paragraphs Wong compares her new Kira doll with the
   other Barbie dolls in her collection. How were they different?

2. In paragraph 4, an eight-year-old Wong wonders why her parents didn't
   get her the doll she wanted, contemplating that "maybe the store didn't
   have any more Princess Barbie dolls, so they had to buy me the leftovers, or the ones that no one wanted." By the end of the essay, however, Wong seems to realize that her parents may have had a different
   reason. Why do you think they chose the Kira doll for their daughter?

3. Wong's essay compares both her Kira doll with Princess Barbie and herself with her best friend, Sarah. In what ways do the dolls function as
   symbols for the girls? (If necessary, see *symbol* in the Glossary.)

4. Based on their context in Wong's essay, try to guess the meanings of any
   of the following words that you don't already know. Test your guesses
   in a dictionary, and then use each new word in a sentence or two of
   your own.

tresses (2)	complement (4)	chirped (15)
coif (3)	scratch (6)	regarding (16)
sly (3)	glamorous (13)	iridescent (17)

Purpose and Audience

1. What do you think might have prompted Wong to write about a doll
   she received as a child? What evidence from the text can you use to
   support your opinion?

2. Although this essay speaks from the perspective of an eight-year-old
   Chinese American girl and was written specifically for a collection aimed
   at young Asian girls, to what extent can other readers—adults, males,
   or Caucasians, for example—sympathize with Wong's experience? How

does she try to make sure that they can do so? Find examples from the essay that show she is addressing people who might not share her experience, as well as girls who may have had similar feelings growing up.

Method and Structure

1. Why is comparison and contrast particularly well suited to Wong's subject and purpose?

2. Where in the essay does Wong focus on similarities between herself and her best friend? Where does she focus on differences? Why do you think she might have chosen to organize her essay as she does?

3. **OTHER METHODS**   Description (Chapter 6) features prominently in Wong's essay. She also uses narration (Chapter 5) to explain her experience. What dimensions do these other methods add to the piece?

Language

1. What is the overall tone of the essay?

2. Throughout "China Doll" Wong uses metaphors and similes to make her comparisons vivid and immediate. Find two or three examples and comment on their effectiveness.

Writing Topics

1. **JOURNAL TO ESSAY**   In your journal entry (p. 242), you wrote about a toy that you wanted as a child. Now think about that toy more critically. Did it carry meanings besides pure entertainment? Make a list of messages that the makers of the toy might intentionally or unintentionally have been sending to children. Using Wong's essay as a model, write an analysis of what the toy represented to you. Your essay may be serious or humorous, but it should include plenty of description so that readers unfamiliar with the toy can picture it in their minds.

2. Although Wong's essay is written with greater skill and range of vocabulary than an eight-year-old would be capable of, it reveals the many facets of a young girl's emotional life. Write an essay in which you analyze the girlish concerns evident in "China Doll," demonstrating how Wong's writing captures a girl's frame of mind. Consider, for example, the way she compares Chinese and white people's attitudes toward food (paragraph 6), or her certainty that "Sarah had gotten the Princess Barbie for Christmas" (paragraph 5). How does the author use diction and point of view to evoke the childhood outlook she no longer has?

3. In her essay Wong explores the complex reasons behind her initial dislike for a doll with Asian features, commenting that "the best dolls, the most glamorous ones, were always the ones that seemed to look like Sarah" (paragraph 13). In other words, the most popular dolls were unmistakably white. Write an essay in which you consider the implications of Wong's observation. To what extent do contemporary fashion dolls (or some other aspect of popular entertainment) reflect, reinforce, or reject racial stereotypes? How might their popularity affect girls' self-esteem? You may draw on Wong's essay or your own experience for examples, or, if none come to mind, consider doing some research on the topic. (See the Appendix for tips on writing from sources.)

4. **CULTURAL CONSIDERATIONS** The inspiration for Barbie was a racy adult doll made in Germany after World War II. In the 1950s, the US toy manufacturer Mattel transformed the original doll into a toy for American girls. What characteristics of Barbie strike you as especially American? How might the doll have been different if it had been designed for girls in other cultures? Why do you think toy manufacturers might feel a need to create alternative versions like Wong's Kira doll or the recently popular Bratz line? Write an essay analyzing Barbie in which you answer these questions. The characteristics you identify may come from Wong's comparisons or your own experience, but be sure to explain why you think they are distinctly American.

5. **CONNECTIONS** Like Wong, Kaela Hobby-Reichstein, in "Learning Race" (p. 83), explores the first time she became aware of race. Though the two authors undoubtedly made parallel discoveries as children, the positions they write from are nearly opposite. Write a comparison of the two essays in which you explore the authors' tones and purposes.

Comparison and Contrast

Select one of the following topics, or any other topic they suggest, for an essay developed by comparison and contrast. Be sure to choose a topic you care about so that the comparison and contrast is a means of communicating an idea, not an end in itself.

EXPERIENCE

1. Two jobs you have held
2. Two experiences with discrimination
3. Your own version of an event you witnessed or participated in and someone else's view of the same event (perhaps a friend's or a reporter's)

PEOPLE

4. Your relationships with two friends
5. Someone before and after marriage or the birth of a child
6. Two or more candidates for public office
7. Two relatives

PLACES AND THINGS

8. A place as it is now and as it was years ago
9. Public and private transportation
10. Contact lenses and glasses
11. Two towns or cities

ART AND ENTERTAINMENT

12. The work of two artists, or two works by the same artist
13. Movies or television today and when you were a child
14. An amateur football, baseball, or basketball game and a professional game in the same sport
15. The advertisements on two very different Web sites

EDUCATION AND IDEAS

16. Talent and skill
17. Learning and teaching
18. A humanities course and a science or mathematics course
19. A passive student and an active student

WRITING ABOUT THE THEME

Evaluating Stereotypes

1. The writers in this chapter wrestle with questions of identity, addressing issues as diverse as the emotional impact of negative stereotypes (Michael Dorris, p. 223; Leanita McClain, p. 230; Cheryl Peck, p. 236; and Alaina Wong, p. 242), the role of peers and family in the development of an individual's sense of self (Julia Álvarez, p. 223, McClain, Peck, and Wong), and the relationship between body image and self-esteem (Peck and Wong). All five authors rely on comparison and contrast, but otherwise they go about their tasks very differently. Most notably, perhaps, their tones vary widely, from irony to vulnerability to anger. Choose the two works that seem most different in this respect, and analyze how the tone of each helps the author achieve his or her purpose. Give specific examples to support your ideas. Does your analysis lead you to conclude that one tone is likely to be more effective than another in comparing stereotypes with reality? (For more on tone, see pp. 41–43.)

2. Michael Dorris, Leanita McClain, and Cheryl Peck refer to misperceptions of a minority group on the part of the dominant society. Think of a minority group to which you belong. It could be based on race, ethnicity, language, sexual orientation, religion, physical disability, or any other characteristic. How is your minority perceived in the dominant culture, and how does this perception resemble or differ from the reality as you know it? Write an essay comparing the perception of and the reality of your group.

3. All of the authors in this chapter suggest that stereotypes play a significant part in our perceptions of others and ourselves. Dorris refers to the "white noise" of Indian images in the media, Alvarez to her parents' negative assessments of each other's extended families, McClain to a distorted image of African Americans, Peck to perceptions about overweight individuals, and Wong to her misguided preference for blond Barbie dolls. To what extent, if at all, are these misconceptions the result of media hype or distortion, whether in advertising, news stories, television programming, movies, or elsewhere? What else might contribute to the misconceptions in each case? Write an essay explaining how such notions arise in the first place. You could use the misconceptions identified by the authors in this chapter for your examples, or you could supply examples of your own.

12

DEFINITION
Clarifying Family Relationships

Definition sets the boundaries of a thing, a concept, an emotion, or a value. In answering "What is it?" and also "What is it *not*?" definition specifies the main qualities of a subject and its essential nature. Since words are only symbols, pinning down their precise meanings is essential for us to understand ourselves and one another. Thus we use definition constantly, whether we are explaining a new word like *staycation* to someone who has never heard it, specifying what we're after when we say we want to do something *fun,* or clarify the diagnosis of a child as *hyperactive.*

We often use brief definitions to clarify the meanings of words — for instance, taking a few sentences to explain a technical term in an engineering study. But we may also need to define words at length, especially when they are abstract, complicated, or controversial. Drawing on other methods of development, such as example, analysis, or comparison and contrast, entire essays might be devoted to debated phrases (such as *family values*), to the current uses of a word (*monopoly* in business), or to the meanings of a term in a particular context (like *personality* in psychological theory). Definition is, in other words, essential whenever we want to be certain that we are understood.

Reading Definition

There are several kinds of definition, each with different uses. One is the **formal definition**, usually a statement of the general class of things to which the word belongs, followed by the distinction(s) between it and other members of the class. For example:

	General class	*Distinction(s)*
A submarine is	a seagoing vessel	that operates underwater.
A parable is	a brief, simple story	that illustrates a moral or religious principle.
Pressure is	the force	applied to a given surface.
Insanity is	a mental condition	in which a defendant does not know right from wrong.

A formal definition usually gives a standard dictionary meaning of the word (as in the first two examples) or a specialized meaning agreed to by the members of a profession or discipline (as in the last two examples, from physics and criminal law, respectively). Writers use formal definition to explain the basic meaning of a term so that readers can understand the rest of a discussion. Occasionally, a formal definition can serve as a springboard to a more elaborate, detailed exploration of a word. For instance, an essay might define *pride* simply as "a sense of self-respect" before probing the varied meanings of the word as people actually understand it and then settling on a fuller and more precise meaning of the author's own devising.

This more detailed definition of *pride* could fall into one of two other types of definition: stipulative and extended. A **stipulative definition** clarifies the particular way a writer is using a word: it stipulates, or specifies, a meaning to suit a larger purpose; the definition is part of a larger whole. For example, to show how pride can destroy personal relationships, a writer might first stipulate a meaning of *pride* that ties in with that purpose. Though a stipulative definition may sometimes take the form of a brief formal definition, most require several sentences or even paragraphs. In a physics textbook, for instance, the physicist's definition of *pressure* quoted above probably would not suffice to give readers a good sense of the term and eliminate all the other possible meanings they may have in mind.

Whereas a writer may use a formal or stipulative definition for some larger purpose, he or she would use an **extended definition** for the sake of defining—that is, for the purpose of exploring a thing, quality, or idea in its full complexity and drawing boundaries around it until its meaning is complete and precise. Extended definitions usually treat subjects so complex, vague, or laden with emotions or values that people misunderstand or disagree over their meanings. The subject may be an abstract concept like *patriotism*, a controversial phrase like *beginnings of life*, a colloquial or slang expression like *hype*, a thing like *nanobot*, a scientific idea like *natural selection*, even an everyday expression like *nagging*. Besides defining, the purpose may be to persuade readers to accept a definition (for instance, that life begins at conception, or at birth), to explain (what is natural selection?), or to amuse (nagging as exemplified by great nags).

As the variety of possible subjects and purposes may suggest, an extended definition may draw on whatever methods will best accomplish the goal of specifying what the subject encompasses and distinguishing it from similar things, qualities, or concepts. Several strategies are unique to definition:

- **Synonyms**, or words of similar meaning, can convey the range of the word's meanings. For example, a writer could equate *misery* with *wretchedness* and *distress*.

- **Negation**, or saying what a word does not mean, can limit the meaning, particularly when a writer wants to focus on only one sense of an abstract term, such as *pride*, that is open to diverse interpretations.

The **etymology** of a word—its history—may illuminate its meaning, perhaps by showing the direction and extent of its change (*pride*, for instance, comes from a Latin word meaning "to be beneficial or useful") or by uncovering buried origins that remain implicit in the modern meaning (*patriotism* comes from the Greek word for "father"; *happy* comes from the Old Norse word for "good luck").

These strategies of definition may be used alone or together, and they may occupy whole paragraphs in an essay-length definition; but they rarely provide enough range to surround the subject completely. That's why most definition essays draw on at least some of the other methods discussed in this book. One or two methods may predominate: an essay on nagging, for instance, might be developed with brief narratives. Or several methods may be combined: a definition of *patriotism* might compare it with *nationalism*, analyze its effects (such as the actions people take on its behalf), and give examples of patriotic individuals. The goal is not to employ every method in a sort of catalog of methods but to use those which best illuminate the subject. By drawing on the appropriate methods, a writer defines and clarifies a specific perspective on the subject so that the reader understands the meaning exactly.

Analyzing Definition in Paragraphs

Firoozeh Dumas (born 1966), a California-based writer who emigrated from Iran with her family at the age of seven, hopes to dispel American fears of Iranian people by revealing their "shared humanity." The following paragraph is from her book *Funny in Farsi: A Memoir of Growing Up Iranian in America* (2003).

When we lived in Abadan, we lived near my father's oldest sister, Sedigeh. She is my *ameh*, my father's sister. Her four sons are my *pessar ameh*, "sons of father's sister." Our families spent every free moment together and I always thought of my aunt Sedigeh and uncle Abdullah as a second set of parents. Since my aunt Sedigeh never had a daughter, she regarded me as her own. Always warm and affectionate, she showered me with compliments that stayed with me long after our visits had ended. She often told me that I was smart and patient and that she wished that I were her daughter. She never criticized me, but loved me as only a father's sister could. To me, the word *ameh* still conjures up feelings of being enveloped with love.

Early sentence introduces role to be defined

Roles and qualities of an ameh:

Parent figure

Warm and affectionate

Uncritical and loving

Topic sentence summarizes meaning of word for author

Sandra Cisneros (born 1954) is an award-winning novelist, short-story writer, and poet. This paragraph is adapted from her essay "Only Daughter," first published in *Glamour* magazine in 1990.

Once, several years ago, when I was just starting out my writing career, I was asked to write my own contributor's note for an anthology I was part of. I wrote: "I am the only daughter in a family of six sons. *That* explains everything." . . . I've thought about that ever since, and yes, it explains a lot to me, but for the reader's sake I should have written: "I am the only daughter in a *Mexican* family of six sons." Or even: "I am the only daughter of a Mexican father and Mexican-American mother."

Early definition of author's identity: only daughter in a family of six sons.

Definition clarified by additional distinctions:

Mexican family

Mexican father and Mexican-American mother

Or: "I am the only daughter of a working-class family   Working class
of nine." All of these had everything to do with who   Topic sentence
I am today.   summarizes
definition.

Developing an Essay by Definition

Getting Started

You'll sometimes be asked to write definition essays, as when a psychology exam asks for a discussion of *schizophrenia* or a political science assignment calls for an explanation of the term *totalitarianism*. To come up with a subject on your own, consider words that have complex meanings and are either unfamiliar to readers or open to varied interpretations. The subject should be something you know and care enough about to explore in great detail and surround completely. An idea for a subject may come from an overheard conversation (for instance, a reference to someone as "too patriotic"), a personal experience (a broken marriage you think attributable to one spouse's pride), or something you've seen or read (another writer's definition of *jazz*).

Begin exploring your subject by examining and listing its conventional meanings (consulting an unabridged dictionary may help here, and the dictionary will also give you synonyms and etymology). Also examine the differences of opinion about the word's meanings—the different ways, wrong or right, that you have heard or seen it used. Run through the other methods to see what fresh approaches to the subject they open up:

- How can the subject be described?
- What are some examples?
- Can the subject be divided into qualities or characteristics?
- Can its functions help define it?
- Will comparing and contrasting it with something else help sharpen its meaning?
- Do its causes or effects help clarify its sense?

Some of the questions may turn up nothing, but others may open your eyes to meanings you had not seen.

Forming a Thesis

When you have generated a good list of ideas about your subject, settle on the purpose of your definition. Do you mostly want to explain a word that is unfamiliar to readers? Do you want to express your own view so that readers see a familiar subject from a new angle? Do you want to argue in favor of a particular definition or perhaps persuade readers to look more critically at themselves or their surroundings? Try to work your purpose into a thesis sentence that summarizes your definition and—just as important—asserts something about the subject. For example:

> TENTATIVE THESIS STATEMENT The prevailing concept of *patriotism* is dangerously wrong.

> REVISED THESIS STATEMENT Though generally considered entirely positive in meaning, *patriotism* in fact reflects selfish, childish emotions that have no place in a global society.

(Note that the revised thesis statement not only summarizes the writer's definition and makes an assertion about the subject, but it also identifies the prevailing definition she intends to counter in her essay.)

With a thesis sentence formulated, reevaluate your ideas in light of it and pause to consider the needs of your readers:

- What do readers already know about your subject, and what do they need to be told in order to understand it as you do?

- Are your readers likely to be biased for or against your subject? If you were defining *patriotism,* for example, you might assume that your readers see the word as representing a constructive, even essential value that contributes to the strength of a country. If your purpose were to contest this view, as implied by the revised thesis statement, you would have to build your case carefully to win readers to your side.

Organizing

The introduction to a definition essay should provide a base from which to expand and at the same time explain to readers why the forthcoming definition is useful, significant, or necessary. You may want to report the incident that prompted you to define, say why the subject itself is important, or specify the common understandings, or misunderstandings, about its meaning. Several devices can serve as effective beginnings: the etymology of the word; a quotation from another writer supporting or contradicting your definition; or an explanation of what the word does *not* mean (negation). (Try to avoid the overused opening that cites a dictionary: "According to *The American Heritage Dictionary*, _____ means. . . ." Your readers have probably seen this opening many times before.) If it is not implied in the rest of your introduction, you may want to state your thesis so that readers know precisely what your purpose and point are.

The body of the essay should then proceed, paragraph by paragraph, to refine the characteristics or qualities of the subject, using the arrangement and methods that will distinguish it from anything similar and provide your perspective. For instance:

- You might draw increasingly tight boundaries around the subject, moving from broader, more familiar meanings to the one you have in mind.
- You might arrange your points in order of increasing drama.
- You might begin with your own experience of the subject and then show how you see it operating in your surroundings.

The conclusion to a definition essay is equally a matter of choice. You might summarize your definition, indicate its superiority to other definitions of the same subject, quote another writer whose view supports your own, or recommend that readers make some use of the information you have provided. The choice depends—as it does in any kind of essay—on your purpose and the impression you want to leave with readers.

Drafting

While drafting your extended definition, keep your subject vividly in mind. Say too much rather than too little about it to ensure that you capture its essence; you can always cut when you revise. And be sure to provide plenty of details and examples to support your view. Such evidence is particularly important when, as in the earlier example of patriotism, you wish to change readers' perceptions of your subject.

In definition the words you use are especially important. Abstractions and generalities cannot draw precise boundaries around a subject, so your words must be as concrete and specific as you can make them. You'll have chances during revising and editing to work on your words, but try during drafting to pin down your meanings. Use words and phrases that appeal directly to the senses and experiences of readers. When appropriate, use figures of speech to make meaning inescapably clear; instead of "Patriotism is childish," for example, write "The blindly patriotic person is like a small child who sees his or her parents as gods, all-knowing, always right." The connotations of words—the associations called up in readers' minds by words like *home, ambitious,* and *generous*—can contribute to your definition as well. But be sure that connotative words trigger associations suited to your purpose. And when you are trying to explain something precisely, rely most heavily on words with generally neutral meanings. (See pg. 56 for more on concrete and specific language and figures of speech. See pp. 55–56 for more on connotation.)

Revising and Editing

When you are satisfied that your draft is complete, revise and edit it against the following questions and the information in the box.

- *Have you surrounded your subject completely and tightly?* Your definition should not leave gaps, nor should the boundaries be so broadly drawn that the subject overlaps something else. For instance, a definition of *hype* that focused on exaggerated and deliberately misleading claims should include all such claims (some political speeches, say, as well as some advertisements), and it should exclude appeals that do not fit the basic definition (some public-service advertising, for instance).

- *Does your definition reflect the conventional meanings of the word?* Even if you are providing a fresh slant on your subject, you can't change its meaning entirely, or you will confuse your readers and perhaps undermine your own credibility. *Patriotism,* for example, could not be defined from the first as "hatred of foreigners," for that definition strays into an entirely different realm. The conventional meaning of "love of country" would have to serve as the starting point, though your essay might interpret the meaning in an original way.

FOCUS ON PARAGRAPH AND ESSAY UNITY

When drafting a definition, you may find yourself being pulled away from your subject by the descriptions, examples, comparisons, and other methods you use to specify meaning. Let yourself explore byways of your subject—doing so will help you discover what you think. But in revising you'll need to direct all paragraphs to your thesis, and within paragraphs you'll need to direct all sentences to the paragraph topic. In other words, you'll need to ensure that your essay and its paragraphs are unified. One way to achieve unity is to focus each paragraph on some part of your definition and then to focus each sentence within the paragraph on that part. If some part of your definition requires more than a single paragraph, by all means expand it. But keep the group of paragraphs focused on a single idea. For more on unity in essays and paragraphs, see pages 35–36.

▶ To practice revising for paragraph unity, visit Exercise Central at bedfordstmartins.com/rewriting.

A Note on Thematic Connections

Family is the core topic of this chapter. The authors represented here are all seeking to define, or redefine, a complex set of relationships that many of us take for granted. Firoozeh Dumas, in a paragraph, explains the special place held by the paternal aunt in an Iranian family (p. 253), while Sandra Cisneros, in another paragraph, considers her family's influence in how she defines herself (p. 253). Ashley Rhodes writes about the role a father plays in the lives of his children (opposite). In defining a wife, Judy Brady questions male and female roles in traditional families (p. 264). And Andrew Sullivan, a gay man with conservative values, examines the very personal meanings of marriage as a public institution (p. 269).

Fathers are biological necessities, but social accidents. —Margaret Mead

It is much easier to become a father than to be one. —Kent Nerburn

Fatherhood is pretending the present you love most is soap-on-a-rope. —Bill Cosby

JOURNAL RESPONSE Many people derive comfort from a childhood object throughout life: they may no longer sleep with a teddy bear, but the sight of it on the shelf provides security and a connection with the past. Think of such an object that exists for you—a doll, a model ship or car, a pillow, a ball, something one of your parents gave you. Describe the object as specifically as you can.

Ashley Rhodes

Ashley Rhodes was born in 1990 and grew up on her family's farm in a small town in South Carolina. She graduated from Clinton High School in 2008 and studied for a year at Lander University before transferring to Greenwood Technical College. Rhodes enjoys painting, drawing, and spending time outside with her dogs and her family. After she finishes school, she plans to become a nurse.

Fatherhood Is Essential

(Student Essay)

Rhodes wrote "Fatherhood Is Essential" as a submission for *This I Believe*, National Public Radio's ongoing effort to gather, broadcast, and publish short statements of personal philosophy. In her essay, written in her freshman year at Lander University, Rhodes outlines what she believes are a father's responsibilities to his children.

The one stuffed animal that I still sleep with is a bean-filled dog that my dad bought for me when I was ten. We were in Books-A-Million, and I wanted the dog so bad because it looked like my dog at home. Normally, this sort of thing would have been "nonsense" for Daddy to spend his money on. However, for some reason, he decided to give in this time. I was ecstatic; I got my dad to break down and buy something for me that I know he would normally have never bought because it was a "waste of money." The dog would be special to me. It still is. It has become something that makes me feel safe at night, that can soak up tears when I'm sad, and that can receive tight hugs when I'm excited. It replaces all the stuff my dad is supposed to do. This is why I believe in the importance of fatherhood.

Dads are supposed to be there for their children in the good times 2 and in the bad. A dad has to do more than pay child support: there are far more qualifications for the job of fatherhood. My mom raised me alone. She held all my birthday parties, managed all of my wild sleep-overs, got me up and ready for school every morning, and worked two jobs, staying tired most of the time so that she could make sure I always had the best things she could afford. Don't get me wrong—my dad has always given me birthday presents, has always made sure I had my needs met. I stayed with him on weekends until I was eleven. However, he was never there for the grunt work, like when my kindergarten class needed a parent to chaperone our zoo trip, when my boyfriend dumped me and I cried for three days, when I was having such a hard time with a math teacher that a parent-teacher conference was required, or when I was staying out too late and needed someone to draw the line. My mom dealt with all of that by herself. My dad never knew, and still doesn't know, about any of that.

I will never forget last year when my artwork was entered in our 3 high school art show. It took me a little while to talk my dad into coming, but he finally gave in. He and my stepmom came together.

I have loved to draw since I was little. My mom knows this very well 4 and has always wanted me to take advanced art classes so that I could get even better. Any time my art has ever been shown, my mom has always been the first in line to see it. My dad had never seen my artwork until last year's art show. When the announcer said my name for the first place prize, the look on my dad's face was priceless. My mom was so excited that she was yelling: "I knew you would win!" All my friends' parents congratulated my mom and dad for my win.

All my dad could say was, "Why didn't you ever tell me you drew?" 5 This sums up our whole relationship. At this moment, I realized just how much my dad has never known about his daughter and how much he has missed out on because he never made an effort to know me.

Dads are supposed to be role models for their families and all 6 others around them. I have heard that fathers are supposed to be the earthly example of God, guiding their families and teaching their children a healthy way to live. My parents got divorced when I was three and my brother was thirteen. They had been married for eighteen years. My mom said she just couldn't take the relationship anymore. Daddy treated Mama more like a maid than a wife. He told her that he didn't like to hug and kiss or to say "I love you," that those things made him uncomfortable. He developed a drinking problem and would frequently come home drunk or would not come home at all. My mom would go out looking for him at the local bars late at night. He later developed a gambling problem and got in a bad situation where some men were threatening to kill him if he didn't get them their money. He and my mom had to give up their house to pay the men back. My brother was a baby at the time. I worry sometimes that the instability hurt his chances to grow up into a grounded adult.

Sons and daughters who have close bonds with their fathers seem   7
to be more successful, happier individuals. Each child has certain needs that can't be met by the child's mother alone. There are roles that a father plays in his child's life, and these roles need to be fulfilled in order for the child to feel secure, confident, and supported. Fathers are more than a child support check. Fathers are the foundation of a strong household and are the number one role model for their children. At least they should be. It is too bad that my dad could never understand how his decisions affected me and my brother. It is too late for my dad to take back the effect he has had on our family, my attitude toward men and my body, and the way my brother thinks about relationships and women. However, it is not too late for other dads. The opportunities are there. Dads can change the world by shaping who their children become, if only they decide that fatherhood is essential.

Meaning

1. In her opening paragraph Rhodes describes a stuffed animal that her father gave her when she was young. Why is the toy still special to her?

2. Rhodes refers to "certain needs that can't be met by the child's mother alone" (paragraph 7) but doesn't specify what those needs are. What, if anything, can you infer about her meaning from other passages in her essay?

3. In paragraph 2, Rhodes claims that a father "has to do more than pay child support." She repeats this idea in her conclusion when she writes, "Fathers are more than a child support check" (7). What do these statements reveal about how her father views his responsibilities? Why is the point important to Rhodes?

4. Based on their context in Rhodes's essay, try to guess the meanings of any of the following words that you don't already know. Test your guesses in a dictionary, and then use each new word in a sentence or two of your own.

ecstatic (1)   instability (6)   grounded (6)
chaperone (2)

Purpose and Audience

1. What do you think might have prompted Rhodes to write so personally about her relationship with her father? What evidence from the text can you use to support your opinion?

2. Rhodes writes from the perspective of a daughter raised without a father. To what extent can readers who have not experienced divorce sympathize with Rhodes's feelings? How does she try to make sure that they can do so? Find examples from the essay that show she is addressing people who might not share or understand her experience.

Method and Structure

1. Why is definition particularly well suited to Rhodes's subject and purpose?

2. Analyze the organization Rhodes uses for her definition of what it means to be a father. Where in the essay does she focus on herself? Where does she focus on her father? Why do you think she might have chosen to structure her essay as she does?

3. **OTHER METHODS** Narration (Chapter 5) features prominently in Rhodes's definition, and in paragraphs 6 and 7 she uses cause-and-effect analysis (Chapter 13) to conclude her essay. What dimensions do these other methods add to the piece?

Language

1. What is the overall tone of the essay?

2. In paragraphs 4 and 5, Rhodes quotes comments made by her parents when she took first prize at an art show. How do these quotations reinforce the main idea of her essay?

Writing Topics

1. **JOURNAL TO ESSAY** In your journal entry (p. 259), you described an object of attachment from your childhood. Expand that description

into an essay that explores its significance for you. How did you acquire it? Why is it special? What does it mean to you? Consider both the positive and negative associations the object holds for you.

2. Loving another person can often bring both joys and difficulties. In fact, most people have probably had at least one family or romantic relationship that didn't work out the way they would have liked. Write an essay about a difficult or disappointing relationship you have had. Describe the ups and downs of this relationship, from feelings of support and tenderness to moments of conflict and anger, and consider what you have learned from the experience.

3. **CULTURAL CONSIDERATIONS** Rhodes seems to have definite ideas about what a father's job is and what a mother's is. Write an essay about the division of parental responsibilities in your extended family when you were growing up. Were certain tasks always assumed by the males and others by the females? Did this division seem to occur naturally, or was it a source of conflict? Are certain family roles more suited to one gender than to the other?

4. **CONNECTIONS** Like Rhodes, Sandra Cisneros, in her paragraph from "Only Daughter" (p. 253), explores how the men in her family contributed to her sense of who she is. Though both authors undoubtedly struggled to forge independent identities, the experiences they describe demonstrate how family relationships play into people's definitions of themselves. In a brief essay, analyze how the writers convey their feelings about their relatives and the influences those relatives had on them.

A woman's place is in the home.   —Mid-nineteenth-century proverb

Motherhood and homemaking are honorable choices for any woman, provided it is the woman who makes those decisions.   —Molly Yard

We haven't come a long way, we've come a short way. If we hadn't come a short way, no one would be calling us "baby."   —Elizabeth Janeway

JOURNAL RESPONSE   Write a journal entry about gender roles today. How have they changed in the past few decades? How might they continue to evolve?

Judy Brady

Judy Brady was born in 1937 in San Francisco. She attended the University of Iowa and graduated with a bachelor's degree in painting in 1962. Married in 1960, she was raising two daughters by the mid-1960s. She began working in the women's movement in 1969 and through it developed an ongoing concern with political and social issues, especially women's rights, cancer, and the environment. She believes that "as long as women continue to tolerate a society which places profits above the needs of people, we will continue to be exploited as workers and as wives." Besides the essay reprinted here, Brady has written articles for various magazines and edited *1 in 3: Women with Cancer Confront an Epidemic* (1991), motivated by her own struggle with the disease. She is also cofounder of the Toxic Links Coalition and serves on the board of Greenaction for Health and Environmental Justice.

I Want a Wife

Writing after eleven years of marriage, and before divorcing her husband, Brady here pins down the meaning of the word *wife* from the perspective of one person who lives the role. This essay was published in the first issue of *Ms.* magazine in December 1971, and it has since been reprinted widely. Is its harsh portrayal still relevant today?

I belong to that classification of people known as wives. I am A Wife.   1 And, not altogether incidentally, I am a mother.

Not too long ago a male friend of mine appeared on the scene fresh   2 from a recent divorce. He had one child, who is, of course, with his ex-wife. He is looking for another wife. As I thought about him while I was ironing one evening, it suddenly occurred to me that I, too, would like to have a wife. Why do I want a wife?

I would like to go back to school so that I can become economically **3** independent, support myself, and, if need be, support those dependent upon me. I want a wife who will work and send me to school. And while I am going to school I want a wife to take care of my children. I want a wife to keep track of the children's doctor and dentist appointments. And to keep track of mine, too. I want a wife to make sure my children eat properly and are kept clean. I want a wife who will wash the children's clothes and keep them mended. I want a wife who is a good nurturant attendant to my children, who arranges for their schooling, makes sure that they have an adequate social life with their peers, takes them to the park, the zoo, etc. I want a wife who takes care of the children when they are sick, a wife who arranges to be around when the children need special care, because, of course, I cannot miss classes at school. My wife must arrange to lose time at work and not lose the job. It may mean a small cut in my wife's income from time to time, but I guess I can tolerate that. Needless to say, my wife will arrange and pay for the care of the children while my wife is working.

I want a wife who will take care of *my* physical needs. I want a wife **4** who will keep my house clean. A wife who will pick up after my children, a wife who will pick up after me. I want a wife who will keep my clothes clean, ironed, mended, replaced when need be, and who will see to it that my personal things are kept in their proper place so that I can find what I need the minute I need it. I want a wife who cooks the meals, a wife who is a *good* cook. I want a wife who will plan the menus, do the necessary grocery shopping, prepare the meals, serve them pleasantly, and then do the cleaning up while I do my studying. I want a wife who will care for me when I am sick and sympathize with my pain and loss of time from school. I want a wife to go along when our family takes a vacation so that someone can continue to care for me and my children when I need a rest and change of scene.

I want a wife who will not bother me with rambling complaints **5** about a wife's duties. But I want a wife who will listen to me when I feel the need to explain a rather difficult point I have come across in my course of studies. And I want a wife who will type my papers for me when I have written them.

I want a wife who will take care of the details of my social life. When **6** my wife and I are invited out by friends, I want a wife who will take care of the babysitting arrangements. When I meet people at school that I like and want to entertain, I want a wife who will have the house clean, will prepare a special meal, serve it to me and my friends, and not interrupt when I talk about things that interest me and my friends. I want a wife who will have arranged that the children are fed and ready for bed before my guests arrive so that the children do not bother us. I want a wife who takes care of the needs of my guests so that they feel comfortable, who makes sure that they have an ashtray, that they are passed the hors d'oeuvres, that they are offered a second helping of the food, that their wine glasses are replenished when necessary, that their coffee is served to them as they like it. And I want a wife who knows that sometimes I need a night out by myself.

I want a wife who is sensitive to my sexual needs, a wife who makes   7
love passionately and eagerly when I feel like it, a wife who makes sure that I am satisfied. And, of course, I want a wife who will not demand sexual attention when I am not in the mood for it. I want a wife who assumes the complete responsibility for birth control, because I do not want more children. I want a wife who will remain sexually faithful to me so that I do not have to clutter up my intellectual life with jealousies. And I want a wife who understands that *my* sexual needs may entail more than strict adherence to monogamy. I must, after all, be able to relate to people as fully as possible.

If, by chance, I find another person more suitable as a wife than the   8
wife I already have, I want the liberty to replace my present wife with another one. Naturally, I will expect a fresh, new life; my wife will take the children and be solely responsible for them so that I am left free.

When I am through with school and have a job, I want my wife to   9
quit working and remain at home so that my wife can more fully and completely take care of a wife's duties.

My God, who *wouldn't* want a wife?   10

Meaning

1. In one or two sentences, summarize Brady's definition of a wife. Consider not only the functions she mentions but also the relationship she portrays.

2. Brady provides many instances of a double standard of behavior and responsibility for the wife and the wife's spouse. What are the wife's chief responsibilities and expected behaviors? What are the spouse's?

3. If any of the following words are unfamiliar, try to guess what they mean from the context of Brady's essay. Look up the words in a dictionary to check your guesses, and then use each one in a sentence or two of your own.

nurturant (3)	replenished (6)	monogamy (7)
hors d'oeuvres (6)	adherence (7)	

Purpose and Audience

1. Why do you think Brady wrote this essay? Was her purpose to explain a wife's duties, to complain about her own situation, to poke fun at men, to attack men, to attack society's attitudes toward women, or something else? Was she trying to provide a realistic and fair definition of *wife*? What passages in the essay support your answers?

2. What does Brady seem to assume about her readers' gender (male or female) and their attitudes toward women's roles in society, relations between the sexes, and work inside and outside the home? Does she seem to write from the perspective of a particular age-group or social and economic background? In answering these questions, cite specific passages from the essay.

3. Brady clearly intended to provoke a reaction from readers. What is *your* reaction to this essay: do you think it is realistic or exaggerated, fair or unfair to men, relevant or irrelevant to the present time? Why?

Method and Structure

1. Why would anybody need to write an essay defining a term like *wife*? Don't we know what a wife is already? How does Brady use definition in an original way to achieve her purpose?

2. Analyze Brady's essay as a piece of definition, considering its thoroughness, its specificity, and its effectiveness in distinguishing the subject from anything similar.

3. Analyze the introduction to Brady's essay. What function does paragraph 1 serve? In what way does paragraph 2 confirm Brady's definition? How does the question at the end of the introduction relate to the question at the end of the essay?

4. **OTHER METHODS** Brady develops her definition primarily by classification (Chapter 9). What does she classify, and what categories does she form? What determines her arrangement of these categories? What does the classification contribute to the essay?

Language

1. How would you characterize Brady's tone: whining, amused, angry, contemptuous, or something else? What phrases in the essay support your answer? (If necessary, see pp. 41–43 on tone.)

2. Why does Brady repeat "I want a wife" in almost every sentence, often at the beginning of the sentence? What does this stylistic device convey

about the person who wants a wife? How does it fit in with Brady's main idea and purpose?

3. Why does Brady never substitute the personal pronoun "she" for "my wife"? Does the effect gained by repeating "my wife" justify the occasionally awkward sentences, such as the last one in paragraph 3?

4. What effect does Brady achieve with the expressions "of course" (paragraphs 3 and 7), "Needless to say" (3), "after all" (7), and "Naturally" (8)?

Writing Topics

1. **JOURNAL TO ESSAY**   Using your journal entry (p. 264) and ideas generated by Brady's essay, analyze a role that is defined by gender, such as that of a wife or husband, mother or father, sister or brother, daughter or son. First write down the responsibilities, activities, and relationships that define that role, and then elaborate your ideas into an essay defining this role as you see it. You could, if appropriate, follow Brady's model by showing how the role is influenced by the expectations of another person or people.

2. Combine the methods of definition and comparison (Chapter 11) in an essay that compares a wife or a husband you know with Brady's definition of either role. Be sure that the point of your comparison is clear and that you use specific examples to illustrate the similarities or differences you see.

3. **CULTURAL CONSIDERATIONS**   Brady's essay was written in the specific cultural context of 1971. Undoubtedly, many cultural changes have taken place since then, particularly changes in gender roles. However, one could also argue that much remains the same. Write an essay in which you compare the stereotypical role of a wife now with the role Brady defines. In addition to your own observations and experiences, consider contemporary images of wives that the media present—for instance, in television advertising or sitcoms.

4. **CONNECTIONS**   Both Brady and Ashley Rhodes, in "Fatherhood Is Essential" (p. 259), make reference to the demands of children in a family, mentioning their needs to be fed, clothed, entertained, and guided, among others. Brady complains that most of these tasks fall on women's shoulders and wishes that her spouse would help more, and Rhodes, while lamenting her father's lack of involvement, distinguishes the unique role that fathers play in raising their children. Write an essay in which you examine and compare the roles that mothers and fathers play in raising their children. Are there tasks for which one parent is particularly suited? Or is the gender of the parent less relevant than people sometimes think?

Happiness in marriage is entirely a matter of chance. —Jane Austen

Our nation must defend the sanctity of marriage. —George W. Bush

What is fascinating about marriage is why anyone wants to get married. —Alain de Botton

JOURNAL RESPONSE Contemporary society exerts great pressure on single adults to form lasting romantic partnerships. Many unattached people, however, insist that they are perfectly happy to be alone, and many couples are content to live together without a formal commitment. Is marriage a prerequisite for happiness, or is it overrated? Reflect for a moment on what marriage means to you, and write a journal entry that explains your feelings on the subject.

Andrew Sullivan

Andrew Sullivan was born in 1963 in southern England and raised Catholic in a working-class suburb of London. He studied modern history at Magdalen College of Oxford University and holds an MA in public administration and a PhD in political science from Harvard University. A senior editor of the *Atlantic* and the author of countless articles dealing with issues of homosexuality, AIDS, and conservative politics, Sullivan is perhaps best known for his popular blog the *Daily Dish* (http://andrewsullivan.theatlantic.com) and for his book *Virtually Normal: An Argument about Homosexuality* (1995). Sullivan's other titles include *Same-Sex Marriage: Pro and Con* (1997), *Love Undetectable: Notes on Friendship, Sex, and Survival* (1998), and *The Conservative Soul: How We Lost It, How to Get It Back* (2006). He lives in Washington, DC, and is a frequent guest on television and radio talk shows.

The "M-Word": Why It Matters to Me

"The 'M-Word': Why It Matters to Me" first appeared in a 2004 issue of *Time* magazine devoted to the debate over same-sex marriage. In the essay Sullivan offers a very personal definition of *marriage* to explain why he and many other gay Americans want it for themselves.

What's in a name?   1

    Perhaps the best answer is a memory.   2

    As a child, I had no idea what homosexuality was. I grew up in a   3
traditional home—Catholic, conservative, middle class. Life was relatively simple: education, work, family. I was brought up to aim high in life, even though my parents hadn't gone to college. But one thing was instilled in me. What matters is not how far you go in life, how much money you make, how big a name you make for yourself. What really matters is family, and the love you have for one another. The most important day of your life was not graduation from college or your first day at work or a raise or even your first house. The most important day of your life was when you got married. It was on that day that all your friends and all your family got together to celebrate the most important thing in life: your happiness, your ability to make a new home, to form a new but connected family, to find love that puts everything else into perspective.

    But as I grew older, I found that this was somehow not available to   4
me. I didn't feel the things for girls that my peers did. All the emotions and social rituals and bonding of teenage heterosexual life eluded me. I didn't know why. No one explained it. My emotional bonds to other boys were one-sided; each time I felt myself falling in love, they sensed it, pushed it away. I didn't and couldn't blame them. I got along fine with my buds in a nonemotional context; but something was awry, something not right. I came to know almost instinctively that I would never be a part of my family the way my siblings one day might be. The love I had inside me was unmentionable, anathema—even, in the words of the Church I attended every Sunday, evil. I remember writing in my teenage journal one day: "I'm a professional human being. But what do I do in my private life?"

    So, like many gay men of my generation, I retreated. I never discussed   5
my real life. I couldn't date girls and so immersed myself in schoolwork, in the debate team, school plays, anything to give me an excuse not to confront reality. When I looked toward the years ahead, I couldn't see a future. There was just a void. Was I going to be alone my whole life? Would I ever have a "most important day" in my life? It seemed impossible, a negation, an undoing. To be a full part of my family I had to somehow not be me. So like many gay teens, I withdrew, became neurotic, depressed, at times close to suicidal. I shut myself in my room with my books, night after night, while my peers developed the skills needed to form real relationships, and loves. In wounded pride, I even voiced a rejection of family and marriage. It was the only way I could explain my isolation.

It took years for me to realize that I was gay, years later to tell oth- 6
ers, and more time yet to form any kind of stable emotional bond with
another man. Because my sexuality had emerged in solitude—and without any link to the idea of an actual relationship—it was hard later to
reconnect sex to love and self-esteem. It still is. But I persevered, each
relationship slowly growing longer than the last, learning in my twenties
and thirties what my straight friends found out in their teens. But even
then, my parents and friends never asked the question they would have
asked automatically if I were straight: So when are you going to get
married? When is your relationship going to be public? When will we
be able to celebrate it and affirm it and support it? In fact, no one—no
one—has yet asked me that question.[1]

When people talk about "gay marriage," they miss the point. This 7
isn't about gay marriage. It's about marriage. It's about family. It's about
love. It isn't about religion. It's about civil marriage licenses—available
to atheists as well as believers. These family values are not options for
a happy and stable life. They are necessities. Putting gay relationships
in some other category—civil unions, domestic partnerships, civil partnerships, whatever—may alleviate real human needs, but, by their
very euphemism, by their very separateness, they actually build a wall
between gay people and their own families. They put back the barrier
many of us have spent a lifetime trying to erase.

It's too late for me to undo my own past. But I want above everything 8
else to remember a young kid out there who may even be reading this
now. I want to let him know that he doesn't have to choose between himself and his family anymore. I want him to know that his love has dignity,
that he does indeed have a future as a full and equal part of the human
race. Only marriage will do that. Only marriage can bring him home.

Meaning

1. Where does Sullivan stand on the issue of gay marriage? Does he insist on
   full marriage rights for same-sex couples, or does he accept the alternative of civil unions? Where in the essay does he make his position clear?

---

[1] Sullivan was married to artist Aaron Tone in 2007, three years after this essay
was written. In an article about the wedding, he reported that when the engagement was announced, "everybody involved themselves in our love. They asked
how I had proposed; they inquired when the wedding would be; my straight
friends made jokes about marriage that simply included me as one of them. . . . I
felt an end—a sudden, fateful end—to an emotional displacement I had experienced since childhood." [Editors' note.]

2. Sullivan devotes the beginning of his essay to explaining his family's attitudes toward marriage. What was the significance of marriage in the Sullivan household? How did his family's expectations shape his own desires?

3. In paragraph 7, Sullivan writes, "This isn't about gay marriage. It's about marriage." What does he mean? What difference does he see in the concepts of "gay marriage" and "marriage"?

4. If any of the following words are unfamiliar, try to guess what they mean from the context of Sullivan's essay. Look up the words in a dictionary to check your guesses, and then use each one in a sentence or two of your own.

instilled (3)	anathema (4)	persevered (6)
eluded (4)	neurotic (5)	alleviate (7)
awry (4)	solitude (6)	euphemism (7)

Purpose and Audience

1. Why do you think Sullivan wrote this essay?

2. In his conclusion (paragraph 8), Sullivan mentions the "young kid out there who may even be reading this now" but doesn't speak to him directly. What does this suggest about Sullivan's vision of his readers?

3. How do you think Sullivan expects his audience to react to this essay? Does he seem to assume his audience's agreement, does he write defensively to forestall criticism, or does he assume some other response? What in the essay makes you think as you do?

Method and Structure

1. Why is definition an appropriate method for Sullivan to use in developing his ideas? What specific features of this method serve him?

2. In developing his definition, Sullivan relies heavily on personal anecdotes. What do the anecdotes contribute to his essay? Do they weaken his case in any way?

3. **OTHER METHODS** In what ways does Sullivan use narration (Chapter 5) and cause-and-effect analysis (Chapter 13) as part of his definition? Why are these methods important in developing his point?

Language

1. Why does Sullivan use "the 'M-Word'" instead of *marriage* in his title?

2. Sullivan's opening question—"What's in a name?"—is a line from Shakespeare's *Romeo and Juliet*. How does this reference establish the overall tone of Sullivan's argument? Is his tone appropriate to his subject? Why, or why not?

3. Point out some examples that show Sullivan's use of emotional appeal to argue his point. What is the effect of these examples?

Writing Topics

1. **JOURNAL TO ESSAY** In your journal entry (p. 269), you explained what marriage means to you. Now expand your thoughts into an essay-length definition of *marriage*. Does your definition correspond to traditional assumptions about marriage, or is it unconventional? What characteristics does your definition *not* include?

2. Write a response to Sullivan's essay in which you establish your own position on the debate over gay marriage. Do you agree with Sullivan that marriage between same-sex partners is not only acceptable but also necessary, or do you take the view that marriage should be limited to heterosexual couples? Or does your opinion fall somewhere between the two extremes? Draw on the definition of marriage you constructed for your answer to question 1 as necessary or appropriate, and as much as possible, use examples from your own experience (or from the experiences of those close to you) to support your argument.

3. **CULTURAL CONSIDERATIONS** As Sullivan's experience suggests, our adult relationships are often shaped by the examples set by older members of our families—though not always in the ways they might have expected. In an essay explore how your parents or other relatives have influenced your attitudes toward romance and commitment.

4. **CONNECTIONS** In this essay Sullivan argues that marriage is the primary source of an adult's happiness. Judy Brady, in "I Want a Wife" (p. 264), could hardly disagree more. Write an essay in which you compare and contrast the opinions and tones of these two writers.

Definition

Select one of the following topics, or any other topic they suggest, for an essay developed by definition. Be sure to choose a topic you care about so that definition is a means of communicating an idea, not an end in itself.

PERSONAL QUALITIES

1. Ignorance
2. Selflessness or selfishness
3. Loyalty or disloyalty
4. Responsibility
5. Hypocrisy

EXPERIENCES AND FEELINGS

6. A nightmare
7. A good teacher, coach, parent, or friend
8. A good joke or a tasteless joke
9. Religious faith

SOCIAL CONCERNS

10. Poverty
11. Education
12. Domestic violence
13. Substance abuse
14. Prejudice

ART AND ENTERTAINMENT

15. Jazz or some other kind of music
16. A good novel, movie, or television program
17. Impressionism or some other art movement

IDEAS

18. Freedom
19. Nostalgia
20. Feminism
21. Success or failure
22. A key concept in a course you're taking

WRITING ABOUT THE THEME

Clarifying Family Relationships

1. Sandra Cisneros (p. 253), Ashley Rhodes (p. 259), and Andrew Sullivan (p. 269) all write of the impact that family members have on a child's development into adulthood. How important is family (immediate or extended) in shaping young people's sense of who they are and what they want out of life? To what extent does the larger community—friends, teachers, neighbors—also play a significant role in forming a person's identity? Answer in a brief essay, citing as examples the selections in this chapter and observations of your own.

2. Several of the authors in this section deal with gender roles. Sandra Cisneros believes that being the only girl in a family of boys had a lasting effect on her identity, Ashley Rhodes focuses on the role of the man as father, Judy Brady (p. 264) is concerned with unreasonable demands on married women, and Andrew Sullivan argues that gender should not factor into a couple's ability to marry. In your experience, are traditional gender roles helpful or harmful to individuals in a relationship? to society in general? Write an essay that supports your opinion with examples drawn from your own experience.

3. Firoozeh Dumas (p. 253), Judy Brady, and Andrew Sullivan each question at least one traditional notion of the nuclear family as it is understood in the United States. What, in your mind, constitutes a family? How—if at all—has the typical American family changed since your parents or grandparents were your age? Do you think that these relationships will continue to evolve? What predictions can you make about how families might be structured in the future?

13

CAUSE-AND-EFFECT ANALYSIS
Understanding Business and Consumers

Why did free agency become so important in professional baseball, and how has it affected the sport? What caused the recent warming of the Pacific Ocean, and how did the warming affect the earth's weather? We answer questions like these with **cause-and-effect analysis**, the method of dividing occurrences into their elements to find relationships among them. Cause-and-effect analysis is a specific kind of analysis, the method discussed in Chapter 8.

When we analyze causes, we try to discover which of the events preceding a specified outcome actually made it happen:

What caused Adolf Hitler's rise in Germany?

Why have herbal medicines become so popular?

When we analyze effects, we try to discover which of the events following a specified occurrence actually resulted from it:

What do we do for (or to) drug addicts when we imprison them?

What happens to our foreign policy when the president's advisers disagree over its conduct?

These are existing effects of past or current situations, but effects are often predicted for the future:

How would a cure for cancer affect the average life expectancy of men and women?

How might your decision to take family leave affect your future job prospects?

Causes and effects can also be analyzed together, as the questions opening this chapter illustrate.

Like everyone else, you probably consider causes and effects many times a day: Why is the traffic so heavy? What will happen if I major in art rather than business? In writing you'll also draw often on cause-and-effect analysis, perhaps explaining why the school's basketball team has been so successful this year, what made a bridge collapse, or how a new stoplight has worsened rush-hour traffic. You'll use the method for persuasion, too, as in arguing that the family, not the mass media, bears responsibility for children's violence (focusing on causes) or that adult illiteracy threatens American democracy (focusing on possible effects). Because cause-and-effect analysis attempts to answer *why* and *what if*—two of the most basic questions of human experience—you'll find the method often in your reading as well.

Reading Cause-and-Effect Analysis

Cause-and-effect analysis is found in just about every discipline and occupation, including history, social science, natural science, engineering, medicine, law, business, and sports. In any of these fields, as well as in writing done for college courses, the purpose in analyzing may be to explain or to persuade. In explaining why something happened or what its outcome was or will be, writers try to order experience and pin down the connections in it. In arguing with cause-and-effect analysis, they try to demonstrate why one explanation of causes is more accurate than another or how a proposed action will produce desirable or undesirable consequences.

The possibility of arguing about causes and effects points to the main challenge of this method. Related events sometimes overlap, sometimes follow one another immediately, and sometimes connect over gaps in time. They vary in their duration and complexity. They vary in their importance. Analyzing causes and effects thus requires not only identifying them but also discerning their relationships accurately and weighing their significance fairly.

Causes and effects often do occur in a sequence, each contributing to the next in what is called a causal chain. For instance, an unlucky man named Jones ends up in prison, and the causal chain leading to his imprisonment can be outlined as follows: Jones's neighbor, Smith, dumped trash on Jones's lawn. In reprisal, Jones set a small brush fire in Smith's yard. A spark from the fire accidentally ignited Smith's house. Jones was prosecuted for the fire and sent to jail. In this chain each event is the cause of an effect, which in turn is the cause of another effect, and so on to the unhappy conclusion.

Identifying a causal chain partly involves sorting out events in time:

- **Immediate** causes or effects occur nearest an event. For instance, the immediate cause of a town's high unemployment rate may be the closing of a large manufacturing plant where many townspeople work.

- **Remote** causes or effects occur further away in time. The remote cause of the town's unemployment rate may be a drastic decline in the company's sales or (more remote) a weak regional or national economy.

Analyzing causes also requires distinguishing their relative importance in the sequence:

- **Major** causes are directly and primarily responsible for the outcome. For instance, if a weak economy is responsible for low sales, it is a major cause of the manufacturing plant's closing.

- **Minor** causes (also called contributory causes) merely contribute to the outcome. The manufacturing plant may have closed for the additional reason that the owners could not afford to make repairs to its machines.

As these examples illustrate, time and significance can overlap in cause-and-effect analysis: a weak economy, for instance, is both a remote and a major cause; the lack of funds for repairs is both an immediate and a minor cause.

Since most cause-and-effect relationships are complex, several pitfalls can weaken an analysis or its presentation. One is a confusion of coincidence and cause—that is, an assumption that because one event preceded another, it must have caused the other. This error is nicknamed post hoc, from the Latin *post hoc, ergo propter hoc*, meaning "after this, therefore because of this." Superstitions often illustrate post hoc: a basketball player believes that a charm once ended her shooting slump, so she now wears the charm whenever she plays. But post hoc also occurs in more serious matters. For instance, the office of a school administrator is vandalized, and he blames the incident on a recent speech by the student-government president criticizing the administration. But the administrator has no grounds for his accusation unless he can prove that the speech incited the vandals. In the absence of proof, the administrator commits the error of post hoc by asserting that the speech caused the vandalism simply because the speech preceded the vandalism.

Another potential problem in cause-and-effect writing is oversimplification. An effective analysis must consider not just the causes and effects that seem obvious or important but all the possibilities: remote as well as immediate, minor as well as major. One form of oversimplification confuses a necessary cause with a sufficient cause:

- A **necessary** cause, as the term implies, is one that must happen in order for an effect to come about; an effect can have more than one necessary cause. For example, if emissions from a factory cause a high rate of illness in a neighborhood, the emissions are a necessary cause.

- A **sufficient** cause, in contrast, is one that brings about the effect *by itself*. The emissions are not a sufficient cause of the illness rate unless all other possible causes—such as water pollution or infection—can be eliminated.

Oversimplification can also occur if opinions or emotions are allowed to cloud the interpretation of evidence. Suppose that a writer is examining the reasons a gun-control bill she opposed was passed by the state legislature. Some of the evidence strongly suggests that a member of the legislature, a vocal supporter of the bill, was unduly influenced by lobbyists. But if the writer attributed the passage of the bill solely to this legislator, she would be exaggerating the significance of a single legislator and ignoring the opinions of the many others who also voted for the bill. To achieve a balanced analysis, she would have to put aside her personal feelings and consider all possible causes for the bill's passage.

Analyzing Causes and Effects in Paragraphs

Barbara Ehrenreich (born 1941) is an essayist, historian, and investigative journalist. A contributing writer for a wide range of periodicals, she is probably best known for her books about contemporary class struggles in the United States, especially *Nickel and Dimed: On (Not) Getting By in America* (2001), the book in which the following paragraph appears.

The problem of rents is easy for a noneconomist, even a sparsely educated low-wage worker, to grasp. . . . When the rich and the poor compete for housing on the open market, the poor don't stand a chance. The rich can always outbid them, buy up their tenements or trailer parks, and replace them with condos, McMansions, golf courses, or whatever they like. Since the rich have become more numerous, thanks largely to rising stock prices and executive salaries, the poor have necessarily been forced into housing that is more expensive, more dilapidated, or more distant from their places of work. . . . Insofar as the poor have to work near the dwellings of the rich—as in the case of so many service and retail jobs—they are stuck with lengthy commutes or dauntingly expensive housing.

> Cause (topic sentence underlined): competition for housing between rich and poor
>
> Effects:
>
> Rich can buy inexpensive properties for themselves
>
> Poor are forced to pay more, accept less, or move

Pico Iyer (born 1957) is a British travel writer of Indian heritage who was educated in England and America and lives in Japan. The following paragraph is adapted from "The Joy of Less," his commentary on the benefits of giving up consumer goods, first posted as a blog entry for the New York Times in 2009.

I still live in the vicinity of Kyoto, in a two-room apartment that makes my old monastic cell look almost luxurious by comparison. . . . I have no bicycle, no car, no television I can understand, no media—and the days seem to stretch into eternities, and I can't think of a single thing I lack. I'm no Buddhist monk, and I can't say I'm in love with renunciation in itself, or traveling an hour or more to print out an article I've written, or missing out on the NBA Finals. But at some point, I decided that, for me at least, happiness arose out of all I didn't want or need, not all I did. And it seemed quite useful to take a clear, hard look at what really led to peace of mind or absorption (the closest I've come to understanding happiness). Not having a car gives me volumes not to think or worry about, and makes walks around the

> Effect (topic sentence underlined): happiness
>
> Causes:
>
> Freedom from worry

neighborhood a daily adventure. Lacking a cell phone and high-speed Internet, I have time to play ping-pong every evening, to write long letters to old friends, and to go shopping for my sweetheart (or to track down old baubles for two kids who are now out in the world).

Daily exercise and adventure

Interacting with loved ones

Developing an Essay by Cause-and-Effect Analysis

Getting Started

Assignments in almost any course or line of work ask for cause-and-effect analysis: What caused the Vietnam War? In the theory of sociobiology, what are the effects of altruism on the survival of the group? Why did costs exceed the budget last month? You can find your own subject for cause-and-effect analysis from your experiences, from observation of others, from your course work, or from your reading outside school. Anytime you find yourself wondering what happened or why or what if, you may be onto an appropriate subject.

Remember that your treatment of causes or effects or both must be thorough; thus your subject must be manageable within the constraints of time and space imposed on you. Broad subjects like those in the following examples must be narrowed to something whose complexities you can cover adequately.

BROAD SUBJECT   Causes of the increase in American industrial productivity

NARROWER SUBJECT   Causes of increasing productivity on one assembly line

BROAD SUBJECT   Effects of cigarette smoke

NARROWER SUBJECT   Effects of parents' secondhand smoke on small children

Whether your subject suggests a focus on causes or effects or both, list as many of them as you can from memory or from further reading. If the subject does not suggest a focus, then ask yourself questions to begin exploring it:

- Why did it happen?
- What contributed to it?

- What were or are its results?
- What might its consequences be?

One or more of these questions should lead you to a focus and, as you explore further, to a more complete list of ideas.

But you cannot stop with a simple list, for you must arrange the causes or effects in sequence and weigh their relative importance: Do the events break down into a causal chain? Besides the immediate causes and effects, are there also less obvious, more remote ones? Besides the major causes or effects, are there also minor ones? At this stage, you may find that diagraming relationships helps you see them more clearly. The following diagram illustrates the earlier example of the plant closing (see p. 278):

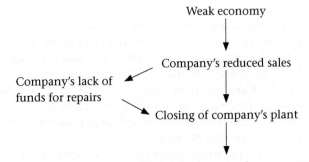

Town's high unemployment rate

Though uncomplicated, the diagram does sort out the causes and effects and shows their relationships and sequence.

While you are developing a clear picture of your subject, you should also be anticipating the expectations and needs of your readers. As with the other methods of essay development, consider especially what your readers already know about your subject and what they need to be told:

- Do readers require background information?
- Are they likely to be familiar with some of the causes or effects you are analyzing, or should you explain every one completely?
- Which causes or effects might readers already accept?
- Which ones might they disagree with? If, for instance, the plant closing affected many of your readers—putting them or their relatives out of work—they might blame the company's owners rather than economic forces beyond the owners' control. You would have to address these preconceptions and provide plenty of evidence for your own interpretation.

Forming a Thesis

To help manage your ideas and information, try to develop a working thesis sentence that states your subject, your perspective on it, and your purpose. For instance:

> EXPLANATORY THESIS SENTENCE   Being caught in the middle of a family quarrel has affected not only my feelings about my family but also my relations with friends.

> PERSUASIVE THESIS SENTENCE   Contrary to local opinion, the many people put out of work by the closing of Windsor Manufacturing were victims not of the owners' incompetence but of the nation's weak economy.

Notice that these thesis sentences reflect clear judgments about the relative significance of possible causes or effects. Such judgments can be difficult to reach and may not be apparent when you start writing. Often you will need to complete a draft of your analysis before you are confident about the relationship between cause and effect. And even if you start with an idea of how cause and effect are connected, you may change your mind after you've mapped out the relationship in a draft. That's fine: just remember to revise your thesis sentence accordingly.

Organizing

The introduction to a cause-and-effect essay can pull readers in by describing the situation whose causes or effects you plan to analyze, such as the passage of a bill in the legislature or a town's high unemployment rate. The introduction may also provide background, such as a brief narrative of a family quarrel; or it may summarize the analysis of causes or effects that the essay disputes, such as townspeople blaming owners for a plant's closing. If your thesis is not already apparent in the introduction, stating it explicitly can tell readers exactly what your purpose is and which causes or effects or both you plan to highlight. But if you anticipate that readers will oppose your thesis, you may want to delay stating it until the end of the essay, after you have provided the evidence to support it.

The arrangement of the body of the essay depends primarily on your material and your emphasis. If events unfold in a causal chain with each effect becoming the cause of another effect, and if stressing these links coincides with your purpose, then a simple chronological sequence will probably be clearest. But if events overlap and vary in significance, their organization will require more planning. Probably the most effective

way to arrange either causes or effects is in order of increasing importance. Such an arrangement helps readers see which causes or effects
you consider minor and which major, while it also reserves your most
significant (and probably most detailed) point for last. The groups of
minor or major events may then fit into a chronological framework.

To avoid being preoccupied with organization while you are drafting
your essay, prepare some sort of outline before you start writing. The outline
need not be detailed so long as you have written the details elsewhere or
can retrieve them easily from your mind. But it should show all the causes
or effects you want to discuss and the order in which you will cover them.

To conclude your essay, you may want to restate your thesis—or
state it, if you deliberately withheld it for the end—so that readers are
left with the point of your analysis. If your analysis is complex, readers
may also benefit from a summary of the relationships you have identified. And depending on your purpose, you may want to specify why
your analysis is significant, what use your readers can make of it, or what
action you hope they will take.

Drafting

While drafting your essay, strive primarily for clarity—sharp details,
strong examples, concrete explanations. To make readers see not only
what you see but also *why* you see it, you can draw on just about any
method of writing discussed in this book. For instance, you might narrate the effect of a situation on one person, analyze a process, or compare and contrast two interpretations of cause. Particularly if your thesis
is debatable (like the earlier example asserting the owners' blamelessness
for the plant's closing), you will need accurate, representative facts to
back up your interpretation, and you may also need quotations from
experts such as witnesses and scholars. If you do not support your assertions specifically, your readers will have no reason to believe them. (For
more on evidence in persuasive writing, see pp. 321–22. For more on
finding and documenting sources, see the Appendix.)

Revising and Editing

While revising and editing your draft, consider the following questions
and the box to be sure your analysis is sound and clear.

- *Have you explained causes or effects clearly and specifically?* Readers
  will need to see the pattern of causes or effects—their sequence

and relative importance. And readers will need facts, examples, and other evidence to understand and accept your analysis.

- *Have you demonstrated that causes are not merely coincidences?* Avoid the error of post hoc, of assuming that one event caused another just because it preceded the other. To be convincing, a claim that one event caused another must be supported with ample evidence.

- *Have you considered all the possible causes or effects?* Your analysis should go beyond what is most immediate or obvious so that you do not oversimplify the cause-and-effect relationships. Your readers will expect you to present the relationships in all their complexity.

- *Have you represented the cause-and-effect relationships honestly?* Don't deliberately ignore or exaggerate causes or effects in a misguided effort to strengthen your essay. If a cause fails to support your thesis but still does not invalidate it, mention the cause and explain why you believe it to be unimportant. If a change you are proposing will have bad effects as well as good, mention the bad effects and explain how they are outweighed by the good. As long as your reasoning and evidence are sound, such admissions will not weaken your essay; on the contrary, readers will appreciate your fairness.

- *Have you used transitions to signal the sequence and relative importance of events?* Transitions between sentences can help you pinpoint causes or effects (*for this reason, as a result*), show the steps in a

FOCUS ON CLARITY AND CONCISENESS

While drafting a cause-and-effect analysis, you may need to grope a bit to discover just what you think about the sequence and relative importance of reasons and consequences. As a result, your sentences may grope a bit, too, reflecting your need to circle around your ideas in order to find them. You might discover, for example, that sentence subjects and verbs do not focus on the main actors and actions of the sentences, that words repeat unnecessarily, or that word groups run longer than needed for clarity. As you edit, then, focus on moving your main ideas up front, on using subjects and verbs to state what the sentences are about, and on cutting unneeded words. For help with editing for clarity and conciseness, see pages 48–52.

▶ To practice editing for clarity and conciseness, visit Exercise Central at *bedfordstmartins.com/rewriting*.

sequence (*first, second, third*), link events in time (*in the same month*), specify duration (*a year later*), and indicate the weights you assign events (*equally important, even more crucial*). (See also *transitions* in the Glossary.)

A Note on Thematic Connections

Analyzing the economy often prompts writers to ask what leads to success or failure or what may result from a business decision. The authors in this chapter all attempt to pinpoint a cause-and-effect relationship between business practices and consumer behaviors. In a paragraph (p. 280), Barbara Ehrenreich considers how the real estate market makes housing less affordable. In another paragraph (p. 280), Pico Iyer explains the emotional benefits of getting by with less. In essays, student writers Stephanie Alaimo and Mark Koester (opposite) and journalist Dana Thomas (p. 292) discuss the consequences of our shopping choices, while Charlie LeDuff contemplates what happens to a factory town when its factory is closed (p. 300).

There is no reason that the universe should be designed for our convenience. —John D. Barrow

All of the biggest technological inventions created by man—the airplane, the automobile, the computer—say little about his intelligence, but speak volumes about his laziness. —Mark Kennedy

Besides black art [such as voodoo and witchcraft], there is only automation and mechanization. —Federico García Lorca

JOURNAL RESPONSE Write a short journal entry about a modern convenience that you dislike. (Examples might include online banking, cruise control, or automated call centers.) Why don't you care for it? In what ways is this technology harmful or just more trouble than it's worth?

Stephanie Alaimo and Mark Koester

Stephanie Alaimo (born 1984) and Mark Koester (born 1983) studied at DePaul University of Chicago and the Université de Strasbourg in France. Alaimo, a Spanish major while at DePaul, volunteered as a tutor in English as a second language and as an intern with the Interfaith Committee for Worker Justice. She is currently a graduate student studying the sociology of migration and development at the University of California, San Diego. Koester, a native of Omaha, Nebraska, majored in philosophy. He now teaches English in Hangzhou, China, and ponders philosophy, language, and politics on his blog, *The Mystic Atheist* (http://mysticatheist.blogspot.com).

The Backdraft of Technology
(Student Essay)

How important is it to save a few minutes in the supermarket? Would you stand in line to save someone else's job? Alaimo and Koester think you should—and they explain why by analyzing the causes and effects of self-service checkout machines. They collaborated on this op-ed piece for the *DePaulia*, a student newspaper, in 2006.

You have picked up the bread and the milk and the day's miscellaneous 1
foodstuffs at your local grocery store. The lines at the traditional, human-
operated checkouts are a shocking two customers deep. Who wants to
wait? Who would wait when we have society's newest upgrade in not
having to wait: the self-checkout?

Welcome to the automated grocery store. "Please scan your next 2
item," a repetitively chilling, mechanical voice orders you.

If you have yet to see it at your nearest grocer, a new technologi- 3
cal advance has been reached. Instead of waiting for some minimally
waged, minimally educated, and, most likely, immigrant cashier to
scan and bag your groceries for you, you can now do it yourself. In a
consumer-driven, hyperactive, "I want" world, an increase in speed is
easily accepted thoughtlessly. We're too busy. But, in gaining efficiency
and ease, a number of jobs have been lost, particularly at the entry level,
and a moment of personal, human engagement with actual people has
vanished.

It seems easy enough to forget about the consequences when you 4
are rushed and your belly is grumbling. The previously utilized checkout lanes at local grocery stores and super, mega, we-have-everything
stores are now routinely left unattended during the peak hours. In these
moments, your options are using the self-checkout or waiting for a real
human being. Often in a hurried moment we choose the easiest, fastest,
and least mentally involved option without much consideration.

We forget to consider that with the aid of the self-checkout at least 5
two jobs have been lost. As a result, a human cashier and grocery bagger
are now waiting in the unemployment line. Furthermore, self-checkout
machines are probably not manufactured in the United States, thus
shipping more jobs overseas. And sadly, the job openings are now shrink-
ing by putting consumers to work. The wages from these jobs are stock-
piled by those least in need—corporations and those who own them.

The mechanization of the service industry has been occurring 6
throughout our lifetimes. Gas stations were once full-service. Human
bank tellers handled simple cash withdrawals, instead of ATMs. Even
video stores are being marginalized from people ordering online from
companies like Netflix. And did you know that you can now order a
pizza for delivery online without even talking to a person?

Sure, these new robots and computers reduce work, which could 7
potentially be a really good thing. But these mechanizations have only
increased profit margins for large corporations and have reduced the
need to hire employees. Jobs are lost along with means of providing for
one's self and family.

For those who find the loss of grocery store labor to be meaningless 8 and, quite frankly, beyond impacting their future lives as accountants or lawyers, it does not seem to be entirely implausible that almost any job or task could become entirely technologically mechanized and your elitist job market nuked.

We are a society trapped in a precarious fork in the road. We can either 9 eliminate the time and toil of the human workload and still allow people to have jobs and maintain the same standard of living, though working less, or, in a darker scenario, we can eliminate human work in terms of actual human jobs and make the situation of the lower classes more tenuous. Is it our goal to reduce the overall time that individuals spend laboring? Or is it our goal to increase corporate profits at the loss of many livelihoods?

At present, corporations and their executives put consumers to work, 10 cut the cost of labor through the use of technology such as self-checkouts and ATMs, and profit tremendously. But a host of workers are now scrambling to find a way to subsist. To choose the self-checkout simply as a convenience cannot be morally justified unless these jobs remain.

The choices we make on a daily basis affect the whole of our society. 11 Choosing convenience often translates to eliminating actual jobs that provide livelihoods and opportunities to many. Think before you simply follow the next technological innovation. Maybe it could be you in their soon-to-be-jobless shoes. Say "No!" to self-checkout.

Meaning

1. What do you make of the title of this essay? What is a backdraft, and what does it have to do with technology?

2. In paragraph 4, Alaimo and Koester write, "Often in a hurried moment we choose the easiest, fastest, and least mentally involved option without much consideration." Do they condemn this tendency?

3. Try to guess the meanings of the following words, based on their context in Alaimo and Koester's essay. Test your guesses in a dictionary, and then try to use each word in a sentence or two of your own.

stockpiled (5)	implausible (8)	tenuous (9)
marginalized (6)	precarious (9)	subsist (10)

Purpose and Audience

1. Do you believe that Alaimo and Koester are writing mainly to express their viewpoint or to persuade readers to do something? Make specific references to the text to support your opinion.

2. Who is the "you" being addressed in the two opening paragraphs? What do these paragraphs and the rest of the essay tell you about the authors' conception of their audience?

Method and Structure

1. Why do you think Alaimo and Koester rely on cause-and-effect analysis to develop their ideas? What are some causes of long checkout lines, in their opinion? What is the effect of the option to serve ourselves rather than wait for a cashier?

2. The authors open and close their essay by having their readers imagine waiting in line at the supermarket. What is the effect of this scenario?

3. In your opinion, is the cause-and-effect analysis in this essay sufficiently thorough and convincing? Why, or why not?

4. **OTHER METHODS**   In addition to cause-and-effect analysis, Alaimo and Koester rely on example (Chapter 7) and argument and persuasion (Chapter 14). What does each of these other methods contribute to their essay?

Language

1. How would you describe the authors' tone? Are they angry? optimistic? passionate? earnest? hesitant? friendly?

2. Alaimo and Koester begin paragraph 7 with the interjection "Sure." They also use phrases such as "miscellaneous foodstuffs" (1), "super, mega, we-have-everything stores" (4), "nuked" (8), and "fork in the road" (9). How would you characterize this language? What does it add to (or take away from) the essay?

Writing Topics

1. **JOURNAL TO ESSAY**   On the basis of your journal entry and your reaction to the quotations at the beginning of this essay (p. 287), expand your ideas about the drawbacks of a modern convenience. Do you agree with Alaimo and Koester that "the choices we make on a daily basis affect the whole of our society" (paragraph 11)? When do technological conveniences help us? At what point does convenience for ourselves become harmful and destructive for others? Write to persuade your readers to change their behavior, as Alaimo and Koester do, or from a narrower personal perspective. If you choose the latter course, however, be sure

to make your experience meaningful to others with plenty of details and examples.

2. Alaimo and Koester challenge their readers to reject self-service opportunities because they believe mechanization deprives unskilled workers of desperately needed jobs. But are such menial, low-paying jobs really worth saving? Write an essay that offers an alternative solution to the employment issue Alaimo and Koester describe. Define the problem as you interpret it, and explain its causes. In your proposal, outline the changes you would like to see take place, identify who would have to make them, and predict how they would improve things.

3. **CULTURAL CONSIDERATIONS** In paragraph 3, Alaimo and Koester say that many cashiers are immigrants; later they express concern that American jobs are being shipped to other countries (paragraph 5). What is your response to these remarks? Write an essay that considers the impact of foreign labor on the US job market. What are some sources of friction? What are some advantages? To what extent should the United States encourage immigration and globalization, and to what extent should the country restrict them? Why? Use examples from your own experience, observations, and reading.

4. **CONNECTIONS** Like Alaimo and Koester, Brandon Griggs, in "The Most Annoying Facebookers" (p. 174), questions the need for a modern technology while understanding why people use it anyway. But whereas Alaimo and Koester take their subject quite seriously, Griggs draws on humor to make his point. Compare and contrast these writers' strategies in an effort to determine when humor is appropriate and when it detracts from a writer's purpose. How, for example, would "The Backdraft of Technology" have worked if the authors had taken a more lighthearted approach? What would be lost in Griggs's essay if he hadn't tried to make his readers laugh?

A bargain is in its very essence a hostile transaction. Do not all men try to abate the price of all they buy? I contend that a bargain even between brethren is a declaration of war. —Lord Byron

Every time you see the Wal-Mart smiley face, whistling and knocking down the prices, somewhere there's a factory worker being kicked in the stomach. —Sherrie Ford

Real happiness is cheap enough, yet how dearly we pay for its counterfeit. —Hosea Ballou

JOURNAL RESPONSE Are name brands and designer logos important to you? Have you ever knowingly purchased something that pretended to be a luxury product but obviously wasn't, such as fake Versace sunglasses or an imitation Coach wallet? Do you have any reservations about making such purchases? Why, or why not? In your journal, write a few paragraphs exploring your thoughts about counterfeit goods.

Dana Thomas

Fashion journalist Dana Thomas (born 1964) grew up in an upscale neighborhood of Philadelphia and attended the American University in Washington, DC. She taught journalism at the American University in Paris, wrote about style for the *New York Times Magazine* and *Newsweek*, and contributed articles to the *New Yorker*, *Harper's Bazaar*, *Vogue*, and several international newspapers before taking her current post as the European editor for *Condé Nast Portfolio*. Noticing in the 1990s that high-end fashion brands such as Louis Vuitton, Gucci, and Prada had begun marketing low-end versions of their products, Thomas was inspired to research and write *DeLuxe: How Luxury Lost Its Luster* (2007), an exposé of diminishing standards in the luxury industry that quickly became an international bestseller. She lives in Paris with her husband and daughter.

The Fake Trade

Thomas been praised for offering an unexpected look at luxury merchandise and its impact on the people who make, sell, and buy it. In this article from *Harper's Bazaar Australia*, she relates a story about a little girl and a fake

Louis Vuitton purse to explain why trading in counterfeit goods is not the victimless crime many shoppers assume it to be.

On a cool August evening, my family and I visited the preppy town 1
of Mill Valley, California, outside San Francisco. In the town square
was an all-American sight: a couple of kids behind a card table selling homemade lemonade. My six-year-old wanted some, so I gave
her a quarter and sent her over to the booth. After a few minutes, I
joined the kids and noticed that one, a cute eight- or nine-year-old
girl with a blonde blunt cut, had a little Murakami[1] pouch slung over
her shoulder.

"Nice handbag," I said to her. 2

"It's Louis Vuitton," she responded proudly. 3

"No," I thought to myself as I gave it a good look-over. "It's a coun- 4
terfeit Louis Vuitton. And it was probably made by a Chinese kid the
same age as you in a slum halfway around the world."

Though the fashion business has muscled up its fight against coun- 5
terfeiting, with many brands investing millions of dollars each year, the
battle is ongoing. Since 1982, the global trade in counterfeit and pirated
goods has grown from an estimated $5.5 billion to approximately
$600 billion annually. Experts believe that counterfeiting costs American
businesses $200 billion to $250 billion annually and is directly responsible for the loss of more than 750,000 jobs in the United States.

What's counterfeited? Everything. A couple of years ago, a counter- 6
feit investigator discovered a workshop in the Thai countryside that produced fake versions of the classic Ferrari P4. Ferrari itself originally made
only three P4s back in 1967. The Food and Drug Administration has said
that counterfeit medicine could account for upwards of 10 percent of all
drugs worldwide. Unknowingly taking a fake version of your medicine
could have horrific effects on your health. European Union officials have
seen a dramatic rise in the seizure of counterfeit personal-care items such
as creams, toothpastes, and razor blades. The television series *Law &
Order: Criminal Intent* recently highlighted this problem in an episode in
which several children died after ingesting counterfeit mouthwash that
had been made with a poisonous chemical found in antifreeze. "There
have been counterfeit perfumes tested by laboratories that have found
that a major component was feline urine," says Heather McDonald, a
partner at the law firm Baker Hostetler in New York who specializes in

---

[1] Japanese cartoon character. [Editors' note.]

anticounterfeiting litigation. Counterfeit automotive brakes made with compressed grass and wood have been found in US stores.

One of the primary reasons counterfeiting keeps flourishing is that, 7 as the little girl in Mill Valley proved, people keep happily buying fakes. According to a study published last year by the British law firm Davenport Lyons, almost two-thirds of UK consumers are "proud to tell their family and friends that they bought fake luxury [fashion items]." And according to a 2003 survey carried out by Market & Opinion Research International in Great Britain, around a third of those questioned would consider buying counterfeits. Why? Because we still think of counterfeiting as a "victimless crime." Buying a counterfeit Vuitton bag surely doesn't affect the company, we reason. The parents of that Mill Valley girl probably wouldn't have invested in a real Vuitton Murakami for her, so it wasn't a loss of sales for the company.

But the reality is that we're all victims of counterfeiting, whether 8 from the loss of jobs or of tax revenue that could fund our schools and our roads, or because by buying counterfeit goods, we are financing international crime syndicates that deal in money laundering, human trafficking, and child labor. Each time I read the horrid tales about counterfeiting from my book, *Deluxe: How Luxury Lost Its Luster*—like the raid I went on in a clandestine factory in the industrial city of Guangzhou, China, where we found children making fake Dunhill and Versace handbags—audience members or radio listeners tell me they had no idea it was such a dark and dangerous world and that by purchasing these goods they were contributing personally to it. Then they invariably swear that they will never knowingly buy another fake good.

Brands as well as law enforcement have cracked down on the coun- 9 terfeit business severely in the past few years, here in the US and abroad. I saw a difference in Hong Kong, for example: a decade ago, you could buy a fake Vuitton handbag or Burberry knapsack for a couple of bucks from a vendor in the subway; today you can't even find them on the street. There are still dealers, but now they lurk in doorways, whispering, "Rolex? Chanel?" and you hurry down dark streets to armored hideaways to close the deal. To say it's scary is an understatement. "If you can keep the stuff out of the public eye, you are halfway to winning the battle," McDonald says. "The brands that are doing aggressive enforcement are hidden in back alleys and not on the street corners."

As long as there is a demand, however, there will be a supply. Tra- 10 ditionally, the supply chain worked like this: an order of ten thousand handbags would be divided into ten groups of one thousand to be made—often by children—in hidden workshops in Guangzhou. Once completed, the items would be wrapped up and deposited in a neutral place, like the courtyard of a local school, where they were picked up by a local transporter, often simply a guy on a bike with a cart. The transporter delivered the package to the wholesaler, who would take it to another neutral place to be picked up by the international shipping agent and put in a shipping container. The goods were often packed in shipments of foodstuffs or legitimately manufactured clothing to escape detection by receiving customs officials. Each time the goods changed hands, the prices doubled. All transactions were done in cash.

But as fashion companies grew wise to the process and went after the   11
sources in China, leading to raids on workshops and busts at ports, the counterfeit-crime rings came up with new routes to supply fake goods: produce them, or at least finish them, in the destination country. Law enforcement witnessed this firsthand during a big bust this past October. The New York Police Department raided a commercial building in Queens, arrested thirteen, and seized around $4 million in counterfeit apparel that carried the logos of major brands including Polo, Lacoste, Rocawear, the North Face, and 7 for All Mankind. Officers also found a stash of fake labels and buttons for Tommy Hilfiger, Nike, and Adidas as well as embroidery machines. Investigators believe that the site was a finishing facility. Workers took generic items that may have been imported legally and sewed on fake logos and labels, turning the items into counterfeit branded goods.

Another trick is to import counterfeit items that are hiding under a   12
legitimate face. "Some of the counterfeiters put a whole separate coating on the bag, and you peel it off like contact paper to see the logo fabric underneath," McDonald tells me. "We seized a load of Lacoste men's dress shirts, and on the left breast pocket, where the alligator should be, there was a little generic label that read, 'Metro.' When you pulled out the threads and removed the Metro label, you found the alligator."

There's another method that is catching on rapidly: counterfeiters   13
who will take a legitimate logo, tinker with it slightly, apply for a trademark for the new design, then import those items under a false pretense of legality, showing the official application paperwork as their defense. For example, a company takes the Ralph Lauren polo-horse-and-rider logo and puts the polo mallet down instead of up in the air. The counterfeiter files a trademark application with the US Patent and Trademark Office and gets a document that states the application is pending. "It's a legitimate document fraudulently secured, and the application will probably be rejected in six months," the intellectual-property counsel for a luxury brand explains to me. "But between now and then, the customs agents will approve the importation of the items—believing, incorrectly, that the pending application proves the importer must have a legitimate right to the trademark."

By the time the brand realizes what's going on, the lawyer says, 14
thousands of items will have been imported and the counterfeiter will
have "made millions" and fled. Luxury companies discovered one operation using this technique about two years ago, and now several more
have popped up. "We must be doing a good job, since counterfeiters are
looking for such complicated ways to get in," the lawyer says.

People often ask me, "How do you know it's fake?"   15

Well, if it's being sold at a fold-up table on a sidewalk corner or on 16
the back of a peddler on the beach, chances are it's fake. Or if it's at a flea
market. Or a church fundraiser. Or in Wal-Mart or Sam's Club or other
discount mass retailers. In June 2006, Fendi filed suit in a US district court
against Wal-Mart Stores, Inc., asserting that the world's largest retailer was
selling counterfeit Fendi handbags and wallets in its Sam's Club stores.
For example, one bag was offered for $295; the legitimate Fendi handbag
of the same design normally retailed for $925. In the suit, Fendi stated
that Wal-Mart has never purchased Fendi products and never checked
with Fendi to see if the items were real. The case was settled out of court
last summer after Sam's Club agreed to pay Fendi an undisclosed sum.

If you want to guarantee that your luxury-brand purchases are   17
legitimate, don't shop in wholesale markets like those in Chinatown in
Manhattan or Santee Alley in Los Angeles. "We'll go on raids on Chinatown wholesalers, and we'll find five or six suburban women standing
there—customers," New York security expert Andrew Oberfeldt has told
me. "We'll say to these women, 'The dealers take you down dark cor-
ridors, through locked doors. The police say, "Open up!" The lights are
turned out and everyone is told to be quiet. At what point did you realize that something was amiss here?'"

If you find an item for sale on the Internet for a price so low that 18
it seems too good to be true, it probably is too good to be true. Last
fall, the UK-based Authentics Foundation, an international nonprofit
organization devoted to raising public awareness about counterfeiting, launched myauthentics.com, a Web site that helps Internet shoppers determine if the products they are eyeing on the Web are real. It
includes blogs and forums, news, myths, and tips on how to spot fakes;
eBay now has links to the site. EBay also works with brands in its VeRO
(Verified Rights Owner) program to find out if the items for offer on the
site are genuine. If the brand deems a particular item to be counterfeit,
the sale will be shut down. However, not all online sales sites have
such verification processes in place. Besides, counterfeiters are known
to post photos of genuine items to sell fakes. So as the old saying goes,
buyer beware.

Of course, the best way to know if you are buying a genuine product 19 is to buy it from the brand, either in directly operated boutiques or in a company's shop in a department store. If you are curious about the authenticity of a used Vuitton item you purchased at a vintage shop or online, you can always contact one of the brand's boutiques.

Most important, we need to spread the word on the devastat- 20 ing effects counterfeiting has on society today. I didn't tell the girl in Mill Valley that her bag was fake. It wasn't her fault her family had given it to her. But if I had met her parents, I would have said something. Awareness is key. Counterfeiting will never go away—it's been around since the dawn of time—but we can surely cut it down to size if we just stop buying the stuff. Without the demand, the supply will shrink. It's up to us.

Meaning

1. Throughout her essay, Thomas repeats the words *counterfeit* and *legitimate*. How does she define these terms? Why is the distinction between the two important?

2. In paragraph 7, Thomas says that consumers believe counterfeiting is a "victimless crime." What does that mean? Does she believe it herself? Why does she bring it up?

3. Although Thomas stresses the importance of raising awareness of counterfeiting, she does not say anything to the girl with the fake designer handbag. Why not? Do you think she was right to keep quiet?

4. If any of the following words are new to you, try to guess their meanings from their context in Thomas's essay. Look up the words in a dictionary to check your guesses, and then use each word in a sentence or two of your own.

pirated (5)	flourishing (7)	pretense (13)
ingesting (6)	syndicates (8)	fraudulently (13)
feline (6)	clandestine (8)	counsel (13)
litigation (6)	invariably (8)	devastating (20)

Purpose and Audience

1. What seems to be Thomas's primary purpose in this piece? Does she want to express her opinion about counterfeit goods? persuade consumers not to buy them? educate her readers? How can you tell?

2. To whom does Thomas seem to be writing here? Why do you think so?

Method and Structure

1. How well does cause-and-effect analysis suit Thomas's subject? How does this method provide Thomas with an effective means of achieving her purpose?

2. "The Fake Trade" explores both causes and effects of counterfeiting. What, according to Thomas, are the main reasons for the practice? What are the most significant consequences?

3. Analyze the organization of Thomas's essay by creating an outline of her major points. What is the effect of this structure?

4. A journalist, Thomas supports her ideas with information from published studies and quotations from interviews with experts. Locate at least two examples of each. How effective do you find this evidence? Is it more, or less, persuasive than the examples she takes from her own experience? Why do you think so?

5. **OTHER METHODS**   Thomas provides many examples (Chapter 7) of counterfeit goods, and she uses process analysis (Chapter 10) to describe how they are manufactured, distributed, and sold. What does she accomplish by using these methods?

Language

1. How does Thomas use transitions to guide readers through her cause-and-effect analysis?

2. How would you characterize Thomas's tone? Is it appropriate, given her purpose and her audience?

Writing Topics

1. **JOURNAL TO ESSAY**   In your journal entry (p. 292), you wrote about your attitude toward counterfeit goods. Now that you've read "The Fake Trade," has your attitude changed in any way? Has Thomas persuaded you that counterfeiting has "devastating effects," or are you unmoved by her analysis? Why? Drawing on your own experience with fake goods and on what Thomas has to say, write an essay that argues for or against buying counterfeits. (If you share Thomas's concerns, be careful not just to repeat her points; look for additional examples of counterfeit products and add your own reasons for rejecting them.)

2. Thomas focuses on luxury goods, but in paragraph 6 she mentions that medicine is frequently counterfeited as well, compromising the health and threatening the lives of people who inadvertently buy ineffective

or tainted drugs. Many supporters of health-care reform have raised the same point to argue that drug makers charge excessive prices for medications and that such costs should be controlled through government action. Write an essay that explores your thoughts on this issue. Should everyone have access to safe and effective medications, regardless of cost? Who should pay? Should some drugs be made available to all while other drugs are available only to those who can afford them? Do pharmaceutical companies have an obligation to make drugs affordable, or do they have a right to profit from the fruits of their research and development efforts? What, if anything, can be done to strike a fair balance between patients' and corporations' needs?

3. **CULTURAL CONSIDERATIONS** Thomas suggests that American culture promotes a desire for luxury, or at least an approximation of it. Many cultures, however, actively discourage indulgence, prizing thrift and generosity over personal acquisition. Write an essay that defends or argues against consumption for its own sake, making a point of explaining what, in your mind, constitutes a necessity and a luxury. Do we have a right—even an obligation—to spend money on things we don't truly need? Why, or why not?

4. **CONNECTIONS** In "The Fake Trade," Thomas shows how efforts to get a bargain can impose high costs on people in less affluent countries. Similarly, Barbara Kingsolver, in "Stalking the Vegetannual" (p. 210), asserts that importing off-season produce from distant parts of the world carries an environmental price tag. Write an essay that compares the two authors' beliefs about the benefits and drawbacks of a global economy. What assumptions, if any, do both writers share? Where do their perspectives diverge? How do their attitudes reinforce or conflict with your own views?

For years I thought what was good for our country was good for General Motors, and vice versa. The difference did not exist. Our company is too big. It goes with the welfare of the country.   —Charles Wilson

Where I come from, when you see a snake, you kill it. At GM the first thing you do is form a committee on snakes, next you hire a consultant, then you talk about it for a year.   —H. Ross Perot

The phrase "bankrupt General Motors" . . . leaves Americans my age in economic shock. The words are as melodramatic as "Mom's nude photos."   —P. J. O'Rourke

JOURNAL RESPONSE   The United States—indeed, most of the world—officially entered a recession in 2008. How, if at all, has the economic downturn affected you, your family, and your friends? Answer this question in a short journal entry.

Charlie LeDuff

Charlie LeDuff was born in 1967 in Virginia and grew up in the suburbs of Detroit, Michigan, where he is a registered member of the Sault Ste. Marie tribe of Chippewa. He earned a BA in political science from the University of Michigan and an MA in journalism from the University of California at Berkeley. Before fully embarking on his writing career, LeDuff worked as a bartender, cannery worker, gang counselor, baker, carpenter, and middle-school teacher. He was a national correspondent for the *New York Times* from 1995 to 2007 and was awarded a Pulitzer Prize for his contributions to a series of articles about race in America. He has recently branched out into television journalism and has written, produced, and hosted series for the Discovery Times Channel and the BBC. LeDuff is also the author of two books: *Work and Other Sins: Life in New York City and Thereabouts* (2004) and *US Guys: The True and Twisted Mind of the American Man* (2006). He is currently a multimedia reporter for the *Detroit News*.

End of the Line

For decades one of the largest employers in the United States, General Motors declared bankruptcy in June 2009, announcing that it would close many of its manufacturing plants and sending shockwaves throughout a country already stunned by global economic collapse. The company emerged from bankruptcy less than two months later, but most of its former employees and factory sites have not shared in its recovery. In September 2009, LeDuff wrote about the local effects of one GM plant closure for *Mother Jones* magazine. A photo essay by Danny Wilcox Frazier accompanied the essay, and we include some of the images here.

Driving through Janesville, Wisconsin, in a downpour, looking past 1 the wipers and through windows fogged up with cigarette smoke, Main Street appears to be melting away. The rain falls hard and makes a lonesome going-away sound like a river sucking downstream. And the old hotel, without a single light, tells you that the best days around here are gone. I always smoke when I go to funerals. I work in Detroit. And when I look out the windshield or into people's eyes here, I see a little Detroit in the making.

A sleepy place of 60,483 souls—if the welcome sign on the east side 2 of town is still to be believed—Janesville lies off Interstate 90 between the electric lights of Chicago and the sedate streets of Madison. It is one of those middle-western places that outsiders pay no mind. It is where the farm meets the factory, where the soil collides with the smokestack. Except the last GM truck rolled off the line December 23, 2008. Merry Christmas, Janesville. Happy New Year.

Janesville Assembly was one of General Motors' oldest plants, employing 4,000 people at its height, turning out classic Chevy and GMC vehicles. In December, the last GM truck rolled off the line. Photo: Danny Wilcox Frazier.

The Janesville Assembly Plant was everything here, they say. It was 3 a birthright. It was a job for life and it was that way for four generations. This was one of General Motors' oldest factories—opened in 1919. This was one of its biggest—almost five million square feet. Nobody in town dared drive anything but a Chevy or a GMC. Back then GM was the largest industrial corporation in the world, the largest carmaker, the very symbol of American power. Ike's man at the Pentagon—a former GM exec himself—famously said, "What was good for our country was good for General Motors, and vice versa."[1] Kennedy, Johnson, Obama, they all campaigned here. People here can tell you of their grandparents who came from places like Norway and Poland and Alabama to build tractors and even ammunition during the Big War. Then came the Impalas and the Camaros. In the end they were cranking out big machines like the Suburban and the Tahoe, those high-strung, gas-guzzling hounds of the American Good Times.

Today, some $50 billion in bailouts later, GM is on life support **4** and there is a sinking feeling that the country is going down with it. Those grandchildren are considering moving to Texas or Tennessee or Vegas. Who is to blame? Detroit? Wall Street? Management? Labor? NAFTA? Does it matter? Come to Janesville and see what we've thrown away.

For years, the people here heard rumors that the plant was on its **5** way out. But no one ever believed it, really. Something always came along to save it. Gas prices went down or cheap Chinese money floated in. Janesville was too big to ignore. Too big to close.

And then they closed it.   **6**

The local UAW[2] union hall is quiet now. A photograph from a 1925 **7** company picnic hangs there. The whole town is assembled near the factory, the women in petticoats, the children in patent leather, the men in woolen bowlers. The caption reads, "Were you there Charlie?"

Todd Brien's name still hangs in the wall cabinet—Recording **8** Secretary, it reads. But that is just a leftover like a coin in a cushion. Brien, forty-one, moved to Arlington, Texas, to take a temp job in a GM plant down there in April. He left his family up here. He is one of the lucky ones. Most of the other 2,700 still employed after rounds of downsizing had no factory to go to. But now, what with the bankruptcy of GM, he's temporarily laid off from Texas and back in Janesville to gather his family and head south.

---

[1] "Ike" was a popular nickname for Dwight D. Eisenhower, president of the United States from 1953 to 1961. LeDuff is referring to Eisenhower's secretary of defense, Charles Wilson, whose line was often misquoted as "What's good for GM is good for the country." [Editors' note.]

[2] United Auto Workers. [Editors' note.]

"It was always in the back of my mind around here . . . They can 9
take it away," Brien says. "Well, they did. Now what? Can't sell my
house. Main Street's boarding up. The kids around here are getting into
drugs. You wonder when's the last train leaving this station? I just never
believed it was going to happen." Today, freight trains leaving from
Janesville's loading docks take auctioned bits and pieces of the plant
to faraway places: welding robots, milling machines, chop saws, drill
presses, pipe threaders, drafting tables, salt and pepper shakers.

Janesville is still a nice place. They still cut the grass along the river- 10
bank. The churches are still full on Sunday. The farmers still get up before
dawn. But there are the little telltale signs, the details, the darkening
clouds.

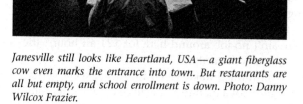

*Janesville still looks like Heartland, USA—a giant fiberglass
cow even marks the entrance into town. But restaurants are
all but empty, and school enrollment is down. Photo: Danny
Wilcox Frazier.*

The strip club across the street from the plant is now an Alcoholics 11
Anonymous joint. There are too many people in the welfare line who
never would have imagined themselves there. Dim prospects and empty
buildings. A motel where the neon "Vacancy" sign never seems to say
"No Vacancy."

The owner is Pragnesh Patel. He is thirty-six, looks a dozen years 12
older. He left a good job near Ahmedabad, India, as a supervisor in a
television factory, he says. He came to try his luck in America. He got
a job in a little factory in Janesville that makes electronic components
for GM. He also bought the motel just up the hill from the assembly
plant. Now with the plant closed, he's down to three shifts a week at
the components factory and having to make $2,500 monthly payments

on his motel on Highway 51. He charges forty-five bucks a night and today it's mostly the crackheads and the down-at-their-heels who come in for a crash landing. Welcome to America, except Patel has to raise his children amid this decay. "I'm trying, really trying to survive," he says. "I don't know anymore. I mean, I'm an American. I cast my lot here. But I have to tell you, on many days, I regret that I ever came."

There is a bar on the factory grounds that has become a funeral 13 parlor. Yes, a bar on the factory grounds, not five-hundred feet from the time clock! Genius! It has been here since at least the Depression if the yellowed receipt from 1937 is to be believed. Five cases of beer for eight dollars and thirty cents.

And in some way, that bar on the factory grounds might explain 14 what happened here. "We used to have a drive-through window," says one of the former UAW workers gathered at Zoxx 411 Club and drinking a long, cool glass of liquor at three in the afternoon. He is about fifty, about the age when a man begins to understand his own obsolescence. "Used to put two or three down and go back to work. Now those were the days, yes-siree."

You feel sorry for that autoworker until you hear he draws nearly 15 three-quarters of his old salary for the first year of his layoff and half his salary for the second year of his layoff—plus benefits.

"It don't make sense to work," says the autoworker, buying one for 16 the stranger.

If he finds a job, he says, they'll take his big check away. 17

"There ain't no job around here for $21 an hour," the autoworker 18 says. "I might as well drink."

A taxpayer-funded wake. Good for him. Except you get the feeling 19 that it's not good for a man to drink all day. Two years comes faster than a man thinks.

A little Detroit in the making, except Detroit has General Motors 20 and Ford and Chrysler. Detroit is an industry town. Janesville had only General Motors. Janesville was a company town. You didn't have to go to college—but you might be able to send your kid there—because there was always GM. GM—Gimme Mine. GM—Grandma Moo, the golden cow. Now GM has Gone Missing. GM has Gone to Mexico.

"We took it for granted," says Nancy Nienhuis, seventy-six, a retired 21 factory nurse who farms on the outskirts of town. She did everything at that plant a nurse could do: tended to amputations, heart attacks, shotgun wounds inflicted by a jilted lover, even performed an exorcism of spiders from a crazy man's stomach. Whatever it took to keep those lines moving.

"The rumor would start, they're talking about closing the plant. No 22 one would believe it. Then you saw the Toyota dealership open on the east side of town and still they didn't believe it. The manager and the worker sat next to each other in church, you see? They went to high school together. Understand? The good worker got no recognition over the bad worker. Nobody made waves about a guy drunk or out fishing on the clock. In the end, the last few years, management rode them pretty good. But by then it was a little too late."

Richard, a former welder at the plant, puts a pastry box in Nurse   23 Nancy's car. Richard begins to weep. He looks over his shoulder, wipes his nose on his sleeve and says, "I don't want my wife to see this. I'm sixty-two and I'm delivering doughnuts. What am I going to do?'"

Most laid-off GM assembly workers are paid severance for two years. "There's going to be hell to pay when those unemployment checks stop coming," says one resident. Photo: Danny Wilcox Frazier.

Desperation comes in subtler ways than a grown man crying. The   24 winner of the cakewalk at the local fair got not a cake—but a single, solitary cupcake. Parents don't come to the PTA as much anymore. A lot of kids will have left by the beginning of the school year, the superintendent says. Unemployment here is near 15 percent. The police blotter is a mix of Mayberry[3] and Big City: Truancy, Truancy, Shots Fired at 2 PM, Dog Barking, Burglary at 5 PM, Burglary at 6 PM.

At 7 PM they fry fish at the VFW hall. Beers two bucks. Two-piece   25 plate of cod $6.95. Charlie Larson runs the place. You can see the factory from Charlie's parking lot, the Rock River running lazily beside it. Charlie tried the factory in 1966. His father got him in, but he was drafted into

---

[3] A fictional small town from the 1960s television series *The Andy Griffith Show.* [Editors' note.]

the jungles of Nam in 1967. "It's a discouraging thing," Charlie, sixty-one, says of the plant closing down, smoothing a plastic tablecloth. "It was the lifeblood of this town. It was the identity of this town. Now we have nothing, nothing but worry. Aw, there's going to be hell to pay when those unemployment checks stop coming."

Blame the factory worker if you must. Blame the union man who   26
asked too much and waited too long to give some back. Blame the guy for drinking at lunch or cutting out early. But factory work is a nine-to-five sort of dying. The monotony, the accidents. "You're a machine," says Marv Wopat. He put bumpers on trucks. A six-foot man stooping in a four-foot hole, lining up a four-foot bumper. Three bolts, three washers, three nuts. One every minute over an eight-hour shift. Wopat, sixty-two, has bad shoulders, bad knees, bad memories. "You got night-mares," he says. "You missed a vehicle or you couldn't get the bolt on. You just went home thinking nothing except the work tomorrow and your whole life spent down in that hole. And you thinking how you're going to get out. Well, now it's gone and alls we're thinking about is wanting to have it back."

And maybe they will have it back. The recession is loosening its   27
grip, some say. Some towns will rebound. Some plants will retrofit. Wind, solar, electric—that's the future, Washington says. But you get a pain-in-the-throat feeling that it is not the future. Not really. At least not as good a future as the past. There's no twenty-eight bucks an hour for life in that future. No two-car garage. No bennies. No boat on Lake Michigan. Because in the new world they can build that windmill, or a solar panel, or an electric battery in India, where the minimum pay is less than $3 a day. Just ask Patel, the motel owner living at the edge of a dead factory in Janesville, Wisconsin. "You cannot compete with poverty unless you are poor."

Meaning

1. In his opening paragraph, LeDuff writes, "I always smoke when I go to funerals." Why does he share this personal information? What does it have to do with his subject or his main idea?

2. Does LeDuff believe that Janesville will recover from the effects of the GM plant closure? Point to evidence from his essay to support your answer.

3. LeDuff's last sentence, "'You cannot compete with poverty unless you are poor,'" is quoted from a struggling motel owner. What does he mean? How does the line sum up LeDuff's underlying message?

4. If any of the following words are new to you, try to guess their meanings from their context in LeDuff's essay. Check your guesses in a dictionary, and then use each word in a sentence or two of your own.

birthright (3)   obsolescence (14)   exorcism (21)
bailouts (4)   wake (19)   cakewalk (24)
petticoats (7)   amputations (21)   monotony (26)
bowlers (7)   jilted (21)   retrofit (27)
components (12)

Purpose and Audience

1. What seems to have inspired LeDuff to write this essay? How is "End of the Line" a reaction to a particular cultural moment?

2. Is LeDuff writing primarily for residents of Janesville, Wisconsin? for managers of General Motors? for the federal government? Or is he writing for a broader audience? How can you tell?

3. What assumptions does LeDuff seem to make about his readers' familiarity with company towns and General Motors? What details help clarify the context of his analysis for those who don't already know it?

Method and Structure

1. In paragraphs 4 and 26, LeDuff lists several possible causes that might explain why General Motors went bankrupt, but he doesn't say anything more about them. Why does he devote his essay mainly to effects? What does he accomplish by dismissing causes as unimportant?

2. Examine the quotations from residents that LeDuff uses to explain the situation in Janesville. What do their own words convey that he could not? Why do you think he quotes them so extensively?

3. Take a close look at the photographs taken by Danny Wilcox Frazier. How would you characterize these images? What do they contribute to LeDuff's main idea?

4. **OTHER METHODS** In what ways does LeDuff use comparison and contrast (Chapter 11) as part of his cause-and-effect analysis? Why is this method important in developing his point?

Language

1. LeDuff's essay is full of sentence fragments, most notably in paragraphs 11, 19, 26, and 27. Choose one paragraph and edit it to eliminate the fragments, ensuring that every sentence is complete (for help with

sentence fragments, see p. 48). Compare your edited version to LeDuff's original. Which is more effective, and why? How does LeDuff's deliberate use of fragments contribute to the overall effect of his essay?

2. How would you describe LeDuff's tone in this essay? Why is it particularly appropriate to his subject and purpose?

Writing Topics

1. **JOURNAL TO ESSAY**   Building on your journal entry (p. 300), write an essay in which you analyze the effects of the current recession on your immediate family or on someone close to you. How have things changed for these people, and what has been their response? To what extent are the individuals involved responsible for their own situation? Can they do anything to improve it?

2. Think of a place to which you feel a special connection. The place may be rural or urban or suburban, and it need not be far away. In an essay, describe the place for readers who are completely unfamiliar with it and who may be skeptical about your enthusiasm for it. Use concrete, specific details and, if appropriate, figures of speech to show clearly why you value the place.

3. How do you react to LeDuff's essay? Do you agree that Janesville, Wisconsin, is dead, or is it simply on life support? Does it matter, as LeDuff asks, why the plant closed? In an essay, examine the writer's assumptions and explain why you either agree or disagree with his conclusions.

4. **CULTURAL CONSIDERATIONS**   In the United States, people often define themselves—and others—by the work they do. Write about a job you have had. Was it something you did just for money, because you wanted to, or because your parents forced you to? Did you enjoy the experience? What lessons did you learn from your employment? In what ways did your job influence your sense of who you are or who you want to become?

5. **CONNECTIONS**   Dave Barry, in "Humvee Satisfies a Man's Lust For Winches" (p. 149), openly mocks one of General Motors' trademark vehicles. Although GM no longer manufactures Hummers (they sold the line as part of bankruptcy restructuring), consider how Barry's attitude toward them may help explain the company's financial troubles and eventual collapse.

Cause-and-Effect Analysis

Select one of the following questions, or any question they suggest, and answer it in an essay developed by analyzing causes or effects. The question you choose should concern a topic you care about so that your cause-and-effect analysis is a means of communicating an idea, not an end in itself.

PEOPLE AND THEIR BEHAVIOR

1. Why is a past or present politician, athlete, police officer, or firefighter considered a hero?
2. What does a sound body contribute to a sound mind?
3. Why is a particular friend or relative always getting into trouble?
4. Why do people root for the underdog?
5. How does a person's alcohol or drug dependency affect others?

WORK

6. At what age should a person start working for pay, and why?
7. What effects do you expect your education to have on your choice of career and your performance in it?
8. Why would a man or woman enter a field that has traditionally been filled by the opposite sex, such as nursing or engineering?
9. What effect has the job market had on you and your friends?

ART AND ENTERTAINMENT

10. Why do teenagers like hip-hop music?
11. Why have art museums become so popular?
12. What makes a professional sports team succeed in a new city?
13. Why is (or was) a particular television show or movie so popular?

CONTEMPORARY ISSUES

14. Why does the United States spend so much money on defense?
15. How can a long period of involuntary unemployment affect a person?
16. Why is a college education important?
17. Why do marriages between teenagers fail more often than marriages between people in other age groups?
18. Why might someone resort to a public act of violence, such as bombing a building?

Understanding Businesses and Consumers

1. Most of the writers in this chapter examine the unintended consequences of actions taken by companies and consumers. Stephanie Alaimo and Mark Koester's warning against self-service checkout (p. 287) and Dana Thomas's exposé on counterfeiting (p. 292) are most notable in this respect, but even Barbara Ehrenreich's analysis of high rents (p. 279) suggests how difficult it is to predict the social effects of a purchase, and Charlie LeDuff's look at the effects of a GM factory closing (p. 300) shows how business decisions can haunt a community. Think of a contemporary product or service that you believe holds the potential to do unexpected harm — or that could bring unanticipated benefits — and write an essay predicting its consequences. (Be sure to review the cause-and-effect guidelines on pp. 281–86 before beginning your analysis.)

2. Pico Iyer (p. 280), Dana Thomas, Stephanie Alaimo and Mark Koester, and Charlie LeDuff all consider the stigma attached to a particular consumer option: Iyer suggests that reducing consumption is the key to happiness; Alaimo and Koester attempt to persuade readers that self-checkout machines are morally wrong; Thomas stresses that we should not buy fake luxury goods because doing so hurts people thousands of miles away; and LeDuff, writing about a GM factory town, mentions that "Nobody . . . dared drive anything but a Chevy or a GMC." Write an essay in which you consider the power of negative publicity. Can regular people influence the behavior of large corporations by boycotting what they have to offer? To what extent does big business control the marketplace regardless of how customers might object? Center your discussion on a particular business or practice that concerns you. Perhaps you'd like to propose a boycott of your own. Just be sure that your essay has a clear, limited thesis and plenty of details to support it.

3. Although the writers represented in this chapter all touch on problems of poverty or underemployment, their tones vary widely, from objective to moralistic to resigned. Choose the two authors who seem most different in tone, and analyze how their tones help clarify their points. Is one author's tone more effective than the other's? If so, why? (For more on tone, see pp. 41–43.)

14

ARGUMENT AND PERSUASION
Debating Law and Order

Since we argue all the time—with relatives, with friends, with the auto mechanic or the shop clerk—a chapter devoted to argument and persuasion may at first seem unnecessary. But arguing with an auto mechanic over the cost of repairs is quite a different process from arguing with readers over a complex issue. In both cases we are trying to find common ground with our audience, perhaps to change its views or even to compel it to act as we wish. But the mechanic is in front of us; we can shift our tactics in response to his or her gestures, expressions, and words. The reader, in contrast, is "out there"; we have to anticipate those gestures, expressions, and words in the way we structure the argument, the kinds of evidence we use to support it, even the way we conceive of the subject.

A great many assertions that are worth making are debatable at some level—whether over the facts on which the assertions are based or over the values they imply. Two witnesses to an accident cannot agree on what they saw; two scientists cannot agree on what an experiment shows; two economists cannot agree on what measures will reduce unemployment; two doctors cannot agree on what constitutes life or death. We see such disagreements play out in writing all the time, whether we're reading an accident report, a magazine article claiming the benefits of unemployment rates, or an editorial responding to a Supreme Court decision.

Reading Argument and Persuasion

Technically, argument and persuasion are two different processes:

- **Argument** appeals mainly to an audience's sense of reason in order to negotiate a common understanding or to win agreement with a claim. It is the method of a columnist who defends a president's foreign policy on the grounds of economics and defense strategy.

- **Persuasion** appeals mainly to an audience's feelings and values in order to compel some action, or at least to win support for an action. It is the method of a mayoral candidate who urges voters to support her because she is sensitive to the poor.

But argument and persuasion so often mingle that we will use the one term *argument* to mean a deliberate appeal to an audience's reason and emotions in order to create compromise, win agreement, or compel action. Making an effective case for an opinion requires upholding certain responsibilities and attending to several established techniques of argumentation, most of them dating back to ancient Greece.

The Elements of Argument

All arguments share certain elements.

- The core of any argument is an assertion or proposition, a debatable claim about the subject. Generally, this assertion is expressed as a thesis statement. It may defend or attack a position, suggest a solution to a problem, recommend a change in policy, or challenge a value or belief. Here are a few examples:

    The college should give first priority for on-campus jobs to students who need financial aid.

    School prayer has been rightly declared unconstitutional and should not be reinstituted in any form.

    Smokers who wish to poison themselves should be allowed to do so, but not in any place where their smoke will poison others.

- The central assertion is broken down into subclaims, each one supported by evidence.

- Significant opposing arguments are raised and dispensed with, again with the support of evidence.

- The parts of the argument are organized into a clear, logical structure that pushes steadily toward the conclusion.

A writer may draw on classification, comparison, or any other rhetorical method to develop the entire argument or to introduce evidence or strengthen the conclusion. For instance, in a proposal arguing for raising a college's standards of admission, a dean might contrast the existing standards with the proposed standards, analyze a process for raising the standards over a period of years, and predict the effects of the new standards on future students' preparedness for college work.

Appeals to Readers

Effective arguments appeal to readers: they ask others to listen to what someone has to say, judge the words fairly, and, as much as possible, agree with the writer. Most arguments combine three kinds of appeals to readers: ethical, emotional, and rational.

Ethical Appeal

The ethical appeal is often not explicit in an argument, yet it pervades the whole. It is the sense a writer conveys of his or her expertise and character, projected by the reasonableness of the argument, by the use of evidence, and by tone. A rational argument shows readers that the writer is thinking logically and fairly (see pp. 315–17). Strong evidence establishes credibility (see pp. 315–17 and 321–22). And a sincere, reasonable tone demonstrates balance and goodwill (see pg. 325).

Emotional Appeal

The emotional appeal in an argument aims directly for the readers' hearts—for the complex of beliefs, values, and feelings deeply embedded in all of us. We are just as often motivated by these ingrained ideas and emotions as by our intellects. Even scientists, who stress the rational interpretation of facts above all else, are sometimes influenced in their interpretations by emotions deriving from, say, competition with other scientists. And the willingness of a nation's citizens to go to war may result more from their fear and pride than from their reasoned considerations of risks and gains. An emotional appeal in an argument attempts to tap such feelings for any of several reasons:

- To heighten the responsiveness of readers
- To inspire readers to new beliefs

- To compel readers to act
- To assure readers that their values remain unchallenged

An emotional appeal may be explicit, as when an argument against capital punishment appeals to readers' religious values by citing the Bible's Sixth Commandment, "Thou shalt not kill." But an emotional appeal may also be less obvious, because individual words may have connotations that elicit emotional responses from readers. For instance, one writer may characterize an environmental group as "a well-organized team representing diverse interests," while another may call the same group "a hodgepodge of nature lovers and irresponsible businesspeople." The first appeals to readers' preference for order and balance, the second to readers' fear of extremism and disdain for unsound business practices. (See pp. 55–56 for more on connotation.)

The use of emotional appeals requires care:

- The appeal must be directed at the audience's actual beliefs and feelings.

- The appeal must be presented dispassionately enough so that readers have no reason to doubt the fairness in the rest of the argument.

- The appeal must be appropriate to the subject and to the argument. For instance, in arguing against a pay raise for city councilors, a legislator might be tempted to appeal to voters' resentment and distrust of wealthy people by pointing out that two of the councilors are rich enough to work for nothing. But such an appeal would divert attention from the issue of whether the pay raise is justified for all councilors on the basis of the work they do and the city's ability to pay the extra cost.

Carefully used, emotional appeals have great force, particularly when they contribute to an argument based largely on sound reasoning and evidence. The appropriate mix of emotion and reason in a given essay is entirely dependent on the subject, the writer's purpose, and the audience. Emotional appeals are out of place in most arguments in the natural and social sciences, where rational interpretations of factual evidence are all that will convince readers of the truth of an assertion. But emotional appeals may be essential to persuade an audience to support or take an action, for emotion is a stronger motivator than reason.

Rational Appeal

A **rational appeal** is one that, as the name implies, addresses the rational faculties of readers—their capacity to reason logically about a problem. It establishes the truth of a proposition or claim by moving through a series of related subclaims, each supported by evidence. In doing so, rational appeals follow processes of reasoning that are natural to all of us. These processes are induction and deduction.

Inductive reasoning moves from the particular to the general, from evidence to a generalization or conclusion about the evidence. It is a process we begin learning in infancy and use daily throughout our lives: a child burns herself the three times she touches a stove, so she concludes that stoves burn; a moviegoer has liked four movies directed by Clint Eastwood, so he forms the generalization that Clint Eastwood makes good movies. Inductive reasoning is also very common in argument: a nurse administrator might offer facts showing that chronic patients in the state's mental hospitals receive only drugs as treatment and then conclude that the state's hospitals rely exclusively on drugs to treat chronic patients.

The movement from particular to general is called an **inductive leap** because we must make something of a jump to conclude that what is true of some instances (the chronic patients whose records were available) is also true of all other instances in the class (the rest of the chronic patients). In an ideal world we could perhaps avoid the inductive leap by pinning down every conceivable instance, but in the real world such thoroughness is usually impractical and often impossible. Instead, we gather enough evidence to make our generalizations probable. The evidence for induction may be of several kinds:

- Facts: statistics or other hard data that are verifiable or, failing that, attested to by reliable sources (for instance, the number of drug doses per chronic patient, derived from hospital records).

- The opinions of recognized experts on the subject, opinions that are themselves conclusions based on research and observation (for instance, the testimony of an experienced hospital doctor).

- Examples illustrating the evidence (for instance, the treatment history of one patient).

A sound inductive generalization can form the basis for the second reasoning process, **deductive reasoning**. Working from the general to the particular, we start with such a generalization and apply it to a new situation in order to draw a conclusion about that situation. Like induction, deduction is a process we use constantly to order our experience. The child who learns from three experiences that all stoves burn then sees a new stove and concludes that this stove also will burn. The child's thought process can be written in the form of a **syllogism**, a three-step outline of deductive reasoning:

> All stoves burn me.
> This is a stove.
> Therefore, this stove will burn me.

The first statement, the generalization derived from induction, is called the **major premise**. The second statement, a more specific assertion about some element of the major premise, is called the **minor premise**. And the third statement, an assertion of the logical connection between the premises, is called the **conclusion**. The following syllogism takes the earlier example about mental hospitals one step further:

> MAJOR PREMISE   The state hospitals' treatment of chronic patients relies exclusively on drugs.
>
> MINOR PREMISE   Drugs do not cure chronic patients.
>
> CONCLUSION   Therefore, the state hospitals' treatment of chronic patients will not cure them.

Unlike an inductive conclusion, which requires a leap, the deductive conclusion derives necessarily from the premises: as long as the reasoning process is valid and the premises are accepted as true, then the conclusion must also be true. To be valid, the reasoning must conform to the process outlined earlier. The following syllogism is *not* valid, even though the premises are true:

> All radicals want to change the system.
> Georgia Allport wants to change the system.
> Therefore, Georgia Allport is a radical.

The flaw in this syllogism is that not *only* radicals want to change the system, so Allport does not *necessarily* fall within the class of radicals just because she wants to change the system. The conclusion, then, is invalid.

A syllogism can be valid without being true if either of the premises is untrue. For example:

> All people who want political change are radicals.
> Georgia Allport wants political change.
> Therefore, Georgia Allport is a radical.

The conclusion here is valid because Allport falls within the class of people who want political change. But the conclusion is untrue because the major premise is untrue. As commonly defined, a radical seeks extreme change, often by revolutionary means. But other forms and means of change are also possible; Allport, for instance, may be interested in improving the delivery of services to the poor and in achieving passage of tougher environmental-protection laws—both political changes, to be sure, but neither radical.

In arguments, syllogisms are rarely spelled out as neatly as in these examples. Sometimes the order of the statements is reversed, as in this sentence paraphrasing a Supreme Court decision:

> The state may not imprison a man just because he is too poor to pay a fine; the only justification for imprisonment is a certain danger to society, and poverty does not constitute certain danger.

The buried syllogism can be stated thus:

> MAJOR PREMISE The state may imprison only those who are a certain danger to society.

> MINOR PREMISE A man who is too poor to pay a fine is not a certain danger to society.

> CONCLUSION Therefore, the state cannot imprison a man just because he is too poor to pay a fine.

Often, one of a syllogism's premises or even its conclusion is implied but not expressed. Each of the following sentences omits one part of the same syllogism:

> All five students cheated, so they should be expelled. [Implied major premise: cheaters should be expelled.]

> Cheaters should be punished by expulsion, so all five students should be expelled. [Implied minor premise: all five students cheated.]

> Cheaters should be punished by expulsion, and all five students cheated. [Implied conclusion: all five students should be expelled.]

Fallacies

Inappropriate emotional appeals and flaws in reasoning—called **fallacies**—can trap writers as they construct arguments. Writers must watch out for the following:

- **Hasty generalization:** an inductive conclusion that leaps to include *all* instances when at best only *some* instances provide any evidence. Hasty generalizations form some of our worst stereotypes:

  > Physically challenged people are mentally challenged, too.
  >
  > African Americans are good athletes.
  >
  > Italian Americans are volatile.

- **Oversimplification:** an inductive conclusion that ignores complexities in the evidence that, if heeded, would weaken the conclusion or suggest an entirely different one. For example:

  > The newspaper folded because it couldn't compete with television.

  Although television may have taken some business from the newspaper, hundreds of other newspapers continue to thrive; thus television could not be the only cause of the newspaper's failure.

- **Begging the question:** assuming a conclusion in the statement of a premise, and thus begging readers to accept the conclusion—the question—before it is proved. For example:

  > We can trust the president not to neglect the needy because he is a compassionate man.

  This sentence asserts in a circular fashion that the president is not uncompassionate because he is compassionate. He may indeed be compassionate, but the question that needs addressing is what will he do for the needy.

- **Ignoring the question:** introducing an issue or consideration that shifts the argument away from the real issue. Offering an emotional appeal as a premise in a logical argument is a form of ignoring the question. The following sentence, for instance, appeals to pity, not to logic:

  > The mayor was badly used by people he loved and trusted, so we should not blame him for the corruption in his administration.

- **Ad hominem** (Latin for "to the man"): a form of ignoring the question by attacking the opponents instead of the opponents' arguments. For example:

  > O'Brien is married to a convict, so her proposals for prison reform should not be taken seriously.

- **Either-or:** requiring that readers choose between two interpretations or actions when in fact the choices are more numerous.

  > Either we imprison all drug users, or we will become their prisoners.

  The factors contributing to drug addiction, and the choices for dealing with it, are obviously more complex than this statement suggests. Not all either-or arguments are invalid, for sometimes the alternatives encompass all the possibilities. But when they do not, the argument is false.

- **Non sequitur** (Latin for "it does not follow"): a conclusion derived illogically or erroneously from stated or implied premises. For instance:

  > Young children are too immature to engage in sex, so they should not be taught about it.

  This sentence implies one of two meanings, both of them questionable: only the sexually active can learn anything about sex, or teaching young children about sex will cause them to engage in it.

- **Post hoc** (from the Latin *post hoc, ergo propter hoc*, "after this, therefore because of this"): assuming that because one thing preceded another, it must have caused the other. For example:

  > After the town banned smoking in closed public places, the incidence of vandalism went up.

  Many things may have caused the rise in vandalism, including improved weather and a climbing unemployment rate. It does not follow that the ban on smoking, and that alone, caused the rise.

Analyzing Argument and Persuasion in Paragraphs

Jenny Price (born 1960) is an environmental historian and freelance writer. The following paragraph is from "Gun Violence at UC Irvine," an article she wrote for the *Los Angeles Times* in response to readers' shock that a woman was shot to death in a neighborhood generally considered safe. The paragraph offers an inductive argument.

Twelve thousand people are shot to death in the
United States every year—accounting for more than
two out of every three killings. That's an average of
33 people daily. An additional 240 people get shot and
injured every day, and more than 65 million Americans
own a total of 283 million firearms. Where, exactly,
do we expect the 12,000 homicides to happen? Do we
really think that the places with gangs and high crime
rates are the only places where people are going to use
their guns? The widespread numbness to the especially
high murder rates in our poor inner-city neighborhoods is egregious enough. But that's matched by the
widespread denial that the epidemic of gun violence is
playing out every day in every kind of neighborhood
across America.

Evidence:

Number of
gun-related
killings

Number of
nonfatal
shootings

Extent of gun
ownership

The generaliza-
tion (underlined):
shootings can
happen anywhere

Martin Luther King, Jr. (1929–1968) was a revered and powerful
leader of the civil rights movement during the 1950s and 1960s. When leading
sit-ins, boycotts, and marches, he always insisted on nonviolent resistance. In
this paragraph from "Letter from Birmingham Jail" (1963), King uses deduction to argue in favor of civil disobedience.

You express a great deal of anxiety over our willingness to break laws. This is certainly a legitimate concern. Since we so diligently urge people to obey the
Supreme Court's decision of 1954 outlawing segregation in the public schools, at first glance it may seem
rather paradoxical for us consciously to break laws.
One may well ask: "How can you advocate breaking
some laws and obeying others?" The answer lies in the
fact that there are two types of laws: just and unjust. I
would be the first to advocate obeying just laws. One
has not only a legal but a moral responsibility to obey
just laws. Conversely, one has a moral responsibility to
disobey unjust laws. I would agree with St. Augustine
that "an unjust law is no law at all."

Major premise:
laws should be
obeyed

Minor premise:
some laws are un-
just and therefore
are not laws

Conclusion: unjust
laws should not
be obeyed

Developing an Argumentative and Persuasive Essay

Getting Started

You will have many chances to write arguments, from defending or opposing a policy such as progressive taxation in an economics course to justifying a new procedure at work to persuading a company to refund your money for a bad product. To choose a subject for an argumentative essay, consider a behavior or policy that irks you, an opinion you want to defend, a change you would like to see implemented, or a way to solve a problem. The subject you pick should meet certain criteria:

- It should be something you have some knowledge of from your own experience or observations, from class discussions, or from reading, although you may need to do further research as well.

- It should be limited to a topic you can treat thoroughly in the space and time available to you—for instance, the quality of computer instruction at your school rather than in the whole nation.

- It should be something that you feel strongly about so that you can make a convincing case. (However, it's best to avoid subjects that you cannot view with some objectivity, seeing the opposite side as well as your own; otherwise, you may not be open to flaws in your argument, and you may not be able to represent the opposition fairly.)

Once you have selected a subject, do some preliminary research to make sure that you will have enough evidence to support your opinion. This step is especially important with an issue like welfare cheating or tax advantages for the wealthy that we all tend to have opinions about whether we know the facts or not. Where to seek evidence depends on the nature of your argument.

- For an argument derived from your own experiences and observations, such as a recommendation that all students work part-time for the education if not for the money, gathering evidence will be primarily a matter of searching your own thoughts and also uncovering opposing views, perhaps by consulting others.

- Some arguments derived from personal experience can be strengthened by the judicious use of facts and opinions from other sources. An essay arguing in favor of vegetarianism, for instance, could mix the benefits you have felt with those demonstrated by scientific data.

■ Nonpersonal and controversial subjects require the evidence of other sources. Though you might strongly favor or oppose a massive federal investment in solar-energy research, your opinions would count little if they were not supported with facts and the opinions of experts.

For advice on conducting research and using the evidence you find, see the Appendix.

In addition to evidence, knowledge of readers' needs and expectations is absolutely crucial in planning an argument. In explanatory writing, detail and clarity alone may accomplish your purpose, but you cannot hope to move readers in a certain direction unless you have some idea of where they stand. You need a sense of their background in your subject, of course. But even more, you need a good idea of their values and beliefs, their attitudes toward your subject—in short, their willingness to be convinced. In a composition class, your readers will probably be your instructor and your classmates, a small but diverse group. A good target when you are addressing a diverse audience is the reader who is neutral or mildly biased one way or the other toward your subject. This person you can hope to influence as long as your argument is reasonable, your evidence is thorough and convincing, your treatment of opposing views is fair, and your appeals to readers' emotions are appropriate to your purpose, your subject, and especially your readers' values and feelings.

Forming a Thesis

With your subject and some evidence in hand, you should develop a tentative thesis. But don't feel you have to prove your thesis at this early stage; fixing it too firmly may make you unwilling to reshape it if further evidence, your audience, or the structure of your argument so demands.

Stating your thesis in a preliminary thesis sentence can help you form your idea. Make this sentence as clear and specific as possible. Don't resort to a vague generality or a nondebatable statement of fact. Instead, state the precise opinion you want readers to accept or the precise action you want them to take or support. For instance:

VAGUE   Computer instruction is important.

NONDEBATABLE   The school's investment in computer instruction is less than the average investment of the nation's colleges and universities.

PRECISE Money designated for new dormitories and athletic facilities should be diverted to constructing computer facilities and hiring first-rate computer faculty.

VAGUE   Cloning research is promising.

NONDEBATABLE Scientists have been experimenting with cloning procedures for many years.

PRECISE Those who oppose cloning research should consider the potentially valuable applications of the research for human health and development.

Since the thesis is essentially a conclusion from evidence, you will probably need to do some additional reading to ensure that you have a broad range of facts and opinions supporting not only your view of the subject but also any opposing views. Though it may be tempting to ignore your opposition in the hope that readers know nothing of it, it is dishonest and probably futile to do so. Acknowledging and, whenever possible, refuting significant opposing views will enhance your credibility with readers. If you find that some counterarguments damage your own argument too greatly, then you will have to rethink your thesis.

Organizing

Once you have formulated your thesis and evaluated your reasons and evidence against the needs and expectations of your audience, begin planning how you will arrange your argument.

The introduction to your essay should draw readers into your framework, making them see how the subject affects them and predisposing them to consider your argument. Sometimes a forthright approach works best, but an eye-opening anecdote or quotation can also be effective. Your thesis sentence may end your introduction. But if you think readers will not even entertain your thesis until they have seen some or all of your evidence, then withhold your thesis for later.

The main part of the essay consists of your reasons and your evidence for them. The evidence you generated or collected should suggest the reasons that will support the claim of your thesis—essentially the minor arguments that bolster the main argument. In an essay favoring federal investment in solar-energy research, for instance, the minor arguments might include the need for solar power, the feasibility of its widespread use, and its cost and safety compared with the cost and safety of other energy sources. It is in developing these minor arguments that you are most likely to use induction and deduction consciously—generalizing from specifics or applying generalizations to new information. Thus the minor arguments provide the entry points for your evidence, and together they should encompass all the relevant evidence.

Unless the minor arguments form a chain, with each growing out of the one before, their order should be determined by their potential effects on readers. In general, it is most effective to arrange the reasons in order of increasing importance or strength so as to finish powerfully. But to engage readers in the argument from the start, try to begin with a reason that they will find compelling or that they already know and accept; that way, the weaker reasons will be sandwiched between a strong beginning and an even stronger ending.

The views opposing yours can be raised and dispensed with wherever it seems most appropriate to do so. If a counterargument pertains to just one of your minor arguments, then dispose of it at that point. But if the counterarguments are more basic, pertaining to your whole thesis, you should dispose of them either after the introduction or shortly before the conclusion. Use the former strategy if the opposition is particularly strong and you fear that readers will be disinclined to listen unless you address their concerns first. Use the latter strategy when the counterarguments are generally weak or easily dispensed with once you've presented your case.

In the conclusion to your essay, you may summarize the main point of your argument and state your thesis for the first time, if you have saved it for the end, or restate it from your introduction. An effective quotation, an appropriate emotional appeal, or a call for support or action can often provide a strong finish to an argument.

Drafting

While you are drafting the essay, work to make your reasoning clear by showing how each bit of evidence relates to the reason or minor argument being discussed and how each minor argument relates to the main argument contained in the thesis. In working through the reasons and evidence, you may find it helpful to state each reason as the first sentence in a paragraph and then support it in the following sentences. If this scheme seems too rigid or creates overlong paragraphs, you can always make changes after you have written your draft. Draw on a range of methods to clarify your points. For instance, define specialized terms or those you use in a special sense, compare and contrast one policy or piece of evidence with another, or carefully analyze causes or effects.

Revising and Editing

When your draft is complete, use the following questions and the box to guide your revision and editing.

- ▪ *Is your thesis debatable, precise, and clear?* Readers must know what you are trying to convince them of, at least by the end of the essay if not up front.

- ▪ *Is your argument unified?* Does each minor claim support the thesis? Do all opinions, facts, and examples provide evidence for a minor claim? On behalf of your readers, question every sentence you have written to be sure it contributes to the point you are making and to the argument as a whole.

- ▪ *Is the structure of your argument clear and compelling?* Readers should be able to follow easily, seeing when and why you move from one idea to the next.

- ▪ *Is the evidence specific, representative, and adequate?* Facts, examples, and expert opinions should be well detailed, should fairly represent the available information, and should be sufficient to support your claim.

- ▪ *Have you slipped into any logical fallacies?* Detecting fallacies in your own work can be difficult, but your readers will find them if you don't. Look for the following fallacies discussed earlier (pp. 317–19): hasty generalization, oversimplification, begging the question, ignoring the question, ad hominem, either-or, non sequitur, and post hoc. (All of these are also listed in the Glossary under *fallacies*.)

FOCUS ON TONE

Readers are most likely to be persuaded by an argument when they sense a writer who is reasonable, trustworthy, and sincere. A rational appeal, strong evidence, and acknowledgment of opposing views do much to convey these attributes, but so does tone, the attitude implied by choice of words and sentence structures. Generally, you should try for a tone of moderation in your view of your subject and a tone of respectfulness and goodwill toward readers and opponents. See pages 41–43 for suggestions and examples.

A Note on Thematic Connections

Argument and persuasion is the ideal method for presenting an opinion or a proposal on a controversial issue, making it a natural choice for the writers in this chapter, all of whom wanted to make a case about criminal justice. In a paragraph (p. 319), Jenny Price insists that we should expect gun violence, not be shocked by it. In another paragraph (p. 320), Martin Luther King, Jr. urges readers to condone civil disobedience. Anna Quindlen (opposite) asserts that changing our attitude toward mental illness may help to prevent school shootings. Linda Chavez's essay (p. 333) warns that a proposal to lower the legal drinking age would create more problems than it solves. In an essay drawing on careful research and his own experience as an inmate, Charlie Spence (p. 338) argues that trying juveniles as adults is morally wrong. And in the final two essays, Ira Glasser (p. 345) and James R. McDonough (p. 351) take opposing positions on the war on drugs.

I am not insane. I am angry. . . . I killed because people like me are mistreated every day. —Luke Woodham

He just seemed strange. . . . He didn't seem dangerous in any way.
—Karan Grewal

The reality is that schools are very safe environments for our kids.
—Jim Mercy

JOURNAL RESPONSE School shootings seem to have become an epidemic in the United States. Most notoriously, in 1999 two students at Columbine High School killed thirteen people, and in 2007 a student at Virginia Tech killed thirty-three people. Because of such tragedies, many high-school (and even grade-school) students now must pass through metal detectors on their way to class, and several school districts have initiated "zero tolerance" policies that call for the removal of children who show any potential to do harm. How do you feel about the violence and its consequences? In a journal entry, comment on the problem of student violence. How extensive is it? What causes it? What should be done about it?

Anna Quindlen

Winner of the Pulitzer Prize for commentary in 1992, Anna Quindlen writes sharp, candid columns on subjects ranging from family life to social issues to international politics. She was born in 1953 in Philadelphia, where she grew up, as she puts it, "an antsy kid with a fresh mouth." After graduating from Barnard College, Quindlen began writing for the New York Post and then joined the New York Times, where she worked her way up from a city hall reporter to a regular columnist. Since 1999 she has written a biweekly column for Newsweek magazine. Her columns have been collected in Living Out Loud (1988), Thinking Out Loud (1993), and Loud and Clear (2004). Quindlen is also the author of A Short Guide to a Happy Life (2000); the novels Object Lessons (1991), One True Thing (1994), Black and Blue (1998), Blessings (2002), and Rise and Shine (2006); and the memoir Good Dog. Stay (2007).

The C Word in the Hallways

Quindlen wrote this selection in November 1999, a few months after the massacre at Columbine High School. Similar events since then have made her message as urgent as ever.

The saddest phrase I've read in a long time is this one: psychological   1
autopsy. That's what the doctors call it when a kid kills himself, and they
go back over the plowed ground of his short life, and discover all the
hidden markers that led to the rope, the blade, the gun.

There's a plague on all our houses, and since it doesn't announce   2
itself with lumps or spots or protest marches, it has gone unremarked
in the quiet suburbs and busy cities where it has been laying waste. The
number of suicides and homicides committed by teenagers, most often
young men, has exploded in the last three decades, until it has become
routine to have black-bordered photographs in yearbooks and murder
suspects with acne problems. And everyone searches for reasons, and
scapegoats, and solutions, most often punitive. Yet one solution continues to elude us, and that is ending the ignorance about mental health,
and moving it from the margins of care and into the mainstream where
it belongs. As surely as any vaccine, this would save lives.

So many have already been lost. This month Kip Kinkel was sentenced   3
to life in prison in Oregon for the murders of his parents and a shooting
rampage at his high school that killed two students. A psychiatrist who
specializes in the care of adolescents testified that Kinkel, now seventeen,
had been hearing voices since he was twelve. Sam Manzie is also seventeen. He is serving a seventy-year sentence for luring an eleven-year-old
boy named Eddie Werner into his New Jersey home and strangling him
with the cord to an alarm clock because his Sega Genesis was out of reach.
Manzie had his first psychological evaluation in the first grade.

Excuses, excuses. That's what so many think of the underlying   4
pathology in such hideous crimes. In the 1956 movie *The Bad Seed*, little
Patty McCormack played what was then called a "homicidal maniac" and
the film censors demanded a ludicrous mock curtain call in which the
child actress was taken over the knee of her screen father and spanked.
There are still some representatives of the "good spanking" school out
there, although today the spanking may wind up being life in prison.
And there's still plenty of that useless adult "what in the world does
a sixteen-year-old have to be depressed about" mind-set to keep depressed
sixteen-year-olds from getting help.

It's true that both the Kinkel and the Manzie boys had already been   5
introduced to the mental health system before their crimes. Concerned
by her son's fascination with weapons, Faith Kinkel took him for nine
sessions with a psychologist in the year before the shootings. Because
of his rages and his continuing relationship with a pedophile, Sam's
parents had tried to have him admitted to a residential facility just days
before their son invited Eddie in.

But they were threading their way through a mental health system 6
that is marginalized by shame, ignorance, custom, the courts, even by
business practice. Kip Kinkel's father made no secret of his disapproval
of therapy. During its course he bought his son the Glock that Kip would
later use on his killing spree, which speaks sad volumes about our peculiar standards of masculinity. Sam's father, on the other hand, spent days
trying to figure out how much of the cost of a home for troubled kids his
insurance would cover. In the meantime, a psychiatrist who examined
his son for less time than it takes to eat a Happy Meal concluded that he
was no danger to himself or others, and a judge lectured Sam from the
bench: "You know the difference between right and wrong, don't you?"

The federal Center for Mental Health Services estimates that at least 7
six million children in this country have some serious emotional distur-
bance and, for some of them, right and wrong take second seat to the
voices in their heads. Fifty years ago their parents might have surren-
dered them to life in an institution, or a doctor flying blind with an ice
pick might have performed a lobotomy, leaving them to loll away their
days. Now lots of them wind up in jail. Warm fuzzies aside, consider this
from a utilitarian point of view: psychological intervention is cheaper
than incarceration.

The most optimistic estimate is that two-thirds of these emotion- 8
ally disturbed children are not getting any treatment. Imagine how we
would respond if two-thirds of America's babies were not being immu-
nized. Many health insurance plans do not provide coverage for necessary treatment, or financially penalize those who need a psychiatrist
instead of an oncologist. Teachers are not trained to recognize mental
illness, and some dismiss it, "Bad Seed" fashion, as bad behavior. Parents
are afraid, and ashamed, creating a home environment, and national
atmosphere, too, that tells teenagers their demons are a disgrace.

And then there are the teenagers themselves, slouching toward 9
adulthood in a world that loves conformity. Add to the horror of creeping depression or delusions that of peer derision, the sound of the *C* word
in the hallways: crazy, man, he's crazy, haven't you seen him, didn't you
hear? Boys, especially, still suspect that talk therapy, or even heartfelt
talk, is somehow sissified, weak. Sometimes even their own fathers think
so, at least until they have to identify the body.

Another sad little phrase is "If only," and there are always plenty of 10
them littering the valleys of tragedy. If only there had been long-term
intervention and medication, Kip Kinkel might be out of jail, off the tax-
payers' tab, and perhaps leading a productive life. If only Sam Manzie
had been treated aggressively earlier, new psychotropic drugs might have

slowed or stilled his downward slide. And if only those things had happened, Faith Kinkel, William Kinkel, Mikael Nickolauson, Ben Walker, and Eddie Werner might all be alive today. Mental health care is health care, too, and mental illness is an illness, not a character flaw. Insurance providers should act like it. Hospitals and schools should act like it. Above all, we parents should act like it. Then maybe the kids will believe it.

Meaning

1. What is Quindlen's main idea, and where do you find it in the essay?

2. What examples of teen violence does Quindlen give? What reason does she provide to explain these students' behavior?

3. Why is Quindlen so alarmed about our attitudes toward mental illness? Whom does she blame for the problems experienced by troubled teenagers?

4. In paragraph 6, Quindlen writes that William Kinkel's purchase of a gun for his son "speaks sad volumes about our peculiar standards of masculinity." What does she mean?

5. If you are unsure of any of the following words used by Quindlen, try to determine their meanings from their context in the essay. Check their meanings in a dictionary to test your guesses. Then use each word in a sentence or two of your own.

scapegoats (2)	loll (7)	oncologist (8)
pathology (4)	utilitarian (7)	derision (9)
ludicrous (4)	incarceration (7)	psychotropic (10)
marginalized (6)		

Purpose and Audience

1. What seems to be Quindlen's purpose in writing this essay? Is she writing mainly to express a concern, offer a solution to a problem, influence government decisions, change individuals' attitudes, or do something else? What evidence from the text supports your answer?

2. Who do you think is the author's target audience? How does Quindlen engage these readers' support?

3. Although this essay was written only a few months after the tragedy at Columbine (which at the time was the deadliest school shooting in American history), Quindlen makes no mention of the shooters there, Eric Harris and Dylan Klebold. Why do you suppose she leaves them out of her discussion?

Method and Structure

1. Is Quindlen's appeal mostly emotional or mostly rational? Explain your answer with examples from the essay.

2. Where in the essay does Quindlen address opposing viewpoints? How fair is her depiction of people with conflicting opinions?

3. Quindlen makes two literary references in this essay: "a plague on all our houses" (paragraph 2) is an allusion to Shakespeare's play *Romeo and Juliet,* and "slouching toward adulthood" (9) is an allusion to William Butler Yeats's poem "The Second Coming." What is the effect of these references?

4. **OTHER METHODS**   Quindlen supports her argument with other methods, such as example (Chapter 7), comparison and contrast (Chapter 11), and cause-and-effect analysis (Chapter 13). Locate one instance of each method. What does each contribute to the essay?

Language

1. What is the "*C* word" to which Quindlen refers in her title? Why do you suppose she waits until the end of the essay to use the word itself?

2. How does Quindlen use parallel sentence structure in her conclusion to drive home her point?

3. How would you describe Quindlen's tone? Is it consistent throughout? Is it appropriate for her subject?

Writing Topics

1. **JOURNAL TO ESSAY**   Take off from the comments you made in your journal entry (p. 327) to write an essay that agrees or disagrees with Quindlen. Has the incidence of teenage suicide and homicide really "exploded" (paragraph 2) to the degree that Quindlen describes? Are teenage killers victims of inadequate mental health care? Is better psychological treatment the answer to the problem? Are there other solutions we should consider? Your essay may but need not be an argument: that is, you could explain your answer to any of these questions or argue a specific point. Either way, use examples and details to support your ideas.

2. Although Quindlen's essay demonstrates a large degree of compassion for troubled teenagers, some scholars and psychologists would caution that the cause-and-effect relationship it draws between mental illness and violence is misinformed. Using the library or the Internet,

research articles or studies concerning media stigmatization of the mentally ill. In an essay, discuss whether you think Quindlen's analysis of teen violence reflects negative stereotypes. If you find that it does, consider whether such stereotypes affect the persuasiveness of her argument. (For advice on finding and using research sources, see the Appendix.)

3. **CULTURAL CONSIDERATIONS** At several points in her essay, Quindlen suggests that American codes of masculinity are at least partly to blame for teenage boys' tendency toward violence. Write an essay that explores what our culture expects of boys and men, and how those expectations might translate into inappropriate behavior. How does American culture define manhood? Do we, in fact, pressure boys to keep silent about their emotions? To what extent is masculine aggression encouraged or rewarded? How does society respond to boys—and men—who don't conform to expectations? And to what extent are individuals responsible for their own behavior? In formulating your analysis, consider also how a person from another culture might respond—a resident of, say, Mexico or Japan or France.

4. **CONNECTIONS** Both Quindlen and Andrew Sullivan, in "The 'M-Word': Why It Matters to Me" (p. 269), write with strong emotion about a social issue—mental illness in Quindlen's case, gay marriage in Sullivan's—and both writers use a similar titling strategy. In an essay, explore how the concept of personal shame, or social taboo, informs each writer's approach. Why do these writers hesitate to name their subjects in their titles, and what does this hesitation say about how they imagine their readers will respond to their arguments? How effective is each writer's strategy of tackling a controversial issue from an emotional perspective? What would these essays have lost (or gained) if they had been written from a more psychologically distant point of view?

Research shows the brain is not fully developed until age twenty-one and many things can damage the brain until then. All of those things that you absolutely would not wish on your child come from underage alcohol use. —Michele Compton

Why don't we trust these young adults to make the same kind of responsible decisions about alcohol that we believe them capable of making in the voting booth, in the jury box, on the battlefield?
—John McCardell

Kids are going to try drugs and alcohol; that's part of society.
—Jamie Lee Curtis

JOURNAL RESPONSE   Take a few minutes to describe and comment on the drinking culture among students at your school. Are rowdy parties the norm, or do most students generally refrain from alcohol? Do you approve of the majority behavior, or do you wish things were different? Why?

Linda Chavez

A vocal supporter of conservative causes, Linda Chavez writes passionately about immigration, affirmative action, civil rights, bilingual education, and other fiery subjects. She also hosts a national radio show and provides political analysis for Fox news. Chavez was born in 1947 in Albuquerque, New Mexico, and received a BA in education from the University of Colorado in 1970. She has had a distinguished political career, including appointments as director of the US Commission on Civil Rights and director of the White House Office of Public Liaisons under President Ronald Reagan, and chair of the National Commission on Migrant Education under President George H. W. Bush. In addition to a syndicated column and numerous articles for popular periodicals, Chavez has written three books: *Out of the Barrio: Toward a New Politics of Spanish Assimilation* (1991), *An Unlikely Conservative: The Transformation of a Renegade Democrat (Or How I Became the Most Hated Hispanic in America)* (2002), and, with Daniel Gray, *Betrayal: How Union Bosses Shake Down Their Members and Corrupt American Politics* (2004). She is the founder of the Center for Equal Opportunity, a nonprofit think tank that researches public policy, and currently chairs both that organization and the Latino Alliance, a political action committee.

Redefining the Problem Won't Make It Go Away

Binge drinking—commonly defined as consuming five alcoholic drinks in a row for men and four for women, or simply as drinking to the point of drunkenness—is a persistent problem on college campuses. In this essay published in the online journal *townhall.com* on August 22, 2008, Chavez takes exception to a solution proposed by a group of college presidents.

If ever we needed proof that having an advanced degree doesn't correlate 1 with common sense, we got it this week. A group of college presidents from some of the most prestigious schools in the nation have called on lawmakers to consider lowering the drinking age. They call their effort the Amethyst Initiative. Why Amethyst? On their Web site, the erudite group explains to those of us who aren't fluent in ancient Greek, the word is derived from the prefix *a*—meaning not—and *methustos,* which means intoxicated.

"Twenty-one is not working," the group claims. "A culture of danger- 2 ous, clandestine 'binge-drinking'—often conducted off-campus—has developed," they say, as if the law prohibiting underage drinking has created this culture. Apparently the group believes that if we'd simply lower the drinking age to eighteen, college students will magically stop binge drinking.

By that reasoning, why not lower the drinking age to fourteen? That 3 way, we could wipe out binge drinking among high-school students as well. Heck, maybe we could cure alcoholism by eliminating age limits on drinking altogether. Start kids early and they'll learn to drink responsibly, right?

The facts suggest otherwise. According to a 2007 survey by the US 4 Surgeon General, 45 percent of high-school students reported drinking alcohol within the previous month, and more than one in four said they were binge drinkers. In 2005, drinking led to 145,000 emergency room visits by kids twelve to twenty years old for injuries related to their drinking. Of the nearly 7,500 traffic deaths involving fifteen- to twenty-year-olds in 2005, more than 2,000 had been drinking. And young people who start drinking before they turn fifteen are five times more likely to become problem drinkers or alcoholics later on.

Lowering the drinking age to eighteen won't solve these problems— 5 and would likely make them worse. So why do these college presidents want to open this Pandora's box? It's simple. They don't want to be responsible for enforcing the law on their campuses.

Back in the Dark Ages when I started college (1965), colleges assumed 6 the role of *in loco parentis,* acting in the place of parents for students who were not yet adults. By 1970 when I graduated, most universities had dropped virtually all the old rules. Once forbidden to do so, students were allowed to entertain members of the opposite sex in their dorm rooms (and soon, those dorms would be coed). Curfews were gone. Indeed, the only behavioral rule colleges seemed willing to enforce after the tumultuous sixties was the prohibition against drinking on campus. Now, more than one hundred college presidents have asked to be alleviated of even this responsibility.

College should be a time for students not only to acquire knowl- 7 edge and earn a degree but to form character. College presidents could help fulfill their role in that endeavor by promoting less, not more, alcohol on campus. The National Institute of Medicine and the National Research Council have outlined several proposals to reduce underage drinking. Among their recommendations are increasing alcohol taxes, reducing youth exposure to alcohol advertising, and enforcing underage drinking laws more aggressively, not less. And they call on colleges and universities to collaborate and implement programs to prevent underage drinking.

The average cost of a four-year public college was nearly $13,000 a 8 year in 2006 and more than $30,000 for a private college. You'd think for that kind of money we could get college presidents to do something as simple as to discourage underage drinking on their campuses. Instead, too many don't only look away but want to define the problem out of existence by lowering the legal drinking age.

Alcohol abuse is a serious problem in our culture. It ruins lives and 9 kills thousands of Americans every year on our streets and highways. Alcohol devastates the health and well-being of those who abuse it and destroys innocent family members. We need to do everything we can to discourage drinking, especially among the young. The last thing we need is a bunch of college presidents to pretend that redefining the legal drinking age is a step in that direction.

Meaning

1. Where, if at all, does Chavez state her thesis? What claim does she want readers to accept, and what does she want them to do as a result of reading her essay?

2. What does *in loco parentis* (paragraph 6) mean? In what way is the concept central to Chavez's argument?

3. On what grounds does Chavez oppose lowering the drinking age? Do you find her reasons convincing? Why, or why not?

4. In paragraph 5, Chavez asks, "[W]hy do these college presidents want to open this Pandora's box?" What is she talking about? Why is the reference particularly appropriate, considering how Chavez introduces her subject?

5. If you are unsure of the meanings of any of the following words, try to guess them from their context in Chavez's essay. Look up the words in a dictionary to check your guesses, and then practice using each word in a sentence or two of your own.

correlate (1)	clandestine (2)	endeavor (7)
prestigious (1)	tumultuous (6)	implement (7)
erudite (1)	alleviated (6)	

Purpose and Audience

1. Why do you believe Chavez wrote this essay? To make fun of the Amethyst Initiative? To express her indignation? To argue for or against something? (If so, what?) For some other purpose? What evidence from the text supports your answer?

2. Whom do you believe Chavez imagines as her primary readers? College presidents? Students? Concerned parents? The general population? How might she have adjusted her tactics if she were writing for a different audience?

3. What assumptions does Chavez seem to make about her readers' values? Do those assumptions hold true in your case?

Method and Structure

1. How does Chavez present and handle opposing arguments? Does she seem fair? Why, or why not?

2. Consider how Chavez supports her argument. What kinds of evidence does she provide? How convincing is it, in your opinion?

3. Chavez's argument is both inductive (see Meaning question 3, above) and deductive. Express her argument as a syllogism (see pp. 315–17). Do you detect any flaws in her reasoning? If so, what are they?

4. **OTHER METHODS** Where in her essay does Chavez use cause-and-effect analysis (Chapter 13) to develop her argument? Why is this method important to her purpose?

Language

1. Why does Chavez quote the Amethyst Initiative in paragraph 2? What function does this passage serve?
2. How would you describe Chavez's tone? Is it consistent throughout?

Writing Topics

1. **JOURNAL TO ESSAY** Starting from your journal entry (p. 333), write an essay about alcohol consumption among students at your school. Do you regard underage and binge drinking as critical problems? Do you believe that the school administration is taking adequate steps to prevent drinking by students? Or do you believe that students are responsible for their own choices? Your essay may but need not be an argument: that is, you could explain your answer to any of these questions or argue a specific point. Either way, use examples and details to support your ideas.

2. Choose a social or other kind of problem you care about—it could be overcrowding in public schools, violence in the media, child neglect, or anything else. Describe the problem as you understand it, particularly how it affects people. Then discuss your solution to the problem or some part of it. Be sure at least to acknowledge opposing views.

3. **CULTURAL CONSIDERATIONS** Chavez doesn't mention it, but in the 1970s many states did in fact lower the legal drinking age to eighteen (most raised it back to twenty-one in the mid-1980s, in response to federal pressure and the threat of losing highway funds if they did not). Using the library and the Internet, research the reasons behind lowering the drinking age, as well as the results. (For advice on finding information, see pp. 363–64 in the Appendix.) Based on what you find, write an argument for lowering the drinking age again, for keeping it at twenty-one, or, as some have proposed, for raising it even higher.

4. **CONNECTIONS** Both Chavez and James R. McDonough, in "Critics Scapegoat the Antidrug Laws" (p. 351), invoke the dangers of substance abuse to argue for stronger laws and more aggressive enforcement. But one aspect of the problem is not discussed by either writer: the *reasons* young people turn to drugs and alcohol in the first place. What do you think these reasons are? How might addressing the causes of alcohol and drug use help to prevent it? Drawing on these two writers' stated and unstated assumptions, your own experiences and observations, and any reading you have done on the subject, write an essay exploring this issue. Be sure to offer sufficient evidence to support your claims.

Prison continues, on those who are entrusted to it, a work begun elsewhere, which the whole of society pursues on each individual through innumerable mechanisms of discipline. —Michel Foucault

Man is not made better by being degraded; he is seldom restrained from crime by harsh measures, except the principle of fear predominates in his character; and then he is never made radically better for its influence. —Dorothea Dix

Of the three official objects of our prison system—vengeance, deterrence, and reformation of the criminal—only one is achieved; and that is the one which is nakedly abominable. —George Bernard Shaw

JOURNAL RESPONSE What is the purpose of prison in a civilized society? Do we jail people to punish them, to rehabilitate them, or to protect others from them? Are there other ways to respond to crime? In your journal, write a few paragraphs exploring your thoughts on these questions.

Charlie Spence

Charlie Spence was born in 1980 and grew up in Sacramento, California, with two brothers and a single mother "who always tried her best." At the age of sixteen, Spence was sentenced to a prison term of twenty-six years to life; he is serving his time at San Quentin and has been working with at-risk youth since 2005. He takes college courses from Patten University through the Prison University Project and plans to earn a degree in social psychology. Spence reports that he "strongly desires to be not only free, but a leading voice for change in America's juvenile justice practices." Beyond sentencing reform, his interests include reading and sports.

Sixteen

(Student Essay)

Spence first wrote "Sixteen" for a Patten University composition course in 2009 and revised it for the *Compact Reader* in 2010. Not surprisingly, Spence is opposed to sentencing juveniles as adults. Although we might have reason to suspect his objectivity, he overcomes the problem by presenting his case rationally and by backing up his claims with ample evidence from reliable sources. In accordance with MLA style, Spence names his sources in the text and lists them at the end. (See the Appendix for information on using and citing sources.)

They seemed larger than me that day, the rain drops, as they fell from 1 an endless gray sky. They illuminated the headlights of oncoming traffic in an iridescent and blurred shine. The display of colors seemed only to intensify the fear and magnify the pain I felt inside about yet another tragedy taking place in my life. I sat there dressed in an orange jump-suit, feet shackled together and a waist chain tightly secured around my midsection to restrict my arms firmly to my sides. The sheriff's van traveled at what felt like the speed of light, never allowing me to col-lect my thoughts before arriving at my next destination: life in an adult institution at the age of sixteen. The words compassionately spoken by the sheriff that day have never left the confines of my soul: "I didn't even start to get it together until I was twenty-five," he said. The sheriff will never understand the extent to which his words thrashed about my heart. Had I been tried and convicted as a juvenile, I would have been given a better chance at rehabilitation and a second chance in society at the age of twenty-five. I feel even more strongly now than I did back then that trying juvenile offenders as adults and sentencing them to life in prison is immoral.

In the year 2000, the people of California voted and passed Proposi- 2 tion 21. This allowed for juveniles as young as fourteen who are accused of a serious crime to be tried as adults at the discretion of the district attorney trying the case. Prior to Proposition 21, juveniles accused of such crimes were given what is called a "707(b) hearing" in front of a judge, to determine if they met the criteria to be tried as an adult. Before Proposition 21 was introduced, only in rare and extreme cases of vio-lence were juveniles tried as adults.

It is easy for me to understand the feelings of one who is opposed to 3 my position. Juveniles do commit crimes that are serious and are con-sidered to be "adult crimes." The juveniles who receive life sentences are certainly not receiving them for petty crimes; it is not as if the fourteen-year-old shoplifter is locked up and the key is then thrown away. I would agree, too, that most juveniles have a sense of right and wrong from an early age. Surely children know that they are not supposed to take cookies out of the cookie jar unless given permission by their parents. On a greater scale most adolescents know it is wrong to smoke, use drugs, cheat, or steal and, therefore, know it is wrong to commit crime, period. But it seems only fair that if we are going to take into account the social development of morality within these children, then by that same token we should also consider their mental development and take into account the neuroscience and the high likelihood of rehabilitating these same children.

According to a newspaper article published in the *Los Angeles Times* 4 and a study conducted for the University of San Francisco's Center for Law and Global Justice, 2,387 juvenile offenders have been given life sentences here in the United States (Weinstein; Leighton and de la Vega 2). To understand this prodigious number, and contemplate the depraved nature of this practice, consider that Israel, the *only other* country in the world to hand out such sentences, is a far and distant second with seven. According to the study, Israel has not handed out such sentences since 2004 (Leighton and de la Vega iii). While the populations in these two countries widely differ, these statistics seem to suggest that Israel uses such sentences in extreme cases only. It should be noted that of the juveniles sentenced to life without parole here in the United States, half of those sentences were issued to first-time offenders (Leighton and de la Vega 14). It is alarming that we are willing to sentence, at a staggering number, our youth offenders to life with or without parole considering that juveniles stand the greatest chance to be rehabilitated.

Senator Leland Yee of San Francisco–San Mateo, whose background 5 is in child psychology, states, "Children have the highest capacity for rehabilitation. The neuroscience is clear; brain maturation continues well through adolescence and thus impulse control, planning, and critical-thinking skills are not fully developed" (qtd. in Weinstein). Other studies support this same finding: the San Francisco Center for Law and Global Justice study asserts, "Psychologically and neurologically, children cannot be expected to have achieved the same level of mental development as an adult, even when they become teenagers" (Leighton and de la Vega i). A perfect example of an immature brain is a fourteen-year-old child, with whom I became acquainted in juvenile hall, who had been asked by a peer to beat up a homeless man for twenty-five cents. This child, having never been accepted by a peer group before, proceeded to beat up the homeless man. The subsequent and tragic outcome of the situation was the homeless man died from his injuries and the child was given life in prison, all because he acted on an impulse to be accepted by friends and lacked the critical thinking skills of a fully developed mind. Had this been a mature adult who had been asked to beat up a homeless man for twenty-five cents, I find it hard to believe that he would have done it.

Juvenile offenders should be punished for serious crimes they 6 commit, but as juveniles in juvenile facilities, where a "life" sentence ends at age twenty-five. The oldest that children can be tried as minors is seventeen, an age that allows for eight years of time in which they can serve their punishment and in which we have an opportunity to rehabilitate them. Age sixteen allows for nine years and so on. By placing our youth in adult facilities with life sentences, we are giving up on them. According to the Center on Juvenile and Criminal Justice, fifteen- to twenty-one-year-olds make up 13 percent of our prison population and together they make up 22 percent of all suicide deaths in our institutions. Juveniles are 7.7 times more likely to commit suicide in adult facilities than in juvenile facilities. Whereas only 1 percent of juveniles reported rape in the juvenile system, that actual number is nine times higher in the adult system. It is not just about these numbers, though. At what point do we brand a person for life for the worst thing he or she did as a child?

The lack of mental maturity and development within the minds   7 of juveniles is what sets the stage for a 2005 US Supreme Court ruling in which the Court determined that it is unconstitutional to execute a person under the age of eighteen. In their majority opinion, the Court cited research saying that the mental capacity of juveniles was not the same as that of adults (Roper v. Simmons). Here, the highest court in the United States is acknowledging that juveniles lack careful and exact evaluation and judgment, as well as the ability to control sudden spontaneous inclinations or urges because of their undeveloped minds. Perhaps this is the reason why juveniles are not allowed to choose for themselves whether or not they can go watch an R-rated movie until the age of seventeen. They cannot vote until age eighteen, buy a pack of cigarettes until age eighteen, or buy alcohol until the age of twenty-one. The contrast here is drastic; by one means we are suggesting that seventeen-year-old teenagers are only entering a mature enough mental state to choose whether they wish to watch an R-rated movie, yet by another we are suggesting that they are mature enough to understand the full consequences of a crime they may commit.

Obviously, we as a society recognize the difference between the   8 mental capacity of juveniles and adults too, or we would not have constructed laws based on the age of an individual as a determining factor for conduct. It seems unfair that we only want to recognize the difference in mental development between adult and child up to the point when the child exercises bad judgment. I hate to think that we are so cruel as a society and a country that we would rather place our children in prison because of poor decision making with an immature brain, for a crime they are convicted of, than try to rehabilitate them while their mental capacity for reform is at its pinnacle.

Works Cited

Center on Juvenile and Criminal Justice. *Center on Juvenile and Criminal Justice.* CJCJ, n.d. Web. 2 Feb. 2010.

Leighton, Michelle, and Connie de la Vega. *Sentencing Our Children to Die in Prison: Global Law and Practice.* San Francisco: U of San Francisco School of Law, 2007. Print.

Roper v. Simmons 543 US 551. Supreme Court of the US. 2005. *Supreme Court Collection.* Legal Information Inst., Cornell U Law School, n.d. Web. 10 Feb. 2010.

Weinstein, Henry. "Focus on Youth Sentences." *Los Angeles Times.* Los Angeles Times, 19 Nov. 2007. Web. 2 Feb. 2010.

Meaning

1. According to Spence, what is the purpose of sending people to prison? What *should* be the purpose, as he sees it? Where in the text does he state the central assumption that grounds his argument?

2. Why does Spence believe that sentencing juveniles to life is immoral? Summarize his supporting arguments in your own words.

3. Spence tells readers that he is serving a life sentence, but he doesn't say what crime he committed. Does it matter? Why, or why not?

4. Some of the following words may be new to you. Try to guess their meanings from the context of Spence's essay. Test your guesses in a dictionary, and then use each new word in a sentence or two of your own.

iridescent (1)	prodigious (4)	spontaneous (7)
confines (1)	depraved (4)	inclinations (7)
discretion (2)	capacity (5, 8)	pinnacle (8)
neuroscience (3, 5)	subsequent (5)	

Purpose and Audience

1. What is the purpose of the personal story with which Spence opens his essay? How did it affect you?

2. Who would Spence's ideal readers be? Politicians? Prisoners? Average citizens? Why do you think so?

Method and Structure

1. Examine how Spence uses information and ideas from sources to develop and support his main idea. What might his argument have lost without this material?

2. How would you rate Spence's ethical appeal? What strategies does he use to overcome readers' potential doubts about his objectivity?

3. How does Spence handle opposing viewpoints? What is the effect of acknowledging that juveniles do commit serious crimes and that life sentences for juvenile offenders are not handed down lightly?

4. **OTHER METHODS** In paragraph 4, Spence uses comparison and contrast (Chapter 11) to examine the sentencing practices in the United States and Israel. What are the differences? How does this comparison further Spence's argument that trying juveniles as adults is wrong?

Language

1. How would you describe Spence's attitude toward his subject? What is the overall tone of his argument?

2. Why does Spence take such pains to refer to juvenile offenders as "children" throughout his essay? How does he use repetition of key words to reinforce his main point?

Writing Topics

1. **JOURNAL TO ESSAY** The United States imprisons more of its citizens than almost any other country. Why is this the case? Reread the quotations and the journal entry you wrote before reading Spence's essay (p. 338). Develop your ideas into an essay that explains and supports your thoughts on the uses of imprisonment in America. Do we, as Spence suggests, jail people to punish them for their crimes, or do other motives come into play? Are such motives reasonable? Is imprisonment effective at accomplishing the purposes assigned to it? Is the institution abused or misused in any way? Whatever your position, be sure to support it with plenty of details and examples and to consider how others might disagree with you.

2. Prison is a perennially popular subject in fiction. Find a novel or film that takes prison, or something related to prison (such as involuntary commitment to a mental hospital), as its subject. (For novels, you might consider Charles Dickens's *Little Dorrit*, Malcolm Braly's *On the Yard*, or Kurt Vonnegut's *Hocus Pocus*. Films touching on this subject include

Cool Hand Luke, Escape from Alcatraz, Bad Boys, The Green Mile, and *The Shawshank Redemption,* the last two based on stories by Stephen King.) Write an essay comparing and contrasting the novel's or film's attitudes toward prison with Spence's views. Are the criticisms the same? Where do they differ?

3. **CULTURAL CONSIDERATIONS**   As the quotation from Michel Foucault (p. 338) suggests, laws reflect and reinforce basic social values: What behaviors are acceptable? What transgressions are punishable? How far should we go to enforce social norms? Although incarceration practices might seem reasonable in a contemporary cultural context, viewed from an outsider's perspective they can often be quite surprising. For much of American history, for instance, whole families—including dependent infants—were routinely placed in debtors' prisons for a father's failure to provide for them. And in the early twentieth century, unmarried women could be jailed for pregnancy. Think of a past or current law that strikes you as absurd or extreme and look for the underlying social value that it's meant to enforce. Then write an essay that explains the law to somebody from another culture, or another time, who might have trouble understanding it. You may be ironic or satiric, if you wish, or you may prefer a more straightforward informative approach.

4. **CONNECTIONS**   Spence and Anna Quindlen, in "The C Word in the Hallways" (p. 327), both write about violent crimes committed by teenagers, and both use psychology to suggest that juvenile offenders aren't fully responsible for their actions. While Spence refrains from detailing such crimes, Quindlen indicates that the subjects of her essay are serving life sentences for brutal, premeditated murders. How, if at all, do Quindlen's examples affect the persuasiveness of Spence's argument? Are some crimes so terrible that the perpetrators should be locked away forever, regardless of circumstance? Why do you think so? Write an essay that explains your answers to these questions, drawing for evidence on Spence's and Quindlen's arguments as well as your own opinions.

ON ILLEGAL DRUGS

Just say no. —Nancy Reagan

There seems to be no stopping drug frenzy once it takes hold of a nation. What starts with an innocuous HUGS, NOT DRUGS bumper sticker soon leads to wild talk of shooting dealers and making urine tests a condition for employment—anywhere. —Barbara Ehrenreich

The entire war on drugs disproportionately targets poor people and people of color. —Ethan Nadelmann

JOURNAL RESPONSE Is there any illegal drug that you think should be legal or a legal drug that you think should be illegal? What would be the effects, both positive and negative, of changing the laws on this drug? Consider, for example, whether a change in status would increase or decrease use of the drug, whether it would hurt or harm users, and what the social and economic repercussions might be.

Ira Glasser

Ira Glasser was born in Brooklyn, New York, in 1938. After obtaining degrees from Queens College of the City College of New York (BS, 1959) and Ohio State University (MA, 1960), he taught college mathematics and edited the public affairs magazine *Current* for several years before finding his life's work with the American Civil Liberties Union (ACLU). First as associate director of the organization's New York branch and then as national director from 1978 to 2001, Glasser developed a reputation for protecting the dispossessed from government abuses of power and for taking on unpopular causes in the name of First Amendment rights. He is generally credited with transforming the ACLU from a small legal service to an influential—if often controversial—national presence. Glasser has published essays in periodicals ranging from *USA Today* to *Christianity and Crisis* to *Harper's Magazine*, as well as two books, *Doing Good: The Limits of Benevolence* (coauthored with Willard Gaylin and others, 1978) and *Visions of Liberty* (1991). Now retired from the ACLU, he is president of the board of the Drug Policy Alliance, a lobbying group dedicated to ending the war on drugs.

Drug Busts = Jim Crow

From the 1870s through the first half of the twentieth century, laws in many states denied African Americans the right to use the same public facilities (such as restrooms and water fountains) and institutions (such as schools and housing developments) as the white majority. This widespread and officially sanctioned segregation, called "Jim Crow" after the title of a popular nineteenth-century song, stayed in place until the civil rights movement successfully forced the creation of new laws against racial discrimination in the 1960s. But is legal segregation truly history? In this essay, first published in the *Nation* in 2006, Glasser suggests that it is not.

I was born in 1938, grew up on the working-class, immigrant streets of East Flatbush in Brooklyn during World War II, and came to political consciousness during the postwar years. As children, we were told that World War II was a war fought against racism, against the idea that a whole class of people could be separated, subjugated, and even murdered because of their race or religion. But back home in the United States, racial separation and subjugation remained entrenched by law in the Deep South and by custom nearly everywhere else.

This moral contradiction between what America said it stood for and the way it was actually organized was largely unrecognized by the American public as World War II drew to a close. The first major postwar event that challenged this contradiction and made it unavoidable was the coming of Jackie Robinson to the Brooklyn Dodgers in 1947. It engaged people, including children, in a drama of racial integration, and it created what may have been the first racially integrated public accommodation—at Ebbets Field, where the Dodgers played. The following year President Harry Truman issued an executive order desegregating the armed forces. In 1950 *Brown v. Board of Education* was filed, signaling the start of the modern civil rights era. Four years later a surprisingly unanimous Supreme Court struck down legally enforced racial separation in public schools, and seventeen months after that, Rosa Parks refused to give her seat to a white man on a Montgomery, Alabama, bus. Nine years later, after countless protests, marches, sit-ins, and freedom rides, as well as murders and beatings of civil rights workers, the Civil Rights Act of 1964 was passed, outlawing racial discrimination in public accommodations, employment, and education. A year later the Voting Rights Act of 1965 outlawed racial discrimination in voting, and three years after that, the Fair Housing Act of 1968 outlawed racial discrimination in the purchase and rental of homes. By 1968 the legal infrastructure of Jim Crow subjugation had been destroyed and a new legal infrastructure of federal civil rights enforcement was erected in its place. America had, for the first time, abolished legalized racial discrimination and replaced it with a system of formal legal equality.

As it turned out, actual equality of opportunity did not follow automatically, easily, or quickly from legal equality. But over the succeeding decades it has been assumed that at the very least, no legalized racial discrimination remains, and certainly no new forms of legalized skin-color subjugation have arisen. This is true, with one substantial exception: the system of drug prohibition and its enforcement, which is the major, and still insufficiently recognized, civil rights issue of our day.

In the late 1960s, at the peak of the civil rights movement, there 4 were fewer than 200,000 people in state and federal prisons for all criminal offenses; by 2004 there were over 1.4 million. Another 700,000-plus in local jails brought the total to 2.2 million. This explosion of incarceration has been heavily due to nonviolent drug offenses—mostly possession and petty sales, not involving guns or violence—resulting from the exponential escalation of the "war on drugs," beginning in 1968 and accelerating again after 1980.

Since 1980 drug arrests have tripled, to 1.6 million annually—nearly 5 half for marijuana, 88 percent of those for possession, not sale or manufacture. Since 1980 the proportion of all state prisoners who are in for drug offenses increased from 6 percent to 21 percent. Since 1980 the proportion of all federal prisoners who are in for drug offenses increased from 25 percent to 57 percent.

At the same time, the racial disparity of arrests, convictions, and impris- 6 onment for these offenses has become pronounced. According to federal statistics gathered by the Sentencing Project, only 13 percent of monthly drug users of all illegal drugs—defined as those who use a drug at least once a month on a regular basis—are black, about their proportion of the population. But 37 percent of drug-offense arrests are black; 53 percent of convictions are black; and 67 percent of all people imprisoned for drug offenses are black. Adding in Latinos, about 22 percent of all monthly drug users are black or Latino, but 80 percent of people in prison for drug offenses are black or Latino. Even in presumptively liberal New York State, 92 percent of all inmates who are there for drug offenses are black or Latino.

The fact that so many people arrested, convicted, and imprisoned 7 for drug offenses are black or Latino is not because they are mostly the ones doing the crime; it is because they are mostly the ones being targeted. This is not a phenomenon of the Deep South. It is nationwide. And it is not accidental. As the racial profiling scandals a few years ago showed, blacks are disproportionately targeted while driving cars on the highway; for example, in a lawsuit challenging this practice, it was revealed that although only 17 percent of drivers on a stretch of I-95 in Maryland were black, 73 percent of all the cars stopped and searched for drugs were driven by blacks. Nor was this an isolated example. In Florida blacks were seventy-five times more likely than whites to be stopped and searched for drugs while driving. And it turned out that these racially targeted stops were the explicit result of a Drug Enforcement

Administration program begun in 1986, called Operation Pipeline, that "trained" 27,000 state troopers in forty-eight states to spot cars that might contain drugs. Most of the cars spotted were driven by blacks. And this happened even though three-quarters of monthly drug users are white! . . .

Despite these patterns of racial targeting, it has not been fashionable 8 among liberals to see drug prohibition as a massive civil rights problem of racial discrimination. Perhaps it would be easier if we examined the way racially targeted drug-war incarceration has damaged the right to vote, a right quintessentially part of the rights we thought we had won in the 1960s with the demise of Jim Crow laws.

Until recently (there have been some changes in the past few years 9 in some states), every state but two barred felons from voting — some permanently, some in a way that allowed, theoretically but often not as a practical matter, for the restoration of voting rights. Because of the explosion of incarceration driven by drug prohibition, more than 5 million people are now barred from voting. The United States is the only industrial democracy that does this. And the origin of most of these laws — no surprise — is the post-Reconstruction period after slavery was abolished. Felony disenfranchisement laws, like poll taxes and literacy tests, were historically part of the system that arose after slavery to bar blacks from exercising equal rights and, in particular, equal voting rights. Felony disenfranchisement laws were, to a large extent, part of a replacement system for subjugating blacks after slavery was abolished. . . .

The fact is, just as Jim Crow laws were a successor system to slavery, 10 so drug prohibition has been a successor to Jim Crow laws in targeting blacks, removing them from civil society, and then denying them the right to vote. Drug prohibition is now the last significant instance of legalized racial discrimination in America.

That many liberals have been at best timid in opposing the drug 11 war and at worst accomplices to its continued escalation is, in light of the racial politics of drug prohibition, a special outrage. . . . Liberals especially, therefore, need to consider attacking the premises upon which this edifice of racial subjugation is based. If they do not, who will?

Meaning

1. Where does Glasser identify the issue he is going to address? Where does he state his thesis?

2. What disparity does Glasser see in drug arrest statistics? Why are the numbers problematic?

3. Some of the following words may be new to you. Try to guess their meanings from the context of Glasser's essay. Test your guesses in a dictionary, and then use each new word in a sentence or two of your own.

subjugated (1)	pronounced (6)	demise (8)
infrastructure (2)	presumptively (6)	disenfranchisement (9)
exponential (4)	disproportionately (7)	successor (10)
escalation (4)	quintessentially (8)	edifice (11)

Purpose and Audience

1. For whom is Glasser writing? People who already favor drug law reform? People who think the laws are beneficial? Someone else? What does the author seem to assume about his readers?

2. Why do you think Glasser wrote this essay? What does he hope to accomplish by making his argument?

Method and Structure

1. Which part of the essay is more explanatory than argumentative? Is this part entirely objective? What does it contribute to Glasser's argument?

2. What kinds of evidence does the author provide? Where does it come from, and is it reliable and convincing? Why, or why not? (See pp. 364–65 for information on evaluating sources.)

3. Can you find any reference to opposing viewpoints in Glasser's essay? How, if at all, does his treatment of alternative perspectives on the issue affect the persuasiveness of his argument?

4. **OTHER METHODS** In paragraphs 8–10, Glasser uses cause-and-effect analysis (Chapter 13) to explain how imprisonment can take away convicts' voting rights. What, then, are the political consequences of targeting racial minorities for drug arrests? How does this analysis further Glasser's argument against current law-enforcement practices?

Language

1. How does Glasser's tone help convey the "special outrage" (paragraph 11) he feels about liberals' failure to oppose drug laws more aggressively? Point out three or four examples of language that establishes that mood.

2. Glasser uses several difficult words, many of which appear in the vocabulary list. He also avoids use of the first-person *I* beyond his

introductory paragraphs. How do his diction and point of view relate to his purpose and audience?

3. What is the effect of the question that closes the essay?

Writing Topics

1. **JOURNAL TO ESSAY**   Starting from your journal notes (p. 345), write an argument in favor of changing the existing laws on the drug you have chosen. Make sure to present both sides of the argument and demonstrate why your side makes more sense.

2. Using the library or the Internet, research a political lobbying organization that is concerned with the war on drugs, such as the Drug Policy Alliance, the Sentencing Project, or DARE. In an essay summarize the global vision the organization outlines in its mission statement, which may include goals met to date as well as plans for the future. Then discuss whether you agree with the organization's assessment of current drug issues, its proposed solutions, and its methods for achieving those solutions. (You may need to narrow this discussion to a particular issue.)

3. **CULTURAL CONSIDERATIONS**   Glasser writes that except for drug-enforcement practices that target minorities, "no legalized racial discrimination remains, and certainly no new forms of legalized skin-color subjugation have arisen" in the United States (paragraph 3). What do you think of this statement? Do you agree with Glasser, or can you think of other forms of racial discrimination that are built into current government policies? And to what extent does it matter whether discrimination is legal or not? Write an essay in which you examine the state of racial discrimination in contemporary American politics or culture. You may wish to think broadly about this issue, but bring your essay down to earth by focusing on a specific form of discrimination—perhaps one that you've experienced or witnessed in your own life.

4. **CONNECTIONS**   Unlike Glasser, James R. McDonough, the author of the next essay ("Critics Scapegoat the Antidrug Laws"), is strongly in favor of the war on drugs. On what major points do the authors agree and disagree? How do the tones of the two essays compare? Does either writer seem more convinced of being in the right? Which essay do you find more convincing, and why?

ON DRUG ABUSE

I oppose intrusions of the state into the private realm—as in abortion, sodomy, prostitution, pornography, drug use, or suicide, all of which I would strongly defend as matters of free choice in a representative democracy.   —Camille Paglia

To punish drug takers is like a drunk striking the bleary face it sees in the mirror. Drugs will not be brought under control until society itself changes.   —Brian Inglis

Let us not forget who we are. Drug abuse is a repudiation of everything America is.   —Ronald Reagan

JOURNAL RESPONSE   In a journal entry, comment on one example of an addictive substance, such as cocaine, heroin, tobacco, alcohol, or caffeine. Who uses this substance, and why? How does it affect the user? What effects, if any, does it have on those who do not use it? Does society condone its use or forbid it? Why?

James R. McDonough

Born in 1946 in New York City, James R. McDonough attended Brooklyn Poly-technic Institute and the US Military Academy at West Point, earned a Purple Heart along with several other medals as a troop leader in the Vietnam War, and went on to receive a master's degree in political science at the Massachu-setts Institute of Technology. During a full career as an officer in the US Army, McDonough served in Europe, Africa, Korea, and Bosnia; taught at West Point; and advised the Defense Nuclear Agency and the US State Department. He retired as a lieutenant colonel. McDonough wrote several publications for the military, including *National Compulsory Service* and *Text on International Rela-tions* (both 1977); he has also published the memoir *Platoon Leader* (1985) and two novels, *The Defense of Hill 781* (1988) and *The Limits of Glory* (1991). As director of strategy for the Office of National Drug Control Policy from 1996 to 1999, he influenced many laws that make up the country's ongoing war on drugs. McDonough has also served as director of Florida's Office of Drug Control and as secretary of the Florida Department of Corrections. He is currently a legal representative for the Florida Association of Drug Court Professionals.

Critics Scapegoat the Antidrug Laws

A former drug-enforcement official himself, McDonough strongly supports the war on drugs. As he sees it, drug abuse is not a personal issue but a major social problem that needs to be resolved. In this essay, first published in 2003 in the conservative current events magazine *Insight*, McDonough explains why drug laws are both reasonable and necessary.

An oft-repeated mantra of both the liberal left and the far right is that antidrug laws do greater harm to society than illicit drugs. To defend this claim, they cite high rates of incarceration in the United States compared with more drug-tolerant societies. In this bumper-sticker vernacular, the drug war in the United States has created an "incarceration nation."

But is it true? Certainly rates of incarceration in the United States are up (and crime is down). Do harsh antidrug laws drive up the numbers? Are the laws causing more harm than the drugs themselves? These are questions worth exploring, especially if their presumptive outcome is to change policy by, say, decriminalizing drug use. . . .

In essence, the advocates of decriminalization of illegal drug use assert that incarceration rates are increasing because of bad drug laws resulting from an inane drug war, most of whose victims otherwise are well-behaved citizens who happen to use illegal drugs. But that infraction alone, they say, has led directly to their arrest, prosecution, and imprisonment, thereby attacking the public purse by fostering growth of the prison population.

Almost constant repetition of such assertions, unanswered by voices challenging their validity, has resulted in the decriminalizers gaining many converts. This in turn has begotten yet stronger assertions: the drug war is racist (because the prison population is overrepresentative of minorities); major illegal drugs are benign (ecstasy is "therapeutic," "medical" marijuana is a "wonder" drug, etc.); policies are polarized as "either-or" options ("treatment not criminalization") instead of a search for balance between demand reduction and other law-enforcement programs; harm reduction (read: needle distribution, heroin-shooting "clinics," "safe drug-use" brochures, etc.) becomes the only "responsible" public policy on drugs.

But the central assertion, that drug laws are driving high prison populations, begins to break down upon closer scrutiny. Consider these numbers from the US Bureau of Justice Statistics compilation, *Felony Sentences in State Courts, 2000*. Across the United States, state courts convicted about 924,700 adults of a felony in 2000. About one-third of these (34.6 percent) were drug offenders. Of the total number of convicted felons for all charges, about one-third (32 percent) went straight to probation. Some of these were rearrested for subsequent violations, as were other probationers from past years. In the end 1,195,714 offenders entered state correctional facilities in 2000 for all categories of felonies. Of that number, 21 percent were drug offenders. Seventy-nine percent were imprisoned for other crimes.

Therefore, about one-fifth of those entering state prisons in 2000 6 were there for drug offenses. But drug offenses comprise a category consisting of several different charges, of which possession is but one. Also included are trafficking, delivery, and manufacturing. Of those incarcerated for drug offenses only about one-fourth (27 percent) were convicted of possession. One-fourth of one-fifth is 5 percent. Of that small amount, 13 percent were incarcerated for marijuana possession, meaning that in the end less than 1 percent (0.73 percent to be exact) of all those incarcerated in state-level facilities were there for marijuana possession. The data are similar in state after state. At the high end, the rates stay under 2 percent. Alabama's rate, for example, was 1.72 percent. At the low end, it falls under one-tenth of 1 percent. Maryland's rate, for example, was 0.08 percent. The rate among federal prisoners is 0.27 percent.

If we consider cocaine possession, the rates of incarceration also 7 remain low—2.75 percent for state inmates, 0.34 percent for federal. The data, in short, present a far different picture from the one projected by drug critics such as [Ethan] Nadelmann,[1] who decries the wanton imprisonment of people whose offense is only the "sin of drug use."

But what of those who are behind bars for possession? Are they not 8 otherwise productive and contributing citizens whose only offense was smoking a joint? If Florida's data are reflective of the other states—and there is no reason why they should not be—the answer is no. In early 2003, Florida had a total of eighty-eight inmates in state prison for possession of marijuana out of an overall population of 75,236 (0.12 percent). And of those eighty-eight, forty (45 percent) had been in prison before. Of the remaining forty-eight who were in prison for the first time, forty-three (90 percent) had prior probation sentences and the probation of all but four of them had been revoked at least once. Similar profiles appear for those in Florida prisons for cocaine possession (3.2 percent of the prison population in early 2003). They typically have extensive arrest

---

[1] Ethan Nadelmann is the founder and executive director of the Drug Policy Alliance, a lobbying group opposed to current drug laws. [Editors' note.]

histories for offenses ranging from burglary and prostitution to violent crimes such as armed robbery, sexual battery, and aggravated assault. The overwhelming majority (70.2 percent) had been in prison before. Of those who had not been imprisoned previously, 90 percent had prior probation sentences and the supervision of 96 percent had been revoked at least once.

The notion that harsh drug laws are to blame for filling prisons 9 to the bursting point, therefore, appears to be dubious. Simultaneously, the proposition that drug laws do more harm than illegal drugs themselves falls into disarray even if we restrict our examination to the realm of drugs and crime, overlooking the extensive damage drug use causes to public health, family cohesion, the workplace, and the community.

Law-enforcement officers routinely report that the majority (i.e., 10 between 60 and 80 percent) of crime stems from a relationship to substance abuse, a view that the bulk of crimes are committed by people who are high, seeking ways to obtain money to get high, or both. These observations are supported by the data. The national Arrests and Drug Abuse Monitoring (ADAM) program reports on drugs present in arrestees at the time of their arrest in various urban areas around the country. In 2000, more than 70 percent of people arrested in Atlanta had drugs in their system; 80 percent in New York City; 75 percent in Chicago; and so on. For all cities measured, the median was 64.2 percent. The results are equally disturbing for cocaine use alone, according to Department of Justice statistics for 2000. In Atlanta, 49 percent of those arrested tested positive for cocaine; in New York City, 49 percent; in Chicago, 37 percent. Moreover, more than one-fifth of all arrestees reviewed in thirty-five cities around the nation had more than one drug in their bodies at the time of their arrest, according to the National Household Survey on Drug Abuse.

If the correlation between drug use and criminality is high for adults, 11 the correlation between drug use and misbehavior among youth is equally high. For children ages twelve to seventeen, delinquency and marijuana use show a proportional relationship. The greater the frequency of marijuana use, the greater the incidents of cutting class, stealing, physically attacking others, and destroying other people's property. A youth who smoked marijuana six times in the last year was twice as likely physically to attack someone else than one who didn't smoke marijuana at all. A child who smoked marijuana six times a month in the last year was five times as likely to assault another than a child who did not smoke marijuana. Both delinquent and aggressive antisocial behavior were linked to marijuana use—the more marijuana, the worse the behavior.

Even more tragic is the suffering caused children by substance 12
abuse within their families. A survey of state child-welfare agencies
by the National Committee to Prevent Child Abuse found substance
abuse to be one of the top two problems exhibited by 81 percent
of families reported for child maltreatment. Additional research
found that chemical dependence is present in one-half of the families involved in the child-welfare system. In a report entitled *No Safe
Haven: Children of Substance-Abusing Parents,* the National Center on
Addiction and Substance Abuse at Columbia University estimates
that substance abuse causes or contributes to seven of ten cases of
child maltreatment and puts the federal, state, and local bill for dealing
with it at $10 billion.

Are the drug laws, therefore, the root of a burgeoning prison 13
population? And are the drug laws themselves a greater evil than
the drugs themselves? The answer to the first question is a clear no.
When we restricted our review to incarcerated felons, we found only
about one-fifth of them were in prison for crimes related to drug laws.
And even the minuscule proportion that were behind bars for possession seemed to have serious criminal records that indicate criminal
behavior well beyond the possession charge for which they may have
plea-bargained, and it is noteworthy that 95 percent of all convicted
felons in state courts in 2000 pleaded guilty, according to the Bureau
of Justice Statistics.

The answer to the second question also is no. Looking only at crime 14
and drugs, it is apparent that drugs drive crime. While it is true that no
traffickers, dealers, or manufacturers of drugs would be arrested if all
drugs were legal, the same could be said of drunk drivers if drunken driving were legalized. Indeed, we could bring the prison population down
to zero if there were no laws at all. But we do have laws, and for good
reason. When we look beyond the crime driven by drugs and factor
in the lost human potential, the family tragedies, massive health costs,
business losses, and neighborhood blights instigated by drug use, it is
clear that the greater harm is in the drugs themselves, not in the laws
that curtail their use.

Meaning

1. What two questions does McDonough seek to answer in this essay?
   Where does he state his thesis?

2. According to McDonough, what is the relationship between drug use
   and other crimes? Why is the relationship important?

3. Some of the following words may be new to you. Try to guess their meanings from the context of McDonough's essay. Test your guesses in a dictionary, and then use each new word in a sentence or two of your own.

mantra (1)	benign (4)	correlation (11)
vernacular (1)	decries (7)	burgeoning (13)
presumptive (2)	wanton (7)	blights (14)
fostering (3)	median (10)	instigated (14)

Purpose and Audience

1. For whom is McDonough writing? People who already favor drug law reform? People who think the laws are beneficial? Someone else? What does the author seem to assume about his readers?

2. Against whom is McDonough arguing? Why does he say it is necessary to debate them?

3. Why do you think McDonough wrote this essay? What does he hope to accomplish by making his argument?

Method and Structure

1. What kinds of evidence does the author provide? Where does it come from, and is it reliable and convincing? Why, or why not? (See pp. 364–65 for information on evaluating sources.)

2. McDonough suggests that some of his opponents' arguments are based on faulty reasoning. What logical fallacies does he implicitly or explicitly identify? Does McDonough lapse into any logical fallacies himself? If so, where?

3. Analyze the organization of McDonough's argument. Which of his opponents' major points does he call into question? Where does he introduce new points? How does he use his introduction and conclusion to frame the debate?

4. **OTHER METHODS** McDonough's argument draws on several methods of development, including division or analysis (Chapter 8), classification (Chapter 9), and cause-and-effect analysis (Chapter 13). Locate one instance of each of these methods. How does using them help the author to support his points?

Language

1. How would you describe McDonough's attitude toward his subject? What is the tone of the last paragraph in particular?

2. McDonough puts quotation marks around many of the words he uses to describe his opponents' position on illegal drugs (see, for instance, paragraph 4). What is the purpose of these quotation marks? What is their effect?

3. What is the difference between the decriminalization (paragraphs 2, 3, and 4) and the legalization (14) of drugs? Does McDonough distinguish between the two?

Writing Topics

1. **JOURNAL TO ESSAY** Take off from the comments you made in your journal entry (p. 351) to write an essay about drug abuse. Do you regard drug use or addiction as a critical problem? Do you believe that the government is taking adequate steps to protect society from users and dealers? Do you believe that individuals have the right to indulge in whatever mind-altering substances they choose? Why are some addictive substances socially acceptable while others are forbidden by law? Who, if anybody, is harmed by drugs? Your essay may but need not be an argument: that is, you could explain your answer to any of these questions or argue a specific point. Either way, use examples and details to support your ideas.

2. McDonough asserts in paragraph 11 that youths who smoke marijuana tend to be more violent than those who do not. At your library or online, try to find *Reefer Madness,* a film made in 1936 that shows middle-class teenagers descending from uncontrollable laughter to murder after smoking marijuana. What tactics does the film use to persuade viewers of the dangers of marijuana? What assumptions does it make? Write an essay analyzing the film as a component of a decades-long campaign against drugs. Do you see any parallels between the movie's approach and McDonough's? Can either work be classified as propaganda? Why, or why not?

3. **CULTURAL CONSIDERATIONS** Think of a drug that is or was illegal in the United States but is legal in another country. An example is hashish, which is legal in the Netherlands but not in this country, or absinthe, a reputedly hallucinogenic liqueur that is available in France but banned here. Do some research on the drug and the debates surrounding it. Can the differences in acceptance be accounted for by different cultural contexts in the two countries? Did scientific studies in the two countries yield different results? Is there a historical explanation? Write an essay in which you compare and contrast attitudes toward the drug in the two countries, and try to explain why the authorities in those countries came to different conclusions about its legality.

4. **CONNECTIONS**   Both McDonough and Ira Glasser, in "Drug Busts = Jim Crow" (p. 345), use statistics from published sources to support their arguments. But there seems to be discrepancy in their data. Both writers state that 21 percent of state prisoners are drug offenders (see paragraph 5 in both essays); but while McDonough asserts that only 13 percent of jailed drug offenders were convicted for possession of marijuana (6), Glasser claims that possession of marijuana accounts for nearly half of all drug arrests (5). What might explain the apparent contradiction in these numbers? Take a close look at the use of statistics in both essays, considering the sources from which they were obtained, the authors' reasons for citing them, and the way each author frames the information. Is either author guilty of misrepresentation, or are there subtle differences in how they define their terms? What does the difference in their numbers tell you about the objectivity of statistics? Are all numerical data automatically authoritative, or can writers manipulate numbers to serve their purposes? Explain your answer in an essay, citing examples from both writers' arguments. If time allows, you might want to look up the sources they cite to check their figures yourself.

Argument and Persuasion

Choose one of the following statements, or any other statement they suggest, and support or refute it in an argumentative essay. The statement you decide on should concern a topic you care about so that argument is a means of convincing readers to accept an idea, not an end in itself.

POPULAR CULTURE

1. Pornographic magazines and films should be banned.
2. Television advertisements serve useful purposes.
3. Music recordings should be labeled if their lyrics contain violent or sexual references.
4. Professional athletes should not be allowed to compete in the Olympics.

HEALTH AND TECHNOLOGY

5. Terminally ill people should have the right to choose when to die.
6. Private automobiles should be restricted in cities.
7. Laboratory experiments on dogs, cats, and primates are necessary.
8. Smoking should be banned in all public places, including outdoors.

EDUCATION

9. Students caught in any form of academic cheating should be expelled.
10. The school's costly athletic programs should be eliminated in favor of improving the academic curriculum.
11. Like high-school textbooks, college textbooks should be purchased by the school and loaned to students for the duration of a course.

SOCIAL AND POLITICAL ISSUES

12. Corporate executives are overpaid.
13. Private institutions should have the right to make rules that would be unconstitutional outside those institutions.
14. Public libraries should provide free, unlimited access to the Internet.
15. When adopted children turn eighteen, they should have free access to information about their birth parents.

WRITING ABOUT THE THEME

Debating Law and Order

1. Several of the essays in this chapter discuss crimes committed by young adults, yet the authors write from very different perspectives with widely varied purposes. Linda Chavez (p. 333), for instance, complains that some college presidents are shirking their responsibilities by arguing for a lower drinking age, while Jenny Price (p. 319) reminds readers that college neighborhoods are not immune to gun violence. Anna Quindlen (p. 327) takes an earnest tone in urging authority figures to do more to protect teenagers. Teen offender Charlie Spence (p. 338) asks, "At what point do we brand a person for life for the worst thing he or she did as a child?" (paragraph 6), while James R. McDonough (p. 351) suggests that young offenders aren't punished harshly enough. Think of an illegal or dangerous behavior typical of teenagers or young adults and write an essay that argues your position on how legal authorities should respond to it. For instance, you might write about tagging, reckless driving, or downloading music without paying for it. How harshly should such behavior be punished, if at all? In your essay, be sure to consider the potential consequences of both the behavior and the response and to support your opinion with plenty of examples and details to explain your reasons.

2. Many of the authors in this chapter disagree on the success and failure of prison in American society. Charlie Spence, for instance, argues that lifelong prison terms for juvenile offenders are unreasonable and immoral, Ira Glasser (p. 345) claims that prison sentences for drug arrests have reinstituted legalized racial segregation, and Martin Luther King, Jr. (p. 320), advocating civil disobedience from his prison cell, suggests that incarceration is often unjust. James R. McDonough, in contrast, believes that jail time is the best way to prevent drug-related crimes. Write an essay in which you defend or propose a reform to the American penal system. In your essay, explain what about prison does or doesn't work, what should change, how that change should be effected, and what the outcome might be if your reform was put into effect. (If you don't see a need for reform, write an essay explaining why reform advocates such as Spence and Glasser are wrong to seek a change.)

3. Most of the topics chosen by the writers in this chapter—gun violence, miscarriage of justice, mental illness, prison sentencing, and drug laws—are concerned to some extent with crime prevention and public

safety. Select the topic that you think is the most important for society to focus on. (You may pick a topic discussed in this chapter or identify one of your own choosing.) Predict the outcome, twenty or thirty years from now, if steps are not taken to adequately address this issue. Describe the best way to deal with the controversy surrounding the problem you have chosen.

WORKING WITH SOURCES

Writing is a means of communicating, a conversation between writers and readers—and between writers and other writers. Finding out what others have said about a subject, or looking for information to support and develop your thesis, is a natural part of the composing process.

A **source** is any work that you draw on for ideas or evidence in the course of writing your essay. Whether you are analyzing or responding to an essay in this book or using research to support your interpretation of a subject, the guidelines in this appendix will help you to use the work of others effectively in your own writing.

Writing about Readings

Many of the assignments that follow the readings in this book ask you to respond directly to an essay or to write about it in relation to one or more other essays—to analyze two writers' approaches, to compare several writers' ideas about a subject, or to use the ideas in one reading to investigate the meanings of another. The same will be true of much writing you do throughout college, whether you are examining literary works, psychological theories, business case studies, historical documents, or lesson plans.

In some academic writing, you'll be able to use an idea in a selection as a springboard for an essay about your own opinions or experiences. However, when academic writing requires you to write *about* one or more readings, you will analyze the material (see Chapter 1) and synthesize, or recombine, the elements of that analysis to form an original idea of your own (see pp. 365–68). Your goal is to think critically about what other writers have said and to reach your own conclusions.

When writing about reading, refer to the writer's ideas directly and draw on evidence to support your conclusions. Use summary, paraphrase, and quotation (see pp. 365–67) to give readers a sense of the work, a clear picture of the elements that you are responding to, and a measured understanding of how those elements contribute to your thesis.

Using Research to Support a Thesis

Often, when you draft an essay, you'll discover that you need more information to clarify part of your subject or to develop a few of your points more fully. Other times, you'll want to conduct more extensive research—for instance, when you need several examples to develop your draft, when you are troubled by conflicting assertions in essays you're comparing, or when you want expert opinion to support your argument. Even a little outside material can contribute compelling and informative support for an essay. This section explains the basics of researching sources and using what you find responsibly and correctly.

Finding Sources

You have two basic options for locating sources: the library and the Internet. Although both can be good sources of information, in general you should prefer printed sources or information located through your library's electronic research portals (such as subject directories and databases) over material you might pull up with a popular Web search engine such as *Google*.

When you're looking for sources, never be shy about asking librarians for help, but make a point of familiarizing yourself with the most useful basic research tools.

- *Subject directories* organize material on the Web into categories. Although the open Internet is riskier than the library for research, a good directory can be a helpful starting point. The best are those compiled by librarians, particularly the Librarians' Internet Index (http://www.lii.org) and directories created for individual colleges (check your library's home page).

- *Library catalogs* offer a comprehensive listing of printed materials (books, magazines, newspapers, reference works, and the like) housed in a library. Most are computerized, which means you can plug in a search term—subject keyword, author, or title, for instance—and pull up a list of what the library has. Many colleges also let you search the holdings of related libraries and arrange for interlibrary loan.

■ *Periodical indexes* provide listings of the articles in thousands of magazines, scholarly journals, and newspapers. Electronic subscription services, such as EBSCO and ProQuest, often provide full-text copies of some of the articles located in a search; other times, you will need to use the information listed in the citation to track down the relevant issue on the library shelves.

Evaluating Sources

When you read a written work for an assignment, you read it critically, digging beneath the surface of the words to tease out the author's intentions and analyze the author's use of evidence (see Chapter 1). The same is true when you use sources to support your ideas. Drawing on reliable information and balancing biased opinions strengthen your essay.

You need not read everything you find as closely as you would a reading assignment. Instead, scan potential sources to see how well each one satisfies the following criteria:

■ *Is the source relevant?* Focus on sources that are directly related to your subject.

■ *How current is the information?* In most cases, the more recently your source was published or updated, the better.

■ *What is the author's purpose?* Consider, for instance, whether a source is meant to provide information, argue a point, or sell a product. When you're looking at a Web site, the URL can give you sense of the purpose of the source: sites ending in *.com* (commercial) are generally created to sell, market, or entertain; sites ending in *.gov* (government), *.net* (network), and *.org* (nonprofit organization) more often exist to provide information.

■ *Is the author reliable?* Determine not only who wrote the material but also the writer's qualifications for writing on the subject, and look for any potential biases. Notice how the author uses evidence: reliable writers provide detailed support for their ideas, distinguish between facts and opinions, acknowledge opposing viewpoints, and cite their sources.

Once you've determined that a source is worth using, the checklist for critical reading on page 8 can help you to examine it more closely.

Synthesizing Source Material

When you bring information and ideas from outside sources into your writing, your goal is to develop and support your own thesis. It can be tempting to string together facts and quotations from your sources and to think that they speak for themselves—or for you—but then your own ideas won't predominate. Aim instead for **synthesis**, weaving the elements into a new whole: gather related information and ideas from your sources and summarize, paraphrase, and quote them to support an idea of your own making. Always strive to maintain your own voice when you're writing.

Summarizing

A **summary** is a condensed statement, *in your own words*, of the main meaning of a work. Summaries omit supporting details and examples to focus on the original author's thesis. You can find short summaries of essays throughout this book in the sections "A Note on Thematic Connections," which appear in Chapters 5–14. For example:

> Langston Hughes pinpoints the moment during a church revival when he lost his faith (78–80).

> Perri Klass's essay grapples with why doctors use peculiar and often cruel jargon and how it affects them (133–36).

Notice that each summary names the author of the work being summarized and provides page numbers; it also refrains from using any of the original authors' language.

Summarizing is one of the most effective ways to bring the ideas of others into your writing without losing your voice or bogging down your essay with unnecessary details. Depending on the length of the original work and your reasons for using it, your summary might be a single sentence or paragraph; keep it as short as possible.

Paraphrasing

A **paraphrase** is a restatement, again *in your own words*, of a short passage from another writer's work. While summarizing makes it possible to explain someone else's main idea without repeating specifics, paraphrasing lets you incorporate important details that support your own main idea.

A paraphrase is about the same length as the original, but it does not use any of the other writer's unique words, phrasings, or sentence structures. Simply replacing a few words with synonyms won't suffice; in fact, that shortcut counts as plagiarism (see pp. 368–69). If you cannot avoid using some of the writer's language, put it in quotation marks. For example:

> ORIGINAL PASSAGE "Poverty is defined, in my system, by people not being able to cover the basic necessities in their lives. Indispensable medical care, nutrition, a place to live: all these essentials, for poor people, are often and classically beyond reach. If a poor person needs $10 a day to make ends meet, often he or she only makes eight and a half."
> —Walter Mosley, "Show Me the Money," p. 6.

> PARAPHRASE As Walter Mosley sees it, poverty is a matter of inadequate resources. The poor have difficulty obtaining adequate health care, food, and shelter—things most of us take for granted—not because they have no income at all, but because the money they earn is not enough to cover these basic expenses (6).

> ORIGINAL PASSAGE "Wealth, in my definition, is when money is no longer an issue or a question. Wealthy people don't know how much money they have or how much they make. Their worth is gauged in property, natural resources, and power, in doors they can go through and the way the law works."
> —Walter Mosley, "Show Me The Money," p. 6.

> PARAPHRASE Wealth, in contrast, is defined by freedom. The rich don't have to worry about finances; indeed, their "property, natural resources, and power" confer social and legal privileges far more significant than freely available cash (Mosley 6).

Notice here, too, that a paraphrase identifies the original source and provides a page number. Even if the words are your own, the ideas are someone else's, and so they must be credited.

Quoting

Sometimes a writer's or speaker's exact words will be so well phrased or so important to your own meaning that you will want to quote them. When you are responding to or analyzing passages in a written work, such as an essay or a novel, direct **quotations** will be essential evidence as you develop your points. Even when you are borrowing ideas from other writers, however, quoting can be useful if the author's original wording makes a strong impression that you want to share with your readers.

Be sparing in your use of quotations. Limit yourself to those lines to which you're responding directly and perhaps a handful of choice passages that would lose their punch or meaning if you paraphrased them.

When you do use a quotation, be careful to copy the original words and punctuation exactly, and to identify clearly the boundaries and source of the quotation:

- Put *quotation marks* around all quoted material shorter than four typed lines.

- Use *block quotations* for quoted passages longer than four typed lines. Start the quotation on a new line and indent the whole passage ten spaces or one inch. Don't use quotation marks; the indention shows that the material is quoted.

- *Cite the source of the quotation,* giving a page number as well as the author's name (see pp. 370–72). For short quotations, place a parenthetical citation after the final quotation mark and before the period. For block quotations, place a parenthetical citation after the final period.

You can make changes in quotations so that they fit the flow of your own sentences—say, by deleting a word or sentence that is not relevant to your purpose or by inserting a word or punctuation mark to clarify meaning. However, such changes must be obvious:

- Use an *ellipsis mark,* or three spaced periods (. . .), to show a deletion.
    Stewart and Elizabeth Ewen have suggested that "for hardworking, ill-housed immigrants, . . . clothing offered one of the few avenues by which people could assume a sense of belonging" (156).

- Use *brackets* ([ ]) around any change or addition you make.
    Most fashion historians echo Thorstein Veblen's assertion that "members of each [social] stratum accept as their ideal of decency the scheme of life in vogue in the next higher stratum" (84).

For examples of the use and formatting of quotations, see the sample documented essay by Tae Andrews (p. 381).

Integrating

When you incorporate material from outside sources, make a point to introduce every summary, paraphrase, or quotation and to specify why it's relevant to your thesis. At the same time, make it clear where your thoughts end and someone else's thoughts begin. Three techniques are especially helpful in giving your readers the necessary guidance.

- *Use signal phrases to introduce summaries, paraphrases, and quotations.* A signal phrase names the author of the borrowed material and thus provides a transition between your idea and someone else's. If the information is relevant, you might also explain why the author is an authoritative source or name the article or book you're referring to. Here are some examples of signal phrases:

  > As financial planner Zora Klyberg points out in the pamphlet *Start Saving for Retirement NOW* . . .

  > US Census Bureau data reveal . . .

  > Not everyone agrees. Wilbert Rideau, for example, believes that . . .

  Be careful to craft each signal phrase to reflect your reasons for including a source. Using the same phrase over and over (such as "According to _____") will frustrate your readers.

- *Generally, mark the end of borrowed material with a parenthetical citation identifying at least the page number of your source.* (See pp. 370–72.) In most cases, the citation is required—an exception would be a source lacking page or other reference numbers—and it makes clear that you've finished with the source and are returning to your own argument.

- *Follow up with a brief explanation of how the material supports your point.* You might, for example, comment on the meaning of the borrowed material, dispute it, or summarize it in the context of a new idea. Such follow-ups are especially necessary after block quotations.

For examples of effective integration of source materials, see Tae Andrews's sample essay (p. 381).

Avoiding Plagiarism

Claiming credit for writing that you didn't compose yourself is **plagiarism**, a form of academic dishonesty that can carry serious consequences. Buying an essay online and submitting it as your own, copying a friend's essay and submitting it as your own, or copying just a sentence from a source and including it as your own—these are most obvious forms of plagiarism. But plagiarism is often unintentional, caused not by deliberate cheating but by misunderstanding or sloppiness. Be aware of the rules and responsibilities that come with using the work of others in your writing.

- *Take careful notes.* Thorough and accurate records are essential. If you copy down the exact words of a source, enclose them in quotation marks. If you paraphrase or summarize, make a note that the language is your own, and double-check that you haven't picked up any of the original phrasing. Always record full source information for any material you find, using the models on pages 372–80.

- *Use electronic sources with care.* Any language or idea you find, regardless of where you find it, must be credited to its source. Resist the urge to cut and paste snippets from online sources directly into your working draft: later on you won't be able to distinguish the borrowed text from your own words. Print electronic documents for your records, or save them as clearly labeled individual files.

- *Know the definition of* common knowledge. *Common knowledge* is information that is so widely known or broadly accepted that it can't be traced to a particular writer. Facts that you can find in multiple sources—the date of a historic event, the population of a major city—do not need to be credited as long as you state them in your own words. In contrast, original material that can be traced to a particular person—the lyrics to a song, an article on the Web—must be cited even if it has been distributed widely. Note that even if a piece of information is common knowledge, the wording of that information is not: put it in your own words.

- *Never include someone else's ideas in your writing without identifying the borrowed material and acknowledging its source.* If you use another writer's exact words, enclose them in quotation marks and identify the source. If you summarize or paraphrase, clearly distinguish your ideas from the source author's with a signal phrase and a source citation. Then, at the end of your paper, list all your sources in a works cited list. (See the next section, "Documenting Sources in MLA style.")

When in doubt, err on the side of caution. It's better to have too much documentation in your essay than not enough.

Documenting Sources in MLA Style

In English classes, and in some other humanities as well, you will be expected to document your sources with the system outlined by the Modern Language Association in *MLA Handbook for Writers of Research*

Papers, Seventh Edition (2009). MLA style provides a brief parenthetical citation for each use of a source within the body of the essay and a comprehensive list of works cited at the end.

PARENTHETICAL TEXT CITATION

In the essay "The Box Man" Barbara Ascher says that a homeless man who has chosen solitude can show the rest of us how to "find . . . a friend in our own voice" (13).

WORKS CITED ENTRY

Ascher, Barbara Lazear. "The Box Man." *The Compact Reader: Short Essays by Method and Theme.* 9th ed. Ed. Jane E. Aaron and Ellen Kuhl Repetto. Boston: Bedford, 2011. 9–13. Print.

In-Text Citations

Citations within the body of your essay include just enough information for readers to recognize the boundaries of borrowed material and to locate the full citation in the works-cited list. Generally, they name the author of a source and the page number on which you found the information or idea cited.

Keep in-text citations unobtrusive by making them as brief as possible without sacrificing necessary information. The best way to do this is to name the author of the source in a signal phrase, limiting the parenthetical information to the page number. Otherwise, include the author's name in the parenthetical citation.

AUTHOR NAMED IN THE TEXT

Historian Thomas French notes that Mount Auburn Cemetery was a popular leisure destination for city residents (37).

AUTHOR NOT NAMED IN THE TEXT

Mount Auburn Cemetery was a popular leisure destination for city residents (French 37).

A work by multiple authors

If a source has two or three authors, list all of their names.

Some of the most successful organized tours in New York bring visitors on guided walks or bus rides to locations featured in television shows (Espinosa and Herbst 228).

In the case of four or more authors, you may list all of the names or shorten the reference by naming the first author and following with "et al." (Latin for "and others"). Whichever option you choose, use the same format for your works-cited list. (See p. 373–74.)

> As early as 1988, scholars cautioned against educators' dependence on computers, warning that technology is "accompanied by rapid change, instability, and general feelings of insecurity and isolation" (Ferrante, Hayman, Carlson, and Phillips 1).

> As early as 1988, scholars cautioned against educators' dependence on computers, warning that technology is "accompanied by rapid change, instability, and general feelings of insecurity and isolation" (Ferrante et al. 1).

A work by a corporate or government author

For works written in the name of an organization, company, or government that doesn't list individual authors, treat the name of the group as the author.

> Progressive neurological disorders damage the body in repeated but unpredictable intervals, forcing patients to adapt to new losses several times over (National Multiple Sclerosis Society 2).

Two or more works by the same author(s)

If your essay cites more than one work by the same author(s), include the title of the specific source within each citation. In the following examples, both works are by Fredey, who is named in the text.

> Maura Fredey notes that most of the nurses at the Boston Home have been on staff for more than five years, and at least seven boast a quarter century or more of service ("21st Century Home" 26).

> The home's high level of care includes not only medical, dental, and vision treatments, says Fredey, but also round-the-clock nursing attention and extensive social and rehabilitative services ("Bridges" 13).

If the title is long, you may shorten it. (The complete titles for the articles cited above are "The 21st Century Home: How Technology is Helping to Improve the Lives of Patients at the Boston Home" and "Bridges to Care: The Boston Home Reaches Out").

An anonymous work

If no author is named, include the title within the parentheses. You may shorten the title if it is long.

> The population of Pass Christian, Mississippi, is a less than a third of what it was before Hurricane Katrina ("A New Town Crier" 22).

An indirect source

Use the abbreviation "qtd. in" (for "quoted in") to indicate that you did not consult the source directly but found it quoted in another source.

> As psychologist Robert Sternberg has pointed out, a high IQ does not guarantee success. Just as important is "knowing what to say to whom, knowing when to say it, and knowing how to say it for maximum effect" (qtd. in Gladwell 101).

An electronic source

Treat most electronic sources as you would any other source—cite the author's name if it is available, or cite the title if no author is named. For electronic sources that number paragraphs instead of pages, insert a comma between the author's name and the abbreviation "par." (for "paragraph"). If neither pages nor paragraphs are numbered, include the author's name only.

> At the time *Dr. Strangelove* was released, filmmakers had begun to believe that "the very discourse of nuclearism . . . was contributing to the nuclear threat" by instilling fear in American audiences (Abbot, par. 35).

> One teacher who successfully brought computers into his classroom argues that to use new technologies effectively, teachers need to become "side-by-side learners" with their students (Rogers).

List of Works Cited

The works-cited list provides complete publication information for every source you refer to within your essay. Format the list as follows:

- Start the list on a new page following the conclusion to your essay.
- Center the title "Works Cited" at the top of the page.
- Double-space everything in the list.

- Alphabetize the entries by authors' last names. If a work doesn't have a listed author, alphabetize by title, ignoring the initial words *A, An,* and *The.*

- For each entry, align the first line with the left margin and indent subsequent lines five spaces or one-half inch.

The elements of individual entries will vary somewhat, as shown in the models in this section. The basic content and formatting rules, however, can be summarized in a few general guidelines:

- Start with the author's last name, followed by a comma and the author's first name. (For more than one author, list the names as they appear in the work, reversing only the first author's name.)

- Provide the full title of the work, with all major words capitalized. Italicize the titles of books, periodicals, whole Web sites, and longer creative works such as plays or television series; put quotation marks around the titles of book chapters, periodical articles, pages on Web sites, and short creative works such as stories, poems, and song titles.

- Include complete publication information. At a minimum this includes city of publication, publisher, and date (for books); date and inclusive page numbers (for periodicals); sponsor, date of publication, and access date (for Web sites); and medium of publication (print, Web, television, radio, DVD, CD, lecture, and so on).

- Separate the elements of an entry (author, title, publication information) with periods.

MLA does not require URLs for Web sources, but your instructor might. If so, place the URL at the end of the entry, enclosed in angle brackets and followed by a period. If you must break a long URL to fit, break it only after a slash and do not add a hyphen.

PRINT BOOKS

A book by one author

Ehrenreich, Barbara. *This Land Is Their Land: Reports from a Divided Nation.*
New York: Holt, 2008. Print.

A book by multiple authors

List all of the authors, or, if there are more than three, you may provide the first author's name followed by "et al." (Latin abbreviation for "and others"). Whichever option you choose, use the same format for your in-text citations. (See p. 370–71.)

Cooper, Martha, and Joseph Sciorra. *R.I.P.: Memorial Wall Art*. London: Thames, 1994. Print.

Ferrante, Reynolds, John Hayman, Mary Susan Carlson, and Harry Phillips. *Planning for Microcomputers in Higher Education: Strategies for the Next Generation*. Washington, DC: Assn. for Study of Higher Educ., 1988. Print.

Ferrante, Reynolds, et al. *Planning for Microcomputers in Higher Education: Strategies for the Next Generation*. Washington, DC: Assn. for Study of Higher Educ., 1988. Print.

A book with an author and an editor

Jacobs, Harriet. *Incidents in the Life of a Slave Girl, Written by Herself: With Related Documents*. Ed. Jennifer Fleischner. Boston: Bedford, 2010. Print.

A book by a corporate or government author

For books written in the name of an organization, company, or government that doesn't list individual authors, treat the name of the group as the author.

National Commission on Terrorist Attacks. *The 9/11 Commission Report: Final Report of the National Commission on Terrorist Attacks upon the United States*. New York: Norton, 2004. Print.

More than one work by the same author(s)

Roach, Mary. *Bonk: The Curious Coupling of Science and Sex*. New York: Norton, 2008. Print.

---. *Spook: Science Tackles the Afterlife*. New York: Norton, 2005. Print.

Edition other than the first

Favazza, Armando R. *Bodies Under Siege: Self-Mutilation and Body Modification in Culture and Psychiatry*. 2nd ed. Baltimore: Johns Hopkins UP, 1996. Print.

An illustrated book or graphic narrative

For a book that contains both text and illustrations, begin the entry with the name of the contributor whose work you are emphasizing (author, editor, or illustrator), using the abbreviations "illus." for illustrator and "ed." for editor. Treat a graphic narrative written and illustrated by the same person as you would a book with one author.

Moser, Barry, illus. *Mark Twain's Book of Animals.* Ed. Shelley Fisher Fishkin. Berkeley: U of California P, 2010. Print.

Satrapi, Marjane. *Persepolis: The Story of a Childhood.* New York: Pantheon, 2004. Print.

An anthology

James, Rosemary, ed. *My New Orleans: Ballads to the Big Easy by Her Sons, Daughters, and Lovers.* New York: Touchstone, 2006. Print.

Cite an entire anthology only when you are referring to the editor's material or cross-referencing multiple selections that appear within it, as shown in the next model.

A selection from an anthology

List the work under the selection author's name. Include the page numbers for the entire selection after the publication date.

Peck, Cheryl. "Fatso." *The Compact Reader: Short Essays by Method and Theme.* Ed. Jane E. Aaron and Ellen Kuhl Repetto. 9th ed. Boston: Bedford, 2011. 236–39. Print.

If you are citing two or more selections from the same anthology, you can avoid unnecessary repetition by listing the anthology in its own entry and cross-referencing it in the selection entries. Put each entry in its proper alphabetical place in the list of works cited, and include the medium of publication only in the anthology entry.

Aaron, Jane E., and Ellen Kuhl Repetto, eds. *The Compact Reader: Short Essays by Method and Theme.* 9th ed. Boston: Bedford, 2011. Print.

Hobby-Reichstein, Kaela. "Learning Race." Aaron and Repetto 83–86.

Wong, Alaina. "China Doll." Aaron and Repetto 242–45.

A section of a book

When referring to only part of a book (such as an introduction, foreword, or a specific chapter), name the author and indicate the part of the book you are citing, with page numbers.

Sedaris, David. "The Smoking Section." *When You Are Engulfed in Flames.* New York: Little. 2008. 240–323. Print.

Lipsitz, George. Foreword. *Race Rebels: Culture, Politics, and the Black Working
    Class.* By Robin D. G. Kelley. New York: Free. 1996. xi–xiii. Print.

A reference work

"Social Security." *The Encyclopedia Americana.* 2006 ed. Print.

PRINT OR ONLINE JOURNALS, MAGAZINES, AND NEWSPAPERS

The formats for articles in journals, magazines, and newspapers are
similar whether the publication appears only in print, appears in print
with additional online content, or appears only online. The key
differences are (1) the inclusive page numbers for print articles and some
online journal articles; (2) the sponsor or publisher of the site for online
magazine and newspaper content; and (3) the date you consulted any
online source.

An article in a scholarly journal

Include the author's name, the article title, the volume and any issue
number (separated by a period), the year, and the page numbers. If an
online journal does not have number pages, use "n. pag." instead.

Douglas, Susan J. "The Turn Within: The Irony of Technology in a Globalized
    World." *American Quarterly* 58.3 (2006): 619–38. Print.

Singer, P. W. "Robots at War: The New Battlefield." *Wilson Quarterly* 33.1 (2009):
    n. pag. Web. 18 Oct. 2010.

An article in a monthly or bimonthly magazine

If you consult an online magazine or newspaper, including one that also
has a print version, provide the publisher's or sponsor's name between
the periodical title and the publication date. Use "N.p." if no publisher
or sponsor is named.

Cascio, Jamais. "Get Smarter." *Atlantic Monthly* July-Aug. 2009: 94–100. Print.

McConnico, Patricia Busa. "Being a Super Model." *Texas Monthly.com.* Texas
    Monthly, Sept. 2009. Web. 19 Nov. 2010.

An article in a weekly magazine

Lyons, Daniel. "Don't Tweet on Me: Twitter Proves That Stupid Stuff Sells."
    Newsweek. Newsweek, 17. Sept. 2009. Web. 22 Feb. 2010.

Ordoñez, Jennifer. "Baby Needs a New Pair of Shoes." *Newsweek* 14 May 2007:
    50–54. Print.

An article in an online-only magazine

Dickinson, Debra J. "Not in My Backyard, Either." *Salon.com*. Salon Media Group,
     18 Dec. 2006. Web. 17 Jan. 2011.

An article in a newspaper

Many print newspapers appear in more than one edition, so you need
to specify which edition you used ("New England ed." in the model
below). Give the section label as part of the page number when the
newspaper does the same ("A1" in the model). Otherwise, give the section after the edition (for example, "Natl. ed., sec. 3: 7"). Cite an article
that runs on nonconsecutive pages with the starting page number followed by a plus sign ("+"). For an article in an online newspaper, omit
page numbers and add the site's sponsor or publisher and the date you
accessed it.

Kanter, James, and Andrew C. Revkin. "Scientists Detail Climate Changes, Poles to
     Tropics." *New York Times* 7 Apr. 2007, New England ed.: A1+. Print.

Rodriguez, Gregory. "Answers Can Be Found in Questions." *Los Angeles Times*. Los
     Angeles Times, 29 June 2009. Web. 4 Dec. 2010.

A letter to the editor

Skinner, Briahnna. Letter. *Boston Sunday Globe* 8 Apr. 2007: E8. Print.

An unsigned article or editorial

"The Car Industry: Small Isn't Beautiful." *Economist.com*. The Economist, 17 Sept.
     2009. Web. 14 Jan. 2011.

"Time to Go Back to Government 101." Editorial. *Salem Observer* 12 Apr. 2007: A6.
     Print.

An article in an online database

Cite a full-text source that you obtain through a database in much the
same way as a print article, but instead of ending with "Print" as the
medium, add the database name, the medium "Web," and your access
date.

al-Khalifa, Raya. "Cover-Up: The New Black." *The New Statesman* 23 Oct. 2006: 17.
     Academic Search Premier. Web. 2 Dec. 2010.

OTHER ONLINE SOURCES

An entire Web site

Start with the author(s) or editor(s) of the site, followed by the site title in italics, the name of the sponsoring organization or publisher, the date of publication or most recent update, the medium, and the date you visited the site. If any of this information is unavailable, include as much as you can find. (Use "N.p." if there is no publisher or sponsor and "n.d." if there is no date.)

Carson, Clayborne, ed. *The King Papers Project*. The Martin Luther King, Jr.,
   Research and Educ. Inst., Stanford U., n.d. Web. 9 Dec. 2010.

Songwriter's Resource Network. N.p., 2009. Web. 4 Oct. 2010.

A short work from a Web site

Include as much information from the entire Web site as you can find (see above), as well as a title for the work. If your instructor requires a URL, or if the page would be difficult to find without one, include it at the end of the entry, enclosed in angle brackets.

Dryden-Edwards, Roxanne. "Obsessive-Compulsive Disorder." *MedicineNet*. WebMD,
   3 Sept. 2008. Web. 4 May 2009.

Mikkelson, Barbara. "Organ Nicked: Vegetable." *Urban Legends Reference
   Pages*. Barbara and David P. Mikkelson, 28 July 2006. Web. 4 Nov. 2009.
   <http://www.snopes.com/horrors/robbery/kidney2.asp>.

A blog entry

Follow the preceding guidelines for a short work from a Web site. If an entry is not titled, use "Blog posting" or "Blog comment" as appropriate.

Huffington, Arianna. "The Sad, Shocking Truth About How Women Are
   Feeling." *The Huffington Post*. Huffingtonpost.com, 17 Sept. 2009. Web.
   2 Oct. 2009.

Phoebe2000. Weblog comment. *The Huffington Post*. Huffingtonpost.com, 18 Sept.
   2009. Web. 2 Oct. 2009.

AUDIO AND VISUAL SOURCES

A television or radio program

Provide as much of the following as available: episode or segment title, program or series title, network, local station, broadcast date, and medium.

Include the name of the director ("Dir."), performers ("Perf."), narrator ("Narr."), or host ("Host") if such information is significant.

"Frenemies." *This American Life*. Host Ira Glass. Natl. Public Radio. WBUR, Boston, 11 Sept. 2009. Radio.

"Pole to Pole." *Planet Earth*. Discovery Channel. 25 Mar. 2007. Television.

A sound recording

Vampire Weekend. "California English." *Contra*. XL, 2010. CD.

Zappa, Frank. *Ship Arriving Too Late to Save a Drowning Witch*. Barking Pumpkin, 1982. LP.

A film, video, or DVD

Donnie Darko. Dir. Richard Kelly. Perf. Jake Gyllenhaal, Jena Malone, Drew Barrymore, Noah Wyle, Patrick Swayze, and Mary McDonnell. 2001. 20th Cent. Fox, 2004. DVD-ROM.

International Forum on Globalization. "Greensumption." *YouTube*. YouTube, 24 May 2007. Web. 18 Jan. 2011.

A photograph or other work of art

For original works viewed in person, provide the artistic medium and the museum's or collection's name and location. For reproductions, omit the artistic medium, indicate where the original is located, and provide complete publication information for the source, including a page number if available.

Kandinsky, Wassily. *Improvisation No. 30 (Cannons)*. 1913. Oil on canvas. Art Inst. of Chicago.

Magritte, René. *The Human Condition II*. 1935. Coll. Madame E. Happé-Lorge, Brussels. *Surrealists and Surrealism*. Ed. Gaëtan Picon. New York: Rizzoli, 1983. 145. Print.

Riis, Jacob. *9 Boys Waist Deep in Country Stream*. N.d. Prints and Photographs Div., Lib. of Cong. *Jacob A. Riis Papers*. Web. 25 Sept. 2009.

An advertisement

Ambien. Advertisement. *Reader's Digest* Aug. 2009: 61–66. Print.

Mastercard. Advertisement. NBC. WNKY, Bowling Green, 16 Sep. 2010. Television.

OTHER SOURCES

E-mail

Jones, Liza. Message to the author. 9 May 2011. E-mail.

Stone, Martha. "Your Query re Cordelia Harmon." Message to Stephen Gallant.
   12 July 2006. E-mail.

A personal interview

Conti, Regina. Personal interview. 3 Feb. 2011.

Sample Documented Essay

The sample essay included here was written by Tae Andrews, a student at the University of Notre Dame. Born in San Antonio, Texas, in 1986, Andrews grew up in Long Island, Connecticut, and upstate New York. He majored in American studies and was chosen to be a features editor for the *Observer*, Notre Dame's student newspaper.

Andrews wrote "Urban Neanderthals" for his first-year composition course and revised it for *The Compact Reader*. He chose the topic, he explains, because as both an aspiring journalist and "a multiracial person . . . attending a heavily white campus," he was bothered by stereotypes of young African American men in the media and felt that "the issues at hand were (and are) pressing."

As you read his essay, notice how Andrews integrates primary and secondary sources to develop and support his original ideas without relying on them to speak for him.

Urban Neanderthals:

The Damaging Effects of Media Stereotypes

on Young African American Males

"Bust a n*gga head, smack a ho, shoot the club up." These lyrics from "You Don't Want No Drama," a popular rap song by Eightball and MJG, neatly capture both cause and consequence of stereotyping young black men as violent, women-hating thugs. By falsely portraying what it is to be an African American man, lyrics such as these are fueling a downward spiral for black male youth. At the same time, they contribute to prejudice and discrimination by reinforcing the idea that black men are unintelligent, aggressive brutes. This one-two punch is an extremely damaging combination — both to African Americans and to race relations in America. It is time for the media to start paying more attention to how they portray black men in fields that permeate youth culture, especially in two areas where young African American males are highly visible and successful: hip-hop music and professional sports. The misrepresentations are too prevalent, and too dangerous, to ignore.

Let's look first at music. The songs and videos created by artists such as 50 Cent, Dr. Dre, and Snoop Dogg have built a youth culture centered in violence and disrespect. These negative ideals are perfectly represented in what I will term "the Urban Neanderthal," the image of a "man" projected by hip-hop culture. The Urban Neanderthal wears his pants low, turns his baseball cap backward, and usually has diamond-encrusted jewelry hanging from his neck. His value as a man is determined by his ability to intimidate and physically impose his will on others and to treat women badly. The Urban Neanderthal uses his fists to do his talking.

The danger posed by the Urban Neanderthal lies not in teenagers' copying 50 Cent's look but in their absorbing the social norms presented in his lyrics. Those norms are not real

Shocking quotation grabs attention and sets up main idea; source identified in second sentence

Thesis statement

First major point: music

Andrews's own idea

but invented: rappers, after all, don't use the names on their birth certificates; they create stage names and characters that they play onstage and in their albums. However, as developmental psychologist L. Monique Ward has warned, this invented culture creates codes of conduct for young black males and influences their self-image (284–85). By presenting the edgy Urban Neanderthal as the personification of black masculinity, the media send out two messages with devastating consequences. First, impressionable black adolescents, many of whom are surrounded by the brutality and abuse glorified by the Urban Neanderthal, begin to fashion the idea that behaving violently is what it means to be a man. Second, the white community, observing this self-representation of black manhood, develops the idea that all young blacks are criminals and feels justified in its prejudiced opinions of the black community.

Recording companies champion Urban Neanderthals like 50 Cent because controversy sells records. Although an essential component of hip-hop as a genre is its emphasis on social justice through social commentary, the positive messages have been lost in the mix. Take, for example, the rapper Tupac Shakur. He will forever be remembered more for his bullet-ridden death than for his songs about improving the ghettos and raising the African American community out of poverty. In his single "Changes," Shakur delivers a soapbox sermon on the need for collective action from the black community to end drug abuse and crime. In an interlude during the song, he stops rapping and speaks directly to his audience:

> We gotta make a change. It's time for us as a people
> to start makin' some changes. Let's change the way
> we eat, let's change the way we live, and let's
> change the way we treat each other. You see the old
> way wasn't working so it's on us to do what we
> gotta do, to survive.

Margin notes:

Signal phrase names author and gives credentials

Citation for summary identifies all pages summarized

Andrews applies idea from source to his own idea

Andrews's own idea

Block format for long quotation

No citation because author and title are named in text and lyrics don't have page numbers

Songs of social commentary from the street such as
Shakur's, however, are usually passed over by record company marketers when they identify singles for airwave play.
In the effort to sell records and boost ratings, labels and
disc jockeys ignore positive tracks in favor of harder, more
provocative songs based on the image of the Urban Neanderthal. As a result, instead of hearing quality songs of social
uplift from artists such as the Roots, John Legend, and
Common, we hear 50 Cent rapping about shooting people.

    With hip-hop culture promoting the stereotype of the
Urban Neanderthal so vigorously, perhaps it should be expected that sports journalists would adopt the stereotype in
their portrayals of African Americans. Black quarterbacks in
the National Football League, for instance, are regularly
portrayed as being somehow less intelligent than their white
counterparts, even when they're being praised. Media scholar
Toni Bruce points out that Caucasian play-callers such as
Peyton Manning and Tom Brady are celebrated for their
leadership, sound decision making, and "knowledge of the
game" — skills generally attributed to intelligence and hard
work — while African American quarterbacks such as Daunte
Culpepper and Steve McNair are highly touted for their
"natural athleticism" (861). This seeming compliment is
actually a subtle insult: by implying that black quarterbacks'
success is a result of natural physical prowess, the media
pointedly ignore the hours of hard work and dedication black
athletes put into their training, reinforcing the long-standing
stereotype of the African American male as a stupid brute
blessed with tremendous physical capability but little mental
facility.

    An even more telling example of the Urban Neander-
thal in sports can be found in media coverage of professional
basketball. More than any other sport, professional basketball is composed mainly of young African American

---

Follow-up comments explain significance of direct quotation

Second major point: sports

Source provides a supporting point

Paraphrase integrates direct quotations

Citation includes page number only because author is named in text

Follow-up comments elaborate on meaning of paraphrase

Andrews's own observations and ideas

athletes. Basketball is also the professional sport most closely associated with hip-hop culture. Many crossover promotions feature rap artists — such as rapper Jay-Z — selling basketball shoes, and players — such as Shaquille O'Neal, Allen Iverson, and Ron Artest — releasing rap albums. Not surprisingly, the National Basketball Association (NBA) is portrayed by many sportswriters as a league filled with lazy, overpaid thugs — a league, that is, of Urban Neanderthals.

One of the most common criticisms leveled at the NBA is that pro athletes don't play "real" basketball. This criticism reflects the same bias directed at African American quarterbacks — namely, that the black athletes of the NBA are tremendously gifted physical specimens but lack the intelligence to play a fundamentally sound game. Consider the words of *New York Times Magazine* writer Michael Sokolove, who writes that the NBA's "players are the best athletes in all of pro sports — oversize, swift, and agile — but weirdly they are also the first to have devolved to a point where they can no longer play their own game." Sokolove goes on to criticize the NBA for its emphasis on individual ability as opposed to a team-first concept of basketball: "The concept of being part of a team," he says, "is one that seems to elude a great many [NBA] players." All of the players he praises for breaking this mold and playing unselfish, technically skilled (in other words, intelligent) basketball are either white or foreign-born. At the same time, Sokolove makes no mention of the predominantly African American Detroit Pistons, who won the league championship in 2004 with a commitment to team play. Again, we see a pointed accusation through omission that *black* NBA players are selfish, unintelligent players who don't work together and get by on pure athleticism alone. Omissions such as this are as sharp a slight as a direct criticism would be, perhaps even more damaging for their subtlety.

Andrews's own observations and ideas

Signal phrase names author and gives credentials

Direct quotations used because exact words illustrate Andrews's point; no citation needed because author is named in text and online article doesn't have page numbers

Brackets indicate material inserted for clarity

Follow-up comments analyze quotations

In both sports and hip-hop, African American males
have experienced success not seen in other industries. Unfortunately, this success goes hand in hand with unbalanced
and biased depictions. Media culture has embraced a
stereotype of black men — even successful black men — as
violent, aggressive, and ignorant brutes who regularly engage
in harmful behaviors and threaten society at large. To undo
the damage caused by this stereotype, the media should focus
more on positive examples of black manhood both in hip-hop
and in sports, such as music artist Kanye West or Philadelphia
Eagles quarterback Donovan McNabb. There are plenty of
better role models out there than Urban Neanderthals.

Conclusion sum-
marizes major
points, restates
thesis, and offers
a solution

Works Cited

Bruce, Toni. "Marking the Boundaries of the 'Normal' in
    Televised Sports: The Play-by-Play of Race." *Media,
    Culture & Society* 26.6 (2004): 861–79. *Academic Search
    Premier*. Web. 4 Feb. 2009.

Eightball and MJG. "You Don't Want No Drama." *Living
    Legends*. Bad Boy Entertainment, 2004. CD.

Shakur, Tupac. "Changes." *Greatest Hits*. Interscope, 1998. CD.

Sokolove, Michael. "Clang!" *New York Times Magazine*. New
    York Times, 13 Feb. 2005. Web. 3 Mar. 2009.

Ward, L. Monique. "Wading through the Stereotypes: Positive
    and Negative Associations between Media Use and Black
    Adolescents' Conceptions of Self." *Developmental Psychol-
    ogy* 40.2 (2004): 284–94. Print.

List of works cited
starts on a new
page

Journal article
in an online
database

Sound recording

Sound recording

Article from a
weekly magazine
accessed online

Article from a
scholarly journal
in print

GLOSSARY

abstract and concrete words An **abstract** word refers to an idea, quality, attitude, or state that we cannot perceive with our senses: *democracy, generosity, love, grief*. It conveys a general concept or an impression. A **concrete** word, in contrast, refers to an object, person, place, or state that we can perceive with our senses: *lawn mower, teacher, Chicago, moaning*. Concrete words make writing specific and vivid. See also pp. 56, 97, and *general and specific words*.

allusion A brief reference to a real or fictitious person, place, object, or event. An allusion can convey considerable meaning with few words, as when a writer describes a movie as "potentially this decade's *Star Wars*" to imply both that the movie is a space adventure and that it may be a blockbuster. But to be effective, the allusion must refer to something readers know well.

analysis (also called **division**) The method of development in which a subject is separated into its elements or parts and then reassembled into a new whole. See Chapter 8 on division or analysis, p. 141.

anecdote A brief narrative that recounts an episode from a person's experience. See, for instance, Peck, paragraph 1, p. 237. See also Chapter 5 on narration, p. 63.

argument The form of writing that appeals to readers' reason and emotions in order to win agreement with a claim or to compel some action. This definition encompasses both argument in a narrower sense—the appeal to reason to win agreement—and persuasion—the appeal to emotion to compel action. See Chapter 14 on argument and persuasion, p. 311.

assertion A debatable claim about a subject; the central idea of an argument.

audience A writer's audience is the group of readers for whom a particular work is intended. To communicate effectively, the writer should estimate readers' knowledge of the subject, their interest in it, and their biases toward it and should then consider these needs and expectations in choosing what to say and how to say it. For further discussion of audience, see pp. 4, 14, and 21.

body The part of an essay that develops the main idea. See also p. 28–29.

cause-and-effect analysis The method of development in which occurrences are divided into their elements to find what made an event happen (its causes) and what the consequences were (its effects). See Chapter 13 on cause-and-effect analysis, p. 276.

chronological order A pattern of organization in which events are arranged as they occurred over time, earliest to latest. Narratives usually follow a chronological order; see Chapter 5 on narration, p. 63.

classification The method of development in which the members of a group are sorted into classes or subgroups according to shared characteristics. See Chapter 9 on classification, p. 167.

cliché An expression that has become tired from overuse and that therefore deadens rather than enlivens writing. Examples: *in over their heads, turn over a new leaf, march to a different drummer, as heavy as lead, as clear as a bell.* See also p. 57.

climactic order A pattern of organization in which elements—words, sentences, examples, ideas—are arranged in order of increasing importance or drama. See also p. 39.

coherence The quality of effective writing that comes from clear, logical connections among all the parts, so that the reader can follow the writer's thought process without difficulty. See also pp. 37–39 and 148.

colloquial language The language of conversation, including contractions (*don't, can't*) and informal words and expressions (*hot* for new or popular, *boss* for employer, *ad* for advertisement, *get away with it, flunk the exam*). Most dictionaries label such words and expressions *colloquial* or *informal.* Colloquial language is inappropriate when the writing situation demands precision and formality, as a college term paper or a business report usually does. But in other situations it can be used selectively to relax a piece of writing and reduce the distance between writer and reader. (See, for instance, Hughes, p. 78.) See also *diction.*

comparison and contrast The method of development in which the similarities and differences between subjects are examined. Comparison examines similarities and contrast examines differences, but the two are generally used together. See Chapter 11 on comparison and contrast, p. 220.

conclusions The endings of written works—the sentences that bring the writing to a close. A conclusion provides readers with a sense of completion, with a sense that the writer has finished. Sometimes the final point in the body of an essay may accomplish this purpose, especially if it is very important or dramatic (for instance, see Winik, p. 184). But usually a separate conclusion is needed to achieve completion. It may be a single sentence or several paragraphs, depending on the length and complexity of the piece of writing. And it may include one of the following, or a combination, depending on your subject and purpose:

- A summary of the main points of the essay (see Heat-Moon, p. 109; Chavez, p. 335; and McDonough, p. 355)
- A statement of the main idea of the essay, if it has not been stated before (see Klass, p. 136), or a restatement of the main idea incorporating information from the body of the essay (see Spence, p. 341)
- A comment on the significance or implications of the subject (see Dillard, p. 75; Hobby-Reichstein, p. 86; Jain, p. 130; Erickson, p. 202; and Rhodes, p. 261)
- A call for reflection, support, or action (see Griggs, p. 176; Kingsolver, p. 215; Alaimo and Koester, p. 289; and Glasser, p. 348)

- A prediction for the future (see Sullivan, p. 271; Thomas, p. 297; LeDuff, p. 306; and Quindlen, p. 329)
- An example, anecdote, question, or quotation that reinforces the point of the essay (see Barry, p. 151; Warren, p. 157; and Brady, p. 266)

Excluded from this list are several endings that should be avoided because they tend to weaken the overall effect of an essay: (1) an example, fact, or quotation that pertains to only part of the essay; (2) an apology for your ideas, for the quality of the writing, or for omissions; (3) an attempt to enhance the significance of the essay by overgeneralizing from its ideas and evidence; (4) a new idea that requires the support of an entirely different essay.

concrete words   See *abstract and concrete words.*

connotation and denotation   A word's **denotation** is its literal meaning: *famous* denotes the quality of being well known. A word's **connotations** are the associations or suggestions that go beyond its literal meaning: *notorious* denotes fame but also connotes sensational, even unfavorable, recognition. See also p. 55.

contrast   See *comparison and contrast.*

critical reading   Reading that looks beneath the surface of a work, seeking to uncover both its substance and the writer's interpretation of the substance. See Chapter 1 on reading, especially pp. 5–8.

deductive reasoning   The method of reasoning that moves from the general to the specific. See Chapter 14 on argument and persuasion, especially pp. 315–17.

definition   An explanation of the meaning of a word. An extended definition may serve as the primary method of developing an essay. See Chapter 12 on definition, p. 250.

denotation   See *connotation and denotation.*

description   The form of writing that conveys the perceptions of the senses—sight, hearing, smell, taste, touch—to make a person, place, object, or state of mind vivid and concrete. See Chapter 6 on description, p. 91.

diction   The choice of words you make to achieve a purpose and make meaning clear. Effective diction conveys your meaning exactly, emphatically, and concisely, and it is appropriate to your intentions and audience. **Standard English**, the written language of educated native speakers, is expected in all writing for college, business and the professions, and publication. The vocabulary of standard English is large and varied, encompassing, for instance, both *comestibles* and *food* for edible things, both *paroxysm* and *fit* for a sudden seizure. In some writing situations, standard English may also include words and expressions typical of conversation (see *colloquial language*). But it excludes other levels of diction that only certain groups understand or find acceptable. Most dictionaries label expressions at these levels as follows:

- **Nonstandard:** words spoken among particular social groups, such as *ain't, them guys, hisself,* and *nowheres.*

- **Slang**: words that are usually short-lived and that may not be understood by all readers, such as *tanked* for drunk, *bread* for money, and *honcho* for one in charge.

- **Regional** or **dialect**: words spoken in a particular region but not in the country as a whole, such as *poke* for a sack or bag, *holler* for a hollow or small valley.

- **Obsolete**: words that have passed out of use, such as *cleam* for smear.

See also *connotation and denotation* and *style*.

division or analysis   See *analysis*.

documentation   A system of identifying your sources so that readers know which ideas are borrowed and can locate the original material themselves. Papers written for English and other humanities courses typically follow the MLA (Modern Language Association) documentation system, which requires brief parenthetical citations within the body of the essay and a comprehensive list of works cited at the end. See the Appendix, especially pp. 369–80.

dominant impression   The central idea or feeling conveyed by a description of a person, place, object, or state of mind. See Chapter 6 on description, especially p. 93.

editing   The final stage of the writing process, in which sentences and words are polished and corrected for accuracy, clarity, and effectiveness. See Chapter 4 on editing, p. 47.

effect   See *cause-and-effect analysis*.

emotional appeal   In argumentative and persuasive writing, the appeal to readers' values, beliefs, or feelings in order to win agreement or compel action. See pp. 313–14.

essay   A prose composition on a single nonfictional topic or idea. An essay usually reflects the personal experiences and opinions of the writer.

ethical appeal   In argumentative and persuasive writing, the sense of the writer's expertise and character projected by the reasonableness of the argument, the use and quality of evidence, and the tone. See p. 313.

evidence   The details, examples, facts, statistics, or expert opinions that support any general statement or claim. See pp. 315 and 320–22 on the use of evidence in argumentative writing, pp. 363–64 on finding evidence in sources, and pp. 369–80 on documenting researched evidence.

example   An instance or representative of a general group or an abstract concept or quality. One or more examples may serve as the primary method of developing an essay. See Chapter 7 on example, p. 115.

exposition   The form of writing that explains or informs. Most of the essays in this book are primarily expository, and some essays whose primary purpose is self-expression or persuasion employ exposition to clarify ideas.

fallacies   Flaws in reasoning that weaken or invalidate an argument. Some of the most common fallacies follow (the page numbers refer to further discussion in the text).

- **Hasty generalization,** leaping to a conclusion on the basis of inadequate or unrepresentative evidence: *Every one of the twelve students polled supports the change in the grading system, so the administration should implement it* (p. 318).

- **Oversimplification,** overlooking or ignoring inconsistencies or complexities in evidence: *If the United States banned immigration, our unemployment problems would be solved* (pp. 279, 318).

- **Begging the question,** assuming the truth of a conclusion that has not been proved: *Acid rain does not do serious damage, so it is not a serious problem* (p. 318).

- **Ignoring the question,** shifting the argument away from the real issue: *A fine, churchgoing man like Charles Harold would make an excellent mayor* (p. 318).

- **Ad hominem** ("to the man") **argument,** attacking an opponent instead of the opponent's argument: *She is just a student, so we need not listen to her criticisms of foreign policy* (p. 318).

- **Either-or,** presenting only two alternatives when the choices are more numerous: *If you want to do well in college, you have to cheat a little* (p. 319).

- **Non sequitur** ("It does not follow"), deriving a wrong or illogical conclusion from stated premises: *Because students are actually in school, they should be the ones to determine our educational policies* (p. 319).

- **Post hoc** (from *post hoc, ergo propter hoc,* "after this, therefore because of this"), assuming that one thing caused another simply because it preceded the other: *Two students left school in the week after the new policies were announced, proving that the policies will eventually cause a reduction in enrollments* (pp. 278–79, 319).

figures of speech Expressions that imply meanings beyond or different from their literal meanings in order to achieve vividness or force. See pp. 56–57 for discussion and examples of specific figures.

formal style See *style.*

freewriting A technique for discovering ideas for writing: writing for a fixed amount of time without stopping to reread or edit. See pp. 23–24.

general and specific words A **general** word refers to a group or class: *car, mood, book.* A **specific** word refers to a particular member of a group or class: *Toyota, irritation, dictionary.* Usually, the more specific a word is, the more interesting and informative it will be for readers. See also pp. 56, 97, and *abstract and concrete words.*

generalization A statement about a group or a class derived from knowledge of some or all of its members: for instance, *Dolphins can be trained to count* or *Television news rarely penetrates beneath the headlines.* The more instances the generalization is based on, the more accurate it is likely to be. A generalization is the result of inductive reasoning; see pp. 315–16.

hasty generalization See *fallacies.*

hyperbole Deliberate overstatement or exaggeration: *The desk provided an acre of work surface.* See also p. 57. (The opposite of hyperbole is understatement, discussed under *irony*.)

image A verbal representation of sensory experience—that is, of something seen, heard, felt, tasted, or smelled. Images may be literal: *Snow stuck to her eyelashes; The red car sped past us.* Or they may be figures of speech: *Her eyelashes were snowy feathers; The car rocketed past us like a red missile.* (See pp. 56–57.) Through images, a writer touches the readers' experiences, thus sharpening meaning and adding immediacy. See also *abstract and concrete words*.

inductive reasoning The method of reasoning that moves from the particular to the general. See Chapter 14 on argument and persuasion, especially pp. 315–16.

informal style See *style*.

introductions The openings of written works, the sentences that set the stage for what follows. An introduction to an essay identifies and restricts the subject while establishing the writer's attitude toward it. Accomplishing these purposes may require anything from a single sentence to several paragraphs, depending on the writer's purpose and how much readers need to know before they can begin to grasp the ideas in the essay. The introduction often includes a thesis sentence stating the main idea of the essay (see pp. 26–28). To set up the thesis sentence, or as a substitute for it, any of the following openings, or a combination, may be effective:

- Background on the subject that establishes a time or place or that provides essential information (see Gould, p. 180; Kingsolver, p. 211; McClain, p. 231; and Glasser, p. 346)

- An anecdote or other reference to the writer's experience that forecasts or illustrates the main idea or that explains what prompted the essay (see Dillard, p. 72; Warren, p. 155; Peck, p. 237; Brady, p. 264; and Spence, p. 339)

- An explanation of the significance of the subject (see Jain, p. 128; Alaimo and Koester, p. 288; and Quindlen, p. 328)

- An outline of the situation or problem that the essay will address, perhaps using interesting facts or statistics (see de Zengotita, p. 160; Griggs, p. 174; and LeDuff, p. 301)

- A statement or quotation of an opinion that the writer will modify or disagree with (see Chavez, p. 334, and McDonough, p. 352)

- An example, quotation, or question that reinforces the main idea (see Heat-Moon, p. 107; Kessler, p. 123, and Klass, p. 133)

A good introduction does not mislead readers by exaggerating the significance of the subject or the essay, and it does not bore readers by saying more than is necessary. In addition, a good introduction avoids three openings that are always clumsy: (1) beginning with *The purpose of this essay is . . .* or something similar; (2) referring to the title of the essay in the first sentence, as in *This is not as hard as it looks* or *This is a serious problem*; and (3) starting too broadly or vaguely, as in *Ever since humans walked upright . . .* or *In today's world. . . .*

irony   In writing, irony is the use of words to suggest a meaning different from their literal meaning. An ironic statement might rely on reversal: saying the opposite of what the writer really means. But irony can also derive from understatement (saying less than is meant) or hyperbole (exaggeration). Irony can be witty, teasing, biting, or cruel. At its most humorless and heavily contemptuous, it becomes **sarcasm**: *Thanks a lot for telling Dad we stayed out all night; that was really bright of you.*

metaphor   A figure of speech that compares two unlike things by saying that one is the other: *Bright circles of ebony, her eyes smiled back at me.* See also p. 57.

narration   The form of writing that tells a story, relating a sequence of events. See Chapter 5 on narration, p. 63.

nonstandard English   See *diction.*

oversimplification   See *fallacies.*

paragraph   A group of related sentences, set off by an initial indentation, that develops an idea. By breaking continuous text into units, paragraphing helps the writer manage ideas and helps the reader follow those ideas. Each paragraph makes a distinct contribution to the main idea governing the entire piece of writing. The idea of the paragraph itself is often stated in a topic sentence (see pp. 35–36), and it is supported with sentences containing specific details, examples, and reasons. Like the larger piece of writing to which it contributes, the paragraph should be unified, coherent, and well developed. For examples of successful paragraphs, see the paragraph analyses in the introduction to each method of development (Chapters 5–14). See also pp. 35–36 and 258 (unity), pp. 28–29 and 148 (coherence), and pp. 39–41 and 173 (development).

parallelism   The use of similar grammatical forms for ideas of equal importance. Parallelism occurs within sentences: *The doctor recommends swimming, bicycling, or walking.* It also occurs among sentences: *Strumming her guitar, she made listeners feel her anger. Singing lines, she made listeners believe her pain.* See also pp. 53–54.

paraphrase   A restatement—in your own words—of another writer's ideas. A paraphrase is about the same length as the original passage, but it does not repeat words, phrases, or sentence patterns. See also pp. 365–66.

personification   A figure of speech that gives human qualities to things or abstractions: *The bright day smirked at my bad mood.* See also p. 57.

persuasion   See *argument.*

plagiarism   The failure to identify and acknowledge the sources of words, information, or ideas that are not your own. Whether intentional or accidental, plagiarism is a serious offense and should always be avoided. See pp. 368–69.

point of view   The position of the writer in relation to the subject. In description, point of view depends on the writer's physical and psychological relation to the subject (see pp. 92–93). In narration, point of view depends on the writer's place in the story and on his or her relation to it in time (see pp. 64–65). More broadly, point of view can also mean the writer's particular mental stance or attitude. For instance, an employee and an employer might have different points of view toward the employee's absenteeism or the employer's sick-leave policies.

premise The generalization or assumption on which an argument is based. See *syllogism*.

process analysis The method of development in which a sequence of actions with a specified result is divided into its component steps. See Chapter 10 on process analysis, p. 192.

pronoun A word that refers to a noun or other pronoun: *Six days after King picked up his Nobel Peace Prize in Norway, he was jailed in Alabama.* The personal pronouns (the most common) are *I, you, he, she, it, we,* and *they.* See also pp. 37–38, and 56–57, 64, 198.

proposition A debatable claim about a subject; the central idea of an argument.

purpose The reason for writing, the goal the writer wants to achieve. The purpose may be primarily to explain the subject so that readers understand it or see it in a new light; to convince readers to accept or reject an opinion or to take a certain action; to entertain readers with a humorous or exciting story; or to express the thoughts and emotions triggered by a revealing or instructive experience. The writer's purpose overlaps the main idea — the particular point being made about the subject. In effective writing, the two together direct and control every choice the writer makes. See also p. 14 and 20–21, *thesis*, and *unity*.

quotation The exact words of another writer or speaker, copied word for word and clearly identified. Short quotations are enclosed in quotation marks; longer quotations are set off from the text by indenting. See pp. 366–67.

rational appeal In argumentative and persuasive writing, the appeal to readers' rational faculties — to their ability to reason logically — in order to win agreement or compel action. See pp. 315–17.

repetition and restatement The careful use of the same words or close parallels to clarify meaning and tie sentences together. See also p. 37 and 148.

revision The stage of the writing process devoted to "re-seeing" a draft, divided into fundamental changes in content and structure (revision) and more superficial changes in grammar, word choice, and the like (editing). See Chapter 3 on revising, p. 33, and Chapter 4 on editing, p. 47.

rhetoric The art of using words effectively to communicate with an audience, or the study of that art. To the ancient Greeks, rhetoric was the art of the *rhetor* — orator, or public speaker — and included the art of persuasion. Later the word shifted to mean elegant language, and a version of that meaning persists in today's occasional use of *rhetoric* to mean pretentious or hollow language, as in *Their argument was mere rhetoric.*

sarcasm See *irony*.

satire The combination of wit and criticism to mock or condemn human foolishness or evil. The intent of satire is to arouse readers to contempt or action, and thus it differs from comedy, which seeks simply to amuse. Much satire relies on irony — saying one thing but meaning another (see *irony*).

simile   A figure of speech that equates two unlike things using *like* or *as*: *The crowd was restless, like bees in a hive.* See also p. 56.

slang   See *diction*.

source   Any outside or researched material that helps to develop a writer's ideas. A source may be the subject of an essay, such as when you are writing about a reading in this book, or it may provide evidence to support a particular point. However a source is used, it must always be documented. See the appendix on working with sources, p. 362.

spatial organization   A pattern of organization that views an object, scene, or person by paralleling the way we normally scan things—for instance, top to bottom or near to far. See also pp. 39 and 95.

specific words   See *general and specific words*.

Standard English   See *diction*.

style   The *way* something is said, as opposed to *what* is said. Style results primarily from a writer's characteristic word choices and sentence structures. A person's writing style, like his or her voice or manner of speaking, is distinctive. Style can also be viewed more broadly as ranging from formal to informal. A very formal style adheres strictly to the conventions of Standard English (see *diction*); tends toward long sentences with sophisticated structures; and relies on learned words, such as *malodorous* and *psychopathic*. A very informal style, in contrast, is more conversational (see *colloquial language*); tends toward short, uncomplicated sentences; and relies on words typical of casual speech, such as *smelly* or *crazy*. Among the writers represented in this book, Glasser (p. 345) writes quite formally, Hughes (p. 78) quite informally. The formality of style may often be modified to suit a particular audience or occasion: a college term paper, for instance, demands a more formal style than an essay narrating a personal experience. See also *tone* and Chapter 3 on revising, especially pp. 41–43.

summary   A condensed version—in your own words—of the main idea of a longer work. A summary is much shorter than the original and leaves out most of the supporting details. See also p. 365.

syllogism   The basic form of deductive reasoning, in which a conclusion derives necessarily from proven or accepted premises. For example: *The roof always leaks when it rains* (the major premise). *It is raining* (the minor premise). *Therefore, the roof will leak* (the conclusion). See Chapter 14 on argument and persuasion, especially pp. 311–13.

symbol   A person, place, or thing that represents an abstract quality or concept. A red heart symbolizes love; the Golden Gate Bridge symbolizes San Francisco's dramatic beauty; a cross symbolizes Christianity.

synthesis   The practice of combining elements into a new whole. In writing, synthesis usually involves connecting related ideas from multiple sources to form an original idea of your own. See pp. 365–68.

thesis   The main idea of a piece of writing to which all other ideas and details relate. The main idea is often stated in a **thesis sentence** (or sentences), which asserts something about the subject and conveys the writer's purpose. The thesis sentence is often included near the beginning of an essay. Even when the writer does not state the main idea and purpose, however, they govern all the ideas and details in the essay. See also pp. 13–14, pp. 25–28, and *unity*.

tone   The attitude toward the subject, and sometimes toward the audience and the writer's own self, expressed in choice of words and sentence structures as well as in what is said. Tone in writing is similar to tone of voice in speaking, from warm to serious, amused to angry, joyful to sorrowful, sympathetic to contemptuous. For examples of strong tone in writing, see Barry (p. 149), Griggs (p. 174), McClain (p. 230), Peck (p. 236), and Brady (p. 264). See also pp. 41–43 and 325.

topic sentence   See *paragraph*.

transitions   Links between sentences and paragraphs that relate ideas and thus contribute to clarity and smoothness. Transitions may be sentences beginning paragraphs or brief paragraphs that shift the focus or introduce new ideas. They may also be words and phrases that signal and specify relationships. Some of these words and phrases—but by no means all—are listed here:

- **Space:** above, below, beyond, farther away, here, nearby, opposite, there, to the right
- **Time:** afterward, at last, earlier, later, meanwhile, simultaneously, soon, then
- **Illustration:** for example, for instance, specifically, that is
- **Comparison:** also, in the same way, likewise, similarly
- **Contrast:** but, even so, however, in contrast, on the contrary, still, yet
- **Addition or repetition:** again, also, finally, furthermore, in addition, moreover, next, that is
- **Cause or effect:** as a result, consequently, equally important, hence, then, therefore, thus
- **Summary or conclusion:** all in all, in brief, in conclusion, in short, in summary, therefore, thus
- **Intensification:** indeed, in fact, of course, truly

understatement   See *irony*.

unity   The quality of effective writing that occurs when all the parts relate to the main idea and contribute to the writer's purpose. See also pp. 35–36 and 258.

Acknowledgments (continued from page iv)

Judy Brady. "I Want a Wife." Originally published in *Ms.*, Vol. 1, and No. 1 December 31, 1971. Copyright © 1970 by Judy Brady. Reprinted by permission of the author.

Linda Chavez. "Redefining the Problem Won't Make It Go Away" from *Townhall.com*, Friday, August 22, 2008. Copyright © 2009 Salem Web Network. Reprinted by permissions of Linda Chavez and Creators Syndicate, Inc.

Thomas de Zengotita. "*American Idol* Worship," originally titled "Why We Worship 'American Idol.'" From *The Christian Science Monitor*, February 17, 2006 edition. Copyright © 2006. Reprinted by permission of the author.

Annie Dillard. "The Chase" from *An American Childhood* by Annie Dillard. Copyright © 1987 by Annie Dillard. Reprinted by permission of HarperCollins Publishers, Inc. and by Russell & Volkening as agents for the author.

Lars Eighner. "Dumpster Diving" from *Travels with Lizbeth: Three Years on the Road and on the Streets* by Lars Eighner. Copyright © 1993 by Lars Eighner and reprinted by permission of St. Martin's Press, LLC.

Glenn Erikson. "How to Survive at Chuck E. Cheese" from the *Metropolitan*, 2002. Reprinted by permission of the author.

Amanda Fields. "Cairo Tunnel" from *Brevity*, 2009. Reprinted by permission of the author.

Ira Glasser. "Drug Busts = Jim Crow." Reprinted with permission from the July 10, 2006 issue of *The Nation*. For subscription information, call 1-800-333-8536. Portions of each week's *Nation* magazine can be accessed at http://www.thenation.com.

Jonathan R. Gould, Jr. "The People Next Door." Copyright © Bedford/St. Martin's. Reprinted by permission of Bedford/St. Martin's.

Brandon Griggs. (CNN) "The 12 Most Annoying Types of Facebookers," August 25, 2009. Copyright © 2009 CNN.com. Reprinted by permission of CNN.com.

William Least Heat-Moon. "Starrucca Viaduct" from *Roads to Quoz* by William Least Heat-Moon. Copyright © 2008 by William Least Heat-Moon. By permission of Little, Brown and Company. All rights reserved.

Langston Hughes. "Salvation" from *The Big Sea* by Langston Hughes. Copyright © 1940 by Langston Hughes. Copyright renewed © 1968 by Arna Bontemps and George Houston Bass. Reprinted by permission of Hill and Wang, a division of Farrar, Straus & Giroux, LLC and Harold Ober Associates Incorporated.

Anita Jain. Excerpt from *Marrying Anita: A Quest for Love in the New India* by Anita Jain. Copyright © 2008 by Anita Jain. Reprinted by permission of Bloomsbury USA.

Barbara Kingsolver. "Stalking the Vegetannual" (pp. 63–69) from *Animal, Vegetable, Miracle* by Barbara Kingsolver with Steven L. Hopp and Camille Kingsolver. Copyright © 2007 by Barbara Kingsolver, Steven L. Hopp, and Camille Kingsolver. Reprinted by permission of HarperCollins Publishers.

Perri Klass. "Learning the Language" from *A Not Entirely Benign Procedure* by Perri Klass. Copyright © 1987 by Perri Klass. Used by permission of G. P. Putnam's Sons, a division of Penguin Group (USA) Inc.

Charlie LeDuff. "End of the Line" from *Mother Jones*, September/October 2009. Reprinted by permission of the author.

Leanita McClain. "The Middle-Class Black's Burden" from *A Foot in Each World: Essays and Articles* by Leanita McClain. Copyright © 1986 by Leanita McClain.

James R. McDonough. "Critics Scapegoat the Antidrug Laws" from *Insight on the News.* Copyright © November 11–24, 2003. Reprinted by permission of the author.

Cheryl Peck. "Fatso" from *Revenge of the Paste Eaters* by Cheryl Peck. Copyright © 2005 by Cheryl Peck. Reprinted by permission of Grand Central Publishing. All rights reserved.

Anna Quindlen. "The C Word in the Hallways" from *Loud and Clear* by Anna Quindlen. Copyright © 2004 by Anna Quindlen. Reprinted by permission of International Creative Management, Inc.

Ashley Rhodes. 'This I Believe: Fatherhood Is Essential,' 2009, from *New Voices*, Lander University. Copyright © 2009 by Ashley Rhodes. Reprinted by permission of the author.

Charlie Spence. "Sixteen." Reprinted by permission of the author.

Andrew Sullivan. "Why the 'M Word' Matters to Me" from *Time* Magazine, February 16, 2004. Copyright © 2004, TIME INC. Reprinted by permission. TIME is a registered trademark of Time Inc. All rights reserved.

Dana Thomas. "The Fake Trade," written by Dana Thomas for the January 2008 edition of *Harper's Bazaar.* Copyright © 1999 Hearst Communications, Inc. Reprinted by permission of Harper's Bazaar. All rights reserved.

Andrew Warren III. "Throwing Darts at *The Simpsons*," originally titled "Paying Off the Interest: The Success of Merchandise and Consumer Sentiment" from *LUX*, a student magazine of the University of Massachusetts, Boston. Fall 2007 Issue. Reprinted by permission of LUX, University of Massachusetts.

Marion Winik. "What Are Friends for?" from *Telling: Confessions, Concessions, and Other Flashes of Light* by Marion Winik. Copyright © 1994 by Marion Winik. Used by permission of Villard Books, a division of Random House, Inc. and Patricia van der Leun Literary.

Alaina Wong. "China Doll" from *Yell-Oh Girls* by Vickie Nam. Copyright © 2001 by Vickie Nam. Reprinted by permission of HarperCollins Publishers.

Art Credits

p. 18, "Homeless Man." Photo by Colin Gregory Palmer.

p. 60, "Homeless Man in Line." Photo by Brant Ward/*San Francisco Chronicle.*

p. 108, "Starrucca Viaduct." From *Roads to Quoz* by William Least Heat-Moon. Copyright © 2008 by William Least Heat-Moon. By permission of Little, Brown and Company.

p. 211, "Vegetables." From *Animal, Vegetable, Miracle* by Barbara Kingsolver with Steven L. Hopp and Camille Kingsolver. Copyright © 2007 by Barbara Kingsolver, Steven L. Hopp, and Camille Kingsolver. Reprinted by permission of HarperCollins Publishers.

p. 301, "GM Plant." Photo by Danny Wilcox Frazier/Redux Pictures.

p. 303, "GM Reading Room." Photo by Danny Wilcox Frazier/Redux Pictures.

p. 305, "GM Prayer." Photo by Danny Wilcox Frazier/Redux Pictures.

INDEX OF AUTHORS
AND TITLES

GUIDE TO THE ELEMENTS OF WRITING

The Compact Reader offers advice on writing from the general, such as organizing and revising, to the particular, such as tightening sentences and choosing words. Consult the page numbers here for answers to questions you may have about the elements of writing. To find the meaning of a particular term or concept, consult the Glossary on pages 386–95.